MW00562983

Peter Cushing

A Life in Film

Peter Cushing

A Life in Film

David Miller

TITAN BOOKS

For Stuart

PETER CUSHING: A LIFE IN FILM
ISBN: 9781781162743

Published by Titan Books, A division of Titan Publishing Group Ltd.
144 Southwark St., London, SE1 0UP

This edition: April 2013
10 9 8 7 6 5 4 3 2 1

First published as *The Peter Cushing Companion* in 2000. This revised edition first published in 2013
Peter Cushing: A Life in Film © 2013 David Miller

Designed by Peri Godbold
Printed in China

Acknowledgments

Special thanks:

To Veronica Carlson, for graciously providing the foreword.

To Peter Nicholson for his glorious collection of photographs and his continued support.

To the BBC Written Archive Centre, Caversham, and particularly to Neil Somerville, whose enthusiasm was so inspiring.

To Adam Newell at Titan, for all his help.

To Graham Skeggs for information about Peter's Hammer work; Marcus Hearn, David O'Leary and Richard Reynolds for their huge support on the original edition; Ingrid Pitt and Tony Rudlin who started the ball rolling; Jonathan Rigby, Mark Gatiss and Jan Vincent-Rudzki for friendship and inspiration.

For their generous hospitality in granting interviews and supplying photographs: Joan Craft, Richard R Greenough, Terence and Gina Morgan, Michael and Ann Redington, Donald Tosh and Derek Whitehurst.

For sharing their memories of Peter: Roy Ward Baker, Ann Bell, James Bernard, Joyce Broughton, Jeremy Bulloch, Hazel Court, William Franklyn, John Fraser, Shelagh Fraser, Tudor Gates, Eunice Gayson, Michael Gough, Val Guest, Bryan Hands, Hugh Harlow, Melvyn Hayes, John Hough, Alice Krige, Christopher Lee, Francis Matthews, Andrée Melly, Caroline Munro, David Prowse, Oscar Quitak, Andrew Ray, Helen Ryan, Jimmy Sangster, Prunella Scales, Ian Scoones, Peter Graham Scott, Barbara Shelley and Madeline Smith.

Also thanks to Brian Murphy, Leslie Schofield, The British Film Institute, The Mander and Mitchenson Theatre Collection, Josephine Botting, Colin Cutler, Donald Fearney, Simon Flynn, David Howe, Ian Jennings, Wayne Kinsey, Mark A Miller, Andrew Pixley and Stuart Targett.

To Mike Hodges for providing interviews with Eugenio Martin, Paul Naschy and Francisco R Gordillo, Adam Jezard for interviews with Roy Ward Baker and Andrew Keir and John Walter Skinner for information about the Connaught Theatre, Worthing.

To Brian Holland for his sterling work for The Peter Cushing Association, and for his kindness in swiftly supplying various films.

To all those who provided such encouragement in the making of this new edition, particularly Mum and Dad, Ian and Michaela, Graham and Astrid, Sol and Edie, David Carlisle, Stephen Graves, Derek and Michelle Handley and family, Peter Hawkins, Julian Knott and Richard Shiner.

Cover image: The Kobal Collection
Frontispiece: *The Skull* (Amicus, 1965)

Contents

Foreword

'I am here to talk about Peter Cushing.' My opening statement at a convention in Washington in 1999 brought the house down. Such cheering, whistling and prolonged applause! I am delighted to introduce this fine book, and honoured to once more say that 'I am here to talk about Peter Cushing.' My first meeting with Peter was fleeting, during Hammer's presentation of the Queen's Award To Industry in 1968. Less than a year later we were reunited when I was cast as Anna in *Frankenstein Must Be Destroyed*.

Any nervousness I may have felt about joining the long-established partnership Peter shared with director Terence Fisher was dispelled when Peter greeted me with a slight bow and kissed the back of my hand.

The filming of my character's death scene says much about Peter's meticulous approach to his craft. 'I've been giving this a lot of thought,' he told Terry Fisher. 'Anna will hopefully still be holding the scalpel with which she inflicted a mortal wound on Brandt. I could simply take her hand, turn it towards her heart and embrace her.' Terry, eager to commit my dramatic demise to film, thought the idea was wonderful. Thus it was.

Shortly before filming ended, Hammer's managing director Jimmy Carreras rushed onto the set, clutching a copy of the script. 'There's not enough sex in this movie!' he exclaimed, thrusting some pages at Terry before abruptly leaving the sound stage. The pages detailed a new scene in which Frankenstein raped Anna. Terry reasoned with Jimmy, explaining that there were only five days' filming left. Peter said it was totally out of character for Frankenstein, and all I could think of was how the scene would affect the continuity of my performance. My reactions to Frankenstein would have been totally different were I aware that the scene was in the script from the outset.

Peter took me out for a lovely meal, though the spectre of the imminent scene loomed large. 'We simply *have* to talk about it,' he said. 'I know that Terry will go along with whatever we work out. You must trust me Veronica.' He placed his hand over mine and gave it a gentle squeeze.

We tried our best to perform the scene 'tastefully', and afterwards Peter found it impossible to hide his distress. 'I'm so sorry darling,' he said as he embraced me. 'Just remember it isn't me.' There was such compassion in Peter, and I loved him for that.

Peter introduced me to his beloved wife Helen at the première of *Frankenstein Must Be Destroyed*. She was so gracious and complimentary, and as we ascended a broad staircase together I noticed she had difficulty breathing. I realised then that she was frail, but I had no idea how ill she really was. By the time I worked with Peter again she had passed away.

My next film with Peter was *The Ghoul*, which was directed by Freddie Francis in 1974. I played a character called Daphne and Peter played Doctor Lawrence. The loss of Helen had changed Peter so much – always thin, he was now almost skeletal in appearance. He had become a very solitary man, and retired to his dressing-room at every available opportunity. The mischievous twinkle in his eyes had gone. To me, it seemed a part of Peter had died along with Helen. I grieved for him.

The filming of one scene in particular is extremely difficult for me to recount. Daphne asks a question to which Doctor Lawrence replies 'My wife is dead...' The tone of utter finality and loss in his voice was absolute. At this point Doctor Lawrence picked up a photograph of his late wife – in actual fact Peter had insisted on using a picture of Helen. This scene was shot about seven times, and each time Peter uttered that awful sentence he became more broken. Finally, tears streaming uncontrollably down his face, he swiftly walked off the set. Freddie Francis simply turned and looked at the floor amid a horrible silence.

In later years I kept up a correspondence with Peter thanks to his long-time friend and secretary Joyce Broughton. When Peter's health was rapidly declining, I dreaded the inevitable phone call from Joyce to tell me that Peter had passed away. 'Sir wanted me to be the one to tell you when this happened,' she said. 'You were one of his favourite people.' I will always be grateful for the kindness she showed me when she herself was heartbroken. We both agreed that he had joined Helen at last.

I don't want to believe that Peter is dead, and I know that I don't have to believe it – this remarkable chronicle of his career, along with the ongoing appreciation of his thousands of fans around the world, will help ensure that he remains alive and well in our hearts.

Veronica Carlson
Florida, May 2000

Introduction

'Growing up I loved *Dracula*. I was such a fan of Peter Cushing in that. All my friends wanted to be Christopher Lee and I wanted to be Peter Cushing.'
Daniel Radcliffe

Peter Cushing was born one hundred years ago, and it is my great privilege and pleasure to return to this book for a new edition in celebration of his centenary. That people are still interested in Cushing's career one hundred years after his birth is a remarkable tribute in itself.

Cushing's fans have always been in esteemed company, and that is no less the case today. Actor Daniel Radcliffe, who wasn't even born when Cushing retired, recently sang the actor's praises as he took up the Cushing mantle in Hammer's new blockbuster hit *The Woman in Black*. Guillermo del Toro, director of *Hellboy* and *Pan's Labyrinth*, cited Cushing as one of his favourite actors, with his performance as Grimsdyke in *Tales from the Crypt* particularly memorable. 'Cushing was a very subtle actor,' says del Toro, 'A very delicate actor, capable of great nuance.'

Those subtleties that del Toro mentions are part of Cushing's magic – his awestruck stare at the Yeti in the conclusion of *The Abominable Snowman*; his expression of exhausted disbelief as Christopher Lee's Dracula is reduced to ashes in a shaft of sunlight; the insane glitter in his eyes as Baron Frankenstein when he determines to bring life to the dead.

I hope that this book conveys something of the times in which Cushing lived and worked, and shows the breadth of his talents and his appeal. He had no less than five careers, in fact, each one following after the other. After repertory theatre in England he starred briefly in Hollywood films, then returned to the stage in London alongside theatre's royalty, Sir Laurence Olivier and Vivien Leigh. He then became one of the first British television stars, and on returning to film became a worldwide success.

What is less well known, but which has come to light in testaments from those who worked with him, is that throughout his film career, Cushing was constantly suggesting additions and improvements, never content with half-measures or 'making do'. His love of theatre and knowledge of film history informed these suggestions with immeasurable details, in some cases, they were the making of whole scenes – the crossed candlesticks in *Dracula*, the harpooning of the Mummy, Grimsdyke's ghastly resurrection.

He also contributed to many scripts, including *Captain Clegg*, *She*, *The Blood Beast Terror* and most of the Amicus films, while his artistic abilities are recorded in the watercolour costume sketches which illuminate his scripts. He even at one point considered directing a film for Hammer. Though this was not to be, we now know more about the enormous contribution he did make to cinema, which he always saw as a collaborative art-form.

Cushing's evocative autobiography in 1986 and its companion volume in 1988 are tributes to the love and support of his wife Helen, whom he first met outside the stage door of the Theatre Royal Drury Lane, and who became his constant companion, his encouragement and his strength. 'My belovèd Helen,' he said, 'shone like a good deed in a naughty world.' When she died in 1971, Cushing said that his life, as he knew and loved it, ended. In writing this book, it was a pleasure to meet those people who knew Peter and Helen at the happiest time of their lives, particularly Joan Craft, the ENSA stage manager who first introduced them, and Michael and Ann Redington, who used to share trips to the rugby with the Cushings and evenings with them enjoying the latest board-games brought back from New York.

In this book you will find a collection of quintessential Cushing moments, many of them in some very famous films. He always had an instinct for a popular success and his association with so many iconic screen figures has helped to ensure his longevity. While there are fans of classic horror and fantasy films, fans of Dracula, Darth Vader and the Daleks, people will come anew to the work of Peter Cushing. Then, I think, they will grow to appreciate an actor of rare depth and sensitivity, who brought humanity, charm and a kind of nobility to all the roles he played.

Here's to the next one hundred years.

Chapter One

Little Horror

Peter Wilton Cushing was born on the morning of Monday 26th May 1913, at 'Normandy', Godstone Road, Kenley, Surrey, to George Edward and Nellie Maria Cushing. George was a quantity surveyor and Nellie was the daughter of a carpet merchant. Little Peter had an elder brother, David, three years his senior.

It seems Nellie Cushing had wanted a girl. 'Wanting "one of each" she had mitigated any disappointment in my arrival by dressing me in girls' frocks,' Cushing explained, 'allowing my hair to grow in long curls, tied with pink ribbon.' Eventually, 'father exerted his gentle authority' and the boy was more appropriately attired. By Peter's own admission, the Cushings were 'by no means a rich family. I should think very middle class with just enough to get by. No... more than "just enough", because tax wasn't a problem in those days. Looking back we always had what was to me a very nice house, and always a very nice garden.'[1]

The family moved to Dulwich during the 1914-18 war and among Cushing's earliest memories was the sight of the Zeppelins overhead. After the war, the family moved back to Surrey, to Purley near Croydon, living near the station and then subsequently at the top of Downs Court Road.

Although there were no theatrical connections in his immediate family, Cushing's lineage included several figures who were performers. The career of Cushing's paternal grandfather, Henry William Cushing, was checkered, but he was listed (among other things) as 'Actor (Tragedian)', in such exalted company as Forbes Robertson, William Terris and Ellen Terry. His step-uncle, Wilton Herriot, after whom Cushing was given his middle name, wrote and performed his own music hall sketches. There was also the flamboyant Aunt Maude, who trod the boards in South Africa, and mysterious Uncle Bertie, who was 'banished' to Australia in 1901 – for no reason Cushing could discover, save that he reportedly had an 'artistic temperament'.

Even as a child Cushing had a formidable imagination – from the age of five he drew strip-cartoons, and would earn money from his long-suffering relations by taking them for make-believe bus rides, with David as the driver. He also gave

Punch and Judy shows. 'Uncle George Gatenby suggested that we not charge an entrance fee, but make a collection as the audience left. We collected what was to us a nice lot of money and my share was about three shillings – which meant something in 1917! It enabled us to indulge in our favourite comic, the *Gem*, and several bags of bullseyes.'[2]

Young Peter's great difficulty with words troubled him all his life. This made school a trial and his academic advancement minimal. 'Ever since I can remember, I have seen things in terms of shapes and movement,' he said in 1955. 'I have always found it easier to draw, paint or mime something than to present it in words.'[3] His fractured spelling became a sort of trademark, and one that he would use to entertain friends, although his later work 'improving' threadbare scripts was legendary and highly effective.

Cushing suffered pneumonia for three successive years in infancy, the third time developing double-pneumonia which in the 1920s was generally fatal. He survived, but this encouraged his mother to cosset him all the more. Despite his close friendship with his brother, Cushing became a rather solitary child, often creating elaborate imaginary scenarios. From a young age he was enchanted by the cinema, and an early hero was the cowboy Tom Mix. 'Returning from the "Picture House" I would re-enact some tales of derring-do which I had just witnessed, using the back garden as a prairie,' he wrote. 'We had a long garden that sloped down from a railway and I would rush along this embankment, fall down and terrify people. I just came crashing down on bruised knees and cut elbows, but I enjoyed every minute of it. I remember hanging myself once, after having seen Tom Mix being hanged in a film. So I hanged myself from my mother's washing line but fortunately she didn't see me. I suppose it's all to do with imagination and trying to copy what one's hero did.'[4] This boundless enthusiasm for play-acting translated directly into Cushing's later work, when it was his mixture of wide-eyed delight, whether for adventures or horrors, mixed with almost reckless physical force that distinguished his performances.

Cushing took his code of honour from the pages of the *Popular*, a weekly comic which featured the escapades of schoolboy Tom Merry – 'true-blue, eye-on-the-ball, no cribbing and no smoking.'[5] He tried to stick to Merry's tenets of honesty and decency all his life – except for the last one, and he only started smoking when he needed to smoke a pipe for a role on stage. In early years he had an insatiable appetite, but he later took to eating in moderation and became a strict vegetarian. After a trip to the Christmas pantomime, he fell in love with Peter Pan, but as he was quick to point out, the 'boy who never grew up' was, in this case, played by a girl. Sex education was rather more rudimentary in those days. When young Peter was invited to a mixed bathing party, Nellie's advice was 'If you see anything you haven't seen before, dear, throw your hat at it.' David filled in the gaps for his little brother, whom he called 'Brighteyes', by taking him off to a nearby farm for a practical demonstration. Still Peter was not convinced. '"But they're animals," I protested. The wise one spoke: "And so Brighteyes," he said profoundly, "are we."'[6]

'The rod was always spared in our home,' Cushing attested, but his mother nevertheless had a particularly chilling method of punishing her little ones. Her tactics were to sing the first few bars from 'Love Will Find A Way', a song made famous by José Collins in the musical *The Maid of the Mountains*, adding her own lyrics. She would sing 'I'm going away, away, away, across the ocean blue...' and then pretend to be dead. This quite terrified the young boy, who loved his mother dearly. 'Don't sing that song mother,' he would

Cushing never lost his love of the stage, and in later years would create elaborate sets for a model theatre

cry, 'it's a horrid song!' The experience left him, he admitted, with a morbid and unreasonable fear of death. Sensible brother David said that if she did it again, he was to pinch her to prove she was play-acting. Cushing couldn't bring himself to do this, but when next his mother tried the trick, he went at her with a slice of bread and marmalade, slapping it in her face. 'The cure was effective immediately,' he reported, 'and Mother's resurrection permanent.'[7] Even so, he could not bear to listen to the song ever again. This fear of death was allied with another fear of the dark – instilled in him by his father who once punished him by locking his son in the cellar. Cushing was later able to overcome this phobia by taking moonlit walks.

At 11, he was packed off to a boarding school at Shoreham-by-Sea in Sussex. He lasted just one

miserable term before he was returned to the family bosom. He was then sent to Purley County Secondary School, which was within a few hundred yards of the Cushing home. 'By the time I was 16, I stood six feet tall and weighed 12 stone 5lb.' As a reaction to his mother's early attempts at transvestitism, he insisted on wearing short trousers in all weathers to show off his scarred knees. 'I even refused to have my rugby injuries bandaged,'[8] he said. These athletic pursuits served him well in later life, however, when he admitted he was rarely in a film where he didn't have to fall or get knocked down.

Cushing's favourite teacher at Purley was Mr D J Davies, the physics master. 'He needed no gift of insight to conclude that I was no budding Einstein,' said Cushing. 'In fact, had he not been the producer of the school plays, I'm sure he would have had me banned from the physics classes on the grounds that I was mentally deficient.' Davies encouraged Cushing's acting, and cast him as the lead in many of his school productions, which included Sheridan's *The Rivals*. 'I think it was Mr Davies more than anyone else,' said Cushing later, 'who encouraged me to take up acting professionally.'

Davies also let Cushing paint the scenery, which got him out of lessons and enabled him to practice his slapstick in front of the other children. In the evenings, as well as taking part in the school plays, Cushing studied painting and drawing under Mr Percy Rendell at the Croydon College of Art. He would continue these art classes for four years, long after he had left school.

Meanwhile, George Cushing was eager that his sons should make a living for themselves. He set David up in an apprenticeship at a farm in Pulborough and then bought a smallholding for him in Norwood Hill. But as for Peter... 'Just consider my qualifications for the harsh world of commerce and big business – top marks in art, nil for everything else; capped for Rugger, medals for athletics and swimming; played the lead in nearly all the school productions; the ability to fall down a cliff without breaking my neck and, just for good measure, an appetite like several horses.'[9] Cushing senior would not accede to his son's request to go into the theatre, and, 'by pulling a few strings' ultimately secured a position for his younger son with the local council.

Chapter Two

The Madman of Purley

In the summer of 1933, at a salary of one pound ten shillings a week, Cushing started work in the drawing office of the surveyor's department at Coulsdon and Purley Urban District Council. 'The plans I drew up were architect's nightmares,' he remembered. 'One had a garage on the front of the house, leading on to the kerb; another highly decorative chimneys placed in impossible positions. Yet another showed a semi-detached house with a bathroom extending into the adjoining house. It was said of my plans that any resemblance to a real building was entirely coincidental.'

Despite his grand title of surveyor's assistant, Cushing found himself as little more than a glorified office-boy. He remained in this lowly position for nearly three years by going to the most extravagant lengths to avoid doing any work. He knew he was destined for the theatre, and this job was merely a distraction.

Cushing's duties included street-numbering and collecting the money from public conveniences. Whenever he was let out of the office, he endeavoured to make the job last as long as possible, then nipped off home if he thought he could get away with it. In the office, he was put in charge of the numbering machine, and even here he found a chance for unscheduled (and unwanted) performance. He would hand-stamp his papers to the rhythms of popular tunes and invite his co-workers to guess what the tunes were. 'Inviting everyone to stand, I always ended these recitals with a spirited rendition of the National Anthem.'[1]

Work with Cushing in those days may have been a noisy experience, but it was surely never a boring one. He was a member of the National Association of Local Government Officers (number 16851) and was featured in the programme for the Council's ninth annual dinner. This booklet contained ditties and cartoons of NALGO members – 'Twenty personalities libelled in Caricature and Verse' – and under a startlingly accurate profile of young Mr P Cushing it read: 'We're very fond of Peter/He has some charming habits/His brother is a poacher/Who sends us fine fresh rabbits.' This seems rather more libellous towards Cushing's brother, who was actually a trainee farmer – it's difficult to think of Cushing, who thought that fishing was unkind to the *worm* as well as the fish, bringing dead rabbits into the office.

Although several years beyond school, he was able to continue appearing in the school plays thanks to the good offices of his friend and former teacher Mr Davies, and he also appeared in local amateur productions, including W S Gilbert's *Pygmalion and Galatea* (for which he shaved his legs). Despite such theatrical distractions, Cushing was becoming increasingly depressed – as he would at several points throughout his career. So, at the age of only 22, he decided to end it all. He took a bank holiday excursion to Exmouth and made his way along the cliff path to Straight Point, 'on the look-out for a good spot to drop off into oblivion.'[2]

It was a glorious day, however, and he was stopped in his tracks by the majesty of the view and the splendour of the surrounding coastline. While taking in the glory of the Devon countryside, his eye was caught by the antics of a little bird, a wheatear, which deflected him from his more sinister purpose. Cushing followed the bird and ended up in Budleigh Salterton, where he enjoyed a cream tea and decided that 'Life was good'. He left his bus fare to Exmouth as a tip for the waitress and walked back to the station.

From an advert in a discarded newspaper on the home-bound train, he learned that there were acting scholarships on offer at the Guildhall School of Music and Drama, so he went along for an interview. He was duly presented to Allan Aynesworth, a somewhat terrifying actor/manager of the old school. As Cushing wrote later, this was a trying experience.

'He rose to his feet as I was ushered in ... and asked, "Well laddie, and what can I do for you?"

"I wanna go on the stage."

Aynesworth glared. "This isn't an audition," he snapped. "Speak in your normal voice."

"But this *is* me normal voice. I wanna go on the stage!"

The elderly gentleman uttered a cry like a wounded stag, clasped his hands to his ears and boomed "Take him away! His voice offends me!"'[3]

'I didn't know what a dreadful accent I had until I got rid of it,'[4] Cushing said. He was sent away with a list of phrases with which to improve his speech. He called on James Cairns-James, of the original D'Oyly Carte Opera Company, who offered advice and assistance. Cushing was then able to marry his vocal exercises with his love of the countryside. 'To improve my diction and practice voice projection, I used to go for long walks over the nearby downs, bawling such lines as: "How now brown cow? The moon in June is full of beauty." I became known as "the Madman of Purley".' Later in his career, whenever possible, Cushing went on long walks to learn his lines. 'I was also given a device to fit between the teeth,' he said later. 'It was a piece of wood with a notch at each end. I put it between my teeth and talked. It really made your lips and your tongue work!'[5] Impeccable diction and pronunciation would become a Cushing hallmark.

In 1935, Cushing was finally accepted for evening classes at the Guildhall School. 'Never did a more ardent and punctual pupil attend those classes,' he said. 'So different from the slacker at those other schools!' He attended the classes twice a week, travelling up to town on the train. At the end of the year, he performed in *The Red Umbrella* and George Kelly's *The Torch-Bearers*. These he proudly placed on his CV, along with a photograph which, he said 'made me look like a glassy-eyed juvenile delinquent in the last stages of degeneracy.'[6]

Mr. P. CUSHING.

We're very fond of Peter,
He has some charming habits,
His brother is a poacher
Who sends us fine fresh rabbits.

An affectionate caricature of Cushing from the NALGO programme

Meanwhile the day-job in the surveyor's office was not going at all well. 'My chief at the surveying office caught me playing darts with the sharp-pointed surveyor's instruments. "Young man," he said, "as a surveyor you give one of the worst performances I've seen. I'm sure you could do better on the stage."'[7]

Cushing redoubled his efforts to find work in a repertory company and the focus of his first letter-writing campaign (there would be several more) was Bill Fraser, manager of the Connaught Theatre at Worthing in Sussex. Scottish-born Fraser became famous in the 1950s and 60s as Snudge in the popular TV comedy *The Army Game*, but as the 28-year-old actor-manager of Worthing Rep, he was using the rather more fearsome moniker of W Simpson Fraser, and had a formidable reputation. Cushing wrote to him every few weeks asking for a job and eventually, he received a curt request to come down to Worthing.

'When I walked into Bill Fraser's office, he barked: "Who are you?"

"I'm Peter Cushing," I revealed, and waited expectantly. "Look, Mr Cushing," said Fraser wearily,

"I only wanted to see you to tell you this: Please, *please*, stop writing to me for jobs."'[7]

Cushing was 'utterly shattered' by this rebuttal. The sensitive 23-year-old was reduced to tears. But Fraser must have appreciated Cushing's feelings, since he had left a banking job himself at 24 to turn to a career in the theatre. All he could offer was a position as an assistant stage manager at 15 shillings a week, and a walk-on role as one of the creditors in J B Priestley's play *Cornelius*. Cushing was overjoyed – it was nothing less than his passport to a new life.

Apart from stage appearances, the ASM's duties included looking after three lots of props at the same time. He had to return the last week's props to whoever they had been borrowed from, marshal those for the current play and find the props for next week's production. To distinguish them, they were marked green, red and blue. Cushing spent the whole day at the theatre, from 8.00 am to midnight, and his digs – bed and breakfast – cost all of his 15 shillings a week. To get by, he made the best of a huge breakfast and, like some scavenging creature, ate what he could find at the theatre. At least all the food on the stage

NALGO

SOUVENIR
OF THE
9TH ANNUAL DINNER

TWENTY
PERSONALITIES
LIBELLED
IN

CARICATURE
BY

VERSE
BY

was real, supplied by various local companies in return for a mention in the programme. 'I made a point of scanning advance scripts for eating scenes,' Cushing remembered. 'North-country plays were popular with me; they often featured a high tea. Whatever its dramatic merits, I did not care for St John Ervine's *Anthony and Anna*.

The chief character, an American invalid suffering from indigestion, had to be fed on charcoal biscuits and no other food was supplied for the play. By the end of the week I felt I could portray the invalid with more conviction than the leading actor.'[8]

Cushing began to see his name appearing in the cast-lists more frequently. He played the role of Johnson in *It Pays to Advertise* for the week commencing 15th June 1936, Mr Tooke in *Bees on the Boatdeck* by J B Priestley from 29th June, and the police surgeon in *The Man at Six* from 20th July. All these productions were produced and directed by Bill Fraser.

After several weeks, Peter Coleman, who would later run the Palmers Green Intimate Theatre in North London, came to Worthing from Southampton as a guest producer and leading player while Bill Fraser took a holiday. Coleman would oversee Cushing's roles as the expressman in *Potash and Perlmutter* from 3rd August, Boano in *Aloma* from 17th August and Kingsford in *The Midshipmaid* from 24th August.

When Coleman returned to the rather more affluent Grand Theatre in Southampton, he took Cushing with him as an ASM, where he stayed for the next nine months. The salary was higher and the parts were bigger, although if they were not, Cushing did everything in his power to make them so. 'For the small but important role of John Fairweather in *Lean Harvest*, the script described the character as "slightly merry". I staggered onto the stage with balloons tied to the ends of my tie and bottles of gin sticking out of my pockets. So much the "drunk" was I that no one understood a word I said.'[9]

Possibly Cushing's earliest professional appearance as a villain was at Southampton, playing King Rat in *Dick Whittington* at Christmas 1936. To liven things up, he worked out an acrobatic routine which 'nearly killed the actor playing the cat.' Soon he was playing juvenile leads at two pounds a week, which was then a generous salary for repertory actors. There were also character parts, requiring some considerable ingenuity with greasepaint and putty to transform the dashing, rugby-playing juvenile into an elderly traveller (for *Winter Sunshine*) or a Chinese servant (in *Lady Precious Stream*).

Also in the Southampton company was 18-year-old Doreen Lawrence, later the wife of film star Jack Hawkins. She was living locally with her parents, and when she discovered the disgracefully damp state of Cushing's digs, she invited him to stay with her until alternative accommodation could be found. The stage manager, Bill Johnson, was another great friend, and one who would appear later in Cushing's story.

Armed with new confidence and a year's worth of acting experience, Cushing scanned the pages of the actors' newspaper *The Stage* for likely new positions. He left Peter Coleman to join the William Brookfield Players in Rochdale, where he appeared, among other roles, as an army officer in *Marigold*. He later travelled with the company to Scarborough and there were week-long 'special' engagements at Burnley and several other northern theatres.

In 1937, the pinnacle of achievement in repertory was to join Harry Hanson's 'Court Players', a team (in fact, several teams) of actors who toured the country with scaled-down versions of West End hits. To his

Cushing in his repertory days (1937)

delight, Cushing was invited to join the Court Players at the Theatre Royal Nottingham. A fellow traveller on the train up to Nottingham was actor Peter Gray, who recounted his first meeting with Cushing in the foreword to *Past Forgetting*.

Gray had just, in his own words, been 'jilted' and was sitting in a railway carriage like Greta Garbo, wanting to be alone. 'Suddenly ... rumble, crash! The door was flung back and a substantial hunk of masculine brawn ... beamed happily back at me.

"Mind if I join you?" I felt like saying "Of course I mind, *fathead*, can't you see I'm on the rack of unrequited love?" But how could I?... My resistance began to crumble, eroded by the torrent of bonhomie from my companion and his disarming candour.'

By the time they got to Nottingham, Cushing had persuaded Gray to join him in the search for digs, and they ended up at 6 Hampden Street, ten minutes from the Theatre Royal, under the watchful eye of Mrs Robinson (full board, fires in all rooms, 30 shillings a week). 'We had to supply our own clothes for the weekly plays,' Gray recalled, 'but a made-to-measure dinner jacket (of superlative cloth and pure silk facings) cost only three pounds ten shillings at Montague Burton's. Tails were seven pounds.'[10]

Touring brought Cushing and the Players nearer to London (the Penge Empire) in a piece with the alarming title of *The Greeks Had a Word for It*. This ran for a week at the end of March 1938 and the following week Cushing joined in a performance of *Fresh Fields* by Ivor Novello. Back at the Theatre Royal Nottingham at the end of May, Cushing played Mr Lilywhite in *This Money Business* by Cyril Campion.

Cushing had an abiding love for the movies and was entranced by the stars of Hollywood. With a little money saved, he decided that he wanted to fulfil a long-held ambition and seek work in America. But he didn't have enough money for the fare, so asked his father for assistance. Father agreed, and paid for the trip, but only bought a one-way ticket – Cushing would have to 'work his passage home'. Most of the Christmas period was taken up with preparations for the trip, and in the third week of January 1939 he set off. When he returned to England, he would have become, in the meantime, a movie actor and a Broadway star.

But by then, the world would be at war.

Chapter Three

Hooray for Hollywood

Thoughts of war were a long way from Cushing's mind when, on Wednesday 18th January 1939, he set sail for America on the *SS Champlain* out of Southampton. He was 25 years old. After an uneventful voyage, he arrived in New York at the beginning of February and booked in for a week at the YMCA. From there, he attempted to contact the East Coast representatives of the Hollywood film studios, and received the expected polite dismissals. Only one person thought he could help – a Columbia executive with the appropriately benevolent-sounding name of Larney Goodkind. He was as good as his name, too, as he had a contact with Edward Small Productions in Hollywood and, not without a word of friendly warning, agreed to provide Cushing with a letter of introduction.

Also in New York at the time was English actor Robert Morley, who was starring on Broadway as Oscar Wilde. Although Cushing had not met the actor before, he went backstage to ask for advice. Morley told him that he was not alone in wanting to be a Hollywood star, but at least the weather was going to be nice, so he should be sure to take his swimming things. While in New York, Cushing splashed out on a ticket for a Broadway show – albeit in the Gods – to see Franchot Tone and Sylvia Sidney in *The Gentle People*. It was his first experience of Hollywood stars 'in the flesh'.

The next leg of the journey to Hollywood was to be made by rail, crossing 12 states in five days. Cushing boarded the *Challenger* at Grand Central station on 6th February and arrived in Los Angeles five days later in the pouring rain. During the journey he befriended a trio of college students who entertained the passengers with barber-shop songs. As Cushing couldn't sing or play the ukulele, he was elected treasurer and entrusted with passing round the hat.

'After the stuffiness of New York and the days of being cooped up on the train,' Cushing wrote, 'the crisp Californian air and the scent of the orange groves quite went to my head. I began to feel like a film star before I had even set foot in the studio.'[1] He duly checked into the Hollywood branch of the YMCA, where his 'Britishness' won over the desk clerk, who took his watch and $16 as security for a room. Then it was off to follow up Mr Goodkind's lead, at the offices of Edward Small Productions.

Edward Small was a onetime actor and agent who had subsequently become an independent producer. He was about to start a film with the English director James Whale. So, in a weird presentiment of his later career, Cushing's first job in the movies was with Whale, the director of the 1931 version of *Frankenstein* for Universal Studios. There would not be another straight retelling of Mary Shelley's story until Cushing's went into production in 1956.

By 1939, through a combination of studio politics, homophobia and his own disillusionment, James Whale had fallen from grace since his glory days at Universal, and was in the ignominious position of being a director-for-hire. In 1938, Small had signed a five-picture deal with United Artists and wanted Whale to direct his most expensive production, a swashbuckling adaptation of Alexandre Dumas' *The Man in the Iron Mask*. Filming commenced at the General Services studios in Hollywood in the last week of February 1939 with Louis Hayward playing the dual role of the tyrannical Louis XIV of France and his good twin brother Philippe. A double was required to stand in for Louis Hayward whenever he was acting opposite himself, then the two Haywards would be spliced together and the double removed. After little more than a fortnight, Cushing was acting opposite a Hollywood lead for a princely $75 per week. 'Apart from easing my immediate financial anxiety,' he wrote later, 'here was a Heaven-sent opportunity for someone who had never set foot in a film studio before to observe and learn how such old hands as Joseph Schildkraut and the rest of the distinguished cast set about the method of acting in this very technical medium, so different from giving a live performance in the theatre. Furthermore, I would be able to see the daily rushes and correct the many faults I was bound to commit, and so gradually improve. 'I dislike the word "technique" but that was where I learned the technique of screen acting.'[2]

Best of all, Cushing was in a position to refine his performance before the camera, knowing that it was destined for the cutting-room floor. As compensation for all his hard work, and to at least ensure that his

The students (Cushing, as Jones, centre) 'initiate' Stan Laurel and Oliver Hardy in *A Chump at Oxford* (1939)

face was seen on the screen, albeit briefly, Cushing was offered the part of the King's Messenger (or 'Second Officer' as it is presented in the film's credits). His single line is delivered on horseback, he looks young but to his credit not completely terrified. His voice is perhaps lighter than expected but unmistakable.

This 'new' role involved much ferocious swordplay, so Cushing had to convince James Whale that he had been fencing since childhood. He had never fenced in his life, but by sheer bare-faced honesty he got on the good side of the film's fencing master, Fred Cavens, who taught him enough to pass muster in the fight scenes, where, significantly, Cushing is on the side of the baddies.

The script for the film, by George Bruce, was massively overlong. Edward Small disliked and distrusted directors and Whale saw his control of the film slipping away during endless on-set rewrites. Whale did everything he could to antagonise Small, even sitting under the camera puffing on a cigar, letting the smoke drift into shot and necessitating expensive re-shoots. Inevitably, Whale was fired.

The finished film is fast-moving and enjoyable, with at least a few of Whale's trademark touches, like Hayward's effete delivery as the wicked King and the grotesque close-ups of the iron mask in which the King tortures his brother. While not a runaway success, it performed respectably against the big films of the year, which included some of cinema's most enduring classics – *The Wizard of Oz*, *Stagecoach* and

Gone With the Wind. For Peter Cushing, however, this was the start of his career on the big screen.

In his personal life, Cushing made friends easily. Louis Hayward found fellow Englishman Whale aloof and difficult to get on with, but this was clearly not the case with Hayward's English stand-in. Cushing was a frequent visitor to Hayward's home, a villa on the Brentwood heights, and was 'adopted' by Hayward's London-born wife, Ida Lupino. Cushing even tagged along to watch the location filming of Lupino's film *High Sierra*, where her co-star Humphrey Bogart entertained them by shooting coins in mid-air. Lupino, a practical joker, started a story about her 'adopted son' coming to stay. A puzzled columnist followed up the story 'Ida Lupino is always talking about her adopted son who lives in. People are always surprised when they meet him, because he is 6ft 2in Peter Cushing, the RKO actor.' Ida, then only 23, gave Cushing a photo signed 'To my son, love always, Mother.'[3]

On completing his first Hollywood picture, Cushing was once again a free agent, although with his finances now healthier than they had been for some time. In Schwab's Drug Store, a favourite hang-out for actors between engagements, he learned that Hal Roach Studios required English actors for the new Laurel and Hardy picture, *A Chump at Oxford*. Cushing went along, was accepted, and was with the legendary comedy duo for one week.

In this film, street sweepers Stan and Ollie accidentally foil a bank robbery and spend their reward on an Oxford education. They arrive in a hansom cab, wearing Eton collars, much to the amusement of a group of students, among them Cushing, as 'Jones'. He gets noticeably more lines than his fellows, presumably because he had an authentic English accent, and he looks every inch the star in his pencil moustache, waved hair and rakish mortar board. 'I think they're entitled to the royal initiation, don't you?' he pipes.

The 'initiation' involves getting the chumps lost in a maze, and then putting them to bed in the dean's lodgings – a cue for much business with a soda siphon. Cushing gets to play some very energetic slapstick and later sports a huge fake moustache, like 'Monsewer' Eddie Gray from The Crazy Gang. When the students march on the Americans in a bloodthirsty posse, they are one by one flung out of the window by Stan and land in the pond. Cushing remembered that this sequence was filmed in the evening, and that Laurel and Hardy ensured that those actors who got wet were looked after with dry towels and hot drinks. Cushing was lucky to appear in one of Laurel and Hardy's finest comedies, which contains some priceless bits of comic business. Cushing adored comedy – and comedians – all through his life, and doubtless learned a lot from this experience.

After *A Chump at Oxford*, Cushing found himself involved in his longest and most rewarding Hollywood film role, opposite Carole Lombard in *Vigil in the Night*, adapted from A J Cronin's novel. The director, George Stevens, had recently finished the rousing *Gunga Din* with Cary Grant and Douglas Fairbanks Jnr, and would later make Hollywood history twice over with *Shane* in 1952 and *Giant* in 1956. *Vigil in the Night* details the struggles of a young nurse, Anne Lee (Lombard), who takes the blame for a fatal mistake made by her sister Lucy (Anne Shirley), also a nurse. Anne loses her job and joins the staff of an impoverished country hospital, where she finds love with Doctor Prescott (Brian Aherne) but has to deal with a smallpox epidemic. Cushing was asked to play Joe Shand, boyfriend to the selfish Lucy.

The dialogue director for *Vigil* was Robert Coote, whom Cushing had met at a celebrity cricket match with David Niven, C Aubrey Smith and Boris Karloff. 'They were looking,' said Cushing 'for someone who could speak with a modified Lancashire accent that would be understood by American audiences.'[4] Cushing's 'modified Lancashire' sounds a little outlandish and it would surface again, with further modifications, in *From Beyond the Grave*.

Soon after shooting began in July 1939, Carole Lombard was hospitalised with acute appendicitis, and the production was stopped. In the six-week hiatus, Cushing was reportedly offered two other 'substantial' film roles, which, chiefly out of loyalty to Lombard, he declined. He was also reportedly screen tested for *Tom Brown's Schooldays*, directed by Robert Stevenson at RKO.

Cushing was able, however, to accept an offer from Ida Lupino to join her in a stage production of *Love from a Stranger* at Palm Springs. The previous year, Cushing had appeared in the drama, based on Agatha Christie's short story *Philomel Cottage*, with the Court Players at Nottingham. This time, however, he was playing the villain, Bruce Lovell, a role which had been played on film by Basil Rathbone in 1937.

Cushing's Hollywood career was, by any standards, going very well, until the turn of world events all but stopped it in its tracks. On 3rd September 1939, Britain declared war on Germany. At first, Cushing did not believe the headlines, 'but this "sensation" was the real thing.' He later admitted that, like many, when Neville Chamberlain had declared 'peace in our time', he'd believed him and 'got on with the job in hand.'[5] Full of patriotic fervour, Cushing immediately tried to enlist, regardless of his contract. He was classified 4C, however, due to torn ligaments in his knee from an old rugby injury and a perforated eardrum. He failed the medical. 'They are not in need of cannon fodder yet!'[6] Cushing was cheerfully informed by the MO.

Filming on *Vigil in the Night* re-commenced at the end of September, finishing on 30th November, and throughout the shooting Cushing still regarded the Hollywood 'goddesses' as sacrosanct. 'Before starting my first scene with Miss Lombard, I whispered to the director "Am I allowed to touch her?" He looked at me in astonishment and said "You can do what you like with her, as long as you cause no bodily harm."'[7]

RKO reported that George Stevens was so impressed with Cushing's early work on the film that he gave him a specially-written confrontation scene with Lombard and Aherne near the conclusion, in which Joe blames Anne for Lucy's death in the smallpox outbreak. 'More than one male star has hit his stride with just-such high-keyed histrionics,' noted the pressbook. And the scene did indeed make an impression. 'Peter Cushing dominates two dramatic scenes,' reported the *New York Daily News* when the film opened in May 1940. 'His acting has the same forceful quality that distinguishes Spencer Tracy's performances.'

After these several successful engagements, and by thriftily continuing to reside at the YMCA, Cushing was able to purchase a car by instalments. An infection in his heel, however, spread upwards and there was a risk that he would lose the leg. A more acceptable treatment was found but it still required several weeks of painful and costly attention. His leg was saved but the car, alas, had to go. Cushing kept busy with several projects, including *Women in War* with Patric Knowles and *The Howards of Virginia* with

Cary Grant, which was so brief that he didn't bother to mention it on subsequent CVs. Many of these were small roles, requiring little more than a few days' work, although the money was useful.

Cushing's role in *Laddie* (1940) is similarly brief, but interesting because his character is significant to the plot. The film stars Tim Holt as Laddie Stanton, a hardworking young farmer who falls in love with Pamela (Virginia Gilmore), beautiful daughter of the neighbouring landowner Mr Pryor (Miles Mander), an embittered Englishman. Pamela's brother has been dishonourably discharged from the Army and has run away, causing her father to suspect the motives of any suitors. Eventually, Robert reappears, ill with a fever, and the reconciliation between father and son means that Laddie and Pamela can wed. Cushing only has two scenes – and two lines – but plays them for all he is worth, and gets to kiss saucer-eyed Virginia Gilmore into the bargain.

Undoubtedly the strangest subjects that Cushing worked on in Hollywood were the short films in the *Passing Parade* series, produced by John Nesbitt. These were 10-minute MGM support features, generally without dialogue but with a voice-over from Nesbitt, illustrating curious events and scenes from history.

In *Dreams*, directed by Felix E Feist, Cushing is seen in fitful sleep – in his dream, his feet are chained to a railway line and a train is bearing down on him. The narration

As Clive of India in *Your Hidden Master*, part of the *Passing Parade* series (1940)

explains that the dream represents the dreamer's desire to escape from the circumstances of his life, but he is held back by devotion to a loved one. Cushing gives a very affecting impression of inescapable dread in this brief scene. A split second from *Dreams* was used in a montage at the beginning of another short, *The Woman in the House*, but Cushing does not appear in the rest of the film.

Cushing's most memorable *Passing Parade* role was in *Your Hidden Master*. This related an event from the early life of Robert Clive when, in a fit of despair, he tried to take his own life. When Clive brought a revolver to his head, however, the gun would not fire. A second attempt and again, nothing. The third time, Clive aimed at a pitcher of water and the gun fired. He took this as an omen and gave up the attempt.

Cushing's compelling portrayal of the young Clive, influenced no doubt by the actor's own self-destructive feelings before the start of his stage career, led to talk at MGM of grooming him for stardom. However, as the war continued to rage in Europe,

and horrifying news came through of the London Blitz, Cushing's thoughts turned more and more to returning home.

Towards the end of 1940, James Whale was booked to direct a new film for Columbia. *They Dare Not Love*, a story of Nazi persecution in Austria, starred George Brent and Martha Scott. Although the film was intended to revive Whale's failing career, his fee was only $30,000, and the production, which began on New Year's Day 1941, was an uncomfortable one. The director disliked the script ('curiously naïve romantic propaganda'[8] one review called it) and did not get on with either his leading man or the raucous Columbia producer Harry Cohn. Three weeks later, he was asked to leave and the remainder of the film was shot by Charles 'King' Vidor. Whale would never work as a film director again.

Cushing's role was Sub-Lieutenant Blacker, who leads a raid at the end of the film to rescue Brent and Scott. If Cushing did indeed leave Hollywood on 18th January 1941, as he states in his autobiography, then he left *They Dare Not Love* before Whale, and probably knew nothing of the director's dismissal.

Back in New York, Cushing started saving money for his return trip. He worked for NBC radio, in a serial called *The Grandpa Family*, and played Tom Prior in a radio production called *Outward Bound*, as well as participating in several radio commercials. There were other, more colourful jobs, too. After a disastrous morning as a car-park attendant (he was too timid to smash the cars into position), he found himself briefly cast as an assistant to a boss-eyed illusionist. Cushing quickly learned the secrets of the trade, such as various coded signals and different ways to hold the cards, but the engagement only lasted three weeks and he was faced with the prospect of sleeping in a flophouse.

Help came via a chance meeting in Greenwich Village with Canadian actor John Ireland, who recognised Cushing from his film appearances. The two actors teamed up to pool their resources, Ireland telling his new friend that as social security payments had been deducted from his previous salaries he was entitled to $18 unemployment benefit per week. This kept them going until the pair, and Ireland's wife Elaine, found employment in the American equivalent of a repertory company, a summer stock troupe at the picturesque Green Mansions camp near Warrensburg, New York State. Although there were no wages, all expenses were paid by the company and there was a bonus of $100 at the conclusion of the four-month contract. They began in May 1941 and worked through a varied bill, including a production of *Macbeth* presented in modern dress, in which Cushing played Banquo and the Doctor.

Other productions at Warrensburg included an Irish one-act comedy *Pound on Demand*, in which Cushing played an Irish policeman, and this was presented with the short Noël Coward play *Fumed Oak*, with Cushing in the lead as Henry Gow. There followed *The Ghost Train* by Arnold Ridley, *The Petrified Forest* by Robert E Sherwood, *Biography* by S N Behrman and *Night Must Fall*. The troupe were accommodated in spacious log cabins near a lake, among the pine trees of upstate New York, and after four invigorating months, Cushing was eventually able to put $25 into his savings for his return to England.

The Warrensburg shows had been attended by various talent scouts and, as a result of their attentions, Cushing was invited back to New York to take part in a show on Broadway. He had planned to make his way over the Adirondack mountains to Canada, the better to secure a passage home, but fate (briefly) had other ideas. Although he was also offered a part by Gilbert Miller in a play called *RAF*, Cushing joined the cast of the Theatre Associates production of *The Seventh Trumpet* by Charles Rann Kennedy at the Mansfield Theater on Broadway. He played Police Constable Percival, a London 'Bobby' wounded in the Blitz, in what he called 'a mystical war play. It mystified the audiences, the critics and the cast.'[10]

Although this experience enabled Cushing to say, in future years, that he had in fact played on Broadway, it was hardly the most auspicious run in theatre history. The play opened on 21st November and closed on the 29th. Nine days later, world events took a further tragic turn, as the USA declared war on Japan. It now became imperative that Cushing return to England as soon as possible. He redoubled his efforts to raise the fare home and was advised to go to Canada where a working passage would be more easily secured. He eventually left New York in February, sent on his way with donations from friends and colleagues that included a significant sum from Rita Hayworth.

On 8th February 1942 Cushing arrived in Montreal and immediately made his way to the YMCA. His various jobs in Canada were no less varied than they had been in New York, his first being as a cinema usher, in a pill-box hat and an ill-fitting uniform.

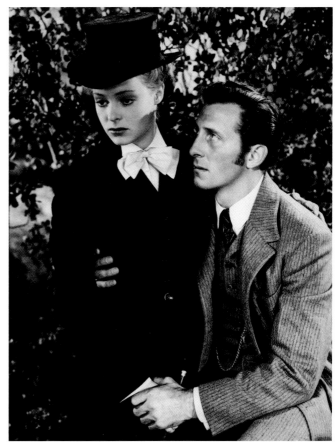

Virginia Gilmore as Pamela Pryor with Cushing as her brother Robert in *Laddie* (1940)

He found work with a local studio who were filming inserts and special effects shots for the film *49th Parallel*. The film was being made in England, directed by Michael Powell, and starring Laurence Olivier and Eric Portman (both of whom Cushing would work with later in his career). Cushing's job for the art department was to manufacture miniature flags depicting the Japanese rising sun and the Nazi swastika. However, his handiwork was discovered by a cleaner in his bedroom at the YMCA and Cushing was arrested as a fifth columnist. A telephone call to the film studio soon set matters right, and the Mounties who apprehended him at least provided some reference for his next job, which was portraying Captain Roberts of the Royal Canadian Mounted Police in the Canadian Ministry Film *We All Help*.

The remuneration from these various activities meant that Cushing finally had enough money to sail for England. He joined the crew of the Merchant Navy ship *Tilpala* and left for England on Sunday 15th March 1942. After three years in America he was on his way home.

Chapter Four

Back to Dear Old Blighty

'I sat in a barrel high up on the mast, my feet in 12 inches of rain water. I was up there for six hours. By the end of the watch my legs had frozen and I could not get down. Two men were sent up to rescue me,' Cushing recounted mournfully. 'My second attempt to help win the war was no more successful than my fiasco as a blood donor. When he heard I was an actor, the Captain muttered some uncomplimentary expletive and put me in charge of the ship's cat for the rest of my service at sea.'[1]

On Friday 27th March 1942, the *Tilpala* neared a severely bomb-damaged Liverpool. It was more than three years since Cushing had seen England, and he remembered how his heart fell at the sight of the wrecked ships in the Mersey. He boarded a train and headed for his brother David's poultry farm at Norwood Hill, near Reigate, where his parents were also staying. His sudden appearance was completely unexpected, and Cushing remembers that his mother took one look at her returned 'prodigal' and fainted quite away. Three days later, Cushing was once again turned down for active service, and headed for the Drury Lane offices of the Entertainment National Services Association – 'ENSA', which the services quickly took to mean 'Every Night Something Awful'.

In charge of the ENSA drama department was actor Henry Oscar, who would later appear with Cushing in *The Brides of Dracula* as the peppery schoolmaster Herr Lang. Cushing recalled that Oscar had been searching everywhere for 'a presentable young man with talent', but they were all in the services or playing leads in the West End. Suddenly, he seemed to have found an actor exempt from service, fresh from Broadway, *insisting* that he work for ENSA. When asked whether he could learn the part in three days, Cushing said 'Yes, of course.' 'For just a few moments,' Oscar recalled, 'I thought he was an escaped lunatic.'[2]

Cushing was placed in a company touring with *Private Lives*, Noël Coward's brittle comedy about a divorced couple who meet up in a French Riviera hotel where they are on honeymoon with their respective new partners. Cushing was to take over the lead, Elyot Chase, a part Coward had written for himself and played to enormous acclaim in the première

run in 1930. Sonia Dresdel was cast as the female lead, Amanda Prynne, the part originally played by Gertrude Lawrence. Miss Dresdel, born Lois Obee in 1909, ultimately made a reputation playing villainous women. Humphrey Morton and Yvonne Hills played the other partners – 'the skittles' as Coward referred to them – originally played by Laurence Olivier and Adrienne Allen.

Members of the ENSA touring parties were paid a comfortable £10 a week, although anything up to £3 was given over for accommodation (generally hostels) and ration-books were surrendered. Joan Craft, who was stage manager for the tour, went on to be one of the first female television producers at the BBC and recalled the ENSA days with great affection. 'We toured Army, Navy and Air Force camps all over England. It was all planned by Drury Lane, so virtually all one had to do was to get into a coach in London and get driven off. We rarely knew where we were going, or where we were when we got there.'

The first engagements were in the relative comfort of the fully equipped garrison theatres, but as time went by, and the locations became more isolated, the company had to take with them a wooden framework which was fitted-up on site and hung with black drapes to form a stage. 'We had a carpenter with us who would help,' Craft remembered, 'and the soldiers would lend a hand – but they didn't really know what to do. We intended to enjoy it, though. Because we had the day free, there was always something to see, and Peter would find something new wherever we went. The show pottered along quite happily. I think it did some good because we ended up in some places that were terribly isolated, it couldn't have been drearier. Not that I'd say the boys really *liked* it, to be honest, but it was a night's entertainment.'

As for what brought Cushing home, Craft is under no doubt. 'It was his patriotism that brought him back to England. I if he had stayed in America he could have been a very good light British actor abroad, another David Niven-type. He was on a cloud when he was in London. He could hardly believe he was back. He went around wide-eyed. It nearly made you weep, the enthusiasm in him when he got back to London.'

Craft and Cushing became good friends. 'He had the most extraordinary laugh,' she recalled. 'We were at the theatre in London, the two of us, I can't remember what we were seeing, but there was this line "I never knew anyone who took sleeping together so literally" and it happened we were sharing a bed in London at that time. There was suddenly this great booming '*Ah-Ha-Ha!!*' Everyone turned around and it was him. It made me laugh like mad or blush like mad, I can't remember which. He was like a very young person, a child, really, in his absolute astonishment at life.'

Sonia Dresdel had been working solidly with ENSA for more than a year. She left the company in May 1942 and the part of Amanda was recast. The new actress was called Helen Beck. 'Peter was cuckoo about her,' Craft remembered , 'in the sweetest way.'[3]

Cushing met his future wife for the first time outside the stage door of the Theatre Royal, Drury Lane. 'At the stage door,' Helen herself remembered, 'I saw a man with an old suitcase listing to starboard and a grubby ancient mackintosh, wearing a *very* old grey velvet hat. It was Peter. He swept the hat off and greeted me as if I were royalty – he seemed unconscious of his appearance. I thought: "This is the strangest individual I've ever met – but the most attractive!"[4]

'I had never met him, yet I knew, deep in my deepest heart, we had been together before. Tall and lean, a pale, almost haggard face, with astonishingly large, blue eyes, a jacket beyond description and repair, spotless white shirt badly frayed at cuffs and collar, a pair of once dark blue corduroy trousers, most of the nap long since worn away through constant wear, down-at-heel shoes of grey suede. Later, I was to discover the soles were as worn down as the heels, and had holes as large as half-crowns in their centres, also woollen stockings that have never known the comfort of a darning needle. He walked with a slight limp, using an ash walking-stick, the ferrule now a mere useless ring of metal around its tip, on his back a huge and obviously heavy kit-bag, such as sailors use.' (The stick, which went with Cushing everywhere, was christened 'Elyot' after his character.) 'There was an aura about this "beloved vagabond". His hands told me he was either a musician or an artist – they reminded me of those drawn by Albrecht Dürer – and when he bent over one of mine to kiss it, a faint and quite delightful waft of tobacco and lavender water hung upon the air. I knew I would love him for the rest of my days – and beyond.'[5]

'Can you think of a more romantic place to meet?'[6] Cushing said later. They were waiting for the coach to take them to their next port of call at Colchester. They sat together on the coach to run through their lines. 'Helen was word-perfect and soon we began to talk of

One of Peter's favourite pictures of Helen, taken during a holiday on the Norfolk Broads

other things...'[7] Helen had much in common with Cushing, including a love of classical music and literature. She also adored whodunnits and Jimmy 'Schnozzle' Durante.

'I wouldn't have said that they fell in love straight away,' says Craft, 'but they got on terribly well in the beginning. Peter wasn't tremendously mature, in fact he never was, there was always a naïveté about him. Helen worshipped him, I think, it was that sort of score. He was terribly fond of her, but she was just smitten by him.'[8]

Violet Helen Beck was born on 8th February 1905 in St Petersburg. Her father, Ernest Beck, was a Lancashire industrialist, proprietor of the James Beck Spinning Company, at the time the largest firm of cotton spinners in Russia. The mills had been handed down for generations by his family, who, though British, had helped to pioneer the textile industry there. In Russia, Ernest Beck married a Nordic beauty of Swedish-Polish parentage, Helen's mother. The Becks lived in luxury until the 1917 Revolution, when, almost penniless, they escaped to Britain with 12-year-old Helen, who was already set on being an actress.

'When I was four,' Helen told the *TV Mirror* in October 1955, 'I spoke fluent French, German, Russian and English, English the worst of all. When I finished school in Switzerland my English was so bad that something had to be done about it. So my father sent me to Kate Rorke, the teacher of voice production who trained so many of our actors and actresses, and there I learned to speak properly. That's how I went into the theatre.'[9]

Helen worked for André Charlot and C B Cochran, who put on revues filled with beautiful young ladies. She was selected from 500 girls to appear in a Cochran revue in America, and at the age of 21 in Hollywood she appeared with Eric Fawcett – later a television producer – in Raoul Walsh's film *What Price Glory?* Later she switched to the stage and toured the United States.

Returning to England, Helen became the English tutor to Yvette la Brousse, who was soon to marry the Aga Khan. Helen declined a permanent job with her in Egypt, opting to stay with her parents in England. She was a secretary to comedian Sonnie Hale and his then-wife, the musical star Jessie Matthews, and went on to join several repertory companies. Helen's previous marriage, to Kenton Redgrave, had been 'disastrous' and she rarely spoke of it.

Actor Michael Redington and his wife Ann became friends with the Cushings in the late 1940s. 'Helen didn't make any demands for herself,' Ann recalls. 'which was bad, really, because I think you have to make demands as a woman. But they were very, very happy together. Helen never really spoke about her previous marriage, because it was so awful. She was very, very unhappy. She had a child, which she lost, and the man deserted her. I think it coloured her whole idea of marriage. So I think, in a way, Peter made up for the child as well as being her husband.'[11]

'Even then, Helen wasn't very well,' Joan Craft added. 'She wasn't very strong. She was very ill towards the end of the run, in Canterbury.'[12] Helen suffered a haemorrhage while staying at Bridge in Kent, and Cushing himself was later diagnosed with congestion of the lung while in Taunton, Somerset. Helen kept him warm and nursed him back to health, a difficult task with the war-time rationing of food and fuel. Soon, it became clear that the ENSA tour had exhausted them both and they were invalided out. Free from one lot of responsibilities, Cushing assumed another. He proposed to Helen.

'After nearly a year of fighting on the stage,' said Cushing, 'we decided to try it at home.'[13] Peter Wilton Cushing and Violet Helen Beck were married on 10th April 1943 at Marylebone Register Office. Helen's parents were the witnesses, Cushing having decided not to tell his own parents, in case of objections. 'I married Helen for money,' he later admitted. 'She had £30 and I had £23 and ten shillings.'[14] After a short holiday in Sussex, the couple took lodgings at 18 Bellingham Mansions, Pitt Street, Kensington, not far from Helen's parents.

Following his de-mob from ENSA, Cushing was taken on by agent Al Parker. Albert Parker was an

ebullient New Yorker, who had been variously a writer, director and actor in silent films, including John Barrymore's *Sherlock Holmes* in 1922. Finding work difficult to come by when the talkies arrived, Parker came to England, where he directed short films until 1938 when he became a full-time agent. In May, Parker secured for Cushing not one but two roles in an optimistically extravagant production of *War and Peace*, directed by Julius Gellner. Cushing played two roles – Captain Ramballe and Alexander I, Emperor of Russia. With him in the cast were Barry Morse, Peter Illing, Paulette Preney, Frederick Valk and his former ENSA boss Henry Oscar.

War and Peace was a mammoth 32-scene production that lasted nearly four hours. The scenery consisted of a series of raised levels and staircases, and the backdrops were projected slides – a revolution in the theatre then. 'Hardly any canvas has been needed,' reported *Illustrated* magazine in a large colour feature announcing the London presentation, 'a valuable saving in these days of fabric scarcity. The backdrop may be ... a palace garden, a clouded sky, Moscow roofs, a bleak plain or a snow-clad forest, by the simple swift means of a coloured lantern slide, which gives a brighter and more sharply defined background than the scenic painter could achieve.'[15]

This was all well and good, but as Cushing recalled, the slides frequently got muddled, were placed in upside down and sometimes didn't appear at all. 'After cavorting around and about in Moscow,' he said, 'to the music of Tchaikovsky, Glinka, Mozart and Rameau, we were transported swiftly to Borodino, where a mighty battle ensued.'[16] Special records were made for the battle of Borodino; the prologue and epilogue of a Moscow Anti-Aircraft battery in 1941 included actual air-raid recordings. Apparently it was sometimes difficult to differentiate between the war onstage and the one going on outside.

Nevertheless, this was one of the most involved pieces to be staged in war-time London, and it received a hefty charge of publicity. In one photograph of the company sitting in the stalls of the Phoenix Theatre, Cushing can be spotted, heavily bandaged for his role as Captain Ramballe.

War and Peace opened at the Grand Theatre Blackpool in June; at the Palace Theatre Manchester in July; and at London's Phoenix Theatre in the Charing Cross Road in August. Reviews praised its scope and ambition. 'Mr Valk's Kutuzov and Mr Illing's Napoleon are notable rivals in vocal power ... and make the artillery seem but a faint accompaniment to their choleric explosions.'[17]

Unfortunately, despite high expectations, the play lasted just 20 performances (6th – 21st August 1943) and as the play closed, there was a rumour that producer Tom Arnold had *intended* the play to be a flop, so that a legitimate loss could be shown on the income tax returns. 'If that was what he wanted,' Cushing said 'that sure was what he got!'[18]

Cushing's next engagement didn't even get to a first performance. Bernard Miles was to star and the director was a refugee from Hitler's purge of the Jews. Cushing's part was a civil engineer. He realised the project was doomed when the director asked 'Doz zis mean you are polite viz zer machines?' The rehearsals limped on for a few days before the whole thing was quietly laid to rest.

Al Parker looked for alternative work for Cushing, and in securing a part for him in a radio play, so began a relationship for the actor that would last for 50 years and lead to some of his greatest successes. In September 1943, Peter Cushing gave his first performance for the BBC.

Since the Blitz, the BBC had decided it was unsafe to broadcast plays from London, so Cushing's first radio role, in *Mendelssohn*, was broadcast from the Bedford Corn Exchange on 8th September. The programme was an hour-long musical biography featuring the BBC Orchestra and Chorus conducted by Sir Adrian Boult. Cushing's fee was ten guineas, plus two nights' subsistence at 20 shillings a night, and a third class return from London to Bedford. There was nothing third class about the cast, however – Basil G Langton played Mendelssohn and Peggy Ashcroft his sister Fanny, with Patricia Wynne and Austin Trevor as Queen Victoria and Prince Albert. The supporting cast included comedy actor Deryck Guyler and Carleton Hobbs, who in the 1950s and 60s would achieve fame with a 17-year run as radio's most popular Sherlock Holmes. Cushing listed his character as 'Paul' although it was not given in the *Radio Times*, and he referred to the production as *Memoirs of Mendelssohn*.

Throughout his career, Cushing's letter-writing was prodigious. Letters of thanks, praise, inquiry, suggestion, correction and criticism. After every broadcast on radio, and later on television – more often than not the very same night – he would write a letter of appreciation to the producer. The following, to Stephen Potter, producer of *Mendelssohn*, is typical of many that followed, although this letter contained a reference to a heartening turn in world events. 'May I express my appreciation for your courtesy and thought in arranging for me to play in the Mendelssohn programme this week. Coupled with the Italian Armistice, it was a most happy experience!'

On 29th September, Peter and Helen moved to Airlie Gardens in Kensington. For £3 a week, they rented the garden flat in a cul-de-sac backing onto the tennis courts. Property in that location is now highly valued, but the Cushings found their home easily because of the general evacuation of London due to the bombing. They had little furniture, and even less money, so Helen decorated the flat with furniture made of wooden crates and boxes found on bomb sites.

The end of 1943 saw the beginning of another long association for Cushing, and one that would help him greatly in times of dire financial straits. He took part in a performance at the 'Q' Theatre, situated near Kew Bridge at Richmond. The tiny independent theatre was run by Jack and Beattie De Leon and was a starting ground for a great array of actors and actresses. Dirk Bogarde, Vivien Leigh, Joan Collins, Anthony Quayle and Margaret Lockwood all trod the boards for the first time at the 'Q'. John Schlesinger, Richard Attenborough, Flora Robson and Michael Hordern appeared there too.

Cushing's first play at the 'Q' was *The Morning Star* by Emlyn Williams, which ran from 16th November, with Charles Hickman as producer. The fee was a single ten-guinea payment for a fortnight's rehearsal and a week-long run of nine shows. Cushing played Cliff Parrilow, and this was the first time, of many, that he would share the bill with the character actress and comedienne Irene Handl.

The 'Q' programmes are crammed with gems of incidental detail. 'This theatre is disinfected throughout with Jeyes' Fluid.' 'Smoking is permitted, "Abdullas" for choice.' The seat prices range from 7/6 to 3/6, or, if you were 'skint', the pit stalls at 2/6. Although the conditions, particularly in war-time, could be spartan, the love and dedication of the De Leons shone like a beacon. 'There will always be a warm place in my heart,' Cushing wrote later, 'for the dear old "Q".'[19]

Cushing then returned to the BBC for two more radio broadcasts, *Destination Unknown*, recorded on 11th November at Bedford College for producer V C Clinton-Baddely (the fee in this case was down to seven-and-a-half guineas) and *The Lay of Horatius* on 16th December 1943 for producer John Burrell (for only six guineas). Burrell was on the board of the Old Vic and later directed Olivier's *Richard III*, in which Cushing would appear during the Old Vic tour of Australasia.

On 14th December 1943, Cushing had had a meeting with producer Sydney Attwood at the BBC. 'Since my return from the USA I have often felt a stranger in my own land,' he wrote to Attwood the following day. 'My visit to you yesterday made me feel as if I had never been away and was urgently needed here! Thank you for this encouragement and the courteous reception which I most warmly appreciated.' To further his cause he enclosed a list of the 'dialects and foreign languages' in which he was proficient. 'French, Welsh and German', he was quick to state, were only 'accents'. The dialects were 'West Country, Lancashire, Cockney, Irish and Scotch'.

As the war continued to rage, Cushing, assisted and supported by his new wife, began to see his career as an actor flourish, but there were still surprises and hardships to come.

Chapter Five

French Without Tears

After Christmas, Cushing was back at the 'Q' for *The Dark Potential* by Joan Morgan. This was a domestic melodrama involving the descent into madness of Olivia Russell, who is prevented from controlling the lives of her son and daughter and tries to poison her husband. The action takes place in the Russells' house near the Crystal Palace, and involves the burning down of the palace on 30th November 1936. For this play, Cushing was reunited with his old ENSA sparring partner Sonia Dresdel, who played Olivia; Peter Copley was the husband and Renée Asherson played the daughter, Fenella, while Cushing played Valentine Christie.

The Dark Potential transferred to the Comedy Theatre with the new title *This Was A Woman* but Cushing declined to join the new production. It ran for more than a year in London and was made into a film in 1948, with Sonia Dresdel and many of the London cast, and it is interesting to speculate what might have happened if Cushing had gone with the play to the West End.

However, during the brief 'Q' run Helen had fallen seriously ill and was admitted to the Samaritan Free Hospital for Women in the Marylebone Road. Cushing was reluctant to leave her alone while she convalesced. In his autobiography, Cushing related simply that 'Helen had to undergo major surgery for a hysterectomy and a lifeless foetus was discovered within her womb.'[1]

After Christmas little was forthcoming from the BBC, so Cushing returned to the 'Q'. He appeared in a play every month or so, beginning with *The Fifth Column* by Ernest Hemingway on 27th March 1944. Next, on 7th May was *The Crime of Margaret Foley*, a play set in Dublin written by actors Percy Robinson and Terence de Marney. Cushing played a character called Kevin Ormond, with Judy Kelly in the title role plus George Merritt, Percy Robinson himself and Ian Fleming (no relation to the James Bond writer). 'The Week's "Q" Thought' given on the programme, shows a hardening of attitudes to the ongoing conflict. 'You are just as safe inside a theatre as anywhere else – why not forget for a little while that you are not as safe anywhere as in peacetime.' Cushing's next 'Q' play was a drama with a German setting, *Watch on the*

Rhine, in mid-June (Helen tutored her husband on his German accent) and he followed this with another turn as Elyot in *Private Lives*.

Cushing tried the BBC for work again, asking Sydney Attwood if there was anything suitable for which he would be considered. 'I do hope you are keeping well,' he wrote 'and are ready for the peace, which I feel is not so far off now, don't you?'

With the autumn came a return to the West End, this time as Private Charles, a Free Frenchman, in a new play called *Happy Few* at the Cambridge Theatre. Once again, Helen taught him the correct inflection for each line. *Happy Few* was written by a 26-year-old Canadian officer who went under the *nom-de-plume* of Paul Anthony – apparently even director William Mollison, who had previously specialised in musical comedies, did not know the writer's real name. The play was set at El Alamein in the nine days leading up to the Eighth Army advance in October 1942, and was described by Beverley Baxter in the *Evening Standard*: '*Happy Few* is simply the story of a young captain with a dozen men who held a hill in the desert. A stretcher-bearer mysteriously joins the beleaguered little garrison. His hands are bandaged because they have been wounded. When the cook's eyes are injured, these wounded hands bandage the poor fellow's eyes. Two days later, these same hands remove the bandages, slowly, tenderly, while all the soldiers stand by to find out if the cook is blinded. When the bandages are removed, the stretcher-bearer says "Open your eyes slowly. Have courage. You will see." And when the cook cries pitifully that he can see, I am sorry for anyone in the theatre whose tears were dry. Yes, it is the Christ theme, *The Servant in the House*, *The Passing of the Third Floor Back*.'[2]

The cast included popular Cockney character actor Wally Patch, Tony Quinn, Derek Blomfield and John Slater. The play opened on 10th October 1944 and though very well reviewed, only ran for a fortnight. During this short run, however, Cushing was seen by Elsie Beyer, general manager with the well-known and influential theatrical management company H M Tennent Ltd. Tennent's were producing Terence Rattigan's comedy *While the Sun Shines* at the Globe Theatre. The play had been running since 1943 and concerned the misadventures of an American soldier, Lieutenant Wiseman, and a Free Frenchman, Lieutenant Colbert, who attempt to woo the eligible Lady Elizabeth Randall away from her intended husband, the Earl of Harpenden. On 12th January 1944 the *Tatler and Bystander* had written 'a Rattigan play is fast becoming a good reason in itself to go to the theatre and in this comedy-cum-farce playgoers will not be disappointed. The slenderness of the plot is cunningly concealed amidst situations amusingly conceived and outrageously dispelled, so much so that the plot itself becomes of secondary importance.'

The play's director was Anthony Asquith, who had directed the film of Rattigan's *French Without Tears* in 1939, and the thriller *Cottage to Let* in 1941. He would go on to direct the film of *While The Sun Shines* in 1946. The original cast included Michael Wilding as the Earl, Hugh McDermott as Wiseman and Eugene Deckers as Colbert. Deckers had to take a break after an 18-month run, and Cushing, with his recent experience playing a Frenchman, was just the man to take over. He joined the production at the end of 1944.

Practical joker Michael Wilding kept the cast amused with his antics during the long run, and became a good friend to the Cushings. So too did veteran actor Ronald Squire, who played The Duke of Ayr and Sterling – the Earl's father – in the original run, and who rejoined the production when it went on tour in March. The cast were in Bolton when the end of the war in Europe was announced on 8th May 1945, and Squire was responsible for organising the V E Day celebrations. He had joked that he would see that Cushing was 'well-placed' and as the tour reached its last week, met up with an old friend, Edith Evans, who was about to direct a production of Sheridan's *The Rivals* with William Armstrong. Squire suggested Cushing for the role of Faulkland and Evans accepted readily.

The Rivals was a celebratory production to re-open the Criterion Theatre, which had been occupied by the BBC during the war. Before coming to London, how-ever, there was a brief tour of the North. In the role of Jack Absolute for this prepatory run was Terence Morgan, who shared a dressing room with Cushing and who would become a good friend. 'I was totally wrong for Jack Absolute,' Morgan recalls. 'I was far too young, so I didn't get to London. Edith had a bizarre way of directing. It was something to do with the movement of stillness. So she stood stock still in the middle of the stage and everyone had to move around her. She didn't really direct at all. Tyrone Guthrie did most of it.'[3] Cushing remembered William Armstrong complaining that co-directing with theatrical *grande dame* Evans was somewhat trying – 'he couldn't see anything going on "from under Edith's thumb" so Guthrie was also enlisted to act as arbitrator. We always knew our performances

A contemporary cartoon for Edith Evans' production of *The Rivals* (1945)

were below par if Guthrie popped his head around the dressing-room door and said "Loved your hat, dear."'[4]

The London production starred Anthony Quayle, whose Jack Absolute was described as 'fresh, hearty, and as likeable as a games master in one of our best public schools.' Edith Evans played Mrs Malaprop, with able support from Morland Graham, Pauline Jameson and Reginald Beckwith. Cushing's character of Faulkland is a jealous and temperamental beau, forever finding fault with his love Julia, although she is faithful and tolerates him. This was Cushing's most prominent stage role so far, and he received considerable acclaim in the first-night reviews. 'Peter Cushing conspires to make that dreary creature Faulkland both comic and sympathetic', said W A Darlington in the *Post* of 26th September. The *Times* praised 'A Faulkland in Peter Cushing who cleverly contrives to relieve that part of the tedium which the doubts and hesitation of the melancholy lover so often arouse.'[5] 'Peter Cushing raves most ardently as Faulkland...'[6] raved the *Tatler and Bystander*.

Although it was generally felt that the whole show, except for Evans, lacked comic gusto, it ran through Christmas and clocked up 166 performances. Oliver Messel's costumes and settings were lavish, bringing a touch of glamour to a war-weary London starved of spectacle. The scenery featured a backdrop depicting 18th-century Bath, Edith Evans looked like a galleon in full sail, while Cushing, in his buckled boots, powdered wig and bicorne hat looked very like Captain Pearson, the character he would play in *John Paul Jones* ten years later.

Also in the cast was Michael Gough, who would later join Cushing in Hammer's *Dracula*. Cushing and Gough shared a dressing room on tour, and in Liverpool their dresser won the pools and went on a spree. 'From the first interval,' Gough remembered 'the pub next door was dispensing free drinks until closing time.' But Cushing was concerned that the man's largesse might have exceeded his actual winnings. As Gough recalled, 'Peter said "If he's only won a few bob, how is he going to pay the pub's bill? I dare say we could help, couldn't we?" Peter would help anyone.'[7]

On 22nd January 1946, the cast of *The Rivals* were invited to the broadcast of a BBC radio play by the producer David Chandler. Cushing wrote afterwards to apologise for his booming laugh. 'It was so kind of you to let my wife and I come to the show last night, and to put up with my noise. But I really did enjoy the show and I'm afraid that was my way of showing it.' There was also discussion about another project. 'I shall be awfully glad to see the script of Frank Richards', if it's no bother to you to look one up.' Chandler replied 'I have now procured a copy of the Richards script from the files. Would you come round one morning or afternoon to read it? Incidentally, I see George Orwell is bringing out a collection of his essays shortly, including the article he wrote for *Horizon* on Richards. Combined with Richards' own ingenious piece, it ought to keep you amused for days!'

'When the run of *The Rivals* ended,' wrote Cushing, 'so began an 18-month period of unemployment. The rent for the flat had risen, ten per cent of all earnings went to my agent and I was now just inside the income tax bracket. Soon I was heavily in debt.'[8]

There is an indication that at one point Cushing fell foul of Hugh 'Binkie' Beaumont, the legendary managing director of H M Tennent, who reputedly held unofficial auditions at his house in Lord North Street reclining in pastel pyjamas on black silk bedsheets. While claims are exaggerated of a 'gay mafia' operating in the London theatre during the war, there were undeniably a large number of homosexual directors, writers and actors, including Noël Coward, Terence Rattigan, John Gielgud, Emlyn Williams and Michael Benthall, with whom the heterosexual, somewhat unsophisticated Cushing had little in common. His idea of a good evening in was to knock over battalions of lead soldiers with a pop-gun, a world away from the social whirl of the theatrical cocktail party. In addition to this, there was another hurdle. Cushing admitted that he was 'the

world's worst at auditions, not once getting the part I had read for at those... humiliating sessions.'[9] Times may well have been extremely hard, but as far as acting roles were concerned, when *The Rivals* finished on 16th February 1946, the next year-and-a-half was not totally barren.

Although not particularly lucrative, there were several more fortnight-long engagements at the 'Q', including the role of Doctor Dorn in Chekhov's *The Seagull* and the Coward triple-bill *Tonight at 8.30*. This trio of short plays saw Cushing in three parts (Chris Faber in *The Astonished Heart*, Karl Sandys in *We Were Dancing* and Henry Gow in *Fumed Oak*) and sharing the bill with Joan Greenwood, who had already appeared in several films, and would achieve lasting fame in the Ealing comedies *Kind Hearts and Coronets* and *The Man in the White Suit*.

There was more radio work and Cushing's first serial for the BBC, a 12-part adaptation of Anthony Trollope's novel *Orley Farm*. Cushing received ten guineas – equivalent to a fortnight at the 'Q' – for each of his four half-hour episodes as Mr Round, Junior. The Rounds, father and son, were a somewhat disreputable pair of solicitors; Round Senior was played by Leo Sheffield, and the cast included Arnold Ridley (who wrote *The Ghost Train* and achieved immortality as Private Godfrey in *Dad's Army*), Barbara Lott, Roderick Lovell and Philip Wade. It was produced by Howard Rose and adapted by H Oldfield Box. The programme was recorded for a weekly repeat and discs were produced for overseas transcription services, so there is a chance that these recordings may still exist in a sound archive or a private collection.

At this time, there were only two radio channels, the Home Service and the Forces' programme. Radio was the principal form of entertainment for the nation, and doggedly cheered the population along with *Music While You Work* and *Wot, No Gloom?* (Home), *The RAF March Past* and Eric Barker in *Merry-Go-Round* (Forces). On 11th December Cushing was back at the Home Service for the *Wednesday Matinee*, *A Fourth for Bridge* with Raf de la Torre. The producer was Hugh Stewart, to whom Cushing wrote the following day. 'Thank you for the kind and helpful way you guided me through our little "piece" yesterday afternoon. Normally, I'm so nervous that my knees knock together like castanets and my voice gets higher and higher with fright! But thanks to your diplomatic guidance and encouragement, I felt comparatively cosy. So much I enjoyed the last few days that I wish they were not over!' It seems that Cushing must have provided some impromptu 'sound effects' for the play, as he adds the PS 'I can also "do" a chicken and a motor horn!'

Interspersed with Cushing's BBC work was the title role in another 'Q' production, *The Curious Dr Robson* by J Lee Thompson, from 26th November to

1st December 1946. The play was a contemporary whodunnit, set in Robson's house in the Devon village of Clevely, involving such characters as a local seamstress and the village schoolmistress.

As a favour to Peter Gray around this time, Cushing joined the cast of Gray's repertory production of *The Rivals* at the Theatre Royal, Windsor, once again playing Faulkland, and he was ribbed mercilessly whenever he sugggested a bit of stage business he had used 'when we did it in London.' Determined to give Helen a spectacular Christmas present, Cushing purloined a square of silk from one of Helen's mother's old ball gowns which was due to be made into dusters. He secured it on a pastry-board and painted it with characters from Dickens, then left it on Helen's pillow on Christmas morning.

Cushing's next play at the 'Q' was one of his most interesting roles in this period – and is the third significant Priestley play that he cannot quite remember in the 1988 documentary *A One-Way Ticket to Hollywood*. It was *They Came to a City*, Priestley's 'fable for our times'. This experimental, allegorical fantasy presents nine disparate characters, including a bank clerk, a charlady, a waitress and a railway-worker, who find themselves one morning at the gates of a city. The doors of the city open and the group enter – some gladly, some fearfully, some out of curiosity. The second half of the play, which takes place the following evening, shows the return of the explorers, who describe their experiences in the city during the day. Cushing played the role of the heroic stoker Joe Dinmore, a role that

Cushing as Osric in *Hamlet* (1947)

was played by John Clements in the 1943 West End production and in the 1944 Ealing film of the play.

Once again, the Priestley magic was to work for Cushing. Helen wore her hand-painted scarf to the first night of *They Came to a City* at the 'Q' where it caught the eye of actress Roberta Huby, who was playing the waitress in the play. She asked to borrow the scarf to show to a friend of hers who was a textile manufacturer in the North of England. Though reluctant to part with it, Helen knew that the contact would prove useful. And so it did.

In his autobiography, Cushing protects the identity of the bluff Macclesfield factory-owner who diddled the insurance to build a new wing for his factory, but posterity owes him a great debt for keeping the Cushings from ruin. For the next ten months, on a freelance basis, Cushing sent drawings that were worked up into printed designs, eventually securing a similar contract from 'Sammy' scarves, a firm who supplied Marks and Spencer.

Helen was still troubled with a persistent cough and was taking in sewing to bring in a little more money. Cushing remembers it was a gruelling period. 'I used to look through my cuttings books, trying to reassure myself that I was destined to be an actor. I had been acting for 11 years. I had reached the goal of repertory actors, Harry Hanson's Court Players, at 24 and I had played second lead to Carole Lombard in Hollywood. I had a role on Broadway, then, roles in London's West End. Even when the play was bad the critics had singled me out for praise. So where had I gone wrong? Later I realised nothing was wrong. I believe those 18 months of disillusionment, depression, and frustration were put into my life to widen my emotions.'[10]

During this period, there were two more radio plays for the BBC. *The Face of Theresa* was broadcast on 25th January 1947 from the Langham Hotel, produced by Hugh Stewart, and Cushing received ten guineas for playing Blane. The *Radio Theatre* production *It Speaks for Itself* came from Broadcasting House on 1st May 1947 for producer Peter Watts.

When Cushing repeated his West End performance as Colbert in *While the Sun Shines* at the 'Q', he was seen by Anthony Bushell, who was then preparing the film version of *Hamlet* with Laurence Olivier. In the autumn of 1946, Cushing had auditioned for Olivier for a production of the American play *Born Yesterday* by Garson Kanin, but had turned down the role of Paul Verrall because he did not think he would be able to carry off an American accent. Bushell was impressed enough with Cushing's French accent to decide that he should play Osric, 'that sinister Beau Brummell of the Danish Court.'

Olivier's first film as director was *Henry V* in 1944. He was awarded a special Oscar and won enormous acclaim at home for producing so rousing a piece of patriotic pageantry. On New Year's Day 1947, Olivier had received word that he had financial backing to realise a long-held ambition to produce a film of *Hamlet*, which he would star in and also direct.

He then spent the first months of the year developing the abstract look for the sets with designer Roger Furse (Olivier wanted 'a hell of a lot of smoke and emptiness all over the place'[11]), planning the script and the technical considerations. There was a family connection for the Cushings, too – associate producer Reginald Beck, who had been a film editor on *Henry V*, was Helen's brother.

Unlike the Technicolor tapestry of *Henry V*, Olivier announced that *Hamlet* was to be filmed in black and white using deep-focus photography, enabling the

Osric holds the dying Laertes (Terence Morgan) in *Hamlet* (1947)

viewer to take in whole tableaux, as on a theatre stage. Banks of powerful lights used for the process made the sets uncomfortably hot, especially for players in heavy costumes and armour. Olivier later revealed that he was engaged in a row with Technicolor at the time, and that he decided to shoot *Hamlet* in black-and-white to spite them. Another version of the story says Technicolor wouldn't let him use their process. Whatever the reason, the stark monochrome photography is one of the film's great strengths.

Filming began at the D&P studios at Denham in early May, on a closed set. This was partly a trick to increase press anticipation, partly to keep the filming on schedule. Because Olivier was already committed to leading the Old Vic company – including his second wife, Vivien Leigh – on a tour of Australia in January 1948, their time was strictly limited, and after a while tempers began to fray.

'When the production started, Larry was a kind, considerate, patient director,' Cushing said. 'But as time went by he became more and more autocratic. At first it was "let's try it this way" or "what do you think about going from here to here instead of from there to there?" But towards the end it was "do it this way, do it that way, and don't argue, goddamit!" We all started calling him Willie behind his back, after the stories we'd heard about William Wyler. But I must say, the directorial method he settled on got great results. Whoever said *Hamlet* couldn't be done on film was made to eat his words by Larry.'[12] During filming it was announced, in the Queen's birthday honours list, that Olivier was to be knighted 'in recognition of his services to England'.

Terence Morgan, who played Laertes, was involved with the film from the earliest screen tests – there were 23 tests for Ophelia alone. Morgan also helped

with the preliminary effects work for the ghost, which involved being filmed with a lit electric bulb in his mouth. It was Olivier's intention to play Hamlet and the ghost, the ghost being seen in negative in the same shot. Unfortunately, this proved beyond the limits of the technology of the time, but the ghost's appearances, accompanied by a monstrous, distorted heartbeat, are still exceptionally eerie, as good as any horror film.

In fact there are several presentiments of things to come. The creeping shots through the corridors of Elsinore prefigure Terence Fisher's camerawork for several sinister prowls around Castle Dracula and when Hamlet goes to face the spectre of his father, Olivier grimly carries his sword hilt-upwards, making the shape of a cross, with the same glint of defiance in his eyes that Cushing would adopt for Van Helsing. There is madness, murder, a ghost – and Jean Simmons' Ophelia looking like nothing so much as a vampire's bride. 'If *Hamlet* had been a Hammer film,' Cushing quipped later, 'they'd say "This is disgusting! Dreadful! All these deaths. Think of the bodies littering the floor!"'[13]

Osric makes his entrance flouncing into the scene with letters from Hamlet, waving his hat, and holding his nose ostentatiously as he ejects the Sea Captain (Niall MacGinnis). His costume is glorious, with details like a tiny moustache, beard and ear-ring adding an exotic touch. Despite Osric's prancing gait, Cushing still has a noticeable limp, but he nevertheless manages an excellent comic pratfall on a flight of steps. Cushing gives Osric a tight-lipped, 'plummy' delivery, and though the character is clearly intended to provide some light relief from the horrors, he is obviously not without influence in the court. In the great procession before the duel, Osric takes the Queen's arm with a deferential nod to the King and, for all his dandified foolishness, this 'water-fly' is a conspirator in Hamlet's murder by giving Laertes the poisoned sword.

Cushing's only problem with *Hamlet* came after the filming was finished. He had suffered an abscess in his soft palette and treatment required the removal of 'three perfectly good front teeth'. The dental work was paid for by his agent Al Parker, but when Cushing joined Olivier for post-synching on the film, he was conscious of his new false teeth and could not project properly. Olivier moved nearer to Cushing and instructed him 'Drown me. It will be a glorious death.'

While filming was still underway, however, and Cushing was sitting in the make-up room with his hair in rollers (for Osric's flowing locks) Olivier came to him with a proposition. Would he join the company for the Australasian tour? Cushing's first thoughts were for Helen – he couldn't bear the thought of leaving her. Olivier's solution was simple. 'There were enough separations during the war. Helen must come with us...!'[14]

Chapter Six

Down Under and Back Again

The programme for the Old Vic tour of Australasia was to comprise three plays: Richard Brinsley Sheridan's *The School for Scandal*, Shakespeare's *Richard III* and Thornton Wilder's 'History of the World in Comic Strip', *The Skin of Our Teeth*, which had been a great success for Vivien Leigh at the Phoenix Theatre in 1945. Olivier's performance as Richard III – 'that bottled spider ... foul bunch-back'd toad' – first seen at the Old Vic in 1944 was already legendary.

The company rehearsed for two months in Donald Wolfit's scenery repository near Holloway Women's Prison. The store was a huge, high building, cluttered with old furnishings and uncomfortably damp. George Relph, one of the senior actors on the tour – and who suffered more than most – said it was damp 'with the tears of all the actors who were never paid.'[1]

Vivien Leigh was affected by the damp atmosphere too, and to make matters worse for the Cushings, no one was paid for the rehearsal period. Things improved once on board ship. Junior members of the cast, including Cushing, Terence Morgan and Michael Redington, were paid half-wages at £15 per week. Helen, along with Georgina Jumel, Morgan's wife, received £6 per week.

The *SS Corinthic*, a 15,000-ton refrigerated cargo ship which carried 100 first-class passengers, set sail from Liverpool on 14th February. Daily rehearsals for *The School for Scandal*, in which Cushing was to play the dashing if shallow Sir Joseph Surface, took place in the dining saloon, generally in the mornings. For the rest of the time the company were able to relax and play deck tennis, housey-housey or swim in the canvas swimming pool constructed near the mast. In the evening, they played 'The Game' – a kind of charades. Michael Redington elaborated: 'The players would be given bits of paper with names on and then they'd have to impersonate people. Peter was brilliant at it, as you can understand. He used to do a terrific impersonation of Sid Field – and Olivier would encourage him. Eventually the passengers used to gather to watch and we asked them to join in. Of course, the passengers were hopeless, so, very kindly,

Peter and the others did these wonderful impressions of the passengers making fools of themselves.'

At the end of February, the ship docked off Cape Town. Table Mountain was unfortunately wreathed in low cloud but – 'the next best thing' wrote Cushing – there was a chance to see Ivor Novello in *Perchance to Dream*, which he was taking on a tour around South Africa. Novello, at 55, was still regarded as something of a matinée idol. He was a good friend of Olivier's and after the show, invited the company to supper.

In the early morning of 14th March, the *Corinthic* docked at Fremantle and the passengers were able to disembark, after being checked over by the ship's doctor. The first show of *The School for Scandal* was to be performed on the following Saturday, so rehearsals commenced almost immediately, punctuated only by various official receptions. The actors flagged in the stifling humidity of a 100-degree late-summer heatwave, but the prospect of seeing the Old Vic company had already sold out the first night at the 2280-seat Capitol Theatre in Perth. However, the

Lady Teazle (Vivien Leigh), Charles Surface (Terence Morgan), Sir Peter Teazle (Laurence Olivier) and Sir Joseph Surface (Cushing) in *The School for Scandal*, as represented by 'Tom Titt' in the *Tatler*

In the Gracious Presence of Her Majesty The Queen

NEW THEATRE
St. Martin's Lane, W.C.2

Lessees THE WYNDHAM THEATRES LTD.
Managing Director and Licensee SIR BRONSON ALBERY   Assistant Managing Director DONALD ALBERY

Tuesday, May 17th 1949

A Special Matinee Performance
of

THE OLD VIC THEATRE COMPANY
in

THE TRAGEDY OF

KING RICHARD III

By WILLIAM SHAKESPEARE

in aid of
KING GEORGE'S PENSION FUND
for ACTORS and ACTRESSES

By Royal Appointment…

theatre was designed as a cinema, the acoustics were very poor, the actors' voices were drowned out by the air-conditioning unit and there were only two dressing-rooms.

Unused to live performances, the Australians were generally disinclined to react and the show was initially a depressing exercise for the players. The first scene passed in silence until Cushing made his entrance as Joseph Surface, seized the initiative and played for all he was worth. Everyone followed suit. Olivier wrote 'We were bashing over Sheridan's trifle like *Hellzapoppin'* with everything we knew or had.'[2]

Whatever the performances were like, the press reviews were rapturous, and after Olivier and Leigh, Cushing led those who received the highest praise. There was great praise too for Cecil Beaton's black-and-white toy-theatre sets, accented with gorgeously coloured costumes.

Wednesday of the second week saw an invitation to Sir Laurence and the company from the Reelers – members of the Australian film industry. It was a dour – and teetotal – experience, but on the coach home Cushing entertained all with an impersonation of the Reelers' MC.

The School for Scandal was the only play performed in Perth, while *Richard III* was rehearsed during

the day. After the final performance at the Capitol Theatre, there was a beach party, and at midnight the company boarded two Skymaster aeroplanes to cross the Nullabor plain to Adelaide.

In *Richard III*, Cushing played the doomed Duke of Clarence – 'false, fleeting, perjured Clarence' – who is drowned in a vat of Malmsey. After Clarence's death, Cushing came back on to play Cardinal Bourchier, the Archbishop of Canterbury. 'It was the scene with the princes in the Tower,' Michael Redington remembered, 'and Peter played that very naughtily. Laurence Olivier used to go up to the princes and they'd say "What's that Uncle?" pointing to his sword. He'd say "Wouldst thou have my weapon?" and nudge the Cardinal. Then Peter would then make this rather outraged expression, and cross himself very quickly. And every night, it got more and more outraged. Pip Barnard and I were holding a canopy, and we got the giggles. And the more we got the giggles, the more this canopy shook. Olivier always had his back to us so we were all right. Except for one night, when he turned around and saw this canopy shaking about. We got in the most terrible trouble, and it was all Peter's fault.'[3]

On the second day in Adelaide, 10th April, after two shows of *Richard III* to ecstatic reviews, the Oliviers gave a party to celebrate the Cushings' fifth wedding anniversary, with oysters and champagne in abundance and dancing until 3.45 am. Olivier was meanwhile preoccupied with setting and lighting *The Skin of Our Teeth*, which he variously called 'the Picasso of our repertoire' the 'Salvador Dali' or the 'Henry Moore'. (The *Sydney Tribune* called it 'a play for morons and lunatics'.) Cushing played several small parts, including a hunchback. 'Peter had a cushion that he tied on his back,' Michael Redington recalls. 'On the thing was written 'P Cushion'. Someone had said "Who's this for?" and someone else said "P Cushing" and that was that.'[4] *The Skin of Our Teeth* was presented in a vaudeville style with the characters deliberately two-dimensional. Though the play baffled many Australians, it was generally well received.

One of the chief delights for the Cushings was the chance to enjoy the local fauna. He wrote 'Our favourite without doubt was the duck-billed platypus, a quite adorable creature. Helen thought it looked like an animated rubber hot-water bottle wearing a fur coat.'[5] Other delights included the brush turkeys, fabulously coloured birds of paradise and parakeets.

The company left Adelaide on 18th April and travelled to Melbourne for an eight-week engagement at the Princess Theatre. Melbourne was cold, in both weather and attitude, and the company were succumbing to fatigue. Olivier's local talent-scouting included an audition for Keith Michell, who subsequently came to England to study at the Old Vic School and in 1963 would play a memorable Mark Antony to Cushing's Cassius in *The Spread of the*

Eagle. Helen Keller, the deaf and blind scholar, visited a performance of *Richard III* and had the play relayed to her by her companion Polly Thomson. Helen Keller would also feature in Cushing's later career.

The day before the Melbourne season ended on 12th June, the Oliviers and some members of the cast, including Cushing, attended the Australian première of *Hamlet*. Then the company was off to Tasmania, travelling to Hobart in a two-engined Dakota. En route, one of the engines caught fire, and the plane was forced to land in Launceston, Northern Tasmania, where it missed the runway and had to be towed back onto the tarmac by tractor.

The tiny Theatre Royal in Hobart was welcoming, but bitterly cold. One of the most famous moments of *The School for Scandal* is the 'screen scene' – in which Lady Teazle is discovered hiding from her husband Sir Peter – and in one Tasmanian performance of the play Cushing remembered catching sight of Leigh behind the screen, huddled in a mink coat by an electric fire.

The cast was allowed a brief holiday, then on 29th June *The School for Scandal* opened at the Tivoli Theatre in Sydney. This was the start of an eight-week run in the city, during which time Cushing was invited to take part in two radio broadcasts for NBC Australia. He played the title role in a production of *Beau Brummell* as well as taking part as a guest in the popular panel game *Twenty Questions*.

Critics wrote in admiration of Olivier's synthesis of eighteenth century theatre with film techniques and, once again, Cushing's performance as Joseph Surface came in for particular praise. Oliver carried on as Richard III despite tearing a cartilage in his knee – he used a crutch, which became an integral part of the character.

On 9th July, Olivier received some bad news from the Old Vic governors, who effectively stated that he was being given the sack as a director. This apparent setback had a happy outcome however – it was the start of the process that would lead to the creation of Britain's National Theatre, Olivier's dream project, and one that he would see to fruition in a purpose-built complex on London's South Bank. Communication was slow between Australia and the homeland, so the matter had to wait. In the meantime there were more pressing things to worry about, such as a performance of *The Skin of Our Teeth* for the Australian Prime Minister Ben Chifley on 19th July.

There was also a cricket match organised between the company and the staff of the Tivoli. Michael Redington remembered Cushing's contribution. 'I was captain of the cricket team, and Peter was in the team, even though he would hold the bat the wrong way round. He was game for anything, but he would have been the

Cushing (far right) as the Duke of Clarence in Olivier's *Richard III*

first to admit he wasn't the best cricket player in the world.'[6] The company won by ten wickets.

Preparations were already underway for the company's return to Britain, when a season at the New Theatre in St Martin's Lane would comprise *The School For Scandal*, *Richard III* and Jean Anouilh's *Antigone*, which John Burrell would direct. The Anouilh play replaced *The Skin of Our Teeth* which had already had a successful London run. There was a final fortnight in Brisbane with *The School for Scandal*, and another cricket match (a draw, this time) before a flight to Auckland for the last leg of the tour in New Zealand.

New Zealand made a refreshing change from Australia – it resembled England somewhat and alleviated the company's homesickness a little. More than 33,000 people attended the 17 performances at the St James Theatre in Auckland and there were similar crowds at the St James Theatre in Christchurch and His Majesty's Theatre in Dunedin. In one of the final performances in Wellington, Olivier's knee locked and he was booked into hospital for an operation to remove the damaged cartilage. He made a swift recovery, but because of his leg in plaster, had to be taken on board the *Corinthic* in a tarpaulin sling along with the luggage.

The return journey for the near-exhausted company began on 16th October 1948 and rehearsals began on board for the season at the West End. A little less than a month later, the company were back in England and were installed in the New Theatre.

Antigone was considered too short to provide a substantial night's entertainment, so it was preceded by Chekhov's one-act comedy *The Proposal*. Cushing was given the lead in this three-hander, playing the hypochondriac Ivan Vasilyevitch Lomov. 'The normal running time was about half-an-hour,' wrote Cushing 'but Sir Laurence suggested we performed it in the fashion of a speeded-up Keystone Kops car chase. Once we got into our stride it was all over and done with in 19 minutes flat. It took me another 19 to recover.'[7]

The Proposal was performed in front of a painted cloth with the actors in heavy make-up looking and acting like marionettes. Michael Redington recalls the performance: 'Physical business was Peter's forte,' he says. 'Because all the furniture was painted on the backcloth, Peter had to "sit" in mid-air on a painted seat. Then there was a point in the script when he had to do a big double-take. He'd done it in rehearsals and we'd all fallen about – Olivier said that I'd be better off out in front because I was laughing so much. So on the first night, Peter did a somersault – right over. It was the most amazing thing. He said "Well, I'd been thinking about it, so I just thought I'd do it."'[8]

Kenneth J Hurren in *What's On in London* was not impressed. '*The Proposal*, a brief farce by Anton Chekhov, was performed by three minor members of the cast got up to look like circus clowns. The play seems to have no distinction and I found the break-neck speed of the production both ludicrous and tedious. Several of my neighbours were laughing quite immoderately; myself, I've had more fun with Abbott and Costello.'[9]

However, in the *Old Vic Yearbook* for 1949, Ivor Brown wrote 'Sir Laurence directed, at lightning speed and with a genuine gusto for the broadest comedy, Chekhov's farcical comedy *The Proposal*. Possibly Chekhov might not have recognised his own little piece by the time the energetic players, well led by Peter Cushing, had done with it. But I'm sure he would have laughed freely at the lively antics of the players. We are too ready to regard the Tsarist Russians as only sweetly sad. Sir Laurence demonstrated their scope for robust absurdity.'[10]

Cushing had now been working without a break since before the film of *Hamlet*. The Australasian tour, the added strain of 'carrying' *The Proposal* as well as roles in *Richard III* and *The School for Scandal* stretched his nerves to the limit, and when the run at the New Theatre finished, he was physically and emotionally spent. During the rehearsals for his next job, Cushing suffered a nervous breakdown.

Since leaving the Old Vic, Olivier had taken on the managership of the St James' Theatre in King Street, between Pall Mall and Piccadilly. The first play to be produced was *The Damascus Blade* by Bridget Boland, about the French Resistance during World War II and starring Peter Finch and John Mills. Olivier offered Cushing the now familiar part of a Free Frenchman. But duing a rehearsal, Cushing repeatedly failed to understand a simple cue and broke down in tears. He was unable to work for six months. In a typical act of generosity, Olivier kept Cushing under contract – and paid – during this period of illness, no doubt as repayment to Peter and Helen for two years of hard work and devoted service. This was something of an ill omen for *The Damascus Blade*, which was cancelled before it even reached London.

During the breakdown, Cushing would lock himself in the lavatory for hours on end, fretting that he had forgotten something. 'Come on out, you silly old Bloggs,' said Helen by way of encouragement. 'It's no good trying to remember things you haven't forgotten yet!'[11] They started writing notes to each other in a kind of nonsensical phonetic language. Helen's pet name for Peter, 'Bois' (pronounced 'boys') would inspire a series of characters and stories, which Cushing eventually published as *The Bois Saga* with his own illustrations.

1950 saw a happy event for Michael and Ann Redington: they were married and Cushing played a leading part. 'He kept dropping hints,' Redington recalled. 'Things like "When are you going to marry m'daughter?" He drew me a card with an outraged father waving a shotgun. Ann's parents weren't very happy about her marrying an actor, so we asked Peter to give Ann away at the altar. He said "Is it a speaking part?" and Ann said "Well, when you're asked 'Who gives this woman to be married to this man?' you have to say 'I do'." So, when the time came, with every ounce of the actor's command and projection, he said "*I do!*" at the top of his voice, and everybody in the church looked at him.'[12]

By September 1950, Cushing was strong enough to return to work and joined the cast of a musical adaptation of Molière's *La Malade Imaginaire*. 'It was called *The Gay Invalid*,' Cushing ruminated. 'I felt like one!'[13]

The Gay Invalid at the Garrick was dubbed 'Molière without Tears' by the *Tatler*. Cushing's part was once again that of an ardent young soldier, this time wooing Daphne Slater as the daughter of the crotchety hypochondriac Crank, played by veteran actor A E Matthews.

The huge set was hinged to depict the inside and outside of a house in Paris – 'The adapter's intentions are chiefly spectacular,' continued the *Tatler*. 'Inside, Crank sits among his thousands of medicine bottles, without a Commedia Dell'Arte troupe cavort in the snow. It is indeed a very theatrical evening, with nothing much omitted, except perhaps the finer points of Molière's comedy.'

The performance saw the much-trumpeted return to the London stage of the Polish-born star Elisabeth Bergner, who had appeared in musical comedy in the 1930s. Playing the quack medico Professor Purge was Tod Slaughter, whose blood-and-thunder melodramas on stage and screen (*Sweeney Todd*, *Maria Marten*, etc) had made him a British horror star, and as such a direct precursor to Cushing. There was later a direct coincidence of subjects – Slaughter's 1948 film *The Greed of William Hart* was a version of the Burke and Hare story written by John Giling – in 1959, Cushing starred in the lead as Dr Knox in Gilling's own remake, *The Flesh and the Fiends*.

Heartwell (Michael Shepley), Crank (A E Matthews), Toinette (Elisabeth Bergner), Professor Purge (Tod Slaughter), Angelica (Daphne Slater), Valentine (Cushing) and Harlequin (Walter Gore) in *The Gay Invalid* (1951)

After an out-of-London tour taking in the Manchester Opera House and the Malvern Festival Theatre, *The Gay Invalid* ran happily in London for two months at the beginning of 1951, concluding on 24th March.

Meanwhile, plans were afoot for the Festival of Britain, a government-sponsored jamboree to help Britain out of its post-war doldrums with an exhibition and funfair on the South Bank next to the newly-built Festival Hall.

At the St James' Theatre, Sir Laurence Olivier was preparing a festival season which would feature Vivien Leigh as Cleopatra in Shaw's *Caesar and Cleopatra* and Shakespeare's *Antony and Cleopatra*. Olivier's intention was to display his wife's versatility in presenting two aspects of Cleopatra's life – the young woman who bewitched Caesar and the ruthless politician, the 'serpent of old Nile' who seduced Mark Antony.

The two plays were directed by Michael Benthall, who was using the season to give *his* partner, the celebrated ballet dancer Robert Helpmann, an opportunity to move into acting as his dancing career was reaching its end. Helpmann's performance as Apollodorus almost overshadowed Olivier and Leigh.

Olivier was aware that Cushing was still in somewhat fragile health and offered him two small

roles – Alexas Diomedes in the Shakespeare and the dandyish Bel Affris in the prologue to the Shaw play. In *Caesar and Cleopatra* Wilfrid Hyde-White played Brittanus, a doleful Briton whom Caesar has employed as his secretary. When Hyde-White left to honour another commitment, Cushing was invited to take over. According to Audrey Cruddas' costume designs, Britannus was decked out in long ringlets and a short blue tunic. 'Larry gave these one-word directions,' says Michael Redington. 'For Brittanus he said "He's a scout-master" and that was that. Peter took that, and that was how he did it.' Brittanus is a comic character, full of his own importance and easily outraged. 'Is it true that when Caesar caught you on that island you were painted all over blue?' asks Cleopatra.

There were plenty of old colleagues in the Festival Season cast – including Niall MacGinnis, from *Hamlet*, Dan Cunningham from the Old Vic tour, Thomas Heathcote – and Henry Oscar again. Cushing befriended the actor Esmond Knight, who was almost blind but who nevertheless could negotiate Roger Furse's revolving set without hazard. A strong female contingent included Maxine Audley, Elspeth March and a young Jill Bennett, while Desmond Llewelyn, who later became Q in the James Bond films, had a walk-on role as a Roman soldier.

During the rigorous schedule of daily performances at the St James', the Cushings relaxed at home by listening to the radio. On 10th July 1951, Cushing wrote to David Davis, producer of *Children's Hour*. 'I just wanted to thank you so *very* much and to congratulate you, if I may, for the charming *Jennifer's Journeys* programmes on the *Children's Hour*. They epitomise the very spirit of England and a feeling of love for this dear country of ours comes shining through to the listener! I hope we shall hear more.'

By the beginning of October, the St James' season was drawing to a close, and there was a blow for the Cushings – Peter was not to be included in the cast for the Broadway run of the plays. Wilfrid Hyde-White was returning as Brittanus, and the other parts would be recast. Perhaps Olivier, in his wisdom, realised that Cushing could do better than these minor roles, and that staying in London would advance his career further. Helen suspected that Larry had been nobbled. 'You have been unaware of jealousy in high places,' she told her husband. 'But I have heard and seen things going on behind your back ... You received an ovation every time you played Lomov and stopped the show as Britannus. That is why you were not asked to repeat your performance on Broadway. Larry was not the instigator of this injustice – we have good reason to be grateful to him – but there are others at court whose influence is very strong. Wilfrid is excellent, but he is older than you and well-established. You are a 'new boy' and represent a threat. They cannot stand that kind of competition.'[15] Among the new players who went to New York were Donald Pleasence, Patrick Troughton, Harry Andrews and Alec McCowen.

Determining that her man should 'become independent', Helen began a letter-writing campaign to a number of radio producers, many of whom Cushing had worked with before. Among the targets were Archie Campbell, Douglas Cleverdon, Val Gielgud, Peter Watts, Martyn Webster and Ayrton Whittaker. Cushing was careful to point out that at the time of writing he was still under contract to Laurence Olivier Productions Limited.

Hugh Stewart, a member of the Old Vic company who joined the Australasian tour, returned to his BBC job as a radio producer and supervised the broadcast excerpts from *Antony and Cleopatra* on 13th August. Cushing had worked with Stewart in 1947 and again in 1949 on *The Alien Corn* while he was still suffering the nervous breakdown.

'I hope there is a possibility of working with you again,' Cushing wrote to Stewart on 9th October, putting a positive spin on his position. 'Having finished the season at the St James's I have decided not to go to America. It would give me tremendous pleasure to resume what was for me a most happy association and experience!' Stewart replied almost immediately. 'It was very nice to hear from you again, and I am glad to take this opportunity of telling you how much I enjoyed your performances in both plays at the St James'. I wish I had known a few weeks ago that you would be free now, as I should certainly have been able to offer you a part in my forthcoming serial *Quentin Durward*. However, I hope something will come along soon!'

On 8th November, the letter-writing campaign to television producers began in earnest. During the 1950s, the BBC used the term 'producer' to cover the role of director. The targets included Ian Acton, Alan Bromly, Pamela Brown, Naomi Capon, Harold Clayton, Cleland Finn, Joy Harrington and Vivian Milroy. Many gave positive but non-committal replies.

Helen used one of her contacts too, and wrote a personal letter to BBC producer Eric Fawcett, with whom she had worked in Hollywood. The letter, on Helen's own notepaper with a monogram of an 'H' in two diamonds, says much about the circumstances of the Cushings at the time, Helen's relationship with Peter, and their situation in late 1951.

'My dear Eric,' she wrote, 'shades of America in 1926! I was then a new and rather horrid beginner. The years have made me see sense enough to give up the whole idea. Anyway, since I have married Peter Cushing I haven't had much of a chance to do much else except join all the other housewives in their daily procession of toil. The last time we met was when you were accidentally ushered into my room at the Samaritan Hospital during the war. You looked most taken aback, as well you might! I am really writing now because Peter wants so much to meet you. He is not going to America with Laurence Olivier (to whom he is under contract) because they both feel it is wiser for Peter to carry on in Britain. He was in the USA for five years [sic] and wants to do a greater variety of work at home before he goes back. Wise – don't you think? Anyway, I enclose some data about Peter, which you will perhaps contemplate at leisure. And let us know if and when it would be convenient to see you? I am so very glad you are doing such fine and interesting work, Eric. It is always such a pleasure to see as the years go by that the people you knew are doing well. With every kind wish for all the very best, sincerely yours, Helen Cushing. PS: In the Dark Ages I was Vi Beck, don't let it worry you if you have forgotten!'

Fawcett would indeed remember his old association with Miss Beck, and agreed to meet Peter shortly afterwards. Although they would not work together until 1954, Fawcett would produce one of Cushing's award-winning television sucesses, the light comedy *Tovarich*. In his autobiography, Cushing states that a script came by 'return of post' and this seems to be no exaggeration. They did not waste time in television production in 1951, and when offered an actor of Cushing's talent there was even less reason to delay.

Chapter Seven

The Pride of Alexandra Palace

BBC Television in 1951 bore little resemblance to the multi-million pound business that exists today. In charge was a talented combination of ex-actors (the producers) and ex-servicemen (upper management) who existed in a kind of bewildered tolerance of each other. Almost all television was broadcast from the London Television Station at Alexandra Palace, although the BBC had by now acquired Gainsborough's Lime Grove film studios, where Hitchcock had made *The Lady Vanishes* in 1938. Programmes were broadcast from late afternoon until 10 or 11 at night, sometimes with breaks of as much as an hour between shows.

All productions were live, that is, broadcast from the studios as they were performed, with little provision for covering mistakes beyond blacking out the screen and the deathless announcement 'normal service will be resumed as soon as possible'. Recordings were not made at this time because of an agreement with the actors' union Equity, who perceived danger to its members' livelihoods if the BBC stockpiled old performances. This same restriction extended to on-screen music, which in many cases was played live off-set by a small orchestra. Provision was made to record some programmes 'for use in a national emergency' but it was generally considered that the quality of telefilming was not acceptable for rebroadcast at this time.

Television plays were generally rehearsed for three weeks beforehand in various drill halls and boys' clubs ('which stank of plimsolls, stale perspiration and attar of cats'[1], Cushing wrote) followed by a day's camera rehearsal in studio, to practise the camera moves before transmission.

The principal drama of the week was the Sunday night play. This was repeated on Thursday night, which involved an entire remount of the production – assembling sets, cast and crew and performing the whole all over again. This was occasionally a risky business. ('Disaster could strike in many forms,' said writer Nigel Kneale of those times. 'Your leading man could fall sick or drop dead. It's remarkable that more didn't do so.'[2]) If the first performance was a success, there was the responsibility of matching its quality

in the repeat. If it had been a failure, the repeat was a dispiriting rerun of the whole embarrassing exercise.

Helen's belief in Peter's reputation was proved absolutely correct. Assistant head of drama Michael Barry wrote back 'Although I am not at the moment producing, I shall use my good offices to bring you to the attention of the producers in television. I greatly admired your crisp and brilliantly-coloured performance as Bel Affris.'

On 12th November, just four days after Helen's letter-writing campaign began, Cushing was called to the BBC's rehearsal room at the Inns of Court, Drury Lane, to begin work on J B Priestley's *Eden End* with producer Harold Clayton. There were the usual three weeks of rehearsals for *Eden End*, and Cushing's fee was 40 guineas. (35 guineas basic, plus an extra five for the repeat performance.) Clayton told him that he had seen him on stage in various disguises in the past nine years and 'wanted to see what Peter Cushing really looked like.'

The work of J B Priestley had already proved a good omen for Cushing, after his first professional stage appearance in *Cornelius* at Worthing and the job painting scarves precipitated by *They Came To A City*.

Eden End concerns the family of Doctor Kirby, in the Yorkshire village of Eden End. Kirby's daughter Lilian (played by Rachel Gurney) discontentedly keeps house for her father, while in love with the local gentleman farmer. The elder daughter, Stella (Helen Shingler), arrives back at the house, separated from her drunken actor husband Charles Appleby (Cushing). Stella has the chance of a new life with her old admirer, the gentleman farmer, but then Lilian brings Charles up to Eden End ... So convincing was Cushing's performance as the inebriated Appleby that his wife suspected him of being a secret tippler.

The technical restrictions were arduous and the performance, in the BBC's tiny studios at Alexandra Palace, was very taxing for a newcomer. Cushing was overcome with nerves. To ensure he could cover for missed lines, he learned the *entire* script. A scene where he had to lean jauntily on a piano almost ended in disaster when the stagehands started to pull it away.

Cushing, not knowing that the set furniture often had to be moved around to accommodate the huge, unwieldy cameras, clung grimly on to the piano until he was frantically signalled to let go.

With no audience reaction to gauge, Cushing felt the production was a wretched failure. He went home, still in his make-up – 'with my clothes sticking to me.'[3] The Cushings did not have a television set and Helen had watched the play with friends. When she returned, she did her best to reassure her husband that success was now guaranteed, but Cushing was far from convinced. A phone call from the BBC the next morning, however, brought a request from producer Fred O'Donovan for Cushing to play the juvenile lead in his forthcoming Christmas Day production of Priestley's *When We Are Married*.

This production forced the Cushings to give up their Christmas dinner at home, since the play was rehearsed in studio during the day of the 25th December. Cushing's fee was higher for this job, however, at 40 guineas for only one performance. After a solid month's work for the BBC, the next job was just as soon coming.

Eden End and *When We Are Married* were successful enough, but it was the next performance that set the seal on Cushing's television popularity. Scotsman Campbell Logan was another former actor turned producer. On 2nd January 1952, he asked Cushing to play the lead in a six-part dramatisation of Jane Austen's *Pride and Prejudice*. This classic story tells of the unlikely romance between the spirited, independent Elizabeth Bennet and the noble Mr Darcy, who is described in Logan's notes as a 'fine tall person, with handsome features, a noble mien, haughty, reserved, but fastidious. His manners, though well-bred, are not inviting...' Daphne Slater, who had starred as Cushing's paramour in *The Gay Invalid*, played Elizabeth Bennet, with Ann Baskett, newly graduated from RADA, as her sister Jane.

The third sister, Lydia Bennet, was played by 'a newcomer to television from the Bristol Old Vic', Prunella Scales. 'It was shot live, of course, at Alexandra Palace,' she remembers. 'There was no audience, but I remember rushing round the back of the set for quick changes, trying not to trip over the lighting and camera cables. Peter was charming and benevolent, and smashing in the part.'

Also in the cast was Lockwood West, who became Miss Scales' future father-in-law. 'He played Mr Collins in the production and gave a very splendid and flamboyant performance. I knew he frequently worked for H M Tennent in the West End so I thought to myself, very privately, "This is probably what is known as an 'old queen'. They are very powerful in the theatre, and I must be very respectful to him!" I subsequently met my future husband in another Campbell Logan production, *She Died Young* (subtitled by the cast "None Too Soon") and on being introduced to Timothy by

Campbell – "This is Timothy, Prunella, Harry Lockwood West's son" – I realised my mistake!'[4]

A budget of £3,222 was allocated for six episodes, which were shown on Saturday nights at 8.15. Rehearsals were held each day from 10.30 to 6.00 at the Mansergh Woodall Boys' Club, 23 Hill Road, St John's Wood, beginning on 14th January.

The period for all furniture and props was specified as 1795, with a great many 'dainties' in evidence ('a dainty chair' 'a dainty bowl of fruit', etc) except in the case of Lydia, who was to be furnished with 'a remarkably ugly bonnet'. One 'short-handled quizzing glass' was provided for Darcy.

On 2nd February, an unforeseen circumstance threatened the whole production for the most mundane of reasons. All British citizens of voting age, apart from convicts, the insane and peers of the realm are called upon by random selection to serve on a jury. Peter Cushing was duly summoned to the Old Bailey on Tuesday 26th February. This would have been four days before the fifth episode of *Pride and Prejudice*. There was no question of recasting, and the serial could not reasonably be postponed.

It seems that this was something of a new occurrence for both the BBC and the courts of criminal justice. Rather ferocious letters thundered back and forth between the Old Bailey and Alexandra Palace. 'This sort of thing was much easier to get round on the radio,' grumbled one BBC elder. Eventually Cushing had to go to the Old Bailey in person on 26th February to explain himself. Finally, and still somewhat grudgingly on the part of the Old Bailey, he was excused.

The *Radio Times* noted that Cushing, as Darcy 'looked surprisingly at ease in the costume of the period.'[5] and Lt-Colonel A B Knight wrote to Campbell Logan on 8th March to say 'I have never had so much pleasure from one of my great-great-Aunt Jane's romances before!'

As *Pride and Prejudice* drew to a close, Cushing wrote to Michael Barry wondering if it would be possible for him to play Stanhope in 'a tele vision [sic] production of *Journey's End*' – if the war theme was acceptable for popular entertainment. Barry returned 'There is a ridiculous situation at present with regard to *Journey's End* by which a television production of this English play is prevented by the American film copyright held by MGM. When it is up, we shall do it again, and I would like to think you'd be in it. Darcy is a most distinguished performance, full of thought and style. Don't be depressed by the unending difficulties and breakdowns!'

Cushing replied to Barry 'So glad you are pleased with Mr Darcy and to know that something comes across apart from prostrating nerves! I was interested and a little melancholy to read of what you say about *Journey's End*. They seem to have *everything*, don't they?'

Meanwhile, the strain of television production was manifesting itself physically with Cushing. 'The symptoms, in my case, were acute pains across the eyes, forcing me to close them for a few seconds every so often.'[6] He sought treatment, and the Cushings' doctor prescribed a new tranquiliser that had just come onto the market. 'After my next TV appearance,' he wrote, 'the doctor rang to ask if they had helped. "Not really," Helen replied.

"How many did he take?"

"Five."

There was a pause. "And is he still *alive*?" The pills were "purple hearts", one being considered potent enough to stun a fully-grown elephant for 24 hours, apart from the danger of turning me into a raving drug addict.'[7]

The last part of *Pride and Prejudice* was broadcast on 6th March, and by the end of the month, Cushing was back in the rehearsal rooms for a play called *Bird in Hand*. This project marked the first time Cushing worked in the Lime Grove studios, which would become a home-from-home in the next two years; it was also the first time he worked directly with Michael Barry, who produced the play with Dennis Vance. Barry and Cushing were well on the way to becoming firm friends. After *Bird in Hand*, Cushing wrote to Vance: 'I really enjoyed working with you and was much less nervous than usual.' Vance replied: 'How anyone with your ability could feel nervous, I can't understand. Let's repeat the dose as soon as possible.'

Cushing's television success raised his profile significantly and he was engaged for a short scene in John Huston's lavish, gorgeously coloured production of *Moulin Rouge*, which was filmed in England and France starring Jose Ferrer on his knees as the artist Henri De Toulouse-Lautrec. Cushing's segment seems to have been filmed around the end of April.

About two-thirds of the way through the film, Cushing appears at a racecourse, beautifully attired in a grey suit and top hat, as Marcel De La Voisier, whose wife Myriamme has left him for Lautrec. Cushing has little to do other than stand there and look handsome, which he does very well. He is a paragon, but one whom the deformed Lautrec can beat with his wit and his talent. The role of cuckolded husband is one that Cushing would essay several

'His manners, though well-bred, are not inviting.' Mr Darcy greets Elizabeth Bennet (Daphne Slater) in the BBC's 1951 serial adaptation of *Pride and Prejudice*

times – 'I suppose he'd got that sort of face,'[8] Joan Craft suggested. Lautrec is unimpressed with his vanquished rival. 'He is as handsome a man as his horse is a horse,' he states, before presenting De La Voisier with a drawing of the horse, Magnifique.

The film does at least record, briefly, the gentle French accent which Cushing had used as a stock-in-trade for several years but his appearance too brief to make much of an impression. The cast for *Moulin Rouge* also included, in the role of Georges Seurat, a young hopeful called Christopher Lee.

On 5th June, 1952, Cushing wrote to Vance asking about the possibility of a part if he was casting a new serial. 'Helen has had to go into hospital, but she is getting along fine now.' 'In the one I am doing there is no Cushing part,' Vance replied 'though I should truly love there to be. I look at every script that comes my way with an eye for finding a juicy piece for you.'

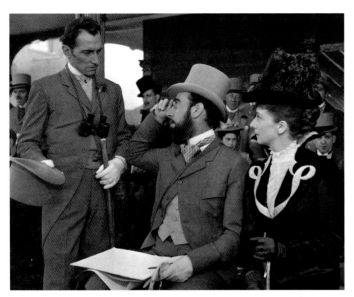

Marcel de la Voisier meets his ex-lover Myriamme (Suzanne Flon) and Henri de Toulouse-Lautrec (José Ferrer) in *Moulin Rouge* (1952)

Helen had ruptured herself badly moving heavy furniture, causing a hernia with complications. She was taken to St George's Hospital for an operation and Cushing visited her every day. The doctor recommended some sea air and a neighbour offered them the use of a cottage in Polzeath, Cornwall. Even with the recent TV work, Cushing's finances were so low that, seeing no alternative, he was forced to ask his father for assistance. This was the deadening day when Cushing senior told his son he was 'nearly 40 – and a failure'. Their holiday on the Cornish Riviera brought Helen back to reasonable health, but Cushing had not told his agent that he was leaving, and may have missed out on several television roles in the meantime. Irene Sutcliffe, a good friend of the Cushings, overheard Robert Helpmann saying that he'd been trying to get in touch with Peter for some time as he had a role for him in the new play he was about to direct. Cushing returned from Cornwall immediately, and was invited to join the cast of *The Wedding Ring*.

This was Helpmann's first play as a director, and was produced by his partner Michael Benthall who had produced the Cleopatra plays at the St James'. *The Wedding Ring* was set in a marriage bureau, and starred two formidable actresses, Adrienne Allen (who had appeared with Coward in the original run of *Private Lives*) and Irene Brown. Also in the cast were Gladys Henson, 'Q' veterans Irene Handl and Shelagh Fraser and a young actor called Patrick Macnee.

Shelagh Fraser, who had also worked with Peter at the 'Q', remembered *The Wedding Ring* well. 'We went on what was called a "Number One" tour, then we

were supposed to be coming to London. The play was written by Simon Waddell and his then-boyfriend Kieran Tunney, who I remember was not such a good writer and a bit of a trouble-maker. We opened in Manchester and, without telling any of us, Tunney went to the Midland Hotel and sought out Noël Coward, who was staying there. He did a bit of a sob story and got him to come to the dress rehearsal of this light comedy in the barn which is the Manchester Opera House. Adrienne, Irene and Gladys Henson were old friends of Coward's and when they found out, the balloon went up. Tunney went from dressing room to dressing room, stirring trouble and eventually the women, who knew each other well, were scarcely speaking.'[9]

'Noël Coward said it was the worst play he'd ever seen,' Patrick Macnee remembered. Macnee, however, made friends with Cushing. 'From Manchester,' he remembers, 'he would walk up into the hills outside Cheshire and paint.'[10]

'We went to Cardiff with *The Wedding Ring*,' recalled Shelagh Fraser. 'Adrienne gave a big party in a local restaurant for everyone. Peter was very broke at the time and living in digs, but he didn't suck up to the two stars, like some did. Adrienne, alas, was a terrible snob and left Peter out of the party. At another time, Adrienne, who loved games, insisted we all played the one where everyone has a label pinned on their backs and they have to guess who they are. Adrienne prided herself on being best at all these things but couldn't guess what Peter had pinned on her. It was "The Iron Butterfly"! Her isolation of him had really backfired.'[11]

Helpmann's encouragement to his suffering actors was 'speed, speed, speed.' 'But,' Cushing wrote dolefully, '*The Wedding Ring* needed something more subtle than speed to attract the customers.'[12] 'There was so much trouble and intrigue...' remembers Shelagh Fraser, 'we never did get to London!' The play is not mentioned in Helpmann's biography – overshadowed, no doubt, by his later worldwide successes directing the likes of Katherine Hepburn and Robert Donat. Cushing's chief reminiscences about the tour concerned a theatrical landlady and his enforced separation from Helen.

Back in London, Cushing was immediately clasped back to the bosom of the BBC for what was to be an unbroken run of 12 productions in as many months. The first of these plays, *If This Be Error*, for director Stephen Harrison, went out on 11th November after the usual two-week rehearsal period. Cushing was reunited with Shelagh Fraser who remembered particularly the 'cut-out' keys, which would cut the sound from the studio so that a live prompt could be given. The cast also included Gillian Lind, the veteran comedy actor Frank Allenby and Dandy Nicholls, the immortal Else from *Til Death Us Do Part*.

Cushing's next role was in the French play *Asmodée*, a complex, allegorical chamber piece. He played the sinister tutor Blaise Lebel, who exerts an almost hypnotic influence over the household of the young widow Marcelle de Barthas and her daughter. His plans are thwarted by the arrival of a guileless young Englishman who represents 'Asmodée' – a devil who takes the roofs off houses and cause havoc among their occupants. For the part of Lebel, producer Harold Clayton suggested that Cushing fill in the sides of his distinctive widow's peak to emphasise the character's vanity. It made a subtle and sinister change to the shape of his face. 'Thank you for your most tremendous help and the trust you put in me,' Cushing wrote back to Clayton. 'And for the brilliant idea of the hair-line! I think it was that that put the proper seal on old Blaisie!'

Shortly after Christmas, Cushing played the Spanish Lord Henriques in the first episode of a children's drama serial that held distinct hints of things to come. *The Silver Swan* was written by C E Webber and produced by Rex Tucker, and involved a young girl who travelled through time with the aid of a magical violin. More than ten years later, Webber and Tucker would help create another children's series with a time-travel theme – *Doctor Who*.

On 16th January, Cushing began rehearsals at the Jewish Lads' Club, Hanway Place, for Charles Irving's play *Number Three*, once again with producer Stephen Harrison. The cast included many popular television names – Ursula Howells, Jack Watling, Raymond Huntley, Terence Alexander and Jack Howarth, who would become the legendary Albert Tatlock in *Coronation Street*. The play was set in an isolated nuclear research centre where the brilliant Professor Brander (Huntley) is attempting to develop a limitless source of cheap electricity. The scientists are all but ignored by the government, until it is discovered that the process could also produce a weapon more powerful than a hydrogen bomb, whereupon the centre is immediately Top Secret and Top Priority. While Brander celebrates what he considers a scientific and patriotic triumph, his assistants realise that they have now created a means to save the world, or annihilate it.

The role of Simpson, the myopic minister in *Number Three*, was the part that secured Cushing the services of a new agent, John Redway. He would remain as Cushing's agent and a good friend until his death. *Number Three* was also Cushing's first involvement with the work of BBC staff writer Nigel Kneale who, with George F Kerr, adapted the play for television. Later in the year, television would terrify the nation for

the first time with the transmission of Kneale's serial *The Quatermass Experiment*.

Asmodée was performed again on 17th February 1953. After this, Cushing wrote to Harold Clayton, 'I think the second Blaisie wasn't up to the standard of the first – hope that's just me!' Clayton's wife, the documentary producer Caryl Doncaster, approached Cushing with a view to doing a project with her but he was now fully booked for the foreseeable future, and had to decline. He was about to embark on another serial, *Epitaph for a Spy*, a six-part mystery for Saturday nights based on a novel by Eric Ambler.

Giles Cooper, who adapted the story for television, set the scene in the *Radio Times*: '*Epitaph for a Spy* addresses one of the author's favourite themes; the intrusion of espionage and other evil into the lives of ordinary harmless men – that spies seldom wear cloaks and carry daggers but... they quite often wear bathing-dresses and carry pictures of their children.' Cooper described Cushing's character of Josef Vadassy as 'the most inoffensive man alive. He is a keen photographer and a conscientious teacher – not in the least the kind of man *to whom things happen*. When they *do* happen to him, Ambler sees to it that we feel that we ourselves would behave in much the same way Vadassy does.'[13]

Epitaph for a Spy was set in the Hotel de la Réserve in the Riviera town of St Gatien in 1937. Vadassy, a language teacher, is stateless – Hungarian by birth, but because of the 1920 Peace Treaty, a Yugoslav by law. He is suspected of photographing a coastal defence installation but Beghin, of French Naval Intelligence, cannot believe in so incompetent a spy. Knowing that the enemy agent must be in the Hotel, Beghin forces Vadassy to investigate his fellow guests at the Réserve. But the real spy knows that he is being spied upon, and Vadassy the hunter is also the hunted...

Stephen Harrison was once again in charge for the weekly broadcasts from Alexandra Palace. The cast included Ferdy Mayne, Raf de la Torre, Philip Leaver and John Vere. Cushing's fee for each half-hour episode was a substantial 30 guineas. Meanwhile, he was having to cope with the new sensation of being a national celebrity, and he relates this demonstration of public affection in his autobiography.

'Visiting the city one day to call on my solicitor, I stopped opposite the bank ... awaiting the chance to nip across the tarmac. Emulating *In Town Tonight*, a constable on point duty stopped the mighty roar of London's traffic from all directions and beckoned me gravely to the other side. When I reached it, he winked "Can't have you run over Mr Cushing, the wife'll never forgive me if she don't see what happens in the last episode of your serial!"'[14]

On 10th April 1953 Cushing wrote to producer John Irving about his upcoming role as Henry Robbins in the *Wednesday Theatre* production of Max Beerbohm's satire *A Social Success*. 'So glad you liked *Moulin Rouge* and that you spotted me! I think the moustache idea for Henry is an excellent one. I'll try to grow it as I *can't bear* that glue!'

The transmission of *A Social Success* on 29th April was followed by a highly enjoyable assignment for Cushing in *Rookery Nook*, undoubtedly the most popular of Ben Travers' famous Whitehall farces, presented by the BBC from the stage of the Scala Theatre, Kingsway on 23rd May. *Rookery Nook* was produced by Lionel Harris and the cast included David Kossoff and Lally Bowers. Further down the cast was a young actress called Beryl Bainbridge, who later achieved great success as a novelist.

William Johnson, who as a stage manager had worked with Cushing in his repertory days in Southampton, went on to become the manager of a department store, Z Dudley Ltd in High St, Kingsland E8. Cushing's model tithe barn, which he began constructing as a kind of therapy during the war was exhibited for the first time at his store in May 1953. Johnson wrote to the BBC encouraging them to show it on television.

'You will doubtless know of Peter Cushing, whose recent performances in Television drama have met with such favourable comment. I am proud to say that we are very old friends and what you will not know is that he is also an extremely gifted artist in other fields. His natural modesty has been, and still is, his own worst enemy, and it is only because I am a businessman rather than an artist that I have managed at last to obtain his permission to borrow and exhibit in my store a model which took him three years to create. It is being officially opened to public exhibition tomorrow – but already it has caused real amazement. The model is of an Elizabethan Tithe Barn, which is finished in antique furniture and adapted for use as a modern Elizabethan home. The scale is half-an-inch to the foot, and the detail is simply wonderful. It is hand painted and the ingredients are chiefly plain white paper and seccotine. The lighting is beautiful. I am showing it, at Peter's request, to raise funds for the SSAFFA (Soldiers, Sailors and Air Forces Families' Association) and later I hope to have it shown elsewhere in London.' Unfortunately, it is not recorded whether the BBC took up Johnson's offer or not.

1953 was a historic year for British television. Although pioneering viewers tuned their pre-war TV sets to watch the Coronation procession of King George VI in 1937, it was with coverage of the coronation of Queen Elizabeth II on 2nd June 1953 that television established itself as the eyes of the people. Televising the Coronation for western Europe forged a TV link between Britain and the continent, with both social and political importance for the future. To match the unprecedented spectacle of the groundbreaking outside broadcast, Michael Barry marked Coronation week with an expensive studio production of his play *The Passionate Pilgrim*, based on Charles Terrot's novel about the women who accompanied Florence Nightingale to the Crimea. Peter and Helen enthusiastically attended the performance at Lime Grove. 'My dear Michael,' Cushing wrote later, 'Helen and I would like to express our appreciation of your splendid production and offer our congratulations. It was a most moving production with such glorious shots! Apart from Marion Pryor, of course, also excellent were Anthony Nicholls and Willoughby Gray. Such real human beings!'

Cushing's next performance for the BBC, in *The Road*, was the first of three French plays that he would take part in during the next two months. This adaptation of Jean Jacques Bernard's *Nationale Six* starred Wilfrid Lawson, Josephine Griffin and Bryan Forbes, and concerned a young artist (Cushing) and his father who unexpectedly find happiness in the simple rural home of an old man and his daughter.

In their autobiographies, both Cushing and Christopher Lee relate anecdotes about the treasured Wilfrid Lawson. As a teenage flier during the First World War he crashed his plane in the trenches. He kept himself alive until he was rescued by consuming a large amount of alcohol – a prescription he continued for the rest of his life. Lawson was an almost uncontrollable but often brilliant character actor and can be seen on fine form as a pixie-like bookseller in Cushing's 1960 film *The Naked Edge*.

In Marcelle-Mauret's play *Anastasia* Cushing found himself embroiled in post-Russian-revolutionary capers, doubtless spurred by Helen's connection with the era. The play took as its central conceit the legend that the Tsar's youngest daughter, Anastasia, was not killed by the Bolsheviks and was somehow smuggled out of the country. A criminal syndicate comprising the disreputable émigré Prince Bounine and his discredited fellow-exiles, the former banker Chernov and the drug addict Petrovsky (Cushing) claims that she has been found, and raises money among Russian refugees in Berlin, ostensibly for her care. The scheme works well, and the money rolls in, until the subscribers become impatient to see their long-lost Princess.

Co-producing *Anastasia* with Michael Barry was John Counsell, who produced the play in Windsor, brought it to the BBC and later took it to the St James' Theatre where it was produced by Laurence Olivier. The television version was broadcast on 12th July and the stage production opened in August. Many of the BBC cast, including Helen Haye, Mary Kerridge (Counsell's wife) and Anthony Ireland repeated their roles on stage, and while Cushing did not, he attended the gala first night among a galaxy of stars including Margaret Lockwood, Robert Helpmann, Olivier, Vivien Leigh and Orson Welles. *Anastasia* is preserved in the BBC archive, making it the earliest surviving example of Cushing's television work.

Chapter Eight

Busy Days and a Black Knight

Somerset Maugham's adaptation of *The Noble Spaniard*, a French farce by Grenet-Dancourt, was broadcast on 4th August for producer Stuart Latham. It was set in a villa in Boulogne in 1850 where, wrote James Doran in the *Radio Times*, 'into a party of English tenants arrives a Spanish nobleman, hot in the pursuit of love.' Cushing, of course, played the noble spaniard of the title, the Duke of Hermanos. 'The object of his desire is a beautiful English widow whom he has worshipped at a distance for three long weeks – and he will be kept at a distance no longer. The impetuosity of his wooing bundles the English holidaymakers into a series of ingeniously contrived misunderstandings – most of them matrimonial. The action, in all its improbabilities, is hustled smartly along at the point of a rapier rather than at the end of a cudgel.'[1]

The misadventures of a society artist – with a sideline in jewel robbery – and his wily 'fence' formed the basis of the comic drama *Portrait by Peko* by Philip Walker-Taylor, which was transmitted on 23rd August 1953. Patrick Barr played Peko, with Irene Handl as the wealthy Mrs Hassall, Ursula Howells as Peko's girlfriend and Cushing as Seppi Fredericks – described simply in the BBC casting documents as 'a crook'. That the *Radio Times* described Fredericks as 'rather a work of art in his own right'[2] gives a clue to his ultimate fate – he is sealed up inside Peko's latest statue. Cushing can be seen in the *Radio Times* during rehearsals for *Peko*, wearing an expression of puppy-dog innocence and his palms raised in a 'would-I-lie-to-you?' gesture of supplication.

Irene Handl brought her tiny dog to appear in one scene – producer Lionel Harris stated firmly that the animal's well-being was to be *entirely* the actress's responsibility. The production was budgeted at £989, with the actors' fees taking up just over £600. With the rest, designer Richard Greenough had to create an artist's studio, a town square and a number of special props, including three unfinished portraits and the statue itself, which was supposed to have Cushing's face, although it was specified that this would not require a head-cast to be taken of the actor. The sets held no terror for Greenough who, on the night before *Peko*'s transmission, had been required to reproduce part of Westminster Abbey at Alexandra Palace and fill it with malignant alien vegetation for the concluding instalment of *The Quatermass Experiment*.

Portrait by Peko was chosen to be performed at the Dusseldorf Television Festival, from where it would be broadcast by Nordwestdeutscher Rundfunk on 31st August. The Dutch Television Service, Nederlandse Televisie Stichting Hilversum, also relayed the broadcast. All artists had to ensure that their passports were in order to travel to Germany on the 29th – there would be two days' rehearsals before the evening performance. Helen Cushing accompanied her husband on the trip, although she had to pay her

Richard R Greenough's set for *Portrait by Peko*. Cushing's character, Seppi Fredericks, was sealed up inside the statue.

The Duke of Hermanos woos English widow Marian Nairn (Frances Rowe) in the BBC play *The Noble Spaniard*

The villainous Sir Palamides shows his true colours in a last-reel duel with *The Black Knight*.

BBC plays until after Christmas. He was intended to appear in the role of Charles Price in *The Guilty Party* on 13th September, but his contract was cancelled when he was offered a role in the film *The Black Knight*. Charles Price was eventually played by Ferdy Mayne.

Cushing worked on *The Black Knight* from early September to late November, travelling to Wales and Spain and finishing up at Pinewood Studios for three weeks. No film can be all bad with a cast that includes André Morell, Harry Andrews, Patrick Troughton and Anthony Bushell but *The Black Knight* is squarely aimed at a young audience.

It was directed by Tay Garnett, who had made *A Connecticut Yankee in King Arthur's Court* in 1949 and must have liked Camelot, since this film is set there, too, although he has a quaintly skewed idea of England and the English. The film was produced by Albert R 'Cubby' Broccoli, who later co-produced the James Bond series, and starred Alan Ladd, who was contracted to a series of British films of which this was the last. Despite a heart-warming jaunt to locations in Spain, Ladd was weary of the British drizzle and anxious to return to America.

The exteriors were shot in Castilla le Nueva, which while it provided some substantial granite castles for the backdrops, meant that the 'Stonehenge' sequences featuring a kind of druidic orgy were shot rather unconvincingly on the Spanish plains.

Cushing is in his element as Sir Palamides, acting out on a grand scale the sort of *Boy's Own* adventures that had previously been confined to his living-room floor. Palamides moves through the film like a silver snake – a villain's villain, in dusky make-up with dubious foreign inflections (he talks a lot about 'Sarry-cens' and 'Cammy-lot') and sporting a collection of rather alarming hats. At one point, for reasons too complicated to go into, we have Cushing (from Kenley) playing a Saracen, disguised as a Viking. Not politically correct, certainly, but surely no more unlikely than Alan Ladd in King Arthur's Court.

Cushing looks magnificent throughout, his blue eyes glittering in the dark make-up, his face framed by a dark wig, black beard and earrings. He revels in some faintly camp one-liners and sarcastic put-downs, and though the film is little more than a pantomime in glorious Technicolor, Cushing is never less than convincing. "There is a saying in my country," he spits at Ladd, "when a puppy yelps at his master it is time to clip his tail!"

own expenses throughout. The BBC's itinerary listed her as 'Mrs Peter Cushion'.

A copy of Greenough's set was made by the NWDR designer Herr Joksch in the Europe Hall in Dusseldorf, although the special props, including the infamous statue were transported to Germany. The production was mounted on ground level with the public looking in on the production from a circular gallery halfway up the sides of the walls. The rapt audience was witness to a narrowly avoided disaster when a working Bunsen burner on Peko's bench accidentally set light to some rags. Cushing was able to douse the flames with a jug of water and stop the gas pipe with his foot, while the attentive floor manager, John Jacobs (who had been taken along because he spoke German and was able to act as interpreter), crawled in to turn off the tap to the gas cylinder.

Silent footage of Cushing with Ursula Howells, Patrick Barr, Hilda Fenemore and Michael Barry at the Dusseldorf exhibition, from the 2nd September news item *British Television on View*, is preserved by the BBC.

After returning from Dusseldorf with Helen in September, Cushing did not take part in any more

If 1953 was a defining year for British television, 1954 was a defining year for Cushing, culminating in his most acclaimed television performance. In January, however, he was at work rehearsing *Tovarich*, Jacques Deval's comedy about an exiled Russian Prince and his wife who are forced into domestic service. The play co-starred film actress Ann Todd, whom Cushing nicknamed 'Annoushka' during rehearsals. She had agreed to take part in the play 'only if she could act opposite Peter Cushing'.

Miss Todd, whose film appearances included *The Seventh Veil* (1945) and *The Paradine Case* (1948) was married at the time to the film director David Lean, and her inclusion in a television production was a coup for the BBC. The play was directed by Eric Fawcett, to whom Helen had written at the outset of Cushing's television career.

Barney Keelan explained the plot of *Tovarich* in the *Radio Times*: 'Her Imperial Highness the Grand Duchess Tatiana Petrovna and her husband, Prince Mikail, living the hard life common among Russian exiles, are reduced to a little mild shoplifting in the Paris markets. The Prince has a fortune in the bank, but his promise to the late Tsar, for whom he holds it in trust, forbids him to spend it on the grocer's bills. "Life," as he says, "is very, very sad and very, very beautiful." When the Grand Duchess and the Prince decide that, in their extremity, work is the only solution, life also becomes very, very amusing, and particularly so when the royal couple is played by Ann

Todd, the film-star, and Peter Cushing, a television star in his own right.'[3]

The exiles become butler and parlour-maid in the household of a banker, M Dupont. Their presence

Stars Ann Todd and Cushing appeared on the cover of the *Radio Times* in the BBC's *Tovarich*

Ann Todd and Cushing in *Tovarich*

Peter Cushing, in costume as Beau Brummell, is joined by studio manager Barry Lupino and Helen in the Lime Grove canteen

Daphne Slater, Walter Fitzgerald, producer Campbell Logan and Cushing in rehearsals for *Beau Brummell* (February 1954)

changes the lives, not only of Dupont and his wife but also of the two young members of the family (who learn such Imperial pastimes as osculation – kissing – and fencing), and the play climaxes with a riotous dinner party. 'Russians may be red or white, nice or nasty,' concluded Keelan, 'but they are seldom predictable...'[4] Clive Morton played the blustering Charles Dupont and Richard Marner, best known for his bumbling German colonel in *'Allo 'Allo!* played Commissar Gorotchenko. Michael Newell, later known as a film director as Mike Newell (*Dance with a Stranger* and *Four Weddings and a Funeral*) played the Dupont son, Georges.

Cushing had won the *Daily Mail* Readers' Award for Best Television Actor of the Year 1953, with Irene Worth winning Best Television Actress. He was concerned, however, given the preparation for

Tovarich, that he would not be able to do justice to the presentation ceremony on 30th January, which had previously involved the recipients performing an extract from a play. He wrote to Michael Barry, who had been unwell, on 31st December. 'I'm thrilled at having won the Television Award but ... having won the honour by virtue of the standard of the work, I would not like even ten minutes to be below that standard. A telefilm would not be the same thing to both the live and viewing audience on that night. Irene Worth is inclined to agree with me, and we think it better just to have a two-minute spot each with a prepared speech of thanks, etc, to give the audience a chance to see their "choices" as themselves for a change, and not in character. (I'm told they prefer this anyway.) Please don't think that I'm being uncooperative, but I am truly thinking what would be best for all concerned. *Tovarich* and Irene's play at the Haymarket wouldn't allow us any time at all to work on anything as we would *want* to. Helen joins me in sending you all good wishes for 1954, and an appeal again for you to consider your own health – for all our sakes.'

The awards ceremony went out on the evening of Friday 29th January, the day after the second performance of *Tovarich*.

Cushing had played the lead in a sponsored radio broadcast of *Beau Brummell* in Australia, and it was good practice, he said, for his subsequent appearance on television as George Bryan Brummell, the celebrated dandy and favourite of the Prince Regent, who for 20 years imposed his dress, manners and wit upon the fashionable world. 'Men copied his stylish extravagances, women longed for his favour and all were, in turn, delighted and wounded by his tongue,' wrote Barney Keelan in the *Radio Times*. 'But the pace was hot, and before his inevitable downfall, this play suggests, two people at least saw beyond the brittle frivolity of his character. Brummell's chivalry towards the unfashionable Georgiana and the man who loved her may have been quixotic, but did it not disclose a melancholy yearning for another mode of life? Here, at any rate, is the suggestion, blended with scintillating glimpses of an age devoted to cultivating the highest of high life. In Regency days, above all, the style was the man – and the man was Beau Brummell. In this production, style is in the safe-keeping of Peter Cushing as Brummell and Daphne Slater as the humble girl who makes him hesitate at the height of his triumph. These two players have already shown viewers their skill in presenting another aspect of the period in *Pride and Prejudice*.'5

The action took place in 1816 in London and Brighton, with a cast that included Ferdy Mayne, Peter Copley, Walter Fitzgerald, Prunella Scales (again) and David Peel, who in 1960 would star as the vampire Baron Meinster opposite Cushing in *The Brides of Dracula*. Campbell Logan was the producer, and Cushing's fee was 65 guineas – the first rise in salary he'd had in more than eighteen months. John Paddy Carstairs, guest TV critic for the London *Evening Standard* said that Cushing's 'impeccable diction' as Brummell 'would enthral American viewers.'6 Carstairs, a film producer and director, was the brother of Anthony Nelson Keys, who would produce some of Hammer's greatest successes. Perhaps the seeds were being sown even then. A clear sign of Cushing's growing celebrity can be gleaned from a letter in January 1954 to the *TV Mirror,* the first magazine solely dedicated to television, which suggested a production of *Lorna Doone* bringing together two TV favourites – Petula Clark as Lorna and Peter Cushing as Carver Doone.

Cushing's participation in the popular radio programme *A Book at Bedtime* in 1954 was an epic in miniature. First of all, Helen sent a choice of books to Patrick Harvey, the producer, with Peter stipulating 'No American accents for me please!' Together they decided upon *Natural Causes* by Henry Cecil, to be read in 15 15-minute instalments, Monday to Friday for three weeks.

But first, there was the small matter of the book itself. 'Would you please let us have it back?' entreated the producer's secretary, on dispatching a reading copy. 'We've had to borrow it from the *Times* Library.' Harvey also outlined the *Book at Bedtime* 'ritual', which is endearingly quaint even by BBC standards. Pre-recording was not uncommon on radio at this time, but the instalments were still broadcast live at 10.45pm each night. Cushing received seven guineas for each instalment, and had to all but turn the lights out when he'd finished. As Harvey told him in the '*Book at Bedtime* ritual' – 'Report to the Duty Officer about 10.45 pm and then go to studio 3C. If you can remember, would you please write on the top of your script the time you come off the air? By deducting 16 or so seconds for the opening announcement, we have a timing for the programme as broadcast. Please don't bother about this if it's going to worry you. After transmission, kindly take your script, and the studio manager's, if it is lying around, back to the Duty Officer who will supply you with a drink if you want one.'

The series was a success, and Harvey duly forwarded a letter of congratulation with a letter from an enthusiastic listener. Cushing returned his usual hearty reply. 'My dear Patrick, how jolly nice that

you were satisfied with our mutual effort on *A Book at Bedtime*! I must say I felt a complete fool when I first kicked off, but you were so helpful and co-operative that if I succeeded at all it was because of the sympathetic and tactful guidance you gave me. I must say that nobody was more surprised than I at the reaction to the bibulous solicitor and his associates (I didn't know I had it in me!) I hope that we may one day repeat our double act.'

Cushing took part in two more radio broadcasts in rapid succession, narrating *The Bride in the Bath* on *Morning Story* on 2nd March 1954 and playing the Marquess of Quex in *The Gay Lord Quex* by Arthur Wing Pinero. ('In 1900, Lord Quex, a genial rake, has become engaged to a "typical creamy English girl" but at a country house-party he becomes embarrassingly involved with the Duchess of Strood.') This was recorded on 31st March, and broadcast on the Home Service on 5th April (after *The Goon Show*) The producer was Archie Campbell and the 'special' fee was 18 guineas. As a further indication of Cushing's success, in April 1954, the *TV Mirror* began a serialised autobiography of 'TV's popular star', which ran for five weeks under the title of 'The Peter Cushing Story'. Cushing's story was actually related to Robert Hirst, who later published it along with similarly 'autobiographical' pieces on Terry-Thomas and Arthur Askey, under the title *Three Men and a Gimmick* for the World's Work press.

Cushing was narrator again on a 20-minute TV programme called *May Day* which went out on 1 May from Lime Grove – 'Television recalls some of the customs and ceremonies which are traditional on the first day of May.' 'Thank you for your patience and trust,' Cushing wrote to producer Paul Johnstone 'over what I found an extraordinary ordeal until transmission. Any show of temperament please put down to my not having enough time for "conning" the lines.' As well as the turn as narrator, Cushing suddenly found himself in demand as a 'celebrity guest'. He was on 'expenses only' however, when he appeared on the magic show *Men of Mystery* ('A programme in which an attempt is made to deceive you') on 14th May, with TV magicians David Nixon, David Berglas and 'Chandu'. 'Be at the studio at 9.15,' specified Angela Heathcote, secretary to producer Bill Ward, 'in evening dress (dinner jacket). I am asking the accounts department to forward a cheque for ten guineas to cover all your expenses in connection with this appearance.'

Men of Mystery was recorded while Cushing was beginning rehearsals for a tour of the play *The Soldier and The Lady* by Ian Stuart Black. This new piece was directed by Sam Wanamaker, the American actor and producer who devoted the latter part of his life to the construction of a replica of Shakespeare's Globe Theatre on London's South Bank. Wanamaker was

Henry Miles in happier times with his wife Sarah (Deborah Kerr) in Edward Dmytryk's *The End of the Affair* (1954)

On 13th June 1954, Cushing wrote to Michael Barry: 'Forgive me taking up your precious time, but I wonder if you have any suggestions for a play I could do soon on Television? *The Soldier and The Lady*, in which I'm now touring, I don't think will come to town, and at present we only have two positive dates, a week in each.'

A fortnight later, however, he was under contract for a film, and so had to decline Royston Morley's offer of a starring role in a new production of *Peer Gynt*. He was, however, able to appear in the panel game *Down You Go!* with Kenneth Horne, Patricia Cutts and Elizabeth Gray (who had featured in *Lord Quex*) on 29th July 1954. The show was presented by Ernest Maxim from the Television Theatre, Shepherd's Bush, and on Maxim's request Helen supplied some photographs of her husband, apologising that they were not 'full length' as he had specified. After his appearance on *Down You Go!* Maxim asked Cushing to appear on the show again immediately, but Cushing sadly had to decline. 'My film commitments will prevent me from appearing for some time.'

The film was *The End of the Affair*, based on Graham Greene's complex novel and directed by Edward Dmytryk, who had made several highly regarded *film noir* thrillers, including *Murder My Sweet* and *Crossfire* and came to England because of the anti-Communist blacklisting in America.

The film was produced by David Lewis, the longtime lover of James Whale. Whether Lewis remembered the handsome stand-in for Louis Hayward or not, this was certainly an important part for Cushing to land, opposite Hollywood star Van Johnson and Deborah Kerr. Greene's book was an examination of his own Catholic faith and, although it was not known at the time, was a *roman-à-clef* for the novelist's own adulterous affair with Lady Catherine Walston. The film is shot through with a tone of pessimism and seems weighed down with Greene's own feelings of guilt.

There's a rather flamboyant piano score too, much given to melodramatic bashing on the keyboard at particularly emotional moments. Johnson is miscast and his flat delivery suggests he did not really understand the material. Greene, who vetoed Gregory Peck for the lead was appalled at the choice of Johnson and noted that the actor chewed gum during the love scenes when not in shot. Cushing however, achieves a kind of brilliance with his portrayal of the wronged husband, a man with 'a mind as neatly creased as his trousers' and it is sobering to think that but for *Nineteen Eighty-Four* he might have carried on playing this kind of repressed individual for as long as it was required.

trained in Stanislavsky and the new vogue of 'method' acting, with emphasis on the inner motivation of a character. This had little in common with Cushing's repertory and television training, which had taught meticulous precision simply by volume of work. However, Cushing overcame his suspicions of Wanamaker's approach and gave an acclaimed performance. The play was a happy, if short-lived, experience for the director and star.

Cushing as 'the soldier' played opposite Richard Attenborough's wife, Sheila Sim as 'the Lady', the tour beginning at the Wimbledon Theatre on 31st May, taking in Eastbourne's Devonshire Park Theatre at the end of June and finishing the run in Southsea. Cushing remembered that during rehearsals, Wanamaker would direct the action while doing handstands on a cane chair placed perilously close to the edge of the stage. While finishing the run, Cushing was able to extol the virtues of a subject close to his heart when he appeared on a *Woman's Hour* segment entitled *Woman, Lovely Woman*, dealing with fashion in the 1930s and 40s.

The plot of *The End of the Affair* is fragmented, and told in a series of flashbacks. During the Second World War, American Maurice Bendrix (Johnson) is writing a book on the British civil service when he meets Henry Miles, who works in service pensions. Miles presents Bendrix to his devoted wife Sarah (Deborah Kerr) – and soon Bendrix and Sarah are having an affair. (What they actually *do*, however, is left terribly vague.) After an air-raid, Sarah suddenly becomes cold to Bendrix and returns to Miles. The rest of the film reveals the reasons for her sudden change of heart.

Though stuffy and pompous, Miles is genuinely in love with Sarah. As time passes and her behaviour remains erratic, he considers employing a private detective to investigate her, but ultimately cannot. 'They always say, don't they, that the husband is the last to know...' Miles is equally unable to answer his wife's questions about her faith. When she asks her husband if he prays, he is at a loss. 'I was *taught* to. In church, whenever I go ... Really, this isn't the sort of thing to go into over a cup of tea!'

Towards the end of the film, Miles is a man on the point of despair and Cushing's performance is deeply affecting. 'I know I'm dull for you, Sarah ... frightfully dull...' he sobs. 'But I couldn't start again. It's too late, do you see?' As Sarah succumbs to a fatal fever, Cushing descends the stairs with a blank expression, unable to comprehend. It is another meticulous and disciplined performance, and Deborah Kerr is a graceful and generous co-star.

After nearly three months at Shepperton Studios, it was back to the Jewish Lads' Club for rehearsals for *The Face of Love* from 17th September to 3rd October. This was a contemporary retelling of the story of Helen of Troy featuring Cushing as Mardian. It was transmitted on 5th October from Lime Grove. The producer was Alvin Rakoff, a young Canadian whose TV work Cushing had seen and admired.

Cushing's fee for *The Face of Love* was 74 guineas. After this, there was a considerable leap in salary – his wages almost doubled. There was a general increase in BBC artists' fees, but Cushing's growing standing as a film actor must have given John Redway extra clout. Part of the reason for the rise in wages was the imminent arrival of a new independent television station, as outlined in the government's bill in the summer of 1954. The BBC's biggest drama of the year, its adaptation of George Orwell's *Nineteen Eighty-Four*, was well into pre-production, and Cushing was to star. Before that, however, he had to make a trip to Bavaria to appear in the film *Magic Fire*.

Otto Wesendonk presents a cheque to Richard Wagner (Alan Badel) but he is soon to lose his wife Mathilde (Valentina Cortese) to the composer in *Magic Fire* (1954)

'Republic's Top 1954 Picture – Life of Wagner,' trumpeted the *Daily Cinema*. 'William Dieterle will produce and direct. Production in Technicolor starts in Germany on September 11th. As the launching stage of Republic's major production this year, *Magic Fire*, the story of Richard Wagner's life and loves, contracts have been signed with Yvonne De Carlo, Rhonda Fleming and Rita Gam for the three feminine leads. This, one of Republic's most ambitious productions, is based on the recently published biography by Bertita Harding.'[7]

The film is slow and heavy-handed, albeit with spectacular reconstructions of famous scenes from Wagner's operas involving giants, valkyries and such. Alan Badel plays the composer who is given to much melodramatic suffering at the harpsichord and whose work is hampered by his roving eye and fierce political convictions. Yvonne De Carlo plays Wagner's first wife Minna, decked out in a series of elaborate Dresden Shepherdess-style costumes.

Cushing appears in the middle of the film as Wagner's friend and sponsor Otto Wesendonk, but the friendship sours when Wagner runs off with Wesendonk's wife Mathilde (Valentina Cortese). Cushing's brief appearance is notable at least for showing him in an outfit like the one he will famously wear as Frankenstein, with frock coat, waved hair and side-whiskers.

Filming took place in Bavaria in October 1954, and Helen was able to accompany her husband to Munich for an enjoyable holiday. With *Magic Fire*, Cushing consolidated his position as an attractive and reliable supporting player, but with his next project, he would earn himself a very different reputation...

Chapter Nine

Nineteen Eighty-Four
And All That

The BBC's adaptation of George Orwell's *Nineteen Eighty-Four* was produced by Rudolph Cartier and broadcast on 12th December 1954. It was British television's first masterpiece.

The production had been first mooted after Cartier's success as producer of *The Quatermass Experiment*, and he was keen to take on the project having first read Orwell's novel in serial form in 1950. Cartier was born in Vienna in 1904 and had worked at the UFA film studios in Berlin, leaving Germany when Hitler came to power in 1933. After the war, Cartier was invited by Michael Barry to join the BBC as a staff director and Cartier, with his usual uncompromising candour, told Barry exactly what he thought of the BBC's drama output. He knew that the way forward was not merely to restage popular stage successes, but to develop new writing specifically for the television medium.

By February 1954 dramatist Hugh Falkus was working on an adaptation with George Orwell's widow, Sonia Blair. A 60-minute TV version of the book had been produced by CBS in America in 1953, but it was, according to Barry, 'restrained to the point of being dull.' There were delays with the project until May. Mrs Blair had sold the film rights to an American company, who granted the rights back to the BBC on the condition that they produced the play within the year. The programme, with a new script by Nigel Kneale, was finally scheduled for December, allowing for a lengthy pre-production period. It was budgeted at £3000, making it the most expensive BBC production to this date. An original costing of £2500 was rejected by Cartier, who eventually used 22 sets in two studios at Lime Grove, 60 actors, a small orchestra and more pre-filmed inserts than had been used for a television drama up to that time.

However, even the BBC's staff were worried at the strength of the material they were being asked to work with. In September 1954 Barry Learoyd, the designer assigned to *Nineteen Eighty-Four*, wrote to Michael Barry. 'This really is no business of mine, but I'm working on *Nineteen Eighty-Four* and I feel so strongly about it that I wonder if others will not do the same. Every time I refer to the script I feel it should not be put on ... I hope you will excuse this interference.' Cartier was more concerned that the sets were looking

shoddy, and demanded that Learoyd be given more money to rectify matters. Jack Kine and Bernard Wilkie of the fledgling visual effects department were set to work on the special props – including the all-seeing telescreens – and a large model of the dried-up River Thames overshadowed by the Ministry of Truth.

Cushing was cast as hero Winston Smith and joined the production for the filming of the location sequences on 10th November. The first filming sessions were at Studio B, Alexandra Palace, and in the adjacent parkland on 10th and 11th November, and the remainder of pre-filming took place at Lime Grove from the 18th – 20th. Rehearsals were then held at the Mary Ward Settlement, Tavistock Place, from 22nd November, and at 60 Paddington Street from 29th November. Studio rehearsals were held at Lime Grove on 11th and 12th December. Cushing was paid 150 guineas, his highest fee yet for a BBC project.

Nineteen Eighty-Four presents a vision of life in Britain in the future where a totalitarian regime has been established. Fronted by the image of 'Big Brother', the government uses surveillance devices – telescreens – to monitor the daily lives of the population, who are divided into three castes – the privileged Inner Party, the Outer Party and the uneducated 'Proles' who are fed computer-written pornography, music and drugs to keep them in a state of placid ignorance.

Winston Smith is an Outer Party worker whose job is to censor archived news reports to conform with the current party line. He keeps a diary in which he secretly questions the omnipotence of Big Brother, and he commits the ultimate crime when he falls in love with a girl called Julia (Yvonne Mitchell). They enjoy a forbidden courtship in the Prole sector, knowing that this is an unforgivable crime and that they can never win but, as Winston says, 'Some kinds of failure are better than others.'

Ultimately there can be no escape. At the Ministry of Love, Inner Party member O'Brien (André Morell) subjects Winston to a barrage of electric shocks, then to the horror of Room 101. 'By itself, pain is not always enough,' O'Brien explains. 'What happens in Room 101 is the worst thing in the world. It can be death by burning, burial alive, or something quite

In the Chestnut Tree café, Syme (Donald Pleasence) confesses to Winston Smith that he has committed 'thoughtcrime'. From *Nineteen Eighty-Four* (1954)

trivial, not even fatal.' In Winston's case, the worst thing in the world is rats. O'Brien presents a mask, attached by a tube to a cage of rats. 'The mask ... fits over the head, leaving no exit. When the plastic door is raised up, the rats will shoot out like bullets. It was a common punishment in Imperial China...' in the climactic scene of the play, Winston breaks. 'Do it to Julia! I don't care what you to her. Do it to Julia! Not me!' The play concludes with Smith a broken man. Cushing's face fills the screen, murmuring 'I love Big Brother. I love Big Brother.'

Although Kneale effectively transformed Orwell's journalistic fable into a compelling play, and Cartier created, with documentary clarity, a nightmarish vision of a ruined, downtrodden London, it was Cushing's performance that gave the production its heart. Without him as 'the guardian of the human spirit' there would surely not have been the huge public outcry that resulted. People were responding to the sight of *Peter Cushing* being tortured – so convincing was the performance. Cushing gave everything to the role – even sacrificing his vanity

(such as it was) by removing his false front teeth to show the brutality of Winston's ordeal.

Detail is the key here. On several occasions, with Cushing's face in extreme close-up, he is acting solely with his wide pale eyes. 'He said that to blink was too much on television,'[1] Joan Craft recalls. 'He served the close screen very well.' Smith bears the horror of 1984 with a weary determination, the traditional bulldog spirit, but distaste and resignation at the grime and the stench, the lack of razor-blades and the revolting 'regulation' stew. It must have had arrowing resonances to those who had lived through the privations of the war – meat rationing had only just been suspended in the summer of 1954.

As well as acting, Cartier also required Cushing to *sing*. 'He said "Zere is a sentimental sonk for ze Proles vich I vish you to sink,"' Cushing remembered, imitating Cartier's Viennese tones. 'So I sunk.'[2] Cushing is heard, off-screen, warbling 'It was Only a Hopeless Fancy' – the synthetic song created for the Proles ('The sentimental ones are issued sparingly,' murmurs O'Brien, 'so they're always popular'). He

Winston Smith and Mrs Parsons (Hilda Fenemore) with the Parsons children (Keith Davis and Pamela Grant)

Julia (Yvonne Mitchell) and Winston unwisely share a toast with O'Brien (André Morell) in *Nineteen Eighty-Four* (1954)

also sings the version of 'Underneath the Spreading Chestnut Tree' which is played in the café.

Cushing always worked well with a strong cast and the support here is exceptional. Yvonne Mitchell was voted Top TV Actress of 1953, and brings beauty and spirit to Julia. It is easy to believe that Winston and Julia are in love. In two intense scenes, Donald Pleasence presents Syme, who is translating the English dictionary into the insidious, economical 'newspeak' with an almost puritanical zeal. But it is André Morell's O'Brien, with whom Cushing shares the last act, who is the most terrifying representation of the regime. In Morell's hands, O'Brien's interrogation scenes are uneasily like seduction. 'My poor friend,' he whispers, 'you are almost well. It is not enough to *obey* Big Brother. You now know ... who it is you must love.'

The second performance of the play was recorded by the BBC, and despite Cushing's insistence that it wasn't a patch on the first performance, it still makes for uncomfortable viewing. The haunting black-and-white photography owes more to European filmmaking than Hollywood, hardly surprising given Cartier's UFA background. Nothing like it had been seen on television before. The most disturbing alternative on the BBC in 1954 was indomitable quiz-show walrus Gilbert Harding hectoring the contestants on *What's My Line?*

'We don't give figures,' said a BBC spokesman, 'but a very considerable number have complained.' And indeed they had. 'Thank God for Wilfred Pickles and *The Grove Family*!' sighed D Hunt of Leicester. 'For weeks on Sundays we have to watch dismal, immoral and sadistically highbrow plays. The persons

responsible for putting on *Nineteen Eighty-Four* are sadists and readers of horror comics.'

'I have a screen television,' wrote Lt Col J B Leicester-Warren, principal of Tabley House School for Boys 'and I had some very senior boys in to watch *Nineteen Eighty-Four*. This kind of play is the antithesis of anything Christian.' 'Unspeakably putrid. I hope you will not again pollute the air with similar muck!' said Mrs Pearl Lee of Colnbrook. 'If that is what the world is going to be like, we might as well put our heads in the gas ovens now.'

On the evening of 15th December there was a televised debate on *Nineteen Eighty-Four* with Cartier and Malcolm Muggeridge. There were questions in the House of Commons about whether such plays were appropriate for a Sunday and a suggestion that the scheduled repeat on Thursday 16th should not go ahead as planned. This repeat was to be a live broadcast of a second performance and the potential risks to personnel and equipment were taken very seriously indeed. On 15th December, even the unflappable Cartier requested extra security at Studios D and E, Lime Grove, for the next day in case anyone broke in to interfere with the transmissions or tamper with equipment.

Alison McLeod in the *Daily Worker* wrote, 'Orwell imagined that talk of "Communist immorality" might sound rather attractive, so sex ... was forbidden and we were edified by the sight of Peter Cushing and Yvonne Mitchell defiantly taking a roll in the hay for freedom. The final scene, which showed a Socialist torture machine looking like something out of the Festival of Britain ... bore out the BBC's warning that the play was not suitable for children or old people. They might have added "or anyone in between".'[3]

'People were asking me all yesterday,' wrote Cushing in the *Daily Express*, 14th December, 'why I agreed to play the part of Winston Smith. Well, to be frank, it was a job of work. But it was also more than that. People have complained that there is no hope in the play. That was Orwell's point. "Don't let totalitarianism happen," he said, "because if it happens, hope will die and love will die." Some of the critics have likened *1984* to a horror comic. In the play, Orwell shows a factory producing horror comics to debase the minds of the people. If his play is a horror comic, then it is a horror comic to expose what horror comics can do. I do not in the least blame or criticise the people who took offence at the play. I do not like whisky, but I do like tea. This does not mean that I wish to stop people drinking whisky, so long as they do not want to stop me drinking tea. I was reminded in rehearsing *1984* of *Gulliver's Travels*, which Dean Swift wrote as a vicious tirade against governmental abuses. I do not suggest that *1984* will ever become a book for children – but it must be remembered that George Orwell, too, was campaigning against the possibility of gross abuse of power.' Yvonne Mitchell also took up the cause: 'All of us who took part in this TV play were convinced of its importance and were proud to take part in it.'[4]

Not all the comments on *Nineteen Eighty-Four* were hostile. 'Thank Goodness Big Brother Could Not Strangle the BBC' cheered the *Daily Sketch*. 'I estimate that the BBC received about 1,000 calls,' said a reporter in the *Evening News*. 'out of a viewing audience of possibly nine million, this can hardly be regarded as damning evidence of disapproval. It is good to see the BBC doing something adventurous and sticking to its guns.'[5]

Michael Barry met Princess Margaret, who told him that she and her mother had watched on Sunday. 'In her view' he reported, 'it was one of the best productions she had ever seen on television.' Another of the BBC heads, D K Wolfe-Murray, was presented to the Duke of Edinburgh on 15th December, and spent some time talking with him. 'He expressed his admiration for the play and message contained in Cartier's production. He also stated that the Queen herself was of the same opinion. He did not in any way charge me to be his messenger, but I have taken upon myself to inform R C and his three leading actors.'

Without doubt the most succinct and moving communication on the subject was a telegram to the BBC from H Stollery of Ipswich after the first broadcast which said simply: 'Please repeat *Nineteen Eighty-Four*. No doubt some have forgotten Belsen.'

While the furore over *Nineteen Eighty-Four* raged, Cushing was already preparing for his next play, again with a script by

Nigel Kneale, again directed by Cartier and with Barry Learoyd again as designer. The play was called *The Creature*, and concerned the fabled Himalayan creature known as the Abominable Snowman. Cartier was leading an expedition to the Jungfraujoch in the Bernese Oberland in Switzerland for location filming in the first week of the New Year, and there was some concern about possible hazard to the BBC's popular star. But Cushing wasn't going to be left behind, as he told Michael Barry. 'If it is for any reason other than a financial one that you didn't want me to risk doing the film work abroad I couldn't be more willing or eager to go on location for *The Creature*. I'm never keen on the idea of a double being used as I like to know what I'm doing in a play *all* the time. However, I appreciate your thoughts as to my well-being.' Cushing was allowed to participate in the overseas filming, and there was additional shooting at Lime Grove on 10th January. When Hammer remade *The*

The intrepid botanist Doctor John Rollason embarks on a quest for the Abominable Snowman in Rudolph Cartier's production of *The Creature* (1955)

The Lama (Arnold Marle), Tom Friend (Stanley Baker) and Rollason
in Nigel Kneale's play *The Creature* (1954)

Creature as *The Abominable Snowman* two years
later, Cushing repeated his role but was *not* taken
on location.

Cushing played botanist John Rollason, who joins
explorer Tom Friend on an expedition to find the
legendary 'yeti' in the high peaks of Tibet. They are
accompanied by a trapper, Brosset, and a young
man called McPhee who sighted yeti footprints on a
previous climb. When one of the man-like creatures is
captured and killed, the explorers experience various
kinds of telepathic assault, and all but Rollason are
ultimately destroyed by their own fears.

The legend of the yeti in other hands would be no
more than an excuse for a man in a fur suit to run
amok. Kneale's script is his usual rich mix of
mysticism and scientific hypothesis, brimming with
atmosphere and imagination. The use of characters is
economical and they are familiar Kneale types – the
noble scientist, the venal hunter, the 'sensitive' loner.
The script addresses Kneale's beloved themes of
mind-control and ancient intelligence, as well as the
idea that humanity, speeding headlong to his own
destruction, will only continue to argue while greater
powers wait in the wings. The writer's ability to create
a whole civilisation in a handful of words is ably
displayed in the Lama's speeches about 'those who
will succeed man'.

In an interview in *Sight and Sound* magazine in
1959, Kneale recalled the transmission of *The Creature*
for less than auspicious reasons. 'The play ... had
what was intended as a tense, penultimate scene in a
Himalayan ice cave at 22,000 feet. Two heavily-clad
characters were acting hard on transmission when a
figure appeared outside the cave. It wore a dust-coat
and was busily sweeping up the eternal snows. A
booby, it turned out, who was in a hurry to get home
and thought he would clear up early. In those days
plays were repeated live a few days later, so at the
second transmission he was firmly warned. To make
sure, the cave was rendered booby-proof with a black

sky-cloth and a large stack of boxes. But, with a
waywardness that had something wonderful in it,
he managed to appear again.'[6]

Stanley Baker appeared as Friend, Simon Lack
played McPhee and Eric Pohlmann played Brosset.
Kneale's character names McNee and Shelley had
been changed to McPhee and Brosset shortly before
transmission, but were changed back for the film
script. As well as Cushing, Arnold Marle (the Lama)
and Wolfe Morris (Nima Kusang) would repeat their
roles in the film. The play was transmitted on 30th
January and 3rd February from Studio D, Lime
Grove.

The *Times*, which headed its review 'Quest Play on
Television' on 31st January was singularly unimpressed
and, with regard to the script, frankly unfair. 'The
play in performance hovered always on the margin
of the ludicrous, and alas, often overstepped it. Every
conceivable effect of atmosphere – vast snowscapes,
fiercely howling wind, foreboding music, night flares
shining in the mountains, a whole monastery full
of masked monks with Arnold Marle effective as the
cropped, goggle-eyed lama – was put into Mr Rudolph
Cartier's production to help the piece along, but
nothing could raise it from the banal level of its
dialogue and narrative. The main trouble presumably
lies in the subject ... Mr Kneale's yeti in his big animal
mask never became any more of a reality than the
team of explorers with the attitudes and ideas of
schoolboys who set out to catch him. For once even
that good television actor Mr Peter Cushing, playing
their leader, seemed dull.'[7]

The Independent Television Authority was
established on 30th July 1954, and would create
Britain's first commercial television network within 18
months. The opposition to independent television was
vociferous and splenetic – some saw it as nothing
less than the end of civilisation. As soon as the
Independent Television Bill was passed, the BBC's
immediate concern was that their stars would defect to
'the other side' and so began hurried negotiations to
sign exclusive contracts with their most popular stars.
Cushing was offered a contract on 24th December
guaranteeing him eight plays in three years, at a fee of
£1000 per annum. Cushing in turn had to guarantee
a minimum of two performances per year. He could
only appear on BBC television, but the contract
could be suspended for 'a good part' on stage or in
a film. Cushing's agent, John Redway, was part of
the MCA Agency at 139 Piccadilly. As Cushing's film
appearances were increasing but his television roles
were also requiring a considerable amount of attention
it was decided that Kenneth Cleveland, another MCA
agent, would handle television work while Redway
concentrated on the films. Cleveland could, however,
drive a hard bargain and in the course of the next two
years would give the BBC some cause for exasperation.
Nevertheless, he was able to secure, to Cushing's

advantage, a BBC contract for six plays in two years for a total sum of £1800. Little did MCA or the BBC suspect how Cushing's career would take off in the next two years, or how difficult it would be for him to complete the required six plays.

'BBC Sign Up Star of "1984"' wrote the *Observer* on 6th February 1955. 'The BBC have signed up Mr Peter Cushing, star of the televised production of "1984", Miss Anne Crawford, the stage and screen actress, and Miss Gillian Lutyens to appear exclusively in BBC television programmes for the next two years. These are the first of a series of contracts which are intended to give the BBC exclusive rights to the services of actors and actresses.'[8]

Powerful rivals Memnon and Alexander (Richard Burton) in *Alexander the Great* (1955)

The announcement was a little premature. Cleveland was hammering the BBC's various draft contracts into shape and Cushing was not actually signed to the BBC over a sixpenny stamp until 17th March 1955. His first play under contract, however, was *The Moment of Truth*, which began rehearsals on 14th February.

The Moment of Truth was written for the stage by Peter Ustinov, based on the fate of Marshal Petain. It was a broad modern interpretation of *King Lear*, set in an imaginary country with Ustinov as the aged Field Marshal, an annoyed and intractable character who commands respect only by his reputation. Suddenly the Field Marshal finds himself called upon to deal with a new crisis – an atomic war –which he is completely unable to comprehend. Cushing played the Prime Minister, 'an apostle of surrender' as Ustinov wrote in the *Radio Times*. 'He is no villain in the accepted sense of the word; on the contrary he is a Prime Minister of crystalline perception, a man who, in his own words "Will save millions of lives; they will thank me by killing me" ... and who claims to be a better patriot than the ambitious general who wishes to continue the war of attrition.'[9]

Also in the cast were Jeanette Sterke as the Marshal's daughter, Ian Colin as the General, and Hugh Griffith as the compassionate photographer, the everyman figure looking on at the conflict of love, duty, devotion, and honour. This was the third play in a row for Cushing directed by Rudolph Cartier and was it broadcast on 6th and 10th March. In January, Michael Barry had written 'the quality of telerecording is improving so rapidly that it is now more than probable that we shall be making full use of telerecording

facilities within the next three months.' Significantly, *The Moment of Truth* was the last play of Cushing's to have a performed repeat.

The rehearsal period for this heavyweight piece was leavened by the series of lunatic correspondences passed between Ustinov and Cushing which were reproduced in *Past Forgetting*. So involved were these notes, loaded with puns, caricatures and 'faked' newspaper cuttings that it is surprising they got any rehearsing done at all. Ustinov's notes to Cushing are masterpieces of abstract wit, Cushing's replies by comparison are more naïve, with his usual deliberately fractured spellings, as in *The Bois Saga*. On 8th March, between performances of *The Moment of Truth*, Alvin Rakoff suggested 'a Mexican play' (*The Legend of Pepito*) for broadcast on 5th June. Cushing declined.

In mid-March, shortly after signing his BBC contract, Cushing flew with Helen to Spain for his most ambitious film project yet – *Alexander the Great*. This was an epic feature from United Artists, in Cinemascope, directed by Robert Rossen at the Sevilla Studios in Madrid. 30-year-old Richard Burton played the 22-year-old Alexander with an all-star cast including Fredric March, Harry Andrews, Stanley Baker and Claire Bloom while Cushing played Memnon, the Athenian general who opposed Alexander at the Battle of Granicus. In his long black wig and saturnine beard, Cushing cuts a far more heroic figure than poor Richard Burton, who with his peroxide blonde curls looks like nothing so much as an elderly cherub.

Memnon is employed by the Persians (in charge, a blacked-up Harry Andrews) to use his military skills against Alexander. 'My Lords of Persia listen well!'

General Memnon bids 'a bitter farewell' to his wife Barsine (Claire Bloom) in Robert Rossen's *Alexander the Great* (1955)

proclaims Cushing, an index finger stabbing the sky, 'Alexander is like a hungry lion on the scent of blood. He needs a fight, a kill, and he needs it quickly...' The Persians will not agree to Memnon's scorched-earth policy, so he returns to his wife Barsine (Claire Bloom), knowing that a straight fight with Alexander will mean certain death. But Barsine has already fallen in love with Alexander. 'This is a bitter farewell...' murmurs Memnon. Cushing's goodbye scene with Claire Bloom is superb and the actors enjoy a genuine rapport.

The staging of the Battle of Granicus is duly massive, with swarms of teeming actors and Cushing in leather armour leading the attack on horseback. Memnon loses his horse and quickly loses his life, but his death-scene is peculiarly shot and strangely anti-climactic, victim of the director's fondness for (often messy) montage. 'Not a scene is held for a second longer than its worth,' huffed Alexander Walker. 'Greatness is pictured in constant dissolve.'

As befits an epic, Cushing's performance throughout has a perfectly-pitched theatricality, but the emotion there is brilliantly controlled. Among some very powerful actors his is quite possibly the finest performance in the film.

While in Spain, Cushing continued his usual active correspondence with the BBC, considering new roles and reading scripts. On 14th April 1955, he wrote to Michael Barry on specially embossed *Alexander the Great* notepaper, from the Castellana Hilton. 'Dear Michael, I am more than enthusiastic about *The Sun and I*, an enchanting play! I would dearly love to play Charles, and have written in detail to John Redway about it and my time here, which at the moment is highly pro-longed [sic]. I do hope some mutually convenient arrangement could be made to enable me to do the play. My only fear is that it might be somewhat episodic – might it be cut down to an hour-and-a-half? Michael Redington would be ideal as 'David' and I do hope you will bring your good offices to help this young and deserving actor. One cannot help but see Peggy Ashcroft as the wife and Kathleen Harrison as the maid! Do you agree?'

As it turned out, Filming for *Alexander the Great* was indeed pro-longed, much to the fury of several cast members – Richard Burton in particular quickly lost faith with the project. On 29th April Michael Barry made the decision to proceed with *The Sun and I* without Cushing. The play concerned the disappointed life of headmaster Charles Cartwright, a 'big fish in a small pond'. It was directed by Campbell Logan and broadcast on 29th May 1955, starring David Markham (who had appeared with Cushing in *Pride and Prejudice*) as Cartwright and Pauline Jameson as his wife.

Cushing wrote back to Barry on 13th May. 'I am so sorry to miss *The Sun and I* and wish you all success with it. This film is taking much longer than was at first anticipated but we hope to be home early in June. I'm not sure of my future dates yet, and I would like a week or so free when I return (to recover! and deal with the accumulated mail, etc), but I would like to do *The Browning Version* very much sometime this year, if it will fit into the scheme of things to come!'

Chapter Ten

Richard II, Irving Nil

Terence Rattigan's short play *The Browning Version* was fitted into the scheme of things almost immediately. The play was rehearsed the following month from 25th June to 11th July. Rattigan was consulted about the casting and replied by telegram 'Agree Peter Cushing if Eric Portman impossible.' Portman had originated the role on stage. *The Browning Version* presents an hour in the life of a severe public school master, Andrew Crocker-Harris – 'the Crock' as he is nicknamed by his pupils. He is retiring due to a weak heart, he has failed to get the headmastership he once coveted, he has failed to earn the love of his pupils and has singularly failedto keep the love of his wife, Millie, who is having an affair with another master, Frank Hunter.

'Crocker-Harris is the old type of schoolmaster,' wrote Peter Currie in the *Radio Times,* 'a classicist in a world that has no time for the classics. And now, forced into premature retirement, he needs all he can muster of the stoic spirit. Yet in the heart of such a man there is more rejoicing over one pupil who responds more than all the rest and appropriately

Millie Crocker-Harris (Joyce Heron) displays her contempt for her passionless husband Andrew in the BBC's adaptation of Terence Rattigan's *The Browning Version* (1955)

Peter with Helen (and the Jaguar) on holiday in Norfolk, summer 1955

Cushing had been able to purchase his dream car – a powder-blue Jaguar, which was pressed into active service rather sooner than anticipated, as Redington recalls. 'Peter went all the way to Coventry to get this Jaguar, and the rules then were that you could only go at 30 miles per hour with a new car. Helen knew all about our theatre and said "We'd love to come up and stay with you, have a lovely holiday, Peter can do his paintings." So Peter and Helen stayed in a flat in our digs. It was a very simple town hall theatre, not much more than a village hall, and we didn't have any lights, so I asked Peter if he would go to Covent Garden and pick some up. So there he was, in this brand new Jaguar, driving all the way up to Cromer loaded down with my lights. He adored it. He enjoyed being in the countryside, and near to Edward Seago, who lived there, and he had the whole of East Anglia to paint. He was very happy and very relaxed.

'He used to encourage me, because I was running this theatre on my own, and I was only 28. One play we were doing was one of the Whitehall farces, and there were asterisks all over the script. It said "This is for the benefit of amateur performers. An asterisk indicates where the main laughs come." You couldn't see anything remotely funny near any of these asterisks, so I said to Peter please come to the first night, and help us with the laughs. Darling Peter, I shall never forget as long as I live, the curtains drew apart very, very slowly and he laughed. That started the whole thing off and it was terrific.'

Soon after independent television began transmission on 22nd September, Redington became an ITV producer. 'I did the religious programmes, probably because no-one wanted to do them. One thing I wanted to do, as a religious programme, was an interview with the Devil. A sort of *Face to Face* thing, with Peter as the Devil. Christopher Hollis wrote a brilliant script, but in the end we couldn't do it. I think there were some raised eyebrows at the idea.'[3]

By 17th August, discussions were well underway for Cushing to star in a production on the life of the actor Henry Irving. Michael Barry sent a draft script by Christopher Hassall and also suggested 'something that might appeal and work in not too arduously. I am currently completing an adaptation of *The Scarlet Pimpernel* – I dare not tell you how drastically, because the old piece certainly requires it. Nothing would make me happier than to have you with me playing Chauvelin, which I believe you would relish without having to become involved in too much thoughtful work – boot and spur fun.'

it is one of the boys who brings some comfort to Crocker-Harris.'[1] At the end of the play, Crocker-Harris is given a present by his pupil Taplow – a translation of the *Agamemnon* by Robert Browning, inscribed with the quotation 'God from afar looks graciously upon the gentle master.' Because of Taplow's kindness, and because of his wife's vain attempt to spoil the gesture, Crocker-Harris is able finally to take control of his life.

The play was transmitted from Lime Grove on 12th July and the producer was Campbell Logan. Joyce Heron co-starred as Millie Crocker-Harris and Michael Gwynn was her lover, Frank Hunter. (In 1958, Gwynn would play the unfortunate victim of one of Cushing's experiments in *The Revenge of Frankenstein*.)

In the role of John Taplow was Andrew Ray, the wide-eyed child star of Ealing's *The Mudlark* (1950) and *The Yellow Balloon* (1952). 'I remember well appearing with Peter in *The Browning Version*,' says Ray. 'I was only 14 at the time but I remember what a lovely gentle man he was and what a fine actor. He was wonderful as Crocker-Harris and I have often thought since that if he had not taken the Hammer road to horror he would have had a very distinguished career in other areas of theatre. This is not to decry those movies, but in a way his talents were wasted in them, I feel.'[2]

With a profitable blockbuster under his belt and a critical success on television, the Cushings had reason to celebrate in the summer of 1955. They went to stay with Michael and Ann Redington near Cromer, where Redington was running a small repertory theatre for a summer season. With the money from *Alexander*,

Considering that *Irving* was to be broadcast only four days after *The Scarlet Pimpernel*, it is extremely odd that Barry should encourage Cushing to work on the two plays in parallel. Despite his love of 'boot and spur fun' Cushing declined *The Scarlet Pimpernel*, which went ahead on 18th September 1955 with Tony Britton as Sir Percy Blakeney and Douglas Wilmer as Citizen Chauvelin. Wilmer, a popular actor of imperious bearing, would inherit several 'Cushing parts' and in 1965 would become an extremely popular Sherlock Holmes for the BBC.

At the beginning of September 1955, Cushing finally rejected *Irving*. Even Michael Redington, who was with him at the time, can offer little by way of explanation. 'He just didn't want to do it. It was about real people and I just don't think Peter thought it was very true. I know Helen read a lot of the scripts, and she was generally spot on. But I don't know why he didn't want to do *Irving*. Maybe he thought it was too big.'4

On 8th September, Michael Barry wrote to Cushing in some bewilderment. 'Thank you for your letter. In it you say that you thank me for understanding but in this case I do not. I find myself deeply concerned ... and a frank and personal letter appears to me to be the only course. You speak of your rejection of *Irving* in the terms that we mutually understand when discussing this or that play. I submit that this project has never been regarded in that light. From the inception of the programme, in discussions with you early this year, the intention has been to pay tribute. This was clearly understood and I made it the key to all my conversations both within and without the Corporation. The intention was supported by a sense of professional dedication. I deliberately use these words and avoid "obligation" or "moral", but it has seemed to me that the responsibility spread deeply across our profession with an importance that does not begin to exist on the occasion of a normal BBC television play. It was for this reason that we selected with care the work. Skill and affection has been directed towards this project during the past months. A contemporary poet and dramatist of standing has completed a script to the considerable satisfaction of Laurence Irving and myself, backed on this occasion by the unanimous approval of the small group whose critical opinion are used to support me when my script decisions are made ... My own work as a writer ... makes me reluctant to allow criticism to pass completely unchallenged. You Peter have expressed a contrary opinion, although you have yet to give, as far as I am concerned, one valid reason. In the normal course of events, once I am convinced that a respected actor has formed an opinion personal to his art ... I am satisfied. On this occasion, and in the light of the wider background I have tried to remind you of, I am by no means satisfied that the decision

is not too puny for the Peter Cushing I know as a professional colleague.'

However, Cushing was still under contract to the BBC so work went on to find another suitable TV role. Meanwhile, he took part in three radio plays – *Wife For Sale*, the navy comedy *Seagulls Over Sorrento* (Cushing's personal choice, which was presented in a season called *Stars In Their Choices*) and *Escape Me Never*.

In *Wife For Sale*, Cushing was once again called upon to sing. Producer Charles LeFaux had been expecting to get a double for the singing, but it suddenly became necessary to pre-record the song as classical guitarist Julian Bream was only available on one day, 9th September. Cushing wrote to LeFaux on 31st August: 'Please don't imagine that I regard myself as a singer, I am anything but! However, I have done a little in similar parts (including the "prole-ified" song in *Nineteen Eighty-Four* – the budget wouldn't "go" to a professional singer) and I like to do everything that is humanly possible *myself* to the building of a character.

Peter and Helen in front of their digs during the idyllic summer of 1955. Another of Michael and Ann Redington's holiday snaps from Cromer

King Richard is comforted by his young wife Anne (Jeanette Sterke) in the BBC's Christmas production of *Richard of Bordeaux* (1955)

I know that you will have patience with me at the recording of this (and I hope Julian Bream will too!)' Cushing duly recorded the song on the 9th and the rest of *Wife For Sale* on 12th September 1955. His fee was 28 guineas.

At the end of October, another television role was offered – the lead in the BBC's prestigious Christmas production of *Richard of Bordeaux*. Cushing liked the part and was keen that Alvin Rakoff direct but Rakoff turned it down. The director wrote to Cushing, telling him this was 'the sort of thing other people can do so much better than I!' Cushing was quick to argue the contrary. 'Alvin, dear fellow,' he wrote on 7th November. 'I saw yer *Makepeace* last night! It doesn't matter what the play is like as long as you are producing it. Congratulations and ONWARDS to further glories. (Pity about *Richard*!)'

Rakoff's 'Makepeace' was the *Sunday Night Theatre* production of *The New Executive* broadcast on 6th November 1955. This was the last in a cycle of four plays, collectively entitled *The Makepeace Saga*, chronicling the life of an industrial family in the North of England.

Escape Me Never was rehearsed on 23rd and 24th November, and recorded on the 25th. *Seagulls Over Sorrento* was rehearsed and recorded the following week for a fee of 40 guineas. Both plays were made

into transcription discs. The recording of *Seagulls* on 30th November 1955 was obviously trying for Cushing. He wrote to LeFaux: 'Thank you so much for all your great help on *S.O.S.* – what an apt abbreviation! I do hope it was really alright. I had so many doubts afterwards!'

The end of 1955 saw him receiving the Guild of Television Producers and Directors Best Performance Award for *Nineteen Eighty-Four*.

After the radio plays, Cushing was straight into rehearsals on 5th December for *Richard of Bordeaux*. This was to be broadcast on 29th December from Lime Grove. The producer was Victor Menzies.

The *Radio Times* wrote: 'Produced at the New Theatre in 1935, *Richard of Bordeaux* was a historic play in more than the obvious sense. It made John Gielgud, already a fine actor, into a star recognised by an enormous public. What dramatist in England would have had the courage to take Shakespeare's hero and a good many of Shakespeare's subsidiary characters, re-shuffle them, afford them everyday, even casual contemporary speech, and make them into a smash hit? Charm is the play's keynote. It has a light, tragi-comic elegance, a light wit, a light melancholy. Richard is a magically charming, brilliant, many-faceted character – the role is a rewarding one for an actor of variety, pyrotechnical expertise, dazzle and the sort of magic that can enslave an audience. Where chronicle plays are often tedious, involved, and emotionally dead, *Richard of Bordeaux* presents historical events and personages in a graceful and contemporary manner. Romantically rosy, no doubt, but persuasive. London was completely bewitched; the play's last line (and Gielgud's delivery of it) became part of theatrical history: "How Robert would have laughed!" The play is a marvellous context for star performance, and it is fitting that the leading parts tonight should be played by two who largely owe their fame to television – the lean-featured Peter Cushing, and pretty, dark-eyed Jeannette Sterke.'[5] *Richard of Bordeaux* was written by the novelist Josephine Tey (author of *Brat Farrar* and *The Franchise Affair*) who was born Elizabeth MacKintosh in Scotland and wrote plays during the 1930s under the pseudonym Gordon Daviot.

In the early part of the production, Cushing's attempts to present the lovestruck, petulant young Richard are hampered by his high-pitched, flowery delivery, but it is a stretch to expect *any* 42-year-old to play a teenager convincingly. Jeanette Sterke's oo-la-la French accent – ''Ees silly tender 'art betrayed 'im', etc – doesn't help. The chief delights are Richard's bullying uncles – Joseph O'Conor's roaring, bearlike Gloucester ('as tactful as an angry wasp') and George Woodbridge's grumbling Earl of Arundel. With a deft touch, the ever-reliable Robin Bailey plays Richard's brother, the poetically-inclined Earl of Oxford, who is 'searching for a rhyme having failed to find reason.' As Richard matures, so Cushing's performance becomes more assured. The young King is forced to realise that 'to become an expert in murder cannot be so difficult...' Cushing revels in a moment of cutting wit, as Richard tells his enemies 'The only persons I trust are 2,000 archers, paid regularly every Friday.'

The last scenes are touching, as we see Richard, worn down by battle and saddened by the death of Anne, facing exile. 'I should have learned from the archbishop how to do an evil thing gracefully' he sighs. His voice cracks in disbelief as he reads the charges against him: 'Insufficient and useless ... unworthy to rule ... Tyranny. Have I been a tyrant? At least no tyrant has shed less blood.'

He is imprisoned, but still finds time to worry about his worn-out shoes. 'Could I start a new fashion – shoes with no toes? To lose one's kingdom is humbling, but to be *down at heel* is utter humiliation.'

The play is obviously several notches down technically from *Nineteen Eighty-Four*, with clumsy camera moves, threadbare scenery and ponderous, irrelevant filmed inserts, purely for the purposes of covering scene-changes, making Cartier's achievement of a whole year before all the more incredible.

Nevertheless the *Daily Telegraph* praised the 'fluent and successful' production. 'The revival of ... *Richard of Bordeaux* on BBC television last night revealed that the play has lost little of its power ... In this study of Richard II mastering his early defects of character, only to succumb in the end to over-confidence, there is perhaps little depth, but much lightness, fluency and grace. As the King, Peter Cushing gave as usual, an intelligent, carefully thought-out performance, yet a romantic quality in the character, an aspect of which Gielgud made much, escaped him.'[6] A telerecording of *Richard of Bordeaux* is preserved in the National Film Archive.

Jeanette Sterke as Anne of Bohemia with Cushing as the young King Richard in the BBC's *Richard of Bordeaux* (1955)

In the first few months of 1956, Cushing took a rest after the hectic schedule of 1955, and in April was again released from his BBC contract to take part in the West End production of *The Silver Whistle* by Robert McEnroe at the Duchess Theatre. Cushing played Oliver Erwenter, a tramp-like confidence trickster who inveigles his way into an old people's home but ultimately changes the lives of the residents for the better. The part of Erwenter had originally been played on Broadway by Jose Ferrer, and Cushing described it as being something like the character played by Robert Preston in *The Music Man*. The production was supervised by Lee Marvin's brother Mark, and starred, in a presentiment of Cushing's career-changing film of later in the year, 77-year-old Ernest Thesiger. In 1935, Thesiger had played the waspish Doctor Pretorius in James Whale's *Bride of Frankenstein*. Other character players involved in *The Silver Whistle* included Robin Bailey (from *Richard of Bordeaux*), Alfie Bass, Peter Vaughn, Olga Lindo and Mary Merrall.

The play was not, however, destined for a lengthy run. It closed on 12th May after some exceptionally bad notices and only twelve performances. 'It was a very good performance from Peter,' wrote Kenneth Cleveland. 'A pity the critics were not of the same opinion!' The dismayed cast learned shortly afterwards that Mark Marvin had returned to New York and commited suicide.

Later in May, Cushing was invited onto the popular *House* magazine programme to talk about his collection of toy soldiers. The armies were to be brought into the studio – 'the producer to arrange insurance cover and transport'. The producer was Josephine Douglas, who wrote to thank Cushing for agreeing to give up his Whit Sunday to come into the studio. Cushing replied that he was nervous about giving an impromptu talk. This was duly sorted out and Cushing wrote to Douglas again. 'I'm very pleased that Larry Forrester is giving me my words. I am no good at making them up and become quite asinine unless they are written for me.' Jo Douglas, who was also an actress, would eventually go into feature film production and work with Cushing again as the producer of Hammer's *Dracula A.D. 1972*.

Cushing's next role was in the film *Time Without Pity*, directed by Joseph Losey. American director Losey fled Hollywood in 1952 during the Cold War witch-hunts initiated by Senator Joseph McCarthy, by which all those suspected of Communist allegiances, particularly those in the entertainment industry, were blacklisted and prevented from working. (*The End of the Affair*'s director Edward Dmytryk had come to England for the same reason.) Losey was allowed to live and work in England, and directed two films under the alias Joseph Walton. His first credit under his own name on a British film was the 1955 Hammer short *A Man on the Beach*.

Time Without Pity was produced by Leon Clore for his own company Harlequin Films and was backed by distributor Eros to the tune of £100,000. The film was based on Emlyn Williams' play *Someone Waiting*, which Losey and Clore rewrote significantly. Three months of filming began in June 1956 at British National Studios, Elstree, although Cushing was only required between 25th June and 28th July at a fee of £150 per day. The BBC contract was suspended during shooting, the Corporation's bookings manager Holland Bennett noting sternly to Kenneth Cleveland: 'I have given you a good deal of latitude over the interpretation of this contract.'

Cushing was part of a distinguished British cast, including Michael Redgrave (who was on a fee of £5000 for the film) Leo McKern and 'Dear Annoushka' – Ann Todd. Redgrave played alcoholic author David Graham, who is forced to conduct his own frantic investigation when his son is accused of murder and sentenced to death. The film was scarcely noticed in England upon its opening in March 1957 (largely because Losey fell out with his backers, who then refused to promote it) but it apparently caused great excitement among cinephiles when it was released in France three years later.

Losey encouraged some strong performances from his cast – Redgrave's harrowing portrait of a desperate, tragic father, Leo McKern's barnstorming turn as a bullying car magnate – but Cushing has little to work with as lawyer Jeremy Clayton, who is something of an automaton. 'Stop thinking like a lawyer,' wails Graham. 'Tell me what you believe as a *man*!' When Clayton meets Graham at London Airport at the opening of the film, Cushing clearly shows that the lawyer is upset at conveying the devastating news. When Redgrave says 'I couldn't come sooner' Cushing's mute nod conveys everything the lawyer already knows about Graham's alcoholism. Losey presents a portrait of fifties' London as only an outsider could paint, at once modern and stiflingly old-fashioned, but the film conveys a real sense of rising panic and the genuinely terrifying threat of the death penalty. Critic Foster Hirsch stated that the film tried to be 'too many things at once – a chase thriller, a psychological study of dominance, a statement against capital punishment – without having the force or clarity to treat any of its themes in depth.'[7]

Cushing's filming on *Time Without Pity* overran into the rehearsal period for his next BBC project, the popular suburban mystery *Home at Seven*, in which he played David Preston. Four years earlier, in 1952, Ralph Richardson had directed and starred in a film version of the play, which had been a great success on the London stage. The BBC rehearsals were scheduled from 25th July to 11th August, and *Home at Seven* was broadcast on 12th August 1956 from Lime Grove, produced by Stephen Harrison. 'David Preston works in a London bank,' explained Elwyn Jones in the *Radio Times*. 'He is a senior official and hopes to become manager of the branch in Eastbourne. Meanwhile he lives in Bromley, Kent with his wife Janet. It is an ordinary humdrum existence. David and Janet are devoted to each other and have grown to respect each other's susceptibilities. There are not many of these, except that Janet does not really approve of alcohol and is anxious not to have strong drink in the house. David, on the other hand, likes his glass of sherry in the evening, and contrives to have it without offending Janet. Against this conventional, even dull background, R C Sherriff's unexpected drama is played out. David always arrives home at seven. And in his mind tonight is the same as any other night. As the town hall clock begins to strike seven, he puts his latch-key in the door, hangs up his coat and drops his umbrella into the hall-stand. "It's been just an ordinary day, dear," he says "just like any other Monday." The catch is that it *isn't* Monday...'[8]

In the role of Janet Preston was Helen Shingler, who had played Cushing's screen wife before, in his first television play *Eden End*. Shingler's kindness to the desperately nervous beginner on that occasion was never forgotten. Cushing was also delighted to be in a play by R C Sherriff, author of his beloved *Journey's End*.

Aware that Rudolph Cartier was preparing *Cyrano De Bergerac*, Cushing sent him a casting suggestion for the female lead and finished with a nod back to *Nineteen Eighty-Four*. 'To Rudy re: *Cyrano*. Virginia McKenna as Roxanne? Helen joins me in sending you love and the cry "Down with Goldstein!"' McKenna was a co-winner with Cushing of the *Daily Mail* Television Award for 1955. On 17th July, Cushing provisionally agreed to appearing in *Dark Victory* for the BBC on 18th November.

On 7th August, Cleveland wrote to the BBC stating that *Home at Seven* was Cushing's fifth play under contract and *Dark Victory* would be the sixth, thereby concluding the contract. He told the BBC that Cushing had been offered a 'very nice part in a TV film series in about two or three weeks' time.' The series was *The Adventures of Sir Lancelot*, produced by Dallas Bower for Sapphire Films. With William Russell playing Lancelot, it is likely Cushing was being sought to play either King Arthur or Merlin.

The BBC were not pleased at all. Norman Rutherford wrote in the strongest terms to Holland Bennett: 'I feel that Cushing is now such a nuisance that the goodwill of Kenneth Cleveland we could claim by granting this request is more valuable than anything

Peter and Helen Cushing arrive at the Savoy for the Guild of Television Producers and Directors Awards. Cushing received the Best Actor Award for *Nineteen Eighty-Four*

we or our audience will gain by sticking to protocol.' On 9th August, Bennett wrote, with clenched teeth, to Cleveland. 'We have no objections to Cushing doing a series of television films provided you confirm he will be able to do *Dark Victory*.'

On 10th August, Cushing turned down *Dark Victory*. There was no reason given why, and it was a play that Cushing seemed keen to do. By the transmission date of 18th November, however, Cushing would be under contract to Hammer Film Productions.

On 23rd September, *Henry Irving* finally surfaced, a year later than Michael Barry had originally intended. Cushing expressed interest in a production of *Uncle Vanya*, but this went no further. The assistant head of bookings noted of Cushing: 'I gather that this artist has not been particularly helpful over the different parts you have suggested his playing under his long-term contract.' Barry responded immediately that 'this is not the time to drop a valuable property.' The BBC asked Cushing to suggest a play and he nominated the Victorian melodrama *Gaslight*. Before that, however, came *The Curse of Frankenstein*.

Chapter Eleven

Enter Baron Frankenstein

It is understood that Hammer had tried to engage Cushing before 1956, although it is not known in which film he would have appeared. It is very likely, however, that they would have been considering *The Creature* as a subject soon after its transmission in January 1955 as they had already completed the film of first *Quatermass* serial at the end of 1954. Producer Anthony Hinds attests that he and Hammer managing director James Carreras actively pursued Cushing, believing that a popular television name would bring audiences back into the cinema.

Cushing saw the trade advertisements for a new colour version of *Frankenstein*, and recalled the 'marvellous' film starring Boris Karloff and Colin Clive. This could be a potential hit, he felt, and asked John Redway to put his name forward. Also, a lead role in a film would be a considerable step up.

The timing of events here was providential – Cushing's preferred vehicles, the 'well-made' plays of Coward and Rattigan, were facing extinction in the West End following the arrival of John Osborne's anti-establishment tirade *Look Back in Anger*, first staged at London's Royal Court Theatre in May 1956. The Angry Young Man and the 'Kitchen Sink' drama were suddenly the rage and Cushing, like many actors of his generation, could not see himself in work of that style. As it was, he was given a rather different type of angry young man to play.

Cushing was invited to a screening of the newly-completed Hammer film *X the Unknown*, Jimmy Sangster's *Quatermass*-inspired story of a sentient radioactive slime that menaces a remote army base. Cushing enjoyed the film and was sold on the idea of Frankenstein. His contract with Hammer was signed on 26th October and reported in the *Kinematograph Weekly* edition of 8th November.

The Curse of Frankenstein began filming at Hammer's studios at Bray in Berkshire on 19th November 1956 with director Terence Fisher. Cushing's fee, at £1,400, was equivalent to more than a year's pay at the BBC. He was contracted at £100 per day for 14 shooting days in the original schedule, but shooting over-ran by three weeks and details of Cushing's final fee are not recorded. Cushing's contract gave the title of the film as simply *Frankenstein*.

To preclude the legal intervention of Universal, who held copyright in the image of Karloff's flat-headed Creature, screenwriters Jimmy Sangster and (the uncredited) Anthony Hinds had to develop a completely new script from Shelley's story. They cut it down to the basic concepts and a minimum of characters, placing it in a Victorian chocolate-box *milieu* of frock-coats and crinolines. Baron Frankenstein became a Byronic figure, to which Cushing was ideally suited.

Awaiting the guillotine in his prison cell, Frankenstein tells his story to a priest: of how, after years of research, he and his former tutor Paul Krempe had developed a means of bringing life to a dead body. Frankenstein then determined to build a perfect Creature, and went about acquiring materials from charnel houses. He murdered the elderly Professor Bernstein so that the Creature could possess 'the matured brain of a genius' but the brain was damaged, and when the Creature was brought to life, its first and only instinct was to kill...

Such is the economy of storytelling that we are scarcely ten minutes into the film before the grown-up Baron is up to his grisly business in his attic laboratory with Paul (played by Robert Urquhart) looking on. In keeping with his intention that the story was to be presented like a fairy-tale, Fisher leads us through an almost magical array of vividly-coloured liquids, humming machinery and the spinning vanes of the generator. With total control, Cushing conducts a symphony of sparks and flashes, adjusting a retort here, flicking a lever there, his eyes darting from one piece of equipment to the next. Fisher used close-ups judiciously and rarely fills the screen with the Baron's face, except once, after Frankenstein and Paul's first experiment to resurrect a dead puppy. Frankenstein listens for the dog's heartbeat and Cushing's expression of wonder is accentuated by a triumphal key-change in James Bernard's thrilling score.

The great attraction of the Baron's character is his complete delight in his own work. Cushing's charm ensures that the viewer *wants* Frankenstein to succeed, however dreadful his intent. 'Neither wicked nor insane,' says Paul of his former pupil. 'Just so dedicated that he can't see the terrible consequences that could result.' Later Frankenstein shows off a

Paul Krempe (Robert Urquhart) watches as Frankenstein revives a dog in *The Curse of Frankenstein* (1956)

stolen pair of hands with a guileless little smile, like a schoolboy with a prize conker, and sings happily to himself as he pops a pair of eyes into a jar.

Despite criticisms of excessive gore and gristle, Sangster and Hinds' script elucidates more grisly details than we actually see. 'Half the head's eaten away' grimaces Paul of the newly acquired corpse they bring back to the laboratory. Fisher deftly catches the glint of light on a knife and Urquhart's look of suspicion and revulsion as Frankenstein cuts off the head, then idly wipes his bloodied hand on his lapel.

Throughout the film, the Baron is rarely off the screen for more than a few moments, and when he is not delivering his lines Cushing shows us that Frankenstein is listening and thinking, his mind working each new situation to his advantage. When his cousin Elizabeth (Hazel Court) arrives, engaged to marry him under a childhood arrangement, Frankenstein uses her as a housekeeper – while carrying on an affair with the maid Justine (Valerie Gaunt). Then, when he needs a bargaining tool to ensure Paul's co-operation, he threatens to involve Elizabeth. The jealous Justine announces that she is

pregnant, and the Baron throws her to his newly re-born Creature without compunction.

The Creature itself is only on screen for about ten minutes and unconscious for half of those. But its first appearance is a moment of true horror that shows Terence Fisher's ability to deliver a really potent scare when he wanted to. In the role of the creature was 34-year-old Christopher Lee and, after attempting to strangle Cushing to death in their first scene together, went on to be a lifelong friend.

Lee was another client of John Redway – the agent was asked simply to suggest tall actors to play the Creature. Lee was chosen, and then endured an arduous series of make-up tests before a suitable image for the monster was found. For Lee, working on the film was a happy and rewarding experience, not least because of his chief co-star. 'From the first time we met at Bray, Peter Cushing and I were friends,' Lee admits. 'I soon found Peter was the great perfectionist who learned not only his own lines but everybody else's, but withal had a gentle humour which made it quite impossible for anybody to be pompous in his company.'[1]

Derek Whitehurst was working at Bray on a television series with Errol Flynn when he was asked to be first assistant director on *The Curse of Frankenstein*. 'There was nothing at Bray then. There was just the house and one tiny stage. We shot *The Curse of Frankenstein* in the winter, which was bitterly cold. There was no central heating! I don't think Peter knew what he was in for – that this was the start of a career in that sort of thing. Seeing him do anything vicious onscreen was always such a shock, because there was nothing vicious about him at all. He was very charming and very gentle. Helen wasn't around at Hammer in the early days, he didn't need it. But Peter used to flirt deliciously. It meant nothing of course, but it was a delight to see. Just this charming, gentlemanly, courteous flirting. And Peter was very athletic. There was lots of swagger and thrust, and those little sets at Bray couldn't really stand up to it when he was really belting around. But it was *precisely* controlled. He should have done the show with Errol Flynn because Peter was once of the original swashbucklers.

The 'family atmosphere' at Bray seems apparent in this still of director Terence Fisher, Hazel Court and Cushing during the making of *The Curse of Frankenstein* (1956)

'Nobody got very much money – I think Chris Lee got £500. I was 22 or 23 and as an assistant director I was getting £25 a week. At the beginning there were conferences at the Hammer offices in Wardour Street, and everybody used to throw ideas in. Even a lowly junior like me could throw in suggestions. I said Frankenstein should have a Gladstone bag and they kept that in. Peter would come up with lots of suggestions about his wardrobe. At the start of the film, he would always have his props ready. Certainly on the first *Frankenstein* he was very particular about the whole set up, his fob watch, the magnifying glass, the boots and the cane.

'The prison entrance was shot in the main house, where the reception at Bray is now. They just clad it and painted it. You can see the fire-buckets. Next to the house was this little white building, and that was the stage. It was crammed with Frankenstein's workshop – all the machinery – you could hardly move. Everything was jammed in there, and the camera. In one of the first scenes we did with Peter we had a little puppy for the Baron to try out his machinery. Peter was standing at the table and the puppy was given anaesthetic to keep it still. The owner said it was alright just to give it a whiff, but somebody overdid it and it died. It was very sad, Peter was terribly upset. It could never happen now, and it shouldn't have happened then. Every time I go to that stage I think of that poor dog.

'We filmed the scene when the monster has just killed the blind man and it was on the river's edge at Bray on a freezing cold miserable day. Chris was staggering about, and Peter shoots him in eye. Peter does it brilliantly and Chris does it brilliantly, and nature adds the most wonderful touch. As the creature falls, there is just a gust of wind and all the leaves billow around. Chris got the blood behind his contact lens and they had to spend forever washing his eye. Jack Asher photographed it in Eastmancolor, and it looked gorgeous. I think Peter appreciated Jack very much – there was a great affinity between them as technicians. And of course, Peter hit it off with Chris immediately. They were enormously fond of each other.'[2]

On set, Lee would join Cushing in impromptu musical numbers, Victorian patter songs and snatches from grand opera. It could sometimes be a bizarre experience, as Whitehurst recalls. 'One day at the viewing of the rushes, just to entertain us, Peter got up – in costume – with Chris, who had the whole horror thing on, and they did a little dance, a macabre little two-step, in front of the screen.' Lee would also do impersonations. Searching the Bray pantry for something he could eat without ruining his make-up, Lee imitated the exasperated splutter of Sylvester the Cat – 'Bird theed! I'll *thtarve*!!' The phrase, and Lee's delivery of it, would never fail to reduce Cushing to helpless fits of laughter.

For a film now regarded as one of the best and most influential fantasy/horror films ever made, contemporary reviews in Britain were unkind. When the film opened on 2nd May 1957, the *Observer* placed it 'among the half dozen most repulsive films I have encountered in 10,000 miles of film reviewing.'[4]

'The most revolting exhibition I can remember seeing on the screen!'[5] frothed R D Smith in the *Tribune*. And so it continued. Cushing, very wisely, took no notice, and his faith in the project was borne out in a couple of weeks by the spectacular box-office returns. The American reviews were subsequently much kinder, many singling Cushing out for particular praise. 'Cushing enacts the role of ... Frankenstein without overacting,' wrote Jim O'Connor in the *New York Journal* on 7th August. 'You could almost hear the nerves snapping in the audience!'[6]

'The Americans just could not believe that such a quality film could be made for that amount of money in that amount of time,' said Cushing. 'They just *would* not and *could* not believe it. It just took off. It went all over the world, especially in America where they were bonkers about it, then everywhere else. Japan loved it. Adored it. That put the seal on my international "fame".'[7]

Cushing's last days of shooting on *The Curse of Frankenstein* – which wrapped on 3rd January – overlapped with the start of rehearsals for the BBC's *Gaslight* on 27th December. 'Old-fashioned' plays were still a successful staple on television. Patrick Hamilton's celebrated thriller, in which a Victorian villain, Manningham, attempts to drive his wife mad, had already been made into a film twice – in Britain in 1940 with Anton Walbrook and Diana Wynyard, and in Hollywood in 1944 with Charles Boyer and Ingrid Bergman. In this version, produced by Stephen Harrison and broadcast on 13th January 1957 from Lime Grove, Mary Morris starred as Bella Manningham with Billie Whitelaw as Nancy the maid and Mervyn Johns as Sergeant Rough. In the *Radio Times* article accompanying *Gaslight*, it was announced that Cushing's next role for the BBC would be as Cyrano De Bergerac.

There was fierce criticism for Cushing's performance as Manningham from the *Daily Telegraph* on 14th January 1957. 'On BBC television last night the 20-year-old *Gaslight* must have made a gripping entertainment for those unfamiliar with the play. For viewers already acquainted with it, interest

lay in comparing present with past performances, and both Mary Morris and Mervyn Johns were well up to the standard of their predecessors. On the other hand, the usually reliable Peter Cushing as the sadistic adventurer trying to drive his wife into insanity showed an unfortunate tendency to overact and gave what could almost be described as a "sneery" interpretation.'[8]

There was an engineering fault at the start of *Gaslight* and Michael Barry wrote, in an internal memo, 'the fault... has been investigated at the very highest level. I have dropped a note to Peter to reassure him that performances and production have spoken for themselves.' But after a lengthy pre-transmission wrangle with Kenneth Cleveland over Cushing's billing in the *Radio Times*, Barry had suspicions that a rift was growing between the BBC and 'their' star.

On 17th January, Cushing wrote back to Barry. 'I was delighted... that you enjoyed the performance of *Gaslight*. It means so much to be told because, at the end of a play and its rehearsals one has an awful

The villainous Mr Manningham with Mervyn Johns as Sergeant Rough in Stephen Harrison's production of *Gaslight* (1957)

The Lama (Arnold Marle) offers advice to John Rollason while Helen (Maureen Connell) and Peter Fox (Richard Wattis) look on in *The Abominable Snowman* (1957)

feeling of let-down and is never quite sure how it's come across. I was a little distressed that you should think that there was any idea of a rift – this has never occurred to me! Naturally there are things that crop up, from the business angle, that have to be gone into. But I'm sure this happens in the best-respected families. One – of course – is the *Radio Times'* attitude to billing, eh? And I understand that steps are being taken to make this a little more co-operative.' He concluded 'It would be lovely to have dinner with you, dear Michael, but may I defer the pleasure for a little while? I'm starting work on the film of *The Abominable Snowman* on Monday week, with the usual costume fittings prior to this and preparing for *Cyrano De Bergerac* (fencing lessons, nose fittings etc). So as we are all ready for the filming sequences as soon as I finish *A.S.*, it's a pretty tight schedule. I look forward enormously to doing this play with Rudy (with not a few quakings inwardly too!)'

The Abominable Snowman, Hammer's version of *The Creature*, began filming at Bray Studios on 28th January. For his latest Hammer film, Val Guest once again found himself working from a Nigel Kneale storyline. Guest streamlined the script of *The Creature* to simplify some of the relationships and concepts. Cushing's character of John Rollason was given a wife, also called Helen. There was also now some gentle comic relief from Richard Wattis as Rollason's exasperated assistant Peter Fox. Arnold Marle repeated his role as the Lama from *The Creature,* giving a memorably weird performance. 'Act in the name of

mankind and act humbly,' the Lama warns Rollason as he seeks the yeti. 'For man is near to forfeiting his right to lead the world.'

The Abominable Snowman is a beautiful and unjustly neglected film, a priceless record of Kneale's atmospheric play. Arthur Grant's crisp black-and-white photography lends an appropriate majesty to the snowy peaks; Humphrey Searle's score complements this with an epic theme and the subtler strains of gongs and cymbals. Several moments, like the yeti reaching into the explorers' tent and the phantom radio messages are chilling.

Cushing's sensitive and relaxed performance is the centre of the film and he clearly enjoys the chance to return to the part away from the rigours of live television. Rollason is a gentle and inquiring character, with a childlike wonder for the new sights and experiences of Tibet. He is appropriately heroic whether facing the self-serving philosophies of Friend and his hunters, or facing the unknown. 'Suppose they're not some pitiable remnant,' Rollason theorises as they begin to learn the true nature of the yeti. 'Suppose we're the savages. *Homo Vastens*. Man the Destroyer!'

'Peter Cushing was a perfectionist,' Kneale remembered. 'He would always challenge something. He'd say "I don't believe this. Why am I doing this?" And he would want an answer. He would then play to the answer he got and convince you it was possible that he was facing the monster and that there was a monster there to be faced."[9]

Rollason's ultimate encounter with the yeti is breathtakingly moving in its simplicity. After the final avalanche and the sequence in which Rollason calls after Friend (a kind of dry run for the conclusion of Kneale's *Quatermass and the Pit*) he retreats back into the cave and is suddenly aware of other figures – huge, humanoid shapes. Cushing barely moves. With a subtle inclination of the head and an almost imperceptible widening of the eyes, he expresses an overwhelming sense of awe.

Forrest Tucker recalled that Cushing was even concerned about details like the contents of his prop kit-bag, and whether smoking at high altitudes was actually possible. 'I'd say "Pete, I'm going to ******* smoke a cigarette at nine thousand feet and I'll find

Above: The black-hearted Sir Palamides in *The Black Knight* (1954). Previous page: As Osric in Laurence Olivier's film of *Hamlet* (1948)

Above: Cushing as Otto Wesendonk with Valentina Cortese in *Magic Fire* (1954)
Left: 'Peter Cushing begins his own story in this issue' *TV Mirror*, 27th March 1954

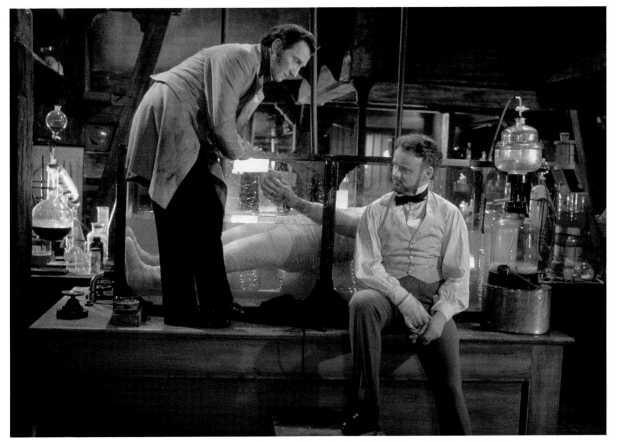

Baron Frankenstein explains his plans to his former tutor Paul Krempe (Robert Urquhart) in *The Curse of Frankenstein* (1956)

Above: Breakfast with the Frankensteins – the Baron with his fiancée Elizabeth (Hazel Court) in *The Curse of Frankenstein*

Left: A dazzling Belgian poster for *The Curse of Frankenstein*. Though Cushing rarely featured on Hammer's British posters, he was given prominence in European promotional artwork

Below: 'Is this your creature of superior intellect? Your perfect physical being, this *animal*?' Krempe (Robert Urquart) is less than impressed with the Baron's handiwork. Christopher Lee plays the luckless creature

Van Helsing on Bernard Robinson's exquisite Castle Dracula set in Hammer's masterpiece *Dracula* (1958).

Good overcomes evil – Cushing himself devised Van Helsing's iconic last stand at the conclusion of *Dracula*. Van Helsing returned in Hammer's *Brides of Dracula* (1960), below

'Since the astonishing success of the Frankenstein picture, the cinema people have been most attentive to me...' Cushing on the cover of *TVMirror* in 1957

As John Rollason in *The Abominable Snowman* (1957) with Maureen Connell as Helen Rollason. Cushing's second film for Hammer was a remake of Nigel Kneale's BBC play *The Creature*, in which Cushing had starred

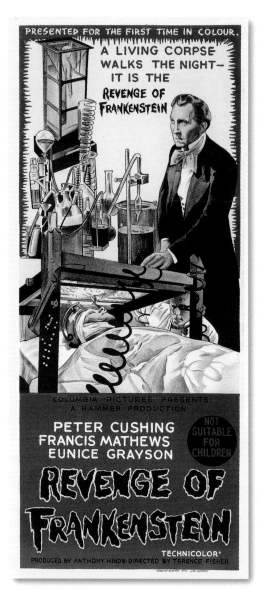

PRESENTED FOR THE FIRST TIME IN COLOUR.

A LIVING CORPSE
WALKS THE NIGHT—
IT IS THE
REVENGE OF
FRANKENSTEIN

COLUMBIA PICTURES PRESENTS
A HAMMER PRODUCTION

PETER CUSHING
FRANCIS MATHEWS
EUNICE GRAYSON

NOT
SUITABLE
FOR
CHILDREN

REVENGE OF
FRANKENSTEIN

TECHNICOLOR®
PRODUCED BY ANTHONY HINDS DIRECTED BY TERENCE FISHER

'Not Suitable for Children' but teenagers loved it –
the Baron returns in *The Revenge of Frankenstein* (1958)

Captain Pearson with Captain Jones (Robert Stack) in *John Paul Jones* (1958)

Holmes and Watson (André Morell) investigate
unspeakable rites on Grimpen Mire in Hammer's
The Hound of the Baskervilles (1958)

Dr Knox looms large over the mayhem in the Belgian poster for John Gilling's *The Flesh and the Fiends* (1959)

Von Brecht and Joe Newman (Stanley Baker) feature on the cover of John Burke's novelisation of *The Man Who Finally Died* (1961)

The saintly Dr Blyss in Hammer's *Captain Clegg* (1961)

'Here is the monster, here is the mad lab and away we go, so to speak' – Director Freddie Francis' recipe for *The Evil of Frankenstein* (1963)

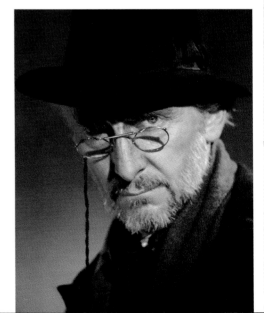

Above: With Anthony Nelson-Keys behind the scenes of *The Gorgon* (1963)
Right: Sinister Dr Schreck from *Dr Terror's House of Horrors* (1964)

a way to get the bastard lit, now you watch me."' But Tucker had to concur that Cushing's mania for research was a valuable asset to a production. 'He can save you thousands of dollars because of what he's gonna do himself. It was an experience for me to watch an actor work that hard in other areas of making a film.' [10]

Val Guest was full of praise for Cushing too, particularly for his mastery of props. 'We rehearsed the scene where he gets the yeti tooth. We went into the take and Peter brought out the file and the tape measure... we got it in the first take because I knew we'd not last through another one without collapsing. The take is in the film and that was the first any of us knew he had he props with him. We used to call him Peter "props" Cushing.'[11]

McNee (Michael Brill), Rollason, Friend (Forest Tucker) and Shelley (Robert Brown) examine the steel net which is no match for the strength of a yeti in *The Abominable Snowman* (1957)

Cushing did oppose Guest for one shot, however. In the final scene on the mountainside, Rollason is discovered standing motionless in the snow. Guest wanted Cushing to keep his eyes open for the shot – even though an aeroplane propeller was being used to blow the fake snow onto the set. Cushing said if Guest wanted him to keep his eyes open he should come in and try it for himself. Guest quickly changed his mind.

Based on Guest's location footage, and on an extremely limited budget, Bernard Robinson created superb snowscapes at Pinewood Studios and a magnificent exterior courtyard for the monastery – the English winter adding an extra detail of making the actors' breaths hang on the air. Jock May's sound plays an important part, suggesting everything from the howling Himalayan winds to the rumbles of the avalanches and the mournful moans of the yeti. Make-up artist Phil Leakey, who had transformed Christopher Lee into Frankenstein's Creature, mimicked Peter Cushing's high forehead and aquiline nose to create the wise face of the barely-glimpsed yeti, played by the Irish actor John Rae. Filming on *The Abominable Snowman* was completed by 5th March.

Meanwhile, back at the BBC, *Cyrano De Bergerac* seemed doomed. At the eleventh hour, it was discovered that the copyright had not been cleared and the production was called off. Kenneth Cleveland wrote to the BBC that as Cushing had prepared for the role and had already learned the lines, this abandoned production should be regarded as his final production

under contract. Cleveland's agenda was clear – he wanted Cushing released from his BBC contract as soon as possible. Michael Barry stood his ground in a letter to Cleveland dated 11th March. 'So far as any claim for exclusivity was concerned, Peter's contract should be regarded as being at an end, and he is now free in that respect. On the other hand, the inability to produce *Cyrano De Bergerac* on 7th April should not put us in the position of writing off the last payment for a production under his contract.' Barry offered two immediate replacements *The Public Prosecutor* and *Eden End*, both of which Cushing declined. 'Your letter,' Barry continued to Cleveland, 'suggests that you wish to interpret the contract strictly without this give-and-take so commonly required in a contract of this kind. I can well understand Peter's disappointment about *Cyrano* but this is shared between us. You and I have a responsibility to the actor in this case. It may well be asking too much for Peter, busy with a film, to make spontaneous suggestions. The idea of *White Cargo*, mentioned between us on the phone and the ideas separately put by him to Cartier seem to me backward-looking suggestions of subjects laden with repertory dust. Should we not be looking forward, and, if we are unable to find something quite new, at least find a vehicle in which his special talents can be shown at their best?'

'I have never been able to decide,' harrumphed an exasperated G M Turnell of the BBC's Long-Term Contracts Department on 19th March, in a letter to Barry. 'whether Cleveland's habitual misconstruction

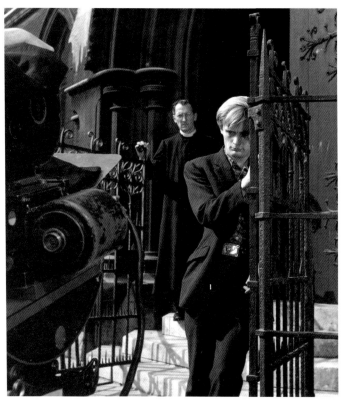

The camera and the law closes in on David McCallum as troubled teenager Johnny, watched by Father Laidlaw, in *Violent Playground* (1957)

the Clock' with a raucous parody called 'Play Rough'. There are earnest but oddly passionless performances from Stanley Baker and Ann Heywood, and David McCallum, at 24, is a bit too old to play a teenage tearaway. Clifford Evans stands out as a gentle, progressive headmaster and appearing as Baker's copper sidekick is the popular but underused actor John Slater, who won the Best TV Actor award for 1952, the year before Cushing.

As Father Laidlaw, Cushing gives a rather severe, tight-lipped performance. His face is pinched and stern, his hair plastered down and his delivery strangely monotonous. Laidlaw never seems at ease, never makes decisions and speaks almost in riddles, drawing conclusions from Baker and McCallum. Even the priest's heroic stand in the final reel, climbing a ladder to talk down the machine-gun wielding Johnny, is an empty gesture as the ladder is pushed over and Laidlaw falls to the ground.

The film is obviously struggling for a message but with strands involving teenage crime, broken families, religion and youth policing in the script, nothing comes across clearly. The *Times*' reviewer found *Violent Playground* a fudge. 'A film which sets out with such self-avowed high purposes degenerates into something dishonest because the issues are avoided. The ineffectual priest, to whose platitudes not even Peter Cushing can give weight, has no reality.'[12]

On 9th March 1958, when the film went on release, Cushing, Baker and McCallum recorded a special excerpt from *Violent Playground* for the radio programme *Follow the Stars*.

On 4th September, Cushing wrote to producer Hal Burton about Burton's production of *Time and the Conways* which was transmitted on 25th August – 'How *good* Gwen Watford was!' Burton subsequently offered Cushing the role of John Robinson in his planned production of *The Night of the Tigers*, but Cushing had to decline, although he enjoyed reading the play – 'It is excellently written, isn't it?'

Cushing signed a contract for *Dracula* on 9th October 1957. John Redway saw that Cushing's contractual fee was now £2,500. With that kind of wage being offered for just six weeks' work, it was hardly surprising that the BBC were increasingly told to bide their time – Cushing was fast becoming a very bankable star. Hammer were clearly aware of this too, and were eager not to lose him, so Cushing was contracted for two Hammer films on the same date – *Dracula* and the sequel to *The Curse of Frankenstein*.

of contracts is due to stupidity or to his rather clumsy attempts to put one over on us. Obviously we want to find some way of having our sixth performance from Cushing without additional payment.'

Cushing and Barry subsequently had a quiet meeting over a meal and matters were calmed down considerably. Barry offered Cushing a play called *The Lover*, to be produced by Johnny Jacobs, but Cushing was not keen. 'The mid-thirties obsession with "sex in the raw",' he wrote, 'seems oddly naïve and a little shocking because its naïvety is no longer important.'

From July, however, he was working with director Basil Dearden on the film *Violent Playground*. The production was undoubtedly intended to address 'modern' themes, but set in the world of rock-and-roll and troubled teenagers, it now seems marooned on the wrong side of Beatlemania.

For a picture set (and partly filmed) in Liverpool, there is a conspicuous lack of scouse accents in the headscarved women clucking disapprovingly on the sidelines. The film lurches from one sensational piece of melodrama to the next, like a whole year of soap opera condensed into 90 minutes. It is a po-faced British copy of 1955's *The Blackboard Jungle,* and even attempts to mimic that film's hit song 'Rock Around

Chapter Twelve

A Feast for the Horror-Gobblers

D*racula* was well underway as the box-office takings of *The Curse of Frankenstein* continued to roll in. The new film had a budget of £82,000, but most of the elements of cast and crew that had made the first colour Hammer horror a success were unchanged. With Christopher Lee as Dracula, Cushing was cast as Van Helsing but was initially unsure how to play the part. 'In the book, Van Helsing was a little old gentleman who almost literally speaks double-Dutch. When I was cast I said to Tony Hinds "oughtn't we to get a little double-Dutchman?" and he said "No, I think the thing to do is to play him as you" – so it became one of my parts. It was always a fascinating character to play.'[1]

Anthony Hinds was wise enough to realise that Cushing's impeccable English was wooing the overseas audiences and there was no need to encumber him with a foreign accent. Peter Cushing they wanted and Peter Cushing they got, notably 'above the title' in *Dracula*.

Jimmy Sangster, who had pruned *Frankenstein* so effectively, cuts Stoker's sea voyages and European treks down to a couple of border-crossing gallops in a coach. Terence Fisher again creates a realistic environment that never once leads us to question that there *are* such things as vampires. To speed the plot further, Van Helsing and his associate Jonathan Harker (played by John Van Eyssen) are fully conversant with vampire lore from the off, and seem, by implication, to belong to a larger band of vampire hunters. So Harker, rather than Stoker's virginal innocent, goes into Castle Dracula on a kind of commando raid – unsuccessfully, as it turns out. Although Harker is able to stake the Count's vampire bride, the first game goes to Dracula.

Castle Dracula itself is sombre and magnificent, featured in the film's title sequence to the accompaniment of James Bernard's forbidding score which uses the rhythm of the word

'Dra-cu-la' like a fanfare. Hammer had constructed a new soundstage at Bray using money from a co-production deal with Columbia Pictures. This gave designer Bernard Robinson enough room to create his exquisite, finely-detailed interiors – including the great hall with its candy-twist columns and animal skins decorating the walls, the 'apartments', the grand staircase and the library.

As Dracula, Christopher Lee came out from behind the creature make-up and immediately proved his magnetic screen presence. Peter Cushing matched it – presenting a man of Van Helsing's moral strength opposite a creature like Dracula reinforces both characters. We are given an indication of Van Helsing's mettle before he is even seen, when he enters the inn at Klausenberg. Fisher keeps Van Helsing's back to camera – in his fur coat and Homburg hat he looks rather like an old-style actor-manager – and we see the apprehensive reactions of the villagers. Then we hear the voice, see the face and are instantly reassured. As with Frankenstein, Cushing

The Count (Christopher Lee) recoils from Van Helsing's crossed candlesticks in the legendary climax of *Dracula* (1957)

— 67 —

Van Helsing informs Arthur Holmwood (Michael Gough) and his wife Mina (Melissa Stribling) of the death of Jonathan Harker in *Dracula* (1957)

makes Van Helsing a living character. He runs his hand through his hair and rubs his neck when he's tired, he looks around while he's kept waiting, he blows into his hands when he's cold.

At Castle Dracula, Van Helsing finds Jonathan Harker in the crypt, transformed into a vampire. Cushing buries his head in his hand, then grimly takes up Harker's discarded stake and mallet. Later Van Helsing visits Arthur Holmwood (Michael Gough) and his wife Mina (Melissa Stribling) to break the news of Harker's death. Holmwood's sister Lucy was Harker's fiancée and Arthur is upset at Van Helsing's apparent indifference. Cushing leaves them with a gentlemanly click of the heels to Mina.

However, Van Helsing is very concerned indeed. Back in his study, he listens to a phonograph recording of his research into vampire lore: 'Certain basic facts established. One: Light. The vampire, allergic to light, never ventures forth in the daytime. Sunlight fatal – repeat – *fatal*. Would destroy them. Two: Garlic. Vampires repelled by odour of garlic. Three: The crucifix, symbolising the power of good over evil. The power of the crucifix in these cases is two-fold. It protects the normal human being, but reveals the vampire, or victim of this vile contagion when in advanced stages.' Cushing enjoys the business with the setting of the machine and his dictation of the 'rules' of vampirism is completely bewitching. Again, it is a question of economy – we are effectively informed

of all the technicalities of what is to follow.

'Established that victims consciously detest being dominated by vampirism, but are unable to relinquish the practice, similar to addiction to drugs. Ultimately death results from loss of blood, but unlike normal death, no peace manifests itself for they enter into the fearful state of the *un-dead*.'

All the elements come together. Cushing knows enough about screen acting to bring his eyes to the camera as he finishes his dictation. 'Since the death of Jonathan Harker, Count Dracula, the propagator of this unspeakable evil, has disappeared. He must be found, and destroyed!' Further to emphasise Van Helsing's words, Fisher cuts suddenly to a startling close-up of Dracula, who has come to prey on Lucy.

Shortly afterwards, Van Helsing is summoned by Mina Holmwood, who tells him that Lucy is very ill. Cushing borrowed much from his theatre training, particularly the dynamic physical style of Olivier, and here uses a trick of distractedly looking out of shot and then turning suddenly to emphasise a particular line – so he spins round, eyes widened as Mina says 'Our family doctor says it's *anaemia*' and would repeat this 'turn', to varying degrees, in many of his films. When Van Helsing discovers a vampire bite on Lucy's neck, Cushing gives an affecting expression of revulsion. 'I cannot impress upon you strongly enough how important it is that you obey my instructions,' he orders. 'Do exactly as I say, and we may be able to save her,' – Cushing holds up his forefinger for emphasis, as he did in *Frankenstein* – this too would become a signatory gesture. 'If you don't, she will die!'

But Van Helsing's advice is not heeded, and Lucy dies. Van Helsing leaves Harker's diary with Mina by way of explanation. As well as furious activity, Cushing could also use stillness to great advantage, as seen when he delivers his condolences to the Holmwoods. But the greater horror for Lucy is yet to come.

In the Holmwood crypt – a setting with moonlight and bare twigs like some fairy-tale illustration – the vampirised Lucy leads the housekeeper's daughter Tanya (Janina Faye) down into the dark. Arthur is there, waiting for her. 'Dear brother...' she croons.

'Come, let me kiss you...' As she advances, Cushing leaps out with a silver crucifix held up in grim determination – the cross brands Lucy's forehead and she flees. Van Helsing takes the little girl to one side and wraps her in his coat protectively. The line is clearly improvised by Cushing. 'You look like a teddy bear now,' he says, giving her a crucifix. 'Will you wear this pretty thing – there? Isn't that lovely?'

Lucy is finally laid to rest with a stake through the heart. Van Helsing asks for Holmwood's help in tracing Dracula. 'The study of these creatures has been my life's work,' he tells him, tapping his cigarette onto the cigarette-case in a little echo of the staking. Van Helsing and Holmwood discover where the coffin has gone, but Mina is already under Dracula's spell. Terence Fisher instructed Melissa Stribling to 'imagine that you have had one whale of a sexual night, *the one* of your sexual experience. Give me that in your face.'[2] And so she did, while Phil Leakey's make-up for the ravished Mina – blusher, a touch more red lipstick – speaks of a new voluptuousness.

Van Helsing gives Mina a crucifix for protection but it instantly burns her hand. As Cushing prises Melissa Stribling's hand open, his expression speaks of the full horror awaiting them.

Holmwood and Van Helsing decide to keep watch outside the house, but Dracula foils them and attacks Mina again. Stribling's expressions are wonderfully ambiguous – she is almost biting her lip like a schoolgirl with a crush. Later, Mina is discovered on the bed, unconscious. Van Helsing immediately performs a transfusion, and Cushing has clearly studied the correct procedure – although he does manage to hook his arm into one of the tubes at one point.

Mina had forbidden the servants to go into the cellar – this is Dracula's hiding-place. Van Helsing goes down to the cellar and puts a crucifix in the coffin he finds there. But Dracula is close behind him – almost on top of him. Cushing leaps over the banisters and smacks the hysterical housekeeper Gerda around the face. But Mina is gone – taken by Dracula.

Cushing drives the gig for the chase after Dracula. The vampire could hide in the castle vaults for years. They would lose him there – and Mina. Van Helsing pursues Dracula through the castle, accompanied by Bernard's insistent chase theme. Dracula catches Van Helsing and tries to throttle him, Van Helsing tricks

Van Helsing protects Tanya (Janina Faye) in the Holmwood crypt in *Dracula* (1957)

Dracula by playing dead, but in the nick of time, leaps up. The vampire and vampire-hunter stand off like tigers. Then Van Helsing makes his final move...

The script dictated that Van Helsing should brandish a crucifix and force Dracula into a shaft of sunlight. Errol Flynn fan Cushing wanted a bit more for his finale. He was all for jumping off a balcony or swinging on a chandelier, but he explained, 'dear Terry wouldn't let me, in case I was injured.' Although a stuntman was used for the jump, it was Cushing's own suggestion that he pelt down the table and rip down the curtains. However, he was bothered by the appearance of yet another crucifix. 'Van Helsing was like a salesman for the things,' he said. 'They were practically coming out of his ears. He gives one to Mina, one to the little girl, he was throwing them in coffins, and so on. At the end he was supposed to pull out *another* one.'[3]

Cushing came up with a clever solution. 'I remembered seeing a film years ago called *Berkeley Square*, in which Leslie Howard was thought of as the devil by this frightened little man who grabbed two candelabra to make the sign of the cross with them. I remembered that this had impressed me enormously. Originally the candelabra we used were the type with four candles on each base. You could tell what I was doing, but it didn't look like a cross. So they were changed to the ones I used in the film.'[4]

Screenwriter Stephen Volk described the final image of light defeating darkness as 'the 20th century equivalent of a stained glass window, in the dark of a movie theatre.'[6]

As Dracula decays, Van Helsing's haunted expression conveys a mixture of exhaustion, revulsion, sadness and relief. Cushing later explained his own feelings about the shot: 'I was reading a book that said, at the end of *Dracula*, there is a look of sadness on Van Helsing's face... He has suddenly achieved his life's quest, and now what is he going to do? I can tell you that I didn't have that in mind at all when we were shooting the film. I stand there and run my hand through my hair and look down out of exhaustion. But that critic was absolutely right. Something in me was communicating that to the audience, and the audience fills in the rest.'[5]

The groundwork that Fisher and his crew did on *The Curse of Frankenstein* pays off a hundredfold here. Something wonderful happens, like alchemy, all the elements come together and the result is a film that is still enchanting and exciting audiences more than fifty years after it was made. It is now regarded as a *bona fide* British screen classic, after many years of being derided as 'just a horror film' and much of the film's lasting power comes from Peter Cushing. He made many fine films, but this, perhaps, is his finest.

The film premièred under its American title *Horror of Dracula* in Milwaukee, Wisconsin on 8th May 1958, taking $1,682 on its first day. The film opened in Britain at the Gaumont Haymarket, with a spectacular front-of-house display featuring Christopher Lee, on 22nd May 1958 and on Broadway a week later.

Though the film was a massive success, reviews were mixed, especially at home. The *Daily Telegraph* forced out a few good words, but could not contain its outrage for long. 'The new version outdoes its Bela Lugosi predecessor in bizarre horror ... There is much erudite play with vampire repellents and crosses and ... stakes; and by way of a climax, we see the Count, several centuries old, with face and hands crumbling to dust. This British film has an "X" certificate. This is too good for it. There should be a new certificate "S" for sadistic or just "D" for disgusting. But I must add that the film is most efficiently produced and is well acted by Peter Cushing, Christopher Lee...'[7]

The *Times* found Cushing 'tight-lipped and resolved' and the film 'by no means an unimpressive piece of storytelling'[8] while *Variety* said Cushing was 'impressive as the painstaking scientist-doctor who solves the mystery.'[9] The *New York Daily News* hit the nail on the head, appreciating that the film had 'allocated time, thought and talent to an enterprise which successfully recaptures the aura and patina of yesterday's middle-Europe. Some of the photography is good enough to frame.'[10]

The *New York Herald Tribune*, on the same day, said 'the cast play their roles straight and capably, giving the impression that they believe every line.'[11] *Daily Cinema* was similarly impressed. 'Not a second is wasted in giving Bram Stoker's great novel the treatment it deserves. Performances are in the right key throughout. Peter Cushing is a dominant figure as the doctor, and Christopher Lee never misses as the horrifying Dracula. This is a classic example of how out-and-out screen thrills can be relayed with a happy combination of punch and conviction. *Dracula* will have audiences terrified in their seats from Land's End to New York.'[12]

Even before the cinematic release of *The Curse of Frankenstein*, word from the studio was so positive that Hammer was planning a sequel. In March 1957, the company's three-picture co-production deal with Columbia promised *The Blood of Frankenstein*. Jimmy Sangster wrote the script, which was eventually retitled *The Revenge of Frankenstein*. In the same way that James Whale accentuated the black comedy and eccentricity present in *Frankenstein* to create the sequel *Bride of Frankenstein*, Terence Fisher used a gleeful injection of humour to give his new scares an added relish. 'There are ... wonderful opportunities to put in intentional laughs,'[13] Fisher

Frankenstein introduces Doctor Hans Kleve (Francis Matthews) to his assistant Karl (Oscar Quitak) in *The Revenge of Frankenstein* (1958)

told the press. Producer Anthony Hinds promised 'all the shake, shudder and wallop'[14] of the first *Frankenstein*, and the public were not disappointed.

The story of *The Revenge of Frankenstein* follows directly on from the finale of *Curse*. The Baron, under sentence of death for the crimes committed by his Creature, was led to the guillotine, but Terence Fisher wisely did not to show the actual execution. As *Revenge* begins, Frankenstein escapes death with the help of a hunchbacked guard, Karl, who is promised a 'perfect' new body. Under the alias 'Doctor Stein', Frankenstein then establishes a respectable medical practice in the town of Carlsbruck, while secretly using the inmates of the poor hospital as donors for his experiments. Assisted by the young Doctor Kleve, Frankenstein transplants

Monkey business with Lucy the chimp, watched by her trainer Molly Badham, at Bray Studios for *The Revenge of Frankenstein* (1958)

Karl's brain into its new body, but when the 'new' Karl is attacked and his brain is damaged, he becomes savage and reveals Frankenstein's true identity. The Baron is attacked by the patients at the poor hospital, and beaten nearly to death, but Kleve is able to transplant Frankenstein's brain into a new body before they escape to London to begin work anew.

On 6th January 1958, just three days after the completion of shooting for *Dracula*, Bernard Robinson's lavish *Dracula* sets were re-dressed and used for the filming of *The Revenge of Frankenstein*. The new cast included Francis Matthews as Kleve, Eunice Gayson as Margaret and Michael Gwynn as the new Creature. The idea of a recurring Frankenstein 'monster', so prominent a feature of the Universal cycle, was dropped, since Christopher Lee's Creature had been utterly destroyed at the conclusion of the last film. Continuity in Hammer's *Frankenstein* cycle was to come from the character of the Baron – and Peter Cushing's Baron, at that. As an extra twist, Sangster has Frankenstein becoming his *own* Creature at the conclusion of *Revenge*.

The work was always of paramount importance to Cushing but with a sympathetic director, a supportive atmosphere and a familiar crew, he is clearly enjoying every second of *The Revenge of Frankenstein*. He revels in some priceless lines too, though there is never a hint of send-up and Cushing's timing must have been the envy of many comedians. When a pickpocket complains that the loss of his arm will mean losing his job, Frankenstein tells him flatly 'You'll have to

find another job ... or use the other hand.' Later, Frankenstein explains to Kleve that after he put the brain of an orang-utan into a chimpanzee, the animal developed cannibal tendencies and ate his wife. 'He ate another *monkey*?' gasps Kleve. With a look of mild outrage, the Baron replies 'What *else* would he be married to?'

Francis Matthews recalls the shooting of the film with great affection. 'The main memory I have of Terry and Peter together is the sheer fun we all had! The seriousness of the material meant that between shots, we all behaved in a ludicrously infantile manner – games, practical jokes and running gags.' In the breaks there were *Times* crosswords and games of battleships (with sound effects) and there was bread-and-butter pudding in the canteen. 'My impression of Peter was of a happy, contented and professionally fulfilled man. He made me feel at home instantly ... It was one of the happiest working relationships I have ever enjoyed.'[15]

Oscar Quitak remembers Cushing fondly too. 'He was wonderful to work with. He was always prepared for every shot, a complete perfectionist.' Quitak, who had to endure painful make-up for the role of the hunchbacked Karl, retreated into Cushing's dressing-room after one shot to find Baron Frankenstein babysitting their simian co-star, Lucy the chimpanzee. On another instance, Cushing was practising his trepanning techniques on a cabbage. 'He was sawing through this cabbage pretending it was a head and it was making such a noise that it was actually worse.'[16]

Kleve (Francis Matthews) and 'Dr Stein' attempt to help Karl (Michael Gwynn), the unfortunate result of Frankenstein's experiments in *The Revenge of Frankenstein* (1958)

In several instances, Cushing displays his unerring ability to carry on with a bit of 'business' while sustaining the performance perfectly. After 'staking' his cigarette-case in *Dracula*, in *Revenge*, he uses his buttonhole to symbolise Frankenstein's aspirations to acceptance and respectability. In the first scene, in the 'posh' consulting room, we see Cushing take up a flower, shake off a drop of water, carefully place it in his coat and sniff it. He repeats this action at the end of the film when Frankenstein has established a practice in Harley Street. But when Frankenstein has been discredited by the medical council, and his consulting room is empty, Cushing flings the buttonhole away in contempt. The Baron is a dandy and a socialite, but strangely, after his womanising in *Curse*, he doesn't give a second glance to his new leading lady. Even when forced to plunge headlong into the bosom of Vera Barscynska, he merely gives a resigned sigh and looks at his watch. Although still shot in glorious Eastmancolor, Terence Fisher lightens the colours in his palette a little for this film, just as the Baron's character is lightened enough to let him escape with honour at the end, beginning his work anew in London.

The supporting cast is once again superb, including many members of Hammer's repertory company. The effete president of the medical council is played by Charles Lloyd Pack, who had played Doctor Seward in *Dracula* and was also in the cast of *Richard of Bordeaux*, as was George Woodbridge, who here plays a brutal janitor. Other notables include Richard Wordsworth as a garrulous patient with Lionel Jeffries and Michael Ripper as a pair of grave-robbers.

For such a funny, pricelessly cast, artfully played piece, the film did not go down at all well with the critics, particularly C A Lejeune, who seemed to take the film as a personal insult. 'This the sequel to an earlier and almost as regrettable Frankenstein travesty made by the same company; and Peter Cushing, who can be an actor of parts when he so chooses, again demeans himself by playing the hero … The actors are more to be pitied than criticised. The whole thing is to my taste a vulgar, stupid, nasty and intolerably tedious business. A crude sort of entertainment for a crude sort of audience. Films of this kind are the last refuge of unimaginative producers who have lost the art of communicating individually with human beings and have fallen back on the appeal to mass hysteria.'[17] Some critics took things less seriously, like Peter Burnup who noted Frankenstein was 'played again by Peter Cushing in forbidding fashion. Miss Eunice Gayson also drops in now and again on the proceedings. Quite why I couldn't quite make out.' Gayson's reduced role is explained by an injury she sustained when a lamp blew while she was filming on horseback. She was thrown from the horse, damaged her back and subsequently had to wear an uncomfortable brace under her costume.

There were the inevitable comparisons to the 1931 model too. 'I am afraid it can't hold a grave-snatcher's candle to the earlier Karloff prototype,' said the *Evening Standard*. 'His was a very terrifying Thing (or so it seemed when I was 12). Frankenstein's revenge is purely to vindicate himself in the eyes of science. He intends to show his product off to the whole medical world in a spirit of They Laughed When I Sat Down To Build A Monster. Peter Cushing is now artistically dedicated to this species of blood chiller.'[18]

At the time of the film's release there was a great deal of negative criticism levelled at the horror genre, with Hammer's James Carreras dubbed the 'King of Nausea' and protest groups frothing at the ever-more-gory front-of-house posters, many of which were far more gruesome than the films they advertised. There was a refreshing note of common sense, however, in this review of *The Revenge of Frankenstein* from the *Daily Express*. 'Frankly I'm not one of those who see anything to worry about in these horror films. This film is preposterous and never tries to be anything else. Moralists can look to life and find their problems there. Here is fantasy. Those who like this sort of thing will love this one, those who don't won't and needn't go.'[19]

Cushing discusses his role as Sir Robert Morton in *The Winslow Boy* with producer Rudolph Cartier

'A man who's good for 14 years stays good to everlasting.' But not the downtrodden Harry Quincey in the BBC's *Uncle Harry* (1958)

On 23rd January 1958, Cushing sent a telegram from Ealing Studios (*Revenge of Frankenstein* was shot at Bray) to Rudolph Cartier about the forthcoming production of Terence Rattigan's *The Winslow Boy*. 'Please consider Gwen Watford Love Peter Cushing' On 28th January 1958 Kenneth Cleveland wrote to Cartier determining that Cushing should get sole star billing above the title of *The Winslow Boy*.

Cushing was so busy and so much in demand at this period that for his appearance on the BBC's popular quiz show *What's My Line* on 9th February, he had to be ferried from the set of *The Revenge of Frankenstein* at Bray.

The Winslow Boy began rehearsal on 20th February 1958, nearly a fortnight before the completion of filming for *The Revenge of Frankenstein*, necessitating some juggling on the BBC and Hammer's part. Cartier, who won the Guild of Television Producers and Directors Award for best drama producer of 1957, had already produced *The Winslow Boy* in Germany in 1956, when it was hailed as 'a shining example of the working of British democracy, showing as it does how even the small man can fight against bureaucracy.'[20] Cushing played the eminent KC Sir Robert Morton, described by Rattigan as 'a man in his early forties, cadaverous and immensely elegant. He wears a long overcoat, and carries his hat and stick. He looks rather a fop, and his supercillious expression bears out this view.' Morton brings the first act to a close with his interrogation of young Ronnie Winslow, who has been accused of stealing a five-shilling postal order, and it is easy to hear Cushing's cadences in Sir Robert Morton's lines. It's a safe bet that the Cushing digit was held aloft more than once. The initially severe character who turns out to be a formidable ally was a role that Cushing would play over and over again. There is more than a little of Van Helsing's steel in Sir Robert and vice-versa.

The Winslow Boy was reviewed in The *Times*: 'Mr Cartier's deliberately suave production laid out

the play for inspection ... he avoided commentary by camera and entrusted the play to his excellent cast. Mr Peter Cushing played Morton without the savagery associated with the part; it was an icy and mercurial performance which preserved the character's paradoxical combination of ruthlessness and gentle reserve.'[21]

The Winslow Boy was the last play of Cushing's BBC contract but he was soon involved in another – Thomas Job's play *Uncle Harry*, again co-starring Mary Morris with Rona Anderson, Beryl Measor and Hugh Morton. The play was set in a small town on the Welsh border and was to be broadcast from the BBC's studios in Cardiff. The *Radio Times* had this to say: '"I've known Harry Quincey" says a character in tonight's play "for 14 years and a man who's good for 14 years stays good to everlasting." As events turn out, this proves to be faulty reasoning, for Harry Quincey – Uncle Harry to everybody because he is such a quiet, gentle sort of chap – lives under a strain, suffocated by the attentions of two quarrelsome sisters, and turned down by the woman he loves. Then one day he conceives a desperate plan to free himself from his bondage.'[22]

The transmission of *Uncle Harry* was unexpectedly put back until 10.00 pm. There was a replay of Manchester United's match against Milan, just days before United's appearance in the FA Cup Final.

'As a rugby fan,' wrote assistant head of drama Norman Rutherford to Cushing on 1st May, 'I cannot expect you to appreciate the significance of this game

In the heat of battle, Captain Pearson of the *Serapis* hails his antagonist to offer a chance of surrender, in *John Paul Jones* (1958)

played with a round ball. But there it is. We must accept it as fact. I asked if we could telerecord *Uncle Harry* but my request was not granted.' However, Rutherford was convinced that 'Mary will hold them to the screen. I am looking forward to the production more than most I will have viewed during the past year as I have always felt that this is a part which you would bring to life most vividly on the television screen.' There was a PS for rugby fan Cushing. 'I am sure you were delighted with Blackheath winning the Middlesex "Sevens" this year!'

'What a skilful re-creator Peter Cushing is!' enthused the *Daily Telegraph*. 'He is always being given characters in television plays created on the stage by a Gielgud, an Emlyn Williams or an Eric Portman, and always putting them successfully through "the sieve of his own personality" as Granville Barker put it. In Thomas Job's psychological murder play *Uncle Harry* on BBC television last night, he was following Michael Redgrave who took the name part in the London production some 15 years ago. This part of a weak, middle-aged bachelor who plans ingeniously to get rid of his two over-possessive spinster sisters so that he can marry suited him far better than some heroic or romantic role, and indeed he gave one of his most satisfying studies. Rona Anderson was also well in character as the girl who attracts him and Mary Morris reminded us what an incisive actress she is as the sister condemned to death for the murder she does not commit – that of her own elder sister.'[23]

With the international success of *The Curse of Frankenstein* and the eagerly anticipated opening of *Dracula*, the Cushings were enjoying unprecedented financial security. They decided to buy a seafront property in the Kent seaside town of Whitstable, where Cushing could paint and where the sea air would help Helen's breathing. On 26th May, Cushing's birthday, this was reported in the *Standard*. 'Actor Peter Cushing, who is 45 today, has bought a white clapboard house on the beach at Whitstable, Kent. He is turning the top floor into a studio. Cushing is an accomplished water colourist and has painted many Whitstable scenes on his visits there in the past 15 years. He says "Now, instead of sitting on a breakwater to paint, I shall be able to work in comfort. I may attempt the wonderful sunsets over the Isle of Sheppey which inspired Turner. It is worth buying a house in Whitstable just to see them!"'[24]

On his birthday, however, Cushing was in New York for the Broadway opening of *Dracula*. The *News of the World* stated that '*Dracula* has ... most profitably ... set the West End of London back on its heels.' While in the US, Cushing was to take part in 'a series of coast-to-coast networked television appearances' promoting *Dracula*, 'not to speak of "personals" before avid Broadway reporters. There'll be quite an ordeal for our Mr Cushing. But so it goes. To the delight, doubtless, of the Chancellor of the Exchequer, Cushing and the goose-fleshed chiller-killer-dillers in which he figures have become rich dollar earners for Britain. The first of the horrific series – *The Curse of Frankenstein* – has already earned 3,000,000 dollars in America.'[25]

Cushing's next job in July and August 1958 was the role of Captain Pearson in *John Paul Jones*, directed by John Farrow. The film is part sprawling American epic and part US Navy propaganda with Robert Stack as the Scottish-born merchant captain John Paul Jones who is adopted as a Naval captain by the newly independent Americas.

Cushing was 'fined down', as he put it, by a mild bout of dysentery on location at Denia in Spain, but is resplendent in powdered wig and period British Naval uniform. The score even gives us a bar or two of 'Hearts of Oak' when he appears. It is 1779, Britain is at war with the Americas, and Pearson, captain of the *Serapis*, engages Jones in a terrific sea battle off Flamborough Head. Jones loses most of his crew but when Pearson hails him to ask for his surrender, Jones gives the film's signatory quote 'I have not yet begun to fight!'

The night-time battle is realistically staged, although Cushing recallede that the explosive charges on deck were sometimes a little too close for comfort. Captain Jones is victorious, and there is a look of real resignation from Cushing as he admits grimly 'it's useless to shed more blood.' Jones refuses to accept Pearson's sword in surrender and later, the erstwhile enemies read the burial ceremony together over their dead. Given Cushing's love of swashbuckling he must have been very happy to make a film like *John Paul Jones*. It was his last prominent role in a big-budget American movie until *Star Wars* in 1976.

Chapter Thirteen

Elementary Exercises

Cushing had been collecting toy soldiers from childhood, and by the late 1950s had an extensive collection. He introduced Alan Ladd to collecting while they were filming *The Black Knight*, and every Cushing co-star who was invited to dinner was given an impromptu review of 'the troops'. Cushing's theories about toys and hobbies were well thought out and somewhat revolutionary for the time, when miniatures were not common, and there is a strong indication of his Peter Pan personality in a piece entitled 'Toys? They're Not Child's Play – says Peter Cushing' which he wrote for the *TV Mirror's* 'On My Soap-Box' column. Cushing changed the column's title to 'On My Hobby-Horse'.

'Hobbies? "Oh," you sigh, "Peter Cushing is going to tell us about his toy soldiers again! Nothing to do with a bold Soap-box subject, surely?" Now I have a theory about hobbies and toys, and I'm quite prepared for you to scoff at me. The theory is quite simple. It is that toys are given to children when they are too young to appreciate them and that because most men "put away childish things" as they reach adulthood, they miss a great deal of happiness at a time in their lives when... they are actually in a much better position to enjoy their toys and hobbies.

'Far too many men are hobby-less ... Without the escapism which comes only from dabbling with adult toys, their minds are prey to all the frustrations and fears of the working day. So many, it seems to me, lose happiness as they grow up. Their entire absorption in their careers and adult responsibilities bring lines of worry and premature old age. It is not silly or childish to have an interest in hobbies... some men develop a passionate interest in costly 35mm cameras and in vintage cars, but what are these things except toys of a rather larger and dearer sort? I am not particularly mechanically-minded, so although I do have a certain interest in mechanical models, I get much greater contentment from miniature figures and costumes. I love collecting old manuscripts and books on period costume too, but of course, that's a branch of art, and not a subject for my hobby-horse.

'H G Wells ... wrote a most interesting book entitled *Little Wars*, which was a serious satire designed to make real war impossible. There is a British Model Soldier Society, including youngsters of nine up to colonels of ninety, and who manoeuvre the soldiers according to the rules which H G outlined in his book, rules which have changed little since the days of Napoleon. When I come home at night and find the TV news or the newspaper headlines more than usually anxious and alarming, I sometimes get out my soldiers and start solving international problems on my lounge carpet. Fearful problems which ... cause international strife at UNO, are settled in a quiet half-hour with my private armies of military men, who are as clever, bold, strategic, and victorious as I can make them. One day, I may be tempted to send to Whitehall, to Washington and to the Kremlin, so that statesmen can find the key... But no. I have no wish to challenge anyone's opinion. I have my own inner contentment with this world-in-miniature ... And you could too. It's not a thing to shout or campaign about, but to discover privately, and to enjoy in one's own heart.'[1]

Cushing with some of his beloved model soldiers, in a picture taken to publicise *The Black Knight* (1953)

'It's a marvellous opportunity,' said Cushing when offered the of Sherlock Holmes in *The Hound of the Baskervilles* (1958)

Cushing's next film would involve him with another subject close to his heart. He was to star as Sherlock Holmes in Hammer's adaptation of *The Hound of the Baskervilles* directed by Terence Fisher. 'Many people said I should play Holmes,' Cushing admitted. 'When I was offered the part I was thrilled. It's a marvellous opportunity when you've got so much detail to base your character on.'[2]

If Cushing played Van Helsing 'more or less as myself,' then Holmes is definitely a performance as a wholly different character. 'Impish, waspish and Wildean'[3] was how *Films and Filming* described it. It is theatrical and not a little arrogant, but appropriately catches the aloof genius of the world's greatest detective. With quizzical expressions and flamboyant gestures, Cushing is perfect for the role. André Morell, reunited with his co-star from *Nineteen Eighty-Four* on much more agreeable terms, is a perfect foil as Watson, restoring honour and a military bearing to a character so often played for comedy.

Kenneth Hyman – son of the American financier Eliot Hyman, James Carreras's partner – acted in a senior role during the production of many Hammer films. *The Hound of the Baskervilles* was one of the few where he took an on-screen credit as producer. Ken Hyman's company Seven Arts had purchased the film rights to *The Hound of the Baskervilles* from Sir Arthur Conan Doyle's estate, and had secured money from distributor United Artists. The film was announced as a forthcoming attraction in March 1958 replacing another proposed literary adaptation – a remake of *Dr Jekyll and Mr Hyde*. Cushing was signed on 1st August, and James Carreras promised 'I shall get him to sex it up a bit.'[4]

Anthony Hinds, however, insisted Holmes would be played 'realistically, not romantically'[5], and Cushing, a longstanding Holmes fan, told the *Evening Bulletin* about his exhaustive research for the role. 'I've based all my costumes on the original *Strand* magazine pictures. Everything is right, down to the old mouse-coloured dressing-gown, which I charred with cigarettes to get the burns Holmes made during his experiments. When he's on a case, he is like a dog following a scent. Holmes is not the pleasantest of characters either. He doesn't suffer fools, and he must have been insufferable to live with.'

Cushing gleefully included canonical details like Holmes writing memos to himself on his shirt-cuff and lighting his pipe with a coal from the fire. The storyline, however, plays rather footloose with Doyle to introduce several 'horrific' elements like a tarantula spider, sacrificial rites (reported but unseen) and a man with a webbed hand.

Following a prologue, which illustrates the story of wicked Sir Hugo Baskerville in the expected Hammer style, we are placed into Bernard Robinson's enchantingly accurate Baker Street set. Cushing is first seen with his hand over his face, smoking his pipe while he listens to Doctor Mortimer (Francis De Wolff) explaining the legend. Holmes solves a chess problem with a snort, and turns to Mortimer with a look of bored indifference. 'There must be hundreds of similar folk stories,' he enunciates fiercely. 'I fail to see why I should find this one of singular interest.' Mortimer explains that Sir Charles – the latest resident of Baskerville Hall on Dartmoor – has recently been found dead, a victim of the 'hound of Hell' that is supposed to take vengeance on all of Sir Hugo's heirs. While he listens to Mortimer, Holmes seems preoccupied with straightening a crooked picture, running his finger through the dust and checking his correspondence which is transfixed to the mantelpiece with a dagger. He later admits that he was deliberately goading Mortimer to find a significant clue – that Sir Charles died of heart failure. Later, Cushing makes Holmes positively coquettish to charm further information out of Mortimer.

As Holmes agrees to meet the Baskerville heir, Sir Henry, the following day, Cushing suggested that they insert an original line from the Doyle canon to send Mortimer on his way – 'My professional charges are on a fixed scale, I do not vary them, except when I remit them altogether.' Christopher Lee makes an attractive hero out of the thankless role of Sir Henry Baskerville, and clearly enjoys his scenes with Cushing. The Cushing digit is brought to bear on Sir Henry as he issues the warning, 'under no circumstances are you to venture out onto the moor at night!' – a definitive Holmes moment in a splendidly enjoyable Cushing performance.

One of the problems with the story of *The Hound of the Baskervilles* is that Holmes is missing for a large chunk in the middle while Watson accompanies Sir Henry to Baskerville Hall – Holmes is meanwhile hiding on the moor, observing and gathering information. For the reunion between Holmes and a baffled

Cushing greets a member of the Sherlock Holmes Society (left) and his old ENSA sparring partner Humphrey Morton (right) on the set of *The Hound of the Baskervilles* (1958)

and angry Watson, Cushing appears in a long black cloak – not unlike his Frankenstein rig. 'Forgive me if my dramatic entrance startled you,' says Holmes with a smile. 'It's been rather lonely up here!'

Meanwhile, Sir Henry has fallen for a local girl, Cecille (Marla Landi), daughter of the farmer Stapleton. Following an intuition, Holmes investigates an abandoned tin-mine and finds that the legendary hound is far from supernatural...

Scriptwriter Peter Bryan's action-packed revision of Doyle's plot gives Cushing some bonus scenes, including one with Miles Malleson as Bishop Frankland, who has clearly been following Holmes' exploits avidly. 'That case of the Bermondsey forgery,' he chortles, 'that was a first class piece of work!' Next to the fluttery Bishop complaining about wordworm in his belfry, Holmes seems particularly steely. The scene demonstrates once again how players of Malleson's calibre ennobled Hammer's output.

Terence Fisher's storytelling and characterisation are first-rate and he uses the same visual language that he used so effectively in *Dracula* to create another dark fairy tale. The settings are magnificent though economical, and Jack Asher's photography is

gorgeous, filling the nooks and crannies with an array of weird colours, particularly the saturated reds and greens which add an other-worldly eeriness to the studio-bound moorland. Once again in a Hammer film James Bernard's driving score gives a sense of energy and excitement throughout.

The only stumbling-block for the filmmakers was the climactic appearance of the hound. There were in fact two dogs – the first, a great dane called Colonel was far too mild-mannered to be a hound of hell. An attempt to film him in a scaled-down set with child actors standing in for Holmes, Watson

'My Lord, I am fighting evil, fighting it as surely as you do!' Holmes consults the forgetful entomologist Bishop Frankland (Miles Malleson) in an enjoyable scene from *The Hound of the Baskervilles* (1958)

and Sir Henry produced footage more laughable than horrible. A second dog was provided by trainer Barbara Woodhouse, but even with the addition of a rabbit fur mask made by Margaret Robinson, wife of designer Bernard, it didn't quite work. Cushing maintained that the Hound had never been realised on screen adequately.

Despite Hammer's hopes that the film may lead to a series of Holmes movies, the response to the film was mixed and plans were dropped. Ten years later, however, Cushing made a series of 15 Holmes adventures for the BBC, which included another version of *The Hound of the Baskervilles*.

Among the reviews for Hammer's version, *Newsweek*'s was particularly encouraging. 'The latest revival of the hair-raising ... classic has among its distinctions actor Peter Cushing, who seems likely to strike oldsters as the best Sherlock Holmes yet ... Tense and taut, with a steely glint on his close-shaven cheekbones, Cushing is the epitome of the classical detective ... A living, breathing Holmes.'[7]

The *Observer*, however, found deficiencies in the film. 'It would seem hard to make a dull picture of *The Hound of the Baskervilles*, but Hammer ... have done it. By cunning changes in the relationships of character, by the invention of new scenes of no relevance whatsoever ... they have managed to evolve a script which misses almost all the salient points of the original. Peter Cushing is the new Sherlock Holmes. Curiously, for he has shown authority in other parts, he seems fussy, finicky and indeterminate in this one. André Morell is the Doctor Watson, and he works hard to avoid the buffoonery in the part. *The Hound of the Baskervilles* is a betwixt-and-between picture; unsatisfactory to the Holmes expert, and providing no full feast to the horror-gobblers.'[8]

The *Sunday Times* found Cushing 'too oversprightly' as Holmes in a 'very mild shocker; a few nocturnal howls, hints of nameless sacrificial rites ... the rest is whodunit and poor hungry doggie.'[9]

While Cushing faced the poor hungry doggie, the BBC was busily planning a production of George Du Maurier's *Trilby* for Christmas 1958, and wanted Cushing for the lead as the hypnotist Svengali, a great theatrical role famously played on screen by John Barrymore in 1931 an Donald Wolfit in 1954.

Ann Redington watches Cushing at his portable easel painting a water-colour of the Norfolk Broads

On 9th September Angela Hepburn, now Cushing's television agent, wrote to Michael Barry. 'I have some more information from Hammer as to their plans for Peter's next production for them, which ... is to be *The Man in Half Moon Street*. At present they plan to start shooting this picture on or about the 10th November (six to seven week schedule – generally six.) *Hound of the Baskervilles*, on which he has just commenced work this week – and the start of *Half Moon Street* gives an available period 20th October to 9th November approximately.'

Despite these restrictions, the BBC was still very keen. 'Svengali belongs to a period that requires the breadth and colour which I believe Peter would join me in appreciating.' Barry explained to Hepburn, adding that they would even consider postponing *Trilby* from transmission on Boxing Day to accommodate Cushing.

But it was not to be. The state of play was spelt out in an exasperated letter from Angela Hepburn to the BBC on 27th November 1958. 'It is with the greatest regret I have to tell you that Peter Cushing will not be available to play Svengali for you on the proposed filming date. As you may or may not know, Peter is under contract to Hammer Films to do five pictures for them within a period of 18 months. This means virtually that he has approximately ten days to a fortnight off between each film and therefore his periods of availability are not only limited but also spaced far apart. In actual fact the film he is about to do (on a 12-week schedule) is not for Hammer but for another company – and therefore it follows that as soon as it is completed he has to return immediately to Hammer to start work on his next film for them. I ... explain this to you so that you can see how very little point there appears to be in postponing your production with the idea of Peter being available at a later date. I have just talked with him on the telephone and he liked the script very much indeed and he is extremely sorry that he will not be able to play it.'

The trouble with *Trilby* seemed to disincline the BBC from involving Cushing in new productions. There would be various inquiries on his part, and an abortive attempt to relaunch *Cyrano de Bergerac*, but he would not appear in a major BBC production until 1963.

There seems no readily apparent reason, either, why Cushing did not make Hammer's *The Man in Half Moon Street,* which was retitled *The Man Who Could Cheat Death* and the lead role was taken by Anton Diffring. He would have been among friends – it was directed by Terence Fisher and co-starred Hazel Court and Christopher Lee. No more is known about the other, non-Hammer film that Angela Hepburn mentions, and Cushing did not start work on another film until the New Year.

It was suggested by Hazel Court that Cushing disliked the violence in the *Half Moon Street* script, or perhaps he simply wanted a break after a lengthy run of film work. It is likely, too, that he wished to devote his attention to a rather different West End appearance. On 3rd December 1958, 'Here and There – An Exhibition of Water-Colours by Peter Cushing' opened at the Fine Art Society, New Bond Street and ran for several months.

The exhibition comprised 54 paintings, many of them views of Whitstable. There was also a painting completed in the garden of artist Edward Seago, studies of the Thames including Lambeth Bridge and a backwater near Richmond, and several scenes around Altea near Alicante, painted while Cushing was filming *Alexander the Great.*

Among the visitors to the exhibition was the assistant controller of the BBC, Cecil Madden, who wrote a letter of appreciation. 'I came along to your water colours at Bond Street. You certainly are a versatile chap! I particularly enjoyed the Spanish pictures.' Cushing replied from Whitstable. 'Thank you so much for going to see the exhibition. I was very sorry not to see you there but I was an hour and a half late due to the fog. I look forward to seeing you again ... with any luck Helen and I will be back in London early in the New Year.'

As it turned out, Cushing's last job of the year *was* for the BBC, but on radio. On 17th December Cushing recorded his selection for one of broadcasting's hardiest perennials, *Desert Island Discs.*

Desert Island Discs was first broadcast in 1942 and even by 1958 was something of an institution. Each week, presenter Roy Plomley interviewed a celebrity 'castaway' who chose eight gramophone records to help him (or her) while away the hours on a desert island. Cushing's selection was a mixture of light classics and popular music including the overture 'Donna Diana' by Reznicek and a piece from Joseph Strauss' *Die Fledermaus,* of which he said: 'It's just so delicious ... It reminds me rather of a Christmas stocking. Whenever you dip into this wonderful piece of music something new and refreshing comes out. It's an awfully difficult choice to take one tiny bit out of such a jewel.'

Cushing repeatedly apologised to Plomley for being a poor Robinson Crusoe, admitting that as a castaway he would be 'absolutely shocking, dear boy ... dreadful!' because his wife did everything for him. As the rules of the island were genially dictated to him, Cushing entered into the spirit of the thing, although he was rather concerned for his creature comforts, chiefly a cup of tea.

He used his next choice, Sibelius' Symphony Number 1 in E minor, to illustrate the feeling he had in America of wanting to get back to England. 'Sibelius always seems to me to have this incredible longing – a longing for something he wants to get to and can't. I'm sure, I know, it was the feeling I had when I was in America – and the same feeling I'll have on this island of yours, to get back to England.'

Then, it was 'from the sublime ... to the sublime' – Jimmy 'Schnozzle' Durante singing 'I'm a Vulture for Horticulture'. 'He's so full of vitality and really the best on the variety and vaudeville stage. You can't help but just go along with Jimmy, he really has something!' Cushing's fifth record was from Richard Strauss' *Der Rosenkavalier.* 'One of my favourite waltzes, from the third act. Amongst all the records that I love, perhaps I love this one a little bit more.'

Next came another change of mood, to a mambo called 'El Limpiabotas' sung by Cuates Castilla, the Mexican Singing Twins. This was followed by Yvonne Printemps singing 'I'll Follow My Secret Heart', from Noël Coward's *Conversation Piece.* 'This is enchantment!' Cushing enthused. 'It is from the era of the theatre that was my favourite and which I loved most dearly. I think it'll come back one day, but I think it's what this time is missing and I'd like a little memory of that, please.' The final selection was 'The Royal Hunt and Storm' from Berlioz' *The Trojans.* 'I think it's most majestic and inspiring and I think it'll help me a lot.'

Cushing opted for the Sibelius as his choice if he were only allowed one record, although he complained that the decision was difficult. In choosing his luxury item, he tried to get one over on the canny Plomley by requesting a full-sized Sopwith Camel aeroplane and a manual on how to fly it. Plomley told him no, so Cushing swapped the complete works of Shakespeare (supplied to all castaways) for a painting set. He also requested his toy soldiers as a luxury item, although 'I'm sure,' he said, 'if that lot was on board it's what sank the boat!'

Cushing's *Desert Island Discs,* which also included plugs for the exhibition and *The Hound of the Baskervilles,* was broadcast on 23rd February 1959. Three weeks later, the castaway was Ernest Thesiger, Cushing's co-star from *The Silver Whistle.* Thesiger's luxury item was also a painting set.

The Cushings stayed in Whitstable over Christmas and through January 1959. They returned for 25th January, when Cushing was back at Bray for his fifth film with Terence Fisher – *The Mummy.*

Chapter Fourteen

That C-r-e-e-p-y Character

'That C-r-e-e-p-y Character' was how David Stone described Cushing in *Everybody's* magazine in February 1959 even though he discovered, like so many others, that there was nothing creepy about at the man all. 'It was at his Whitstable home that I talked to the 45-year-old Peter Cushing. Comfortably clad in a thick sweater, old trousers and fur-lined bedroom slippers, he told me about the hard road he has travelled to reach his present perch at the top. We chatted in the studio which Cushing has built at the top of his house. One wall, almost entirely of windows, floods the room with light, and at the other end of the room is a large work-table, laden with all the apparatus an artist needs.'

Stone continued, 'The critics like to describe him as "suave" "polished" and "silky". He is all these things, and it seems to come from an inner contentment. It is no effort talking to Cushing. He bubbles with a young man's enthusiasm for the world around him. Offstage his voice is surprisingly soft, and he has a tendency to guffaw when something amuses him. He would much rather talk about his hobbies than about himself ... and values his solitary rambles through the English countryside far more than the West End's tinsel glamour.

'It would be impossible to imagine him bothering with "psychological" acting or explaining his art in fancy terms. His approach is essentially that of a man doing a job of work." He is now Peter Cushing Productions Ltd, and in the happy position of having work in the theatre, films and TV as far as the eye can see. But his success does not weigh on his mind in any disturbing way. "I wouldn't mind if I didn't have it, you know. I've got so much more."'[1]

At 45, just five years after his father had made that dread pronouncement of failure, Cushing was a worldwide success. He was greeted with cheers when he visited America with Christopher Lee for the première of *Dracula*, and had signed autographs long into the night. He had little trepidation about following the horror path and becoming typecast; his concern was for Helen, who, after supporting him for so long, deserved something in return. 'Helen's life had been a riches to rags story,' he said. 'I wanted to restore some of the riches again, after all she'd been through.'[2]

Cushing's next project, Hammer's *The Mummy*, began filming on 25th February 1959. It was a lengthy shoot that lasted until 16th April, but he was back with old friends. Christopher Lee was playing Kharis, the Mummy of the title, and Terence Fisher was once again behind the camera.

Cushing had first achieved fame as a romantic actor, and *The Mummy* features one of his gentlest film roles as John Banning, a quiet and scholarly man who is suddenly confronted with the living embodiment of the sins of the father. We first see Banning on an archaeological expedition in Egypt with his father Stephen (Felix Aylmer) and uncle, Joseph Whemple (Raymond Huntley). John has broken his leg but is still full of boyish eagerness and enthusiasm to see the dig. (Because he refuses to have his leg set, he later walks with a limp.) Cushing manages by his wide-eyed performance to portray a young man far better than he did in *Richard of Bordeaux*, though he is clearly abetted by some 'beauty' make-up, courtesy of Roy Ashton, who had taken over from Phil Leakey

John Banning with his wife Isobel (Yvonne Furneaux), the living image of the Egyptian Princess Ananka, in *The Mummy* (1959)

To give 'some sort of logic' to the beam of light passing through the mummy in Hammer's poster, Cushing asked that a scene be included where Banning drove a harpoon through Kharis (Christopher Lee) in *The Mummy* (1959)

as Hammer's chief make-up artist. Jimmy Sangster's script has some subtle jokes, too. When Cushing delivers Banning's wistful line 'I seem to have spent most of my life among the dead,' perhaps Sangster was quietly commenting on Cushing's newfound reputation as a graveyard-dweller.

Stephen Banning has discovered the tomb of Princess Ananka, but a vengeful Egyptian, Mehemet Bey (George Pastell) warns of the ancient curse – 'He who robs the graves of Egypt dies!' Stephen enters the tomb and discovers the Scroll of Life but, unseen to him, a hidden door swings open. When the old man is found later, he has been driven out of his mind and is committed to an asylum. Three years later, however, he suddenly regains his wits and warns John about a living mummy in Ananka's tomb.

There is a touching scene between Banning and his father with Cushing clearly delighted to be performing with veteran actor Aylmer, his co-star from *Hamlet*. Filled with hope that his father is sane, John is bitterly disappointed. 'You're a fool, John,' says Stephen – Cushing visibly winces. Later, when John is

informed that his father will have to put in a padded cell for his own protection, Cushing does a turn-into-shot again, as he did in *Dracula*.

The Mummy has been brought to England by Mehemet Bey, but the crate in which it is contained is accidentally dropped into a marsh. This blood-red bog, filmed at Shepperton because there was no tank facility at Bray, is the focus for one of the film's definitive scenes – the Mummy rising from the mud, sent off by the Bey to destroy the desecrators of Ananka's tomb. The subsequent attack on Stephen Banning in his cell is frighteningly savage. Dripping slime, the Mummy bends back the bars of the cell, slithers in and strangles the old man. Although Kharis is a mute slave of bandage and bone, and moves with an appropriately robotic gait, Christopher Lee once again manages to invest the creature with a personality and motivation using only his eyes. There is no little sadness at Kharis' inevitable destruction.

In Banning's study, John is going through his father's papers. Cushing has a long exchange with Raymond Huntley, during which time he moves about, lights a cigarette, empties his ash-tray into the fire – and the whole speech is filmed in one continuous take, a great achievement that goes almost unnoticed. Cushing then relates the legend of Ananka, and we see Christopher Lee as the High Priest Kharis, looking magnificent in his Egyptian regalia.

When the Mummy attacks his home, Banning can only watch in horror as Whemple is strangled. He rushes to the gun cabinet and empties a pistol into the monster, but it has no effect and convinces the dogged Inspector Mulrooney (Eddie Byrne) that he is dealing with 'fantasies out of Edgar Allan Poe!' Later, as Banning awaits the Mummy's return, he realises that his wife is the image of Princess Ananka – Cushing has a tender scene with Yvonne Furneaux as Isobel. 'She was considered the most beautiful woman in the world,' says Banning, smiling as he adds, 'mind you, the world wasn't such a big place then.' He kisses her and sends her to bed so he may face his enemy alone. The tension is difficult to bear as Banning paces up and down awkwardly on his twisted leg, waiting for the Mummy. The thing duly crashes in and goes for Banning – he is only saved by the intervention of Isobel, whose likeness to Ananka confuses the creature.

Cushing was alarmed to see that the publicity material for the film showed the Mummy with a large hole in his midriff, and a beam of light passing through it. 'This was never referred to in the script,' he recalled, 'so I asked how it got there.

"Oh," said the publicity man. "That's just to help sell the picture." Oh, I thought – that's just not on.' Cushing asked Terence Fisher if he could take the harpoon from the wall in Banning's study and drive it through the Mummy's body, giving at least the idea that light *could* pass through the creature, 'thus giving some sort of logic to the illuminated gap on the posters.'[3] Cushing was always concerned about logic in scripts, believing that it was unwise to treat the audiences as idiots. 'The people who see horror films are very critical,' he noted, 'and they don't like just any old nonsense.'[4]

French-born actress Yvonne Furneaux, who immediately afterwards went to star in Federico Fellini's *La Dolce Vita*, came to *The Mummy* with very low expectations. When she found herself working with people like Cushing and Lee, who treated the material with absolute seriousness, however, she abruptly changed her mind. 'From the start I should have cared just as much as Christopher and Peter.' She noticed how Cushing, diplomatically adding ideas to Fisher's set-ups, raised the bar even further. 'He was so tactful,' she says. 'Every time I was there, I could see that Peter had the ideas. He should have directed films.'[5] Interestingly, Cushing later told writer Bill Kelley that about this time he did discuss directing a film for Hammer. 'Around 1960... I remember saying to Tony Hinds, "If you have a script

you think I could do something with, I'd like to take a crack at it." But nothing ever came of it.'[6]

Three days before the completion of filming of *The Mummy*, on 16th April, Cushing recorded an interview at Bray for the BBC World Service. Broadcast as *Calling Australia* number 211, the subject was 'H for Horror'. Cushing was paid five guineas. Later in the year he was featured in the Light Programme show *Dateline London*, interviewed by Angus McDermid about his collection of model soldiers.

On 25th May 1959, Cushing joined director John Gilling for Robert S Baker and Monty Berman's production of *The Flesh and the Fiends*. Gilling, Baker and Berman formed Triad Productions specifically for this film, which marked the first instance of a company poaching Cushing from Hammer to take advantage of his new reputation.

In comparison with Cushing's last film *The Mummy* – which for all its Eastmancolored elegance is limited to several interior sets and a handful of actors – *The Flesh and the Fiends* in black-and-white is something of an epic, in widescreen, with huge interior and exterior sets stuffed with extras.

The Flesh and the Fiends is set in Edinburgh in 1828, where the 'brilliant, aggressive, provocative, verbose' Doctor Robert Knox teaches medicine and employs the resurrectionists Burke and Hare to acquire bodies for his anatomy classes. Cushing was already familiar with Knox, as he had used the surgeon as one of the components for his portrayal of Frankenstein. 'He was fundamentally doing something for the good of mankind,' Cushing said, 'but against all odds, because the villagers always seem to come and knock on his door and shout "You beast! You beast!"'[7] Knox's plight, Cushing said, helped him to give credibility to his performance as Frankenstein, and you can hear the Baron's metallic tones in Knox's lines: 'Emotion is a drug that dulls the intellect. Approach the science of medicine with a more clinical mind.'

Although the film's middle section is devoted to the performances of Donald Pleasence as Hare and George Rose as Burke, the first quarter-hour is given over almost entirely to a lengthy speech from Cushing as Knox. 'Miracles, gentlemen, are an apology for ignorance and a retreat for fools. To primitive man, the human body was a miracle. To us, it is a structure... a complicated structure, yes, but no longer a miracle.' Knox rarely shies from an insult or an arch observation, and in a searing exchange with the hypocritical Edinburgh elders, spits, 'I can show you the heart, my dear Reverend – can you show me the soul? Beneath the armpit? Between the eyes, deep in the abdomen?' In support are Melvyn Hayes (who had played the young Baron Frankenstein) as the idiot boy Daft Jamie, Renée Houston as the ill-tempered Mrs Burke and Billie Whitelaw as the ill-fated barmaid of the 'Merry Duke'.

'I don't think I have worked with a finer cast,'[8] said John Gilling. And inspired by his actors, he creates an appropriately Dickensian atmosphere of delinquency in the dingy Edinburgh backstreets, with some startlingly brutal scenes. In one, Burke suffocates drunken old Aggie (Esma Cannon) and later, Pleasence gets to copy Cushing's 'terror' scene from *Nineteen Eighty-Four* when Hare sees a rat and goes berserk. As Burke and Hare bring their newest body in, 'fresh as a new-cut cabbage', Knox, roused from his bed, appears in a dressing-gown, waving his handkerchief against Burke's reeking breath.

When Burke and Hare are eventually arrested, Hare immediately turns King's evidence and denounces his former friend, who is hanged. But the mob is not satisfied – they round on Hare and blind him. Knox meanwhile has to face the medical Council, whose only concern is the honour of the profession. Threatened with gaol, Knox is fluorescent with rage. 'Croak your miserable way to the law-courts, if you dare,' he spits. 'I will meet you on the steps with a torchlight to scorch into your souls, and leave them bare as a warning to your future victims.'

Heading home after walking out of the hearing, Knox meets an urchin begging for ha'pennies. The doctor has no money, and asks the girl to come back with him to his house. 'No thank you,' she says politely, 'you might sell me to Doctor Knox!' Knox rises, tears running down his face. Unlike Frankenstein, Knox can still see his soul, can still connect with other people and so is redeemed. 'I've just heard the voice of conscience,' he admits back at the Academy. 'From a small child I heard the truth. It said "You are an ogre, Doctor Knox. You have killed humanity."' Knox is resigned to facing an empty lecture-room, but it is full of his students who applaud as he enters.

The film was another success, with Cushing's performance singled out for more praise than usual, although it was once again remarked upon that Cushing was 'an expert in this sort of fare.' With so many 'horror' performers already sending the genre up, *Variety* noticed that 'Cushing knows... parody is fatal and plays the part with straightforward sincerity, dignity and authority.'[9] The *Times* noted that Gilling's competent direction and concise script was 'well supported by Mr Peter Cushing as the ... sarcastic and autocratic authority figure.' However, the review found fault with Burke and Hare, 'this grotesque and evil pair lose reality in their moments of sardonic

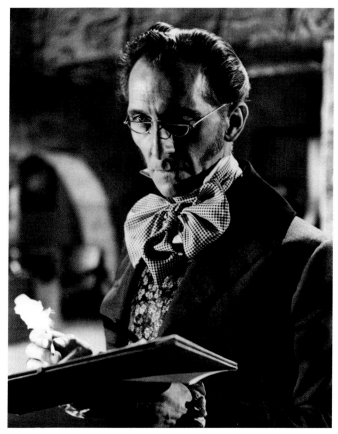

'You are an ogre, Doctor Knox. You have killed humanity.' Cushing as the Edinburgh anatomist who turns a blind eye to grave-robbing and murder in *The Flesh and the Fiends* (1959)

humour, and thus step out of character in a way the director should never have allowed.'[10]

Cushing's next role was Charles Norbury in William Fairchild's play *The Sound of Murder*, directed at the Aldwych Theatre by Fred Sadoff, beginning in August 1959. Norbury, a writer of children's stories, is a cruel tyrant whose despotic behaviour drives his wife Anne (Elizabeth Sellars) to contemplate murdering him. Terence Longdon played Anne's lover Peter Marriott with Patricia Jessell as Norbury's secretary Miss Forbes, who discovers Marriott's murder plot and blackmails him. David Jackson, who later appeared in the science fiction series *Blake's 7*, played PC Nash.

'It's Murder – But It's All Respectable' wrote W A Darlington in the *Daily Telegraph*. 'For years I have been misjudging the inhabitants of Surrey. I imagined behind those smug mock-Tudor facades or in those graciously-beamed cottages the living was gracious and the characters soft. But now I know better – or worse. Successful Charles Norbury... refuses his wife a divorce then within about ten minutes, she and her lover plan

The finger of suspicion points to Lucy Byrne (Virginia Maskell), Professor Sewell, Doctor Shole (Kenneth Griffith) and Bob Marriott (Tony Britton) in the Boulting Brothers' *Suspect* (1959)

to murder him. Neither turns a hair. Obviously violent death is all in a day's work for them. None of the people ... is given any humanity but as cogs in the machine they do their work well enough. Peter Cushing does ... very efficiently his appointed job of being more unpleasant in a shorter space of time than would be credible in an ordinary play. Elizabeth Sellars makes the bloodthirsty Mrs Norbury look like an advertisement for gracious living.'[11]

A review in the *Times* criticised the play's use of technology in the plot. 'It can do no harm to say that the initial breakdown of this plan for a "perfect murder" is brought about by a tape-recording machine. Obviously these modern instruments, which are so easily left on when they should be turned off, will sooner or later have to be banned from the stage, and the sooner the better. The telephone has served the dramatist well, but there can be no future for the mechanical eavesdropper.' The review approved of several ingenious surprises along the way, however, and while 'the moderately clever will anticipate what the penultimate surprise will be ... they will in all probability miss the final turn of the screw and may even be morally aghast at its nature.' Nevertheless, the reviewer found the play 'skilfully directed and no less skilfully acted. Mr Peter Cushing succeeds in making a distinguished writer in the Beatrix Potter vein so odious in his vindictive sadism that he almost deserves to be shot in cold blood.'[12] The play was popular, and ran until February 1960.

In December, however, Cushing started work on *Suspect* for the Boulting Brothers, and after one particularly hair-raising dash from the studios to the stage door decided that it was not sensible to appear on stage while filming. He took advantage of a get-

out clause in his contract and was replaced in the role of Norbury by Michael Goodliffe, who had appeared in *The End of the Affair*.

In the summer, the Cushings had moved house as the lease on their flat in Airlie Gardens expired. They opted to stay in Notting Hill and found a property in Hillsleigh Road, which they had converted to provide a studio with a large window for painting. Reporter Vivien Hislop had a regular feature in the *Evening News*, in which she visited celebrities' homes, commenting on their décor and illustrated her article with a pen-and-ink picture. Hislop visited Peter and Helen at Hillsleigh Road house for a piece entitled 'So *this* is Frankenstein's Real Castle'.

'From actor Peter Cushing, that master of spine-chilling suspense on stage, TV and films, came an invitation ... to see his new home, an old house high on Campden Hill. I found a yellow front door in a whitewashed gable end, halfway up a charming street so steep and narrow it could have been in the depths of the country. Peter's wife, actress Helen Beck, welcomed me in and told me about their "find". It was once a coach-house, then an artist's studio, and it is only a stone's throw away from the two rooms which she and Peter had shared for the past 15 years. First they had to have the builders in. They "imported" five local workmen from Whitstable (where they have a white clapboard house on the beach) and installed them in the attic for ten weeks. "They had wonderful fry-ups at night" says Helen. All the decorating ideas have been hers, except the tiny hall which was planned round Peter's choice of wallpaper – a deep pink pattern of harlequins. The floor is tiled in big black and white squares and the size of the room doubled by a huge old mirror of carved wood and brass. Through the open hall door there is a view of the living room with the spacious north-lit studio beyond.

'All the rooms have Helen's feminine touch. In the living room it is a soft crushed raspberry coloured carpet, pink and white striped wallpaper and graceful regency and early Victorian furniture. Helen loves collecting. Most of her furniture she has bought for a song from a favourite antique dealer in Whitstable. She has a few heirlooms too. One is her great-grandfather's bell-pull, an elaborately beaded affair which she hung for fun near the fireplace.

'The studio is Peter's domain. For an actor who has made a name scaring people out of their wits, Peter is a surprise. He is a quiet, gentle man who lives in a world of his own, an artist and a dreamer whose passion is not the study of murder but model-making. A long glass-fronted showcase holds some of the hundreds of model soldiers he has made or collected since he was a boy. He builds model planes too. They hang overhead suspended from lengths of fishing-line, so high that he keeps an aluminium ladder handy to reach them. Nearest to the roof was a big bomber. "I often take pot shots at it with a model gun" Peter confided. Next we inspected his shipping – model docks, cranes, tugs and liners set out on a sheet of blue plastic. A pair of binoculars was thrust into my hand – upside down for an 'aerial' view. The Cushings have Sir William Russell Flint as a friend and neighbour and somehow Peter finds time to paint in water-colour too.'[13]

On Boxing Day, 26th December 1959, Cushing began work on the thriller *Suspect,* directed by Roy and John Boulting. The Boulting brothers were responsible for such popular British films as *Brighton Rock, The Magic Box* and *Lucky Jim,* and had recently turned to satire with *I'm All Right Jack* starring Peter Sellers. Later in the 1960s they became directors of British Lion Films.

On completion of their latest movie the brothers found that the studio space was still theirs for three weeks. A £1000 wager was made between them that they couldn't complete a film in three weeks, but they did, and *Suspect* was the result. 'It really was one of the quickest pictures I appeared in,' Cushing remarked, 'but it stands to this day as a lesson that such budgets and tight shooting schedules can sometimes work.'[14] The end result is sound but as limited in its setting as a television play of the time would have been. Apparently the strain of working on *Suspect* as well as the *Sound of Murder* in the West End took its toll. Co-star Ian Bannen recalled Cushing repeatedly forgetting his lines on the first day of filming.

For his role as Professor Sewell, Cushing is playing an older man, with a moustache and a severe grey wig. Sewell is a biologist who has developed a cure for bubonic plague but is not allowed to publish his findings for fear of terrorism. Early in the film there is a lengthy exchange on the subject of nationalism with Raymond Huntley (his co-star from *The Mummy*) as the bluff Sir George Gatling, the Minister of Defence. 'You tell me it'd be treason to publish my work because some lunatic might use it to kill Englishmen,' says Sewell. 'It could save half a million lives outside this country, then I say it'd be treason to those half million if I don't!" Like Huntley and Cushing's scenes in *The Mummy,* these exchanges were filmed in lengthy continuous takes, a money-saving device only expedient with the most reliable of actors.

While the settings and the script remain relentlessly grey, *Suspect* relies on its performances to make up for its shortcomings. Sewell is a somewhat flamboyant character with his bow tie and watch-chain, and in

emphasising his odd manner it seems that Cushing is trying his best to give a bit of colour to the part. Thorley Walters is good value as a flustered police inspector and Ian Bannen plays an embittered amputee who manoeuvres young scientist Tony Britton into unknowing espionage. The treasured Spike Milligan, who was still working on *The Goon Show* on radio, provides the comic relief as an Irish janitor and has several scenes with Cushing. Also in the cast were Donald Pleasence, Geoffrey Bayldon, Sam Kydd and Anthony Booth, all of whom would work with Cushing again.

At the beginning of 1960, Cushing was about to start work on Hammer's *The Brides of Dracula* and was scheduled to join the BBC's new production of *Cyrano De Bergerac* shortly afterwards. Then he learned that there was, finally, to be a BBC production of *Journey's End* and wrote to Michael Barry on 10th January. 'I don't know if the rights are now available, whereas most actors' ambition is to play Hamlet, mine has always been to play "Stanhope"! I do realise of course that he is a much younger man than me, although life on the Western Front has aged him prematurely beyond his years. However, I would be very happy to play Osbourne, if the march of time has left its mark too much on me! The biggest fly in the ointment is the question of when you are to transmit this production. As you know, I will be filming up to the point where I begin rehearsing for *Cyrano,* so if it is possible to find a date for *Journey's End* fairly soon after April 10th, I would hold myself available. If I miss this opportunity, it will not come again for the next decade!' He concluded, 'Helen and I are so looking forward to your coming for a meal at our new house as soon as we have a little more free time.'

Despite Cushing's offer to hold himself available, his timing was a little adrift. *Cyrano De Bergerac* proved beyond the BBC's means once again, and the drama department no longer had the luxury of altering transmission slots to accommodate their stars. Michael Barry wrote sadly to Cushing on 14th January: 'No doubt because of your work at the studios you had not heard about *Cyrano,* although I had made sure the word was sent from here as soon as I was given a decision at the end of last week. For three weeks we had been battling with the cost of mounting *Cyrano.* Not until we had striven to solve the problem from every angle did I have to accept the fact that we could not produce. I know this will be a bitter disappointment to you. These financial matters – much as they can affect us all – should not concern you especially when working. I wish I could, in the next breath, come back with *Journey's End,* but it must be done between Monkhouse's *The Conquering Hero* on 28th February and *The Fanatics* on 13th March. I cannot postpone without losing the chance of linking the trilogy of plays together. Sorry, Peter.'

Chapter Fifteen

Swashing His Buckle

After the runaway success of *Dracula* in 1958, the sequel was inevitable. For reasons that remain unclear, Anthony Hinds requested a script that did not rely on the participation of Christopher Lee. Early in 1959 Jimmy Sangster presented *Disciple of Dracula*, featuring a vampire called Baron Meinster. The Baron preyed on the female attendees of a girl's school until he was confronted by the hero, Latour, who summoned Dracula to do away with his disciple. *The Hound of the Baskervilles'* screenwriter Peter Bryan then rewrote the script, and changed the title to *The Brides of Dracula*. Bryan ousted Latour and brought in Doctor Van Helsing, who destroyed Meinster with a swarm of killer bats summoned by an appeal to the powers of darkness to 'do justice to their code'.

It was decided that if Peter Cushing reprised his role as Van Helsing it would provide the necessary continuity in the series. However, Cushing was reportedly unimpressed with the rewritten script. Hinds engaged playwright Edward Percy (whose stage work, including *The Shop at Sly Corner*, Cushing admired)

to add a final polish and shortly before the film went into the studio on 26th January 1960, Hinds himself did further work on the script.

The resulting screenplay is one of Hammer's most lyrical and witty, and Terence Fisher excels himself in creating a richly-coloured world in which an iconic hero takes on a monster – the quintessence of fairy-tale.

The story sees Van Helsing protecting the young schoolteacher Marianne Danielle (Yvonne Monlaur) from the unholy attentions of the vampire Baron Meinster (David Peel). While Van Helsing's bursts of swashbuckling activity were more or less limited to the last reel of *Dracula*, here the whole film is a showcase for Cushing's heroic athleticism. There are a couple of terrific fight sequences – including a deft bit of 'gun-slinging' as he slides a cross along a table to block the vampire's escape, and he later fights off a monstrous bat with his vampire hunter's bag. At the finale, Van Helsing leaps onto the sails of a burning windmill, bringing the mill's shadow into the shape of a cross that destroys the vampire. For that feat, at least, Cushing stood aside for a stunt double.

As Marianne is discovered unconscious in the forest, Cushing emerges from a coach in his opera coat and high-crowned hat, immediately handsome, reassuring and determined. He makes much of little details like breaking open a phial of smelling-salts and gets the best opening lines Hammer had to offer. 'You've been badly frightened, haven't you? But there's nothing to be afraid of now. I'm a doctor. Doctor Van Helsing...' The audience are in need of an ally by this point. In the prologue, Marianne discovers Baron Meinster chained up in his Chateau, apparently by his jealous and cruel mother, the Baroness. Marianne frees the handsome aristocrat, whereupon he immediately kills his mother and escapes into the night. In the

Van Helsing discovers the unconscious form of student teacher Marianne Danielle (Yvonne Monlaur). Location filming in Black Park for *The Brides of Dracula* (1960)

Baron, Terence Fisher created a powerful foe whose appearance switches suddenly from a blonde-haired, Wildean decadent to a red-eyed monster trumpeting with fury. A huge close-up of the Baron, fangs bared, hissing and spitting like a cat cuts to a shot of his grimly determined opponent. For all Christopher Lee's success in *Dracula*, and heretical as it may sound, his presence is not really missed here.

Van Helsing tells the troubled local priest (Fred Johnson) that he is studying a strange sickness 'partly physical, partly spiritual' – the cult of the undead. Cushing has to expound the vampire lore all over again, but in this film he does so while unpacking a suitcase – prop business is used to great effect. He makes the fantastic details of Vampires And How to Kill Them seem all the more believable because, as he is talking, he is putting a bundle of shirts into a wardrobe.

In the climax at the Baron's windmill hide-out, the vampire hunter is bitten by the vampire. His strength failing, Van Helsing hauls himself to a brazier and places a branding-iron into the coals. He sears the bite with the iron and throws holy water on the burn which miraculously heals. Camera operator Len Harris recalled how Cushing put a real iron in the fire then, out of shot, swapped it for a wooden prop which he brought to his neck. 'The strength of the shot is in Peter Cushing's acting, because when he puts the poker on his neck you really feel it!'

'The cast is too good for the material'[1] snorted the *Times* review, but it would take some material to match this cast. Second billing goes to Martita Hunt as the imperious Baroness, who has sheltered and protected her son, procuring victims for him. Her formidably chiselled exterior hides an unbearable loneliness, and Hunt's performance is almost operatic in its grandeur. In return for her indulgence, the (literally) spoiled boy takes everything from his mother, reducing her to a white-faced shadow who shyly hides her vampire fangs from Van Helsing in a gesture of weirdly ambiguous sexuality. The *New York Herald Tribune* noticed 'dabs of Freud and Tennessee Williams.'[2] Hunt was best known for her role as Miss Havisham in David Lean's 1946 film of *Great Expectations*, a role which informs the Baroness' wistful recollections of the 'gay times, balls, dinners … *life*' that once filled the Chateau Meinster.

Cushing shares a powerful scene with Hunt and matches her note for note. On the trail of the vampire, Van Helsing arrives at the chateau. As he explores, the figure of the Baroness creeps into view in the background.

'Who is it that is not afraid?' she asks.

'Only God has no fear,' Van Helsing replies.

'There's no release from this life which isn't life... or death,' the Baroness wails. 'And I know I shall have to do whatever hideous thing he asks me to!'

With a red hot iron, Van Helsing cauterises the bite from Baron Meinster in *The Brides of Dracula* (1960)

Van Helsing brings peace to the Baroness in the only way he can, with a stake through the heart – and with little more than an intake of breath to steel himself, Cushing conveys to the audience the horror of his work. As cock-crow signals daybreak, Van Helsing takes up a stake and a mallet. Then, with a single downward stoke, in an attitude like a Pre-Raphaelite knight, he hammers in the stake. As the blood seeps out, Fisher uses favourite cinematic trick – suddenly, momentarily, he fills the screen with scarlet – a close-up of a red curtain which Van Helsing pulls down to lay over the dead Baroness.

This is the first of Fisher's horror films to have a number of good roles for women. As well as Yvonne Monlaur as Marianne and Andrée Melly as the doll-faced student teacher Gina, Freda Jackson plays Greta, the Baron's old nurse, whose hysterical, triumphant cackles in the prologue set the appropriate key for the events that follow. Later, in the graveyard, a bedraggled Greta hugs the ground as she coaxes the vampire girl out of her coffin. 'The Master's waiting for you...' she coos, 'come on my precious, my little love...' as a white hand claws its way out of the ground. Just as precious is Cushing's ever-widening stare of horror as the coffin lid opens. This is another of Fisher's definitive sequences, a scrap of nightmare committed to film.

Captain Judd makes trouble for veteran pilot Captain Gort (Bernard Lee), while Robinson (Marne Maitland) looks on in *Cone of Silence* (1960)

Other cherishable members of the cast include Miles Malleson as the hypochondriac Doctor Tobler, whom Fisher uses to contrast with the horror of the Baroness's death. (The Doctor briefly becomes a kind of surrogate Watson to Van Helsing's Holmes.) Henry Oscar, Cushing's old ENSA boss, makes something marvellous of the pompous schoolmaster Herr Lang, accompanied by Mona Washbourne in full flutter as his wife. While Lang huffs and puffs, Cushing remains perfectly still – then deftly presents a visiting card from a silver case. Immediately, Lang is all smiles. 'Leiden University?' he coos, 'How could I be expected to recognise a doctor of philosophy, a doctor of theology, a professor of metaphysics by the cut of his trousers?'

Malcolm Williamson provided the score, favouring a reedy organ theme for the suspense sequences at the chateau and the graveyard which adds a faintly ecclesiastical atmosphere to these scenes. To match this, the film is presented in the stained-glass window colours of Jack Asher's luminous photography, never finer than here. The entrance of Chateau Meinster was filmed at Oakley Court, the Victorian Gothic mansion next to Bray Studios, which appeared briefly in *The Curse of Frankenstein* and *The Mummy*. Over the years the house would appear in almost as many horror films as Peter Cushing.

Once again, however, Terence Fisher was without honour in his own country. The *Observer* called the film 'ludicrous monstrosity following a spoor of

Technicolor blood, which lead farther and farther away from the force, pity and near dignity of Bram Stoker's novel.'[3]

This was Cushing's last Hammer horror for some time. He made a conscious effort to make different kinds of films, sensing that he was becoming typecast, and that critics were not responding well to what he knew was work of some quality, not only from him but from all the Hammer personnel.

He would continue to make films for Hammer, but when *The Brides of Dracula* completed filming on 18th March 1960, Cushing would not make another film with a fantasy horror subject for three-and-a-half years.

Cushing's next production, the Bryanston/British Lion film *Cone of Silence*, brought him back down to earth even though it concerned a group of aircraft pilots. The film captures a charming late-fifties *milieu* of Morris Minors, tea bars and aerodromes and the cast includes a host of familiar faces including George Sanders, Bernard Lee, Noel Willman, André Morell and Marne Maitland with Cushing's good friend Gordon Jackson as another pilot. The film was shot in March and April, directed by Charles Frend, who was an editor for Hitchcock and directed such films as *The Magnet* and *The Cruel Sea*.

The film's title plays on a double meaning. The 'cone of silence' refers to an area of radar black-out which pilots must find while flying 'blind' and also decribes the cover-up of a potentially dangerous aeroplane. In America, the film was given the rather more mundane title of *Trouble in the Sky*.

Bernard Lee plays the veteran flyer Captain Gort, who crashes on one of the initial flights of a new plane, the *Phoenix*, designed by Nigel Pickering (an icy Noel Willman). Pickering knows that his career will be finished if the safety of the *Phoenix* is called into question, so he has deliberately been witholding information about a defect in the take-off equipment.

Cushing plays Flight Captain Clive Judd, an urbane and self-serving customer who, while not exactly the villain of the piece, has all the classic traits of a school sneak. Judd charms stewardess Joyce Mitchell (Delphi Lawrence) to get inside information about a romance between Captain Hugh Dallas (Michael Craig) who is investigating the *Phoenix* case and Gort's daughter Charlotte. 'Old Judd's a great organiser but he's not exactly my idea of a gay evening out,' says Dallas.

There is a compelling take-off scene in the *Phoenix*, with Cushing in the full pilot's rig and headphones – the danger that the plane could suddenly go out of control makes the subsequent landing equally heart-stopping. Satisfyingly, Judd gets his come-uppance in the end. Gort was supposed to have caught a piece of hedge in the wheels of his plane at Calcutta, but it transpires that it was Judd's take-off which clipped the hedge.

The film has several thrilling sequences, and the black-and-white photography adds a documentary feel to the whole. Producer Aubrey Baring, of the Baring's banking family served in a similar capacity on *The Abominable Snowman*.

On 23rd May 1960 director Terence Fisher began work on *Sword of Sherwood Forest*, Hammer's Megascope adaptation of the television series *The Adventures of Robin Hood*. The show was one of the first great successes of independent television, making a star of actor Richard Greene in the title role. (Greene acted as co-producer for the Hammer film.) Cushing was cast as the villainous Sheriff of Nottingham, his fee, in second billing, was £3,500. On television, the Sheriff had been played by Alan Wheatley, and Wheatley and Cushing shared many similarities in their careers – Wheatley had previously played Sherlock Holmes and Mr Darcy for the BBC. Terence Fisher had directed several episodes of the TV series so obviously knew the style, but the film is a disappointment. The locations, at County Wicklow in Ireland, are flat and uninteresting, the storyline is convoluted and the dialogue is pallid. Even in widescreen, several elaborate action sequences fail to create any excitement.

Additionally, there is a fundamental problem with the Sheriff. Despite one scene where he offers a man a free pardon and then shoots him, he doesn't do anything particularly wicked. It seems as if Fisher and Cushing are trying very hard to make the Sheriff a three-dimensional human being, in a film where a thoroughgoing villain might have served their purpose better. Certainly Cushing looks every inch the part, immaculate in silver beard and flowing black wig, with no expense spared on his costumes, designed by John McCorry. In almost every scene the Sheriff is wearing a different ensemble in velvet and leather. At home, he wears a sort of flock-wallpaper dressing-gown affair, and he turns up in a black-and-red number with chains for the assizes.

Cushing gives a relaxed and enjoyable performance, particularly in the scenes with Sarah Branch as Maid Marion, whom he always calls 'Madam'. All the familiar gestures are present and correct – he bites his thumb in contemplation and holds his finger aloft

to emphasise that Robin Hood is 'a *very* dangerous criminal'. The real villain of the piece, in a plot to kill the Archbishop of Canterbury, is the Earl of Newark, played at a simmer by Richard Pasco. His henchman is the effete Lord Melton, played by a mincing Oliver Reed with an ill-advised 'snide' accent which is unfortunately comic rather than menacing.

When Robin and Little John seek sanctuary in a priory, the prioress is revealed to be Newark's cousin and part of the plot. The audience should have had seen through her from the outset, however, because she's wearing an awful lot of lipstick for a nun.

As the finale approaches, Newark all for killing off the outlaws but the Sheriff cannot bring himself to murder in cold blood. In a sudden, startling turn, Melton stabs the Sheriff in the back and kills him. It's a good shock, but denies Cushing the traditional last-reel swordfight between Robin and the Sheriff, or indeed, as the story seems to suggest, some kind of reconciliation.

Filming for *Sword of Sherwood Forest* concluded on 8th July and the film was released for the Christmas holidays on 26th December 1960. *Kinematograph Weekly* correctly called it 'jolly, disarmingly naïve adventure comedy melodrama'[4] while in America, *Variety* stated rather baldly that Cushing 'plays the Sheriff the way the Sheriff should be played.'[5]

Cushing discusses the finer points of villainy with director Terence Fisher on location in County Wicklow for *Sword of Sherwood Forest* (1960)

Later in the summer of 1960, Cushing joined the cast of *The Hellfire Club* for Regal Films, directed by Robert Baker and Monty Berman who had made *The Flesh and the Fiends*. The British cast was headed by Peter Arne and Adrienne Corri, with Australian Keith Michell – who was brought to England by Olivier in 1948 – making an impressive starring début as the brawny hero. There is indispensable support from the likes of Bill Owen, David Lodge and Francis Matthews, with Cushing given rightly-earned 'Guest Star' status in the credits. The script was by Jimmy Sangster and Leon Griffiths based on Sangster's original storyline.

While all concerned were doubtless keen to find some potential scares in the legendary coven of debauched noblemen that was the Georgian Hellfire Club, there's more sin in the first five minutes of *The Hound of the Baskervilles* than in the whole of this film. Jason Caldwell (Michell) the heir to Netherden Hall, has been ousted from his country seat by his wicked cousin Thomas (Arne) who carries on the rituals of the Hellfire Club. Jason, who has grown up in a travelling circus, uses his old friends to help him reclaim his title, despite Thomas' associates in the club – 'some of the most influential men in the British government.'

When Lord Netherden dies in 1766, Jason cannot his prove his claim to the estate other than with a locket that belonged to his mother. He visits the family lawyer Mr Merryweather (Cushing) who initially gives him short shrift.

Cushing looks handsome in his beard

Cushing gave a splendidly enjoyable turn as the canny lawyer Merryweather in *The Hellfire Club* (1961)

and black wig, making great play of his snuff-taking and Latin quotations. Merryweather is a wily bird but an endearing ally, like a rather more restrained version of Cushing's Doctor Who. 'Look at you,' says Merryweather, assessing the future Lord Netherden. 'You're dressed like a country clod-hopper! Documents? Nothing! Just some wild story and a locket. Call that proof? I call it impertinence, sir!'

Jason vows to prove his case, and Merryweather, recognising in Jason his 'mother's spirit and his father's temper' agrees to help. The chief piece of evidence in Jason's claim is a letter at Netherden which proves his identity.

Merryweather has a plan. 'If one was dishonest, which of course one is not, one could steal the letter ...'

'And what if one was caught?' asks Jason.

'Then one would need a very good lawyer, my Lord!'

Later, Cushing enjoys himself in a courtroom sequence with Miles Malleson as a hanging judge. Merryweather seems to lose the case, and Jason is sent to Newgate to await execution, but this is all part of the lawyer's plan to keep the young Earl out of danger. Merryweather's trump card is to bring in his friend William Pitt, the Earl of Chatham, who has consented to raise the matter of Jason's title in parliament.

There's nothing wrong with the film – it's another standard British swashbuckler of the time – but there's something magical in Cushing's handful of scenes that makes the rest seem dull when he's not about.

The *New York Herald Tribune* found the film 'nothing more than a routine derring-do melodrama. What went on in those Hellfire caves would have made Fanny Hill blush. The film simply plays up the club as a background ... but the orgies are strictly for Grandma!'[6] (The debauchery in the commonly-seen print is tepid, but there was a spiced-up version of the film, with bosoms bared, produced for Europe.)

The location used for Netherden Hall was Moor Park Golf Club, which would be seen again in *The Vampire Lovers*.

In some filmographies, Cushing listed a German/ British co-production of 1960 called *Im Namen des Teufels* (*The Devil's Agent*). Peter Van Eyck, Christopher Lee and Billie Whitelaw starred in the film and the director was John Paddy Carstairs, who as a journalist had commented so favourably on Cushing's performance in *Beau Brummell* for the BBC. However, Cushing does not appear in the finished film. Christopher Lee maintains that he did not meet Cushing when he made the film, neither did Jeremy Bulloch, who played Peter Van Eyck's son. It has been suggested that Cushing's scenes were deleted, which seems unlikely given how prominent a star he was, so perhaps his role was recast at a very late stage. More than fifty years on, the mystery endures.

Mr Evan Wrack presents the case for the prosecution in Michael Anderson's *The Naked Edge* (1960)

In *The Naked Edge*, however, Cushing *can* be seen, again as a lawyer. The film was directed by Michael Anderson at the end of 1960 with Gary Cooper and Deborah Kerr. It was Cooper's last film – he died before it was released but it gave Cushing a chance to share a scene with the Hollywood legend.

Michael Anderson had directed popular successes *The Dam Busters* and *Around the World in Eighty Days* and significantly, the 1955 film of *Nineteen Eighty-Four* in which American actor Edmond O'Brien took Cushing's role of Winston Smith. In *The Naked Edge*, Anderson's Hitchcock-influenced direction mixes a gritty scenes shot in a tenement block with a psychedelic riot of negative shots, shots through water and diagonal shots. The film was based on Max Ehrlich's novel *Last Train to Babylon,* adapted by Joseph Stefano, who came to the film riding high on the success of his screenplay for *Psycho.*

Donald Heath (Ray McAnally) is on trial for the murder of a co-worker and the theft of £60,000. George Radcliffe (Gary Cooper) is Heath's employer, on whose testimony Heath is ultimately convicted. Some years later, an old blackmail threat comes to light, implicating Radcliffe in the murder and the theft. Radcliffe's wife (Deborah Kerr) begins to suspect her husband and contacts the blackmailer, but in doing so places her own life in grave danger...

Cushing plays Evan Wrack, prosecuting counsel in Heath's trial, shot for the most part in close-up and looking splendid. Wrack is flamboyant of gesture and pedantic of speech, smugly anticipating victory in an open-and-shut case. Shifting his robe on his shoulders when going in for the kill, Cushing deliberately removes his glasses, then uses them as a prop to enunciate his speech for the prosecution. 'Mr Heath, after observing this inhuman, *immoral* effort you are making to save your own neck, I doubt there remains in this court one person who can continue to believe in your protested innocence!'

The film again is a showcase for some excellent characters, notably Wilfrid Lawson (from Cushing's play *The Road*), Hermione Gingold as a blousy gossip and Sandor Eles (who would appear with Cushing in *The Evil of Frankenstein*) as her fey playwright boyfriend. Cushing enjoyed a brief reunion with Deborah Kerr, his co-star from *The End of the Affair*, who made *The Naked Edge* before starting work on the supernatural chiller *The Innocents* in February 1961.

In April, Cushing was back at Bray for the shooting of Hammer's *Cash on Demand*, directed by Quentin Lawrence. This short black-and-white film, which began shooting on 4th April 1961, was based on an ITV play by Jacques Gillies called *The Gold Inside*, also directed by Lawrence, which had been broadcast on 24th September 1960.

Crisply photographed on a handful of tiny sets in a fortnight, the film is no little achievement and shows just what the Hammer personnel were capable of. It features two fascinating central performances from Cushing and his former 'Watson' André Morell (who had appeared in the TV version) in a Pinteresque story of deception and emotional manipulation.

Cushing plays Harry Fordyce, manager of the City and Colonial Bank, Haversham Branch, a petty, vindictive, joyless character who holds the threat of dismissal over his staff because it is practically the only power he has. On the day before Christmas Eve, Fordyce is visited by a man who calls himself Colonel Gore-Hepburn, an inspector from the bank's insurance agency. But Gore-Hepburn, played by Morell at his foxiest, is really a confidence trickster of the most cunning kind.

We first see Cushing looking like black beetle in his bowler hat and steel-rimmed spectacles. He fastidiously cleans a smear off the bank's brass name-plate, and berates his staff for keeping a rusty pen on the counter ('This isn't a post office, you know!') Cushing clearly enjoys playing such a small monster and Morell seems to like playing the brute, mixing avuncular charm with effortless cruelty, although cameraman Len Harris pointed out that the leads could have swapped roles and the piece would still have worked.

By a faked telephone call, Gore-Hepburn makes Fordyce believe that his wife and son are being held hostage. As Morell elaborates with grisly details, there is more than a touch of O'Brien from *Nineteen Eighty-Four*. 'There are two men at your house,' he explains. 'At this moment your wife has an electrode attached to each side of her head. If you fail to co-operate with us in any way whatever they will pass a charge through the circuit. It is extremely painful and I'm afraid the effects of it are permanent. She would never recover her wits.'

'What is it you want?' asks bank manager Fordyce. 'Just some *money...*' replies crooked Colonel Gore-Hepburn (André Morell) in Hammer's modest masterpiece *Cash on Demand* (1961)

Lawrence uses several telling close-ups of Fordyce's appalled, panic-stricken face. 'What is it you want?' he bleats. Gore-Hepburn smiles. 'Just some *money...*'

It is difficult enough to believe that Fordyce has a home life, never mind a wife and child but he is fiercely devoted to them. 'If anything happens to my family, I'll kill you, I swear I will...' he spits.

Gore-Hepburn shows Fordyce how he intends to steal the money – a plot that will involve Fordyce's collaboration in a criminal act.

When, after the suspenseful robbery, Gore-Hepburn has escaped with the loot, the chief clerk, Pearson (Richard Vernon), makes Fordyce admit that he has helped to rob his own bank. In pleading for Pearson's support, Fordyce is reduced to a grizzling wreck – with his hands clenched together in despair. When the police arrive, the staff rally round Fordyce, who at the end of the experience is changed for the better – 'What is the usual sentence?' he asks, in sincere humility, 'For completely failing in my duty towards my staff?' In a film that echoes *A Christmas Carol* and *It's A Wonderful Life*, we discover that there was gold inside Fordyce all along.

Cushing is strong in the role but his performance is more theatrical than usual. Maybe this was because of the tight filming schedule, or perhaps because Fordyce's only characteristic is his meanness, but there are occasions, particularly at the beginning when the character seems over-mannered and rather comically prim. Cushing is playing a little older than his age, but he looks considerably older here, in black-and-white, than he would in colour in *Frankenstein Created Woman* five years later.

Columbia released *Cash on Demand* in America on 20th December 1961, with screenings in New York as late as April. In Britain the film was not released for another two years, although it was received on release as a well-crafted, unpretentious second-feature.

Kinematograph Weekly said 'the film creates considerable tension and excitement without any violent action and without straying at all from the bank itself ... a credit to the script, direction and sound acting by all the cast, especially Peter Cushing as the tortured bank manager and André Morell as the suave robber.'[7]

In his 1997 book *An Autobiography of British Cinema*, critic Brian McFarlane described *Cash on Demand* as 'possibly the best "B" film ever made in Britain.'

Fury At Smugglers' Bay was Cushing's next project, originally titled *The Wreckers*, reuniting him with director John Gilling for a rather run-of-the-mill British swashbuckler filmed on location at Fishguard in Wales, doubling for nineteenth-century Cornwall. Cushing gets top billing as Squire Trevenyan in buckled boots, tricorne hat and a scraped-back wig with a pigtail. His character is something of a martinet, and in the early scenes there seems little logic for his severe behaviour towards his son Chris, played by John Fraser. It eventually transpires that Chris is illegitimate – but Trevenyan has kept this secret from his son. A pirate called Black John (Bernard Lee) was a former groom of Trevenyan's, and knows the secret. The pirate blackmails his former employer, who as justice of the peace and chief arbiter of law in the county is able to turn a blind eye to Black John's smuggling activities.

Cushing gets one good scene with Bernard Lee when the old scoundrel reveals the Squire's wife's indiscretion. 'You hate it, don't ya?' leers Black John. 'It's twisting you, like a knife in the guts.' (Lee's fruity performance has more than a touch of Robert Newton's Long John Silver, from Disney's 1950 version of *Treasure Island*.) Cushing simmers with fury, then snaps and smacks Black John with his horsewhip. Unfortunately, there's no humour in Trevenyan and Cushing's expressions throughout are stiff and unengaging, so different from the sprightly and beguiling Mr Merryweather.

As Cushing pointed out, the film was a British Western. 'The scenario contained all the traditional ingredients: lots of shootin', the inevitable brawl in the saloon, a *High Noon* confrontation between duellists using swords instead of six-shooters and the cavalry charging to the rescue in the nick of time. I had the grumpy-old-dad-who-turns-up-trumps-in-the-end Lee J Cobb part.'[8]

There are notable appearances by George Coulouris as an 'honest' smuggler and William Franklyn as a highwayman known only as 'The Captain'. (The role was intended for Christopher Lee, but he went to France to make *The Hands of Orlac*.) Miles Malleson appears as the Duke of Avon and adds to his memorably funny roster of screen hypochondriacs. On the debit side there are some poorly-choreographed fights and possibly the worst-day-for-night footage ever committed to film. Perhaps the poorest element of the film is the flat script, which allows little in the way of character development for anyone.

At the finale, everybody ends up in Smugglers' Bay for a shoot-out between the smugglers and soldiers. The Captain kills Black John, but not before Trevenyan is shot defending his son. Cushing executes a neat

Cushing as Squire Trevenyan in *Fury at Smugglers' Bay* (1961)

turn as he falls and makes a meal of a rather protracted death-scene in which he manages to give a parting glance to each of the assembled company before rolling his eyes aloft. 'You rode your horse very well, dear fellow,' Cushing recalled Christopher Lee telling him after a television screening of *Fury At Smugglers' Bay*, 'and the expression on your face when you died was exactly the same as when you were told what your salary for the film was going to be.'[9]

John Fraser warmly recalls Cushing's enjoyment of the film and his enthusiasm for the swordfights and horseback chases. 'Peter was the perfect gentleman ... He told me his mother brought him up almost as a girl, and it's a miracle he didn't grow up gay – which of course he didn't – but having missed out a bit on a boys' childhood, his passion was for toy soldiers and boys' games. Every Saturday he used to walk from his home in Holland Park to Hamley's in Regent Street to buy more model soldiers. He had a whole battlefield laid out in his attic. He was a darling man!'[10]

'Even your cloth can't sanctify the mark of the hangman's rope.' Captain Collier (Patrick Allen) feels Dr Blyss's collar in *Captain Clegg* (1961)

character. 'For a happier ending,' Cushing wrote as a postscript, 'which is always more popular, it would be nice if Dr Syn could find his wife.' Quite how Cushing's script relates to the finished film is not known, but it is certainly very different. The annotated typed draft was sold as part of his estate after his death and remains a tantalising 'what if?' in the canon.

Hammer's film gives Cushing the chance to get his teeth into two different characters – the whimsical Dr Blyss (something like Mr Merryweather) and Clegg, a strong and heroic figure who uses the profits from smuggling to help the poor. Cushing is equally good in both roles, and completely at home in the period.

We first see the Reverend Doctor Blyss lustily conducting his flock from the pulpit. We also see Oliver Reed as the Squire's son Harry, lusting after the Innkeeper's adopted daughter Imogene, played by Yvonne Romain. The Reverend gently chivvies his congregation, warning that 'war with France is more than just a possibility,' as the King's revenue men march in, led by Patrick Allen as Captain Collier. Collier has spent many years in pursuit of the notorious pirate Captain Clegg, who is buried in Blyss's churchyard. As the soldiers interrupt the service, Cushing immediately turns his mild steel on Collier. 'Would you be kind enough to remove your hat?'

There is a meeting of the smugglers to decide what to do with the contraband already in the village. Michael Ripper is excellent as Blyss's right-hand man Jeremiah Mipps the coffin maker, and Martin Benson makes a good job of the weasely innkeeper Rash. As Clegg enters, Cushing perfectly times the slam of the door behind him to punctuate his first line. Their plans, he says, will continue as usual.

The smugglers disguise themselves and their horses as the 'Romney Marsh Phantoms' to frighten the locals away from their nocturnal activities. The phantom riders are an unexpectedly chilling image, and the film features some of Hammer's finest day-for-night shooting, streets ahead of Smuggler's Bay.

Cushing effortlessly slips in and out of the benign expression of Doctor Blyss and cheekily makes Collier hold his stick and bible in a priceless bit of prop business. 'They are very devout here,' he explains later of his flock. 'They don't care to meddle with the forces of darkness!' When Clegg sends Collier off on

This portion of Cushing's career could just justifiably been called his 'smuggling period', because his next assignment after *Smugglers' Bay* continued the theme. On 25th September, he took the starring role in Hammer's *Captain Clegg*, directed by Peter Graham Scott. But while the former gave Cushing little to work with, the breadth of story and character in the Hammer film is remarkable.

Captain Clegg is a fast-paced and thrilling adventure film, featuring the expected high Hammer production values and an excellent cast. It was adapted by Anthony Hinds (again writing as John Elder) from Russell Thorndike's novel *Dr Syn*, which had been filmed in 1937 with George Arliss as the Dymchurch vicar who secretly practices smuggling on Romney Marsh. Walt Disney Pictures had secured the rights to the *Dr Syn* title for a film with Patrick McGoohan (not made until 1963) so Hammer's smuggler was given the alias of Doctor Blyss. In all other respects, including the name 'Captain Clegg', Thorndike's story was unchanged, and Cushing is very close in appearance to the character's description in the book.

Cushing clearly adored the chance to tackle the *Dr Syn* story, adding much to the film with his own research. Before filming, in July 1961, he had written a script of his own for a Dr Syn adventure. The story involves a search for Syn's wife, Charlotte and the pirate's old enemy Tappitt, another Thorndike a false trail, Cushing throws his head back in a wild, soundless laugh. Here, as throughout the film, Cushing is every inch the hero. A long black wig with a white streak emphasises the shape of his face and enables him to look both angelic and fierce.

When Harry is arrested as the smugglers' look-out, Clegg takes his phosphorescent friends out for a last job. They distract the excise men long enough to rescue the boy, and the wild ride concludes with an iconic shot of Cushing pulling off his skull-like mask.

Back at the church, with the revenue men's net tightening, Blyss conducts an impromptu marriage between Imogene – who is in fact his daughter – and Harry. Again, the details are everything – Cushing raises an eyebrow when he realises Mipps has used a curtain ring for a wedding ring. Cushing was coached in the wedding service by none less than the vicar of Bray himself.

As the young couple escape, Collier bursts in again, and tears off Blyss' collar to reveal the scars left when Clegg escaped the hangman's rope. Clegg give a final address to his people. 'No man can stand on the gallows without coming face-to-face with his soul. On that day, truly, the old Clegg died. What the new Clegg has done, you all know. When I first came here, I found you in wretchedness and poverty, deprived by harsh laws and heavy taxes of the simple comforts all men have a right to expect. I took upon

Cushing studies the marriage service with the Reverend Sidney Doran, watched by director Peter Graham Scott, during the filming of *Captain Clegg* (1961)

myself the task of changing all that at the expense of the Revenue. What I did, I did for the good of you all.'

Cushing finally gets the swing-on-the-chandelier finale that was denied him in *Dracula*. However, he is, in rapid succession, shot by Collier and then harpooned. The Captain dies heroically saving Mipps, who carries his fallen comrade to the grave that awaits him.

Variety made a good point about Hammer in general when praising the film. 'Pure escapism of course, but notable in that the Hammer imprimatur has come to certify solid values in all production departments, and there's no mystery why these films rate audience allegiance. The histrionics are generally convincing, especially Peter Cushing as the pirate-cum-vicar.'[11]

Director Peter Graham Scott remembered Cushing's considerable contribution to *Captain Clegg*.

'Peter Cushing was a very interesting man. I knew his work, but I had not met him before. He must have been getting on for 50 when we worked with him. He was a proper actor, he was a very good actor, and he knew that those films wouldn't have worked without that. Before we started, [producer] John Temple-Smith and I went and saw Peter. He showed us his soldiers in the attic, all laid out in the battle of Waterloo with Blucher arriving from the right and it was all tremendously interesting. We met Helen, whom he adored, there was no question about it, it was sheer *worship*. She was a lovely woman – I wouldn't have been, let's say, "down on the knee" about her, but there you are, *c'est la vie*.

'Peter said he liked the script, but there were several things he didn't like about it. He said that there wasn't any real characterisation for the Captain. We got a woman called Barbara Harper, an extremely good writer who'd done things for me on television, in on it, and we worked on that, but there was still a sticking point. We had built up the tension and Doctor Blyss was delivering his sermon in the pulpit. And I said, well, he can start the sermon and then we'll get the Navy to burst in, but Peter said "No, he *must* deliver the sermon." We'd got the tension going, and the speed going. He said "No, we must stop the film, and wait while he delivers the sermon." I said well, what are the Navy doing? They're just coming through the forest. He said "It'll just have to be a bigger forest."'

The director revealed that it was Cushing who wrote Clegg's climactic speech to his congregation.

'When we came to shoot it, Peter said "By the way, I've just jotted down a few lines for me to actually utter." So I thought, fine, I'll just let him start off with "My brethren..." and cut away. I didn't rehearse it, I just said "we'll do it". But he delivered this speech, which he'd written, about how Clegg had done all these things for them, on the basis of the smuggling. He delivered it *beautifully*. I thought Peter, you are a crafty old sod. It was the best speech in the film.'[12]

Chapter Sixteen

Abdication, Restoration

On 9th January 1962, Patricia Lewis wrote in the *Daily Express*: 'After a five-year reign as "The King of Horror" actor Peter Cushing plans to abdicate. But not without a courtly bow to the Draculas and Frankensteins who made him an international star. "I was sort of carried along with the cycle," explained this fast-talking greying man of most un-actorish habits, like living in Whitstable, drinking only orange juice and carrying a briefcase. "It was wonderful to work steadily on from one film to the next, but then a few weeks ago I realised that out of the 10 movies I had made for Hammer, six were "X" certificate. Though they made a spectacular impact on the box-office I don't want the public labelling me solely as 'that horror man'." He approaches every role with the same respect but "I have a tremendous eye on the takings" he says. "I don't mind being connected with an artistic success so long as it also takes money. I say to myself 'My ego may want me to play Hamlet, but will people pay to *see* me play Hamlet?' If I were offered two plays at the same time and one was *Macbeth* and the other was *Rookery Nook*, I'd do *Rookery Nook* because I believe it is more attractive for the general public." Cushing studies all his parts with the same attention that he says he would give to *Hamlet*. "But now I'd like to do a film comedy. It's time I got a new identity. Particularly as I have never been the monster in any one of those films."'[1]

The film comedy was, sadly, not forthcoming, and neither was anything else. In a 1965 interview, Cushing wrote of a 'terrible slump in the industry ... three years ago'[2] when he was out of work for 18 months. Cushing had achieved worldwide success but, unbelievably, was unable to find work at home.

On 20th February 1962, Angela Hepburn wrote to the BBC to enquire about the possibility of Cushing appearing on the radio programmes *Frankly Speaking*, *Woman's Hour* and *Let's Find Out*. 'For some time he has wanted to appear on the programmes.' Nothing came of the suggestions immediately, and there was no more enthusiasm from Norman Rutherford, Acting Head of Drama, when Cushing wrote on 21st April to suggest a possible role in a play. 'It is getting on for four years since my last!' he wrote, and suggested the plays *Charles the King* by Maurice Colbourne and

J B Priestley's *They Came To A City* (which he had played at the 'Q'). As was common before, Cushing asked for a list of the forthcoming plays for summer and the autumn, to see if there were any parts he knew and would like to play.

'I am not particularly excited, nor were my council, by the suggestions you have made,' replied Rutherford. 'We have gone a considerable way now in the development of writing for television. The majority of work lies with new writing, so a list of plays would be fruitless as they would mean nothing to you.' Rutherford's reply reflects the changing times at the BBC. New plays were the future of television drama, consequently 'stage' plays and 'stage' actors like Cushing were less and less in demand. There could too have been a touch of prejudice at Cushing's success in what some at the BBC must have regarded as hopelessly low-brow entertainment. This exile, if such it was, did not last long however. There was still a need for theatre-trained actors and the following year they were glad to welcome him back to the fold to play Cassius in *Julius Caesar*.

Cushing only made one film in 1962, *The Man Who Finally Died*. In this, he was again working with director Quentin Lawrence although there is less tension in this rambling tale of middle-European intrigue than in the concentrated atmosphere of their last film together, *Cash on Demand*.

The Man Who Finally Died was based on a 1959 ITV serial by Lewis Greifer, which originally starred Richard Pasco. For the film, Pasco's role was taken by Stanley Baker, with strong support from Mai Zetterling, Eric Portman and Niall McGinnis.

Joe Newman (Baker) arrives in Konigsbaden, Bavaria, following a message from his father Kurt Deutsch, whom he believed had died in 1943. Newman is told that his father was a prisoner of war in Russia for 18 years, and on his escape back to Germany was taken in by Doctor Peter Von Brecht (Cushing), with whom he stayed until he died of a stroke. Von Brecht initially comes across as a completely decent, urbane, generous man, but it soon becomes clear that he is being *too* nice. Deutsch's young widow Lisa (Zetterling) and Police Inspector Hofmeister (Portman) encourage Newman to leave as soon as possible, but as he begins to investigate he finds that no-one is telling the truth. Is it possible that his father is still alive?

The convoluted story betrays its origins as a television serial with every new twist presumably relating to cliffhanging episode endings. As the film wears on, the dialogue becomes more and more forcedly mysterious with a thump on the harpsichord signifying each new revelation.

It is not a taxing role for Cushing, who looks elegant in a dinner suit in the early scenes and who works well with his beautiful Swedish leading lady Mai Zetterling. 'I was never involved in a crime,' says Lisa, as she is forced to lie for Von Brecht. 'You're lucky,' he says wearily, recalling his work in the concentration camps. 'I was involved in six million...'

Cushing gets to stand up to Stanley Baker in one grim scene in a displaced persons' camp and they take part in a disastrous disinterment for which Von Brecht is blamed.

Cushing as Von Brecht with director Quentin Lawrence making *The Man Who Finally Died* (1962)

'I played quite a good chap really,' said Cushing of Von Brecht. 'Although I still went around with a gun in my hand. I have no doubt that people will remember me in this picture as the villain.'[3] It doesn't help that the real villain is kept under wraps until the last reel, while Cushing plays a very obvious, very villainous red herring.

Footage from *The Man Who Finally Died* was turned into Cushing's 1987 Holsten Pils television commercial mixed with newly-shot footage of Griff Rhys Jones. The sequence used in the advert comes from near the beginning of the film when Von Brecht is talking about a fine liqueur ('It's pre-war' he says 'I've only got one more bottle left in the cellar...') although Cushing's lines in the commercial are transposed from their original order.

Cushing's next role was his first for independent television – which had now been running for more than seven years. *Peace With Terror* was a Sunday night play in the *Drama 62* strand, a story about a religious fanatic who plots to blow up the War Office.

An interview in the *TV Times* featured Cushing at home 'inspecting the guard', his collection of model soldiers that 'crowd a glass-fronted cupboard the length of his studio. The British Army is represented through the ages on one shelf. On another are models forming a Coronation procession. Their appeal for

Peter Cushing is not in detail but in their atmosphere of pageantry and contemporary history. Does Peter Cushing enjoy visiting toy shops? "The only sort I ever do visit," he admitted. "My wife has to buy all my clothes!" In spite of the model firearms and gun carriages Cushing is a peaceable man. "Not even soldiers enjoy war," he said. "Only a fanatic ... would think that a bomb in the War Office would do any good – even as a gesture of protest."[4]

Peace With Terror was another play by Jacques Gillies, and the director was once again Quentin Lawrence. (*Cash on Demand* had not yet been released in the UK.) Frederick Parsons (Cushing) heads a sect called The Union for Peace. As accomplice in his bomb plot, Parsons hires Henry Warblow (Brian Wilde), recently released from prison for assaulting a policeman at a disarmament meeting. But Warblow turns out to be an awkwardly large, rather weak character, caught up only accidentally in the disarmament fracas. The chapter-and-verse quoting Parsons is not deterred, however, and goes ahead with his plan.

To research the role, Cushing went on a Sunday morning visit to Speakers' Corner in London's Hyde Park to hear the soap box orators to get some real-life atmosphere into his part. 'There they were,' he said. 'Half a dozen religious fanatics like Parsons.'[5] The cast for the play also included Sheila Manahan as Parsons' indignant wife and George Woodbridge, who was last with Cushing in *The Mummy*, as Sergeant Greenfield.

'Et tu, Brute?' Brutus (Paul Eddington) and Cassius lead the assassination of Julius Caesar (Barry Jones) in the BBC's *The Spread of the Eagle* (1963)

Brian Wilde had appeared in *The Man Who Finally Died*, but had no scenes with Cushing.

The play did not go ahead smoothly, however. An item in the *Daily Telegraph* on 4th June 1962 read 'Unsuitable ITV Play Postponed'. 'The play *Peace With Terror*, by Jack Gillies [sic], was withdrawn by Associated Television last night, because it dealt with a religious fanatic. A spokesman said: "We decided this theme was not entirely suitable for a Sunday evening." It will be broadcast later in the month on a weekday. Peter Cushing was to have taken the part of the fanatic. He had a leading role a few years ago in George Orwell's *Nineteen Eighty-Four* which caused a public outcry when it was televised by the BBC.' ATV kept a copy of the play, which is preserved in their archive and was subsequently acquired by Polygram.

On 10th October 1962, radio producer Charles LeFaux wrote to Cushing suggesting a role in a radio production of M R James' classic ghost story *Oh Whistle And I'll Come To You*, later adapted for television by Jonathan Miller and starring Michael Hordern. 'We are planning a series of half-hour plays and want to have a very good name above the title. I'm sure we could do it in one day in the studio.' Cushing read the play but declined the role.

In January 1963, Cushing embarked on his most involved project for some time. It was a three-part BBC adaptation of Shakespeare's *Julius Caesar*, part of the nine-part cycle called *The Spread of the Eagle*, which included *Corialanus* and *Antony and Cleopatra*. The producer and director was Peter Dews, who in 1960 had overseen a prestigious production called *An Age of Kings* comprising Shakespeare's *Richard II*, *Henry IV*, *V* and *VI*, and *Richard III*.

In *The Spread of the Eagle* Cushing was to play Caius Cassius, one of the conspirators in the murder

of Julius Caesar. Cassius is described by Caesar as having 'a lean and hungry look' – an entirely appropriate description for Cushing. Fellow conspirator Brutus was Paul Eddington, with Barry Jones as Caesar and Keith Michell as Mark Antony.

The setting is Rome 44 BC, where 'the Colossus' – Julius Caesar – is urged to accept supreme power. However, the republicans, including the plain-thinking Brutus and the coldly intellectual senator Cassius, think they see another tyrant in the making. So a conspiracy is forged to assassinate Caesar, while strange supernatural events warn the citizens that tragedy is impending. Caesar's death brings about civil war, and the Republican army led by Brutus and Cassius must confront the forces of Mark Antony, loyal to Caesar's memory. Brutus, troubled by conscience and ghostly visitations, has little heart for the fight; neither has Cassius. The battle goes well for them at first, but their enemies prevail and both conspirators die by their own hands.

With its 1960s graphics and elaborate camera set-ups, *The Spread of the Eagle* boasts a deliberately modern approach, showing how much more sophisticated television production had become since Cushing's last performances. The acting is naturalistic, and Cushing brings force and passion to his delivery of Shakespeare's text, investing the complex speeches with emotion and meaning. In his black wig he looks severe, and the television cameras are noticably less kind to his face than film cameras.

Before rehearsals started on 25th February, Cushing was in contact with Peter Dews to check the pronunciation of certain lines. The series was recorded in Studio 4, Television Centre on 8th March, 25th March and 5th April 1963, with Cushing's fee at 563 guineas per episode. The production was recorded 'as live', which meant that recording breaks were kept to a minimum (to avoid costly editing) and small mistakes had to be worked through if possible. Paul Eddington remembered the problems created by having real horses in the studio – they tended to slip on the rubberised flooring that was used for the battlefield. While Cushing and Eddington struggled to continue with their performances, Keith Michell was fighting a losing battle to keep his horse from wandering into shot. Michell called Cushing's Cassius 'one of the finest Shakespearean performances I have ever seen,' remembering that during rehearsals, Cushing wore doormats and fire-irons in place of his sword and armour, leading the bluff Northerner Peter Dews to remark that he looked like a hearth-tidy.

The newspapers picked up on the return to television of Peter Cushing. This chirpy piece was from James Green in the *Daily Mirror*: 'A few words today from Cassius. Not Cassius Clay of boxing fame. He never said just a few words about anything. This Cassius is the one with the lean and hungry look. Mr Peter Cushing will play him tonight on BBC TV in the Shakespearean play cycle *The Spread of the Eagle*. It is five years since Cushing last acted for the BBC. But having decided that they can be no worse than the horror films he is back with a bang. Mr Cushing as Senator Caius Cassius, will be on view for three Fridays in succession. Take a close look at the togas being worn on TV. If you buy a ticket to see Elizabeth Taylor in *Cleopatra* you will spot the same garments. "The TV people decided to use the film company togas and we had to wait for them to arrive from Rome" says Cassius Cushing. "I suppose if togas have got to come from anywhere they might as well come from Rome. They arrive in two sizes,"

The Spread of the Eagle (1963) – Cassius lends an ear to Mark Antony (Keith Mchell)

he explained. "Large and small. All that needs altering is the hem length. They have an advantage over suits that fittings are not required. The more I wear togas the more I like them. The real thing takes a long time to wind round but these film jobs were in simplified form. A toga is loose and comfortable, does away with collars and ties, and it's easy to learn to swing the train over the left arm." Peter Cushing lives at Whitstable and for much of the year enjoys – if that is the word – a daily swim. He is a kind of Pied Piper to the local children and often joins in their beach games. In fact, the mob can sometimes be seen pushing him into the water. Cassius of the wet and watery look.'

When he had finished *The Spread of the Eagle*, Cushing made an appearance on the BBC's *Living Today* programme on 16th April 1963. He talked about his paintings with interviewer John Anthony.

On 10th September 1963, Cushing recorded a contribution to the *New Comment* radio programme – *The Macabre* was broadcast on the Third Programme on 21st September. On 22nd September he began location filming for a *Comedy Playhouse* episode called *The Plan*, written by Richard Harris and Dennis Spooner, former scriptwriters from Tony Hancock's ITV series. *Comedy Playhouse* was used as a kind of testing-ground for

new comedy situations and characters, some of which (including *Steptoe and Son*) were turned into continuing series. Perhaps there wasn't much mileage in Cushing's character of Albert Fawkes, a disgruntled descendant of the gunpowder plotter, whose appearance in *The Plan* was to be his first and last.

The *Radio Times* introduced *The Plan* thus: 'Just suppose there was an Albert Fawkes who became fed up with having his leg pulled and decided to get his own back. Suppose he enlisted... an ex-member of the IRA, by name Seamus McMichael, in a second attempt to dissolve Parliament the speedy way. Albert's 1963 gunpowder plot is the plot of tonight's *Comedy Playhouse,* written by a team new to BBC-tv – Richard Harris and Dennis Spooner. That well-known Irish actor P G Stephens plays the part of Seamus... "I came over with me young heart bursting to strike a blow for freedom and the only time I've struck in 20 years was for a longer tea break."'

Francis Matthews, who had enjoyed his association with Cushing so much in *The Revenge of Frankenstein* and had a small role in *The Hellfire Club*, appeared as Captain in *The Plan*.

'The only thing I recall about *The Plan*,' he says, 'was the isolated comedy scene which Graham Stark and I played "outside Number 10 Downing Street". We only saw Peter briefly at the read-through. Stark and I were a couple of "whizzo" idiot officers attempting to defuse a bomb.'

Cushing's fee was £420. *The Plan* was rehearsed in the first week of October, recorded on the 7th in Studio 3, Television Centre, and transmitted close to Guy Fawkes' Night on 2nd November. The play is effectively a comic cousin of *Peace With Terror*, and it says much of the times that, in 1963, an ex-member of the IRA would have been considered an acceptable supporting character in a half-hour comedy.

On 14th October work began on *The Evil of Frankenstein* – Cushing's return to Hammer after nearly two years. Helen's worsening illness and its treatment was Cushing's highest priority, so regular money was a necessity, whatever the work.

The Evil of Frankenstein was Cushing's only *Frankenstein* movie not directed by Terence Fisher, who was meanwhile contracted to make two films for

Zoltan (Peter Woodthorpe) attempts to hypnotise the Creature (Kiwi Kingston) watched by Hans (Sandor Elès) and Frankenstein in *The Evil of Frankenstein* (1963)

Hammer's former co-production partner Robert Lippert. Fisher was replaced by Freddie Francis, who had spent many years as a lighting cameraman (including work on Cushing's films *Moulin Rouge* and *Time Without Pity*) and had already directed the psychological thrillers *Paranoiac* and *Nightmare* for Hammer.

Anthony Hinds provided the script for this film, which ignored the Baron's carefully constructed backstory from *Curse* and *Revenge*. Under the terms of a distribution deal with Universal, Hammer were now allowed to use a variation of Jack Pierce's

Director Freddie Francis (standing, left) supervises Sandor Elès and Cushing on location for *The Evil of Frankenstein* (1963)

famous Frankenstein monster make-up, which they did, seemingly regardless of the fact that the first two films had done perfectly well without it. Thus Cushing's Frankenstein is suddenly lumbered with a huge, bolt-necked Creature (played by New Zealand wrestler Ernie 'Kiwi' Kingston) which the character and the canon didn't require.

The story plays like a pastiche of the Universal Horrors, but seems to take its cue from the point when the Universal films were starting to parody themselves. Even Don Banks' bombastic score seems influenced by the musical fanfares of Universal composer Franz Waxman.

At the beginning of the film, Frankenstein's latest experiments in a jerry-rigged watermill laboratory are destroyed by a zealous priest, the Baron determines to return to his former home in Karlstaad with his assistant Hans (Sandor Eles). There he discovers his property ransacked but his old laboratory intact, and preserved in ice nearby is his first half-formed Creature.

The monster is restored to life, but is mindless. A stage hypnotist, 'Professor' Zoltan (Peter Woodthorpe), is engaged to activate the Creature's brain, which he does, but then sends it out to steal and murder. Eventually the Creature turns on Zoltan and kills him, then gets drunk on brandy. Looking around for more alcohol, it drinks chloroform and in raging agony, sets the laboratory ablaze, apparently destroying Baron, creature and all in an inferno.

As Frankenstein, Cushing looks older, often tired and unshaven, some way from the dandy of *Revenge*. Even though he successfully animates his monster, he faces nothing but abuse and betrayal. Hinds determined to 'put more compassion into our horror films'[9] but Frankenstein is only given an out-of-character streak of sentimental self-pity. He is made to seem foolish by deliberately antagonising the citizens of Kalstaad, and then complains when they bother him.

Cushing worked on the script, to ensure that Frankenstein was 'basically the same chap'[10] and there is nothing wrong with his performance, except for a couple of moments of eye-boggling straight to camera. Maybe Cushing came up with some of the saucier lines. 'He has a good brain and excellent eyes,' Frankenstein tells the Zoltan of the monster. 'I won't tell you where I got them, but I can assure you they're perfect.'

Cushing's expression on discovering the monster frozen in ice is full of wonder and a later stand-off with the monster has at least a little of the old Olivier-trained flair.

Francis admits that he had little connection with the material. It was, he says, a case of 'here is the monster, here is the mad lab and away we go, so to speak.'[11] That said, the 'mad lab' itself is truly magnificent, a great cathedral of blue glass, valves and lightning, which Francis uses to great effect. The monster is less memorable, however – an expressionless hulk with none of the childlike innocence that Christopher Lee and Michael Gwynne brought to the role.

Nevertheless, there are some clever sequences, particularly the lead-in to the flashback of the first experiment, which tracks over Cushing's shoulder, down the deserted corridors of the chateau to the laboratory. Unforgivable are the shoddy last-act process shots of Cushing driving a gig, and worse, the long-shot of an obvious stand-in driving the gig on location. Without the support of Terence Fisher, Cushing seems to be having to work very hard to bring the film up to scratch.

'The Evil of Frankenstein ... has its moments,' considered the Times. 'Particularly the full-blooded opening. One or two of the actors get quite out of control, but Mr Peter Cushing is, as ever, authoritative as the idealistic misunderstood Baron and the script ... is engagingly aware of its own absurdity.'[12]

The Evil of Frankenstein finished shooting on 16th November. At the beginning of December, Cushing was reunited with Christopher Lee and Terence Fisher for The Gorgon.

Cushing plays Doctor Namaroff, chief medical officer at the Vandorf Medical Institution. He is an ambiguous figure, devoted to his work but crippled by his love for the enigmatic Carla Hoffmann, who

Professor Namaroff ponders the destiny of Carla Hoffmann (Barbara Shelley) in *The Gorgon* (1963)

is possessed by the spirit of the Gorgon Magaera. 'Namaroff was not a neurotic raving villain,' Cushing remarked, 'but a reserved, thinking man, shy, retiring, rather sad and without much to say. Yet he had the power to collect and sustain around him an aura of undiluted menace. Namaroff sends a cold shudder down your back.'[13] Though Namaroff does indeed have an 'aura of menace', what he knows or doesn't know about Carla's condition is very ambiguous. Namaroff never smiles – he has none of Van Helsing's beguiling charm – it is as if in loving Carla he has been turned to stone already.

Fisher adores the trappings of the ruined Castle Borski where the Gorgon has her lair – there is a thrilling scene in a rainstorm where Paul Heitz (Richard Pasco) sees Magaera in reflection, scored with thunderclaps and bursts of James Bernard's hypnotic novachord-and-percussion score. The idea of a Gorgon who turns bodies to stone is more than usually fantastic for Hammer, but the conviction of Cushing and Barbara Shelley as the beautiful, tormented Carla that makes the conceit believable. Terence Fisher encouraged his cast to play it for absolute truth. Christopher Lee, in a heavy grey wig, turns up as Professor Meinster to badger the locals and eventually see right prevail, but something is adrift. Lee has a whale of a time playing the Van Helsing part, but the story is not set up to properly accommodate one. There are no real heroes or villains in Vandorf.

Janus Cass (Alister Williamson), Inspector Kanov (Patrick Troughton), Carla (Barbara Shelley), Professor Namroff and Professor Heitz (Michael Goodliffe) in *The Gorgon* (1963)

Filming on *The Gorgon* was completed on 16th January 1964 at Bray Studios. Despite the relentlessly downbeat atmosphere of the piece, the filming seemed to go happily enough, though Barbara Shelley was sad that she was not allowed to wear the Gorgon make-up. She even volunteered to have real snakes coiled in her hair, which would have been preferable to the twitching rubber serpents affixed to dancer Prudence Hyman for her appearances as Magaera.

Shelley has fond memories of her time with Cushing on set, singing Gilbert and Sullivan (Giuseppi's song from *The Gondoliers* and the Nightmare song from *Iolanthe*) and taking him on in ferocious contests to see who could sing the fastest without dropping a word. 'It was Chris in the morning with operas and Peter in the afternoon with Gilbert and Sullivan,' Shelley recalls, 'and impersonations of Sylvester the Cat!'

Cushing as Detective Elijah Baley in BBC2's *Story Parade* adaptation of Isaac Asimov's *The Caves of Steel* (1964)

Cushing was up to his old cabbage cutting tricks again, too. 'He did his surgery out of shot on a cabbage and did it *perfectly* – I was expected to keep a straight face. He did, but I couldn't!'

Shelley invited Cushing to participate in a drawing game that she had found. 'You were given two vertical straight lines and you had to incorporate them into a drawing. Most people made the trunk of a tree or something, and you could tell things about their character by what they drew. Peter made the linked letters P and H, for Peter and Helen. No great psychology needed there. I said "You love your wife very much."'[14]

Richard Pasco had first met Cushing at the 'Q' Theatre in 1943, and worked with him and Fisher on *Sword of Sherwood Forest*. He recalled that much of the climactic swordfight between Paul and Namaroff was choreographed by Cushing. *Films and Filming* thought that Christopher Lee was miscast but Fisher had given the film a 'romantic glow'[15] and the acting was unusually sensitive. The film is undoubtedly successful in generating a smothering atmosphere of dread, it looks beautiful and is very well acted, but something is missing in the logic of the plot which stops the film from being a complete success.

Cushing went back to the BBC in March, but there is some mystery surrounding his contribution to the children's programme *Star Story*, a short-lived precursor to *Jackanory*. Star readers in the series included Prunella Scales, Andrew Cruikshank and Stratford Johns, Cushing read a ghost story called *The Yellow Cat* by Michael Joseph. Six stories were broadcast but the seventh, – Cushing's – did not go out. Possibly the story, or Cushing's telling of it, was considered too frightening for the children's television slot.

Cushing did appear on television in June, however, as Elijah Baley, one of science fiction's most beloved heroes, in one of Isaac Asimov's famous robot stories. The BBC 2 adaptation of *The Caves of Steel* in the *Story Parade* series marked Cushing's first association with young Hungarian director Peter Sasdy, with whom he would make the film *Nothing But The Night* in 1972. Asimov's story was adapted by young writer Terry Nation, who had made a name for himself the previous Christmas by devising the Daleks for the new children's science fiction series *Doctor Who*. In May 1965, Cushing would take the role of the Doctor in the film adaptation of Nation's first *Doctor Who* story.

The setting for *The Caves of Steel* is New York City in the distant future. Fourteen million humans live beneath a protective dome, with a workforce of

positronic robots. The city-dwellers live in fear of
the 'Spacers', the former colonists who live in the
Outer World beyond the walls and who wish to
see humanity freed from the domes – the 'caves of
steel'. Detective Elijah Baley (Cushing) is assigned to
investigate the murder of an eminent Outer World
scientist, Doctor Sarton, and to see a fair investigation,
Baley is given an unconventional partner – a lifelike
robot called R Daneel Olivaw (John Carson) who will
act as an observer for the Spacers.

Baley later discovers that Olivaw was a prototype
for a sophisticated new robot created by Sarton in
his own image. After identifying and arresting a
rabble-rouser called Clousarr, who belongs to an anti-
technology 'medievalist' group, Baley is framed for an
attack on another robot. Baley learns that his superior,
Commissioner Enderby (Kenneth J Warren) is
involved with the medievalists and seeking to destroy
their crowning achievement – R Daneel. In the nick of
time, Baley uncovers the truth – Enderby killed Sarton,
believing the scientist was his own robot.

The Caves of Steel was rehearsed from 15th April to
4th May, with filming (for a chase sequence) on 17th
April. The play was recorded in Studio 1, Television
Centre on 7th May. Cushing's fee for the 75-minute
play was £787.

The *Daily Telegraph* noted that *The Caves of Steel*
'proved again that science fiction can be exciting,
carry a message and be intellectually stimulating.'[16]
Although the play no longer exists in the BBC
archives, several extracts featured in *Horizon* and
Tomorrow's World have survived and show the high
production values of the piece, with a surprisingly
graphic sequence for Sarton's murder.

In the mid-1950s, American producer Milton
Subotsky suggested to Hammer that they remake
Frankenstein, submitting his own script for their
approval. They rejected Subotsky's draft but went
ahead with the remake anyway – the rest we know.
Although Subotsky remained philosophical about it,
Hammer's subsequent worldwide success no doubt
stuck in his craw. As soon as he was able, he set to
work making horror films himself with his own
company, Amicus, run with fellow American Max J
Rosenberg. Their intention was to produce movies on
Hammer lines, even if this meant borrowing Hammer
stars Cushing and Lee.

At the end of May, Cushing appeared in his
first film for Amicus – *Dr Terror's House of Horrors*.
This 'portmanteau' film, produced in the style of
Ealing Studios' 1945 film *Dead of Night*, saw the
actor reunited with director Freddie Francis and
Christopher Lee at Shepperton Studios. Also in the
cast were Roy Castle, Donald Sutherland and *Pick of
the Pops* DJ Alan Freeman.

It is fair to say that *Dr Terror's House of Horrors* is not
Dead of Night. It is a garish, lightly comic concoction,

Franklyn Marsh (Christopher Lee) nervously selects a card from
Dr Terror's House of Horrors (1964)

for which Cushing provides the linking banter, peering
out from under a formidable pair of bushy eyebrows
as Doctor Schreck – literally 'Doctor Terror'. The polite
stranger joins five men in a railway carriage and brings
out a tarot deck ('I call it my house of horrors') to offer
them a glimpse of their futures. Each of the five 'futures'
forms a story – the subjects, voodoo, a werewolf, a
creeping vine, vampires and a crawling hand.

By far the best excerpt stars Christopher Lee as
Franklin Marsh, an arrogant and venomous art critic
who is publicly humiliated by one of his 'victims',
artist Eric Landor (Michael Gough). Landor continues
a campaign of embarrassment until eventually,
Marsh runs him over, destroying his right hand and
his livelihood. Then a disembodied hand begins
persecuting Marsh, giving Lee plenty of opportunity
for nervous agitation and horrified reaction. Marsh
eventually throws the hand on the fire but its sudden
reappearance on the windscreen causes him to crash
his car. Marsh, who told us 'I live by my vision', is
blinded in the crash.

Cushing's small role must surely have been a
disappointment for fans, drawn in by his prominent
position on Amicus's lurid poster. He makes the most
of every line, though, with a lilting German accent and
owlish expressions. Eventually, the train pulls up – but
the men in the carriage do not recognise the station.
'Why have you done this? What do you want? *Who
are you?*' demands Marsh. Cushing turns to the camera
and in extreme close-up, smiles 'Have you not guessed?'
Schreck's face is replaced with a grinning skull – their
futures have already happened and he is the Grim
Reaper. The *Daily Cinema* rightly found 'a lot of fun
and irony' in the film, and Cushing 'the ideal choice
for the shabbily sinister Doctor Schreck.' *Monthly Film
Bulletin* praised Cushing's 'unshaven, mittened Death
who ties the stories together, and the denouement has
an appropriately apocalyptic flavour.'[17]

Chapter Seventeen

Men of Steel

After a short break following *Dr Terror's House of Horrors*, Cushing was back with Hammer to play Major Horace L Holly in their adaptation of Henry Rider Haggard's *She*. Location filming took place in Israel from 24th August 1964, returning to the ABPC Studios at Elstree and finishing on 17th October. The film was directed by Robert Day and starred Ursula Andress as the immortal Ayesha with John Richardson, Bernard Cribbins, Christopher Lee and André Morell.

The film begins in Palestine, 1918. Following an encounter with a mysterious and beautiful woman, newly-demobbed Leo Vincey (Richardson) embarks on a quest for the lost city of Kuma with his friend Major Holly and Holly's batman Job (Cribbins). After crossing the desert they are captured by the savage Amahaggers but rescued by Bilali, High Priest of Kuma (Lee). Balali takes them to the 2000-year-old Ayesha, Queen of Kuma, known as 'She Who Must Be Obeyed'. She believes Leo to be the reincarnation of her lost love Killikrates, who must now fulfil his destiny and join her in the flame of eternal life.

After a lacklustre Frankenstein and the emotionally petrified Namaroff, *She* gives Cushing the chance for some traditional derring-do in the sort of entertainment he adored. In this unashamed family film, he proves once more that he could enliven any genre, and that he was particularly suited to action and adventure. The Peter Pan quality that so many have remarked upon in Cushing is at its clearest here, and Major Holly on the back of a camel in the Negev desert is not so very far from little Peter 'Brighteyes' on his bike in Kenley.

In the opening scenes, the three soldiers relax in a hostelry full of dancing girls. ('Well, we've survived the war,' says Holly heartily, 'let's hope we survive this place!') Cushing's expressions calculatedly mix ambiguous feelings of loss and yearning, possibly even premonition, before the reflective mood is dispelled by catching sight of the girls around him ('I say, chaps, look at that!') Holly has clearly been a bit of a rascal in his time, and, advising Job to take his hat off, he joins in with the dancing. The Cushing shimmy is worth the price of admission alone.

Working in the desert was gruelling. The actors had to start filming at 8.00 am because the afternoon heat was unbearable, perspiration evaporated almost immediately and they all had to eat salt to prevent dehydration. Cushing had trouble with a truculent camel called Daisy. In the staging of the spectacular Bedouin attack, a mistimed explosive charge peppered Bernard Cribbins' backside with shrapnel and blew one technician's finger off.

The political situation in Eilat at this time was potentially explosive too. 'The Arabs just sat there with their machine guns in their laps,' said Cushing. 'In the meantime we were popping off our prop guns and hoping we would not be attacked. We were lucky that they seemed to enjoy watching us. It was quite an exciting period.'[1]

John Doran of ABPC Elstree reported on the location filming for *Film Review* magazine, March 1965. 'Standing behind the camera, Bob Day acted each of the parts being played before him; grunting and groaning when things didn't go

'I say, chaps, look at that!' Major Holly, Job (Bernard Cribbins) and Leo Vincey (John Richardson) are entertained by a belly dancer (Lisa Peake) in *She* (1964)

according to plan, enthusing when it went as planned. Peter Cushing sat in the shade and talked. It is a measure of his ability ... that so gentle a man can chill the blood with performances in the horror films with which his name is synonymous. A highly intelligent man, Peter talked ... about the autobiography he has thoughts of writing, a work for which Bernard Cribbins has suggested the title *I'm All Right, Drac*.'[2]

Elstree's interior sets struggle to match the grandeur of the desert exteriors, but Cushing's expression of wonder on entering the halls of Kuma distracts from the deficiencies of the sets.

At Ayesha's side, Christopher Lee positively glows with power as the noble Bilali, who is ultimately corrupted by his desire for immortality. Cushing and Lee share a short but memorable scene when Holly finds Bilali

Holly and Job (Bernard Cribbins) watch as Ayesha crumbles to dust at the conclusion of *She* (1964)

praying amongst the mummies of the previous high priests. Cushing's offhandedness is matched by Lee's restrained strength and the effect is electric. The actors had only shared dialogue in three films thus far, despite co-starring in seven.

Holly has several lengthy speeches on immortality and director Robert Day remembered that Cushing was line-perfect. Leo seeks Holly's advice when Ayesha offers him eternal life, and Cushing's gentle delivery infuses the words with wisdom. 'It's age of the mind that's important, not the body,' Holly says. 'The joy of living is not to be denied, but to know that it will be there for all time, without change – life at a standstill. It's not quite the same thing.'

Holly also discourses on the subject of love and Cushing contributed his own lines here. 'Have you ever been in love, Holly?' asks Leo. 'Oh, many times, and *truly* once,' he smiles. 'A deep sincere love will last most people a lifetime, but even that changes from the frantic yearnings at its beginnings to a quiet unspoken understanding at its end. The physical side of human love wasn't designed to last forever.' Holly is not always so poetic, however. He maintains a constant simmering glare of defiance at Ayesha's cruelty and rages at her when she sacrifices the handmaiden Ustane. Cribbins provides another excellent foil for Cushing and their double-act in *She* is tremendously entertaining. No mean actor, Cribbins equals Cushing's expression of horror as Leo and Ayesha bathe in the blue flame, and She Who Must Be Obeyed withers into hideous old age.

The downbeat ending and several overlong dance sequences hamper the film, other jarring moments include the appearance of André Morell (as the Amahagger leader) dubbed with the familiar tones of George Pastell. However, the performances and a heart-warming 'bank holiday' feeling to the whole count for much. There is also one of James Bernard's most inspiring and lyrical scores, with its two main themes. The 'Desert Quest', which effortlessly captures Holly's boundless spirit of adventure, is matched by Ayesha's fanfare, which trumpets her name – 'She Who Must Be Obeyed!' Bernard stated that he particularly enjoyed this film because it allowed him to use a more romantic palette. Among many effective moments is the point when Leo bids goodbye to Holly, a plaintive echo of the desert theme underscores their farewell.

She was Hammer's most expensive production thus far, and went on UK release on 18th April 1965. Although it was one of the top films of the year, it got a critical pounding. 'Ridiculously old-fashioned' spouted the *New York Times*.[3]

On 3rd September, while still filming *She*, Cushing was a guest on the Light Programme's *Let's Find Out*. Produced by David Carter, the show was broadcast on 20th October 1964.

In August, radio producer Charles LeFaux wrote to Cushing offering him the lead in *Loyal Servant*, a specially commissioned play about the Duke of Marlborough, Winston Churchill's noble forebear, the BBC's tribute for Churchill's 90th birthday.

Director of Photography John Wilcox adapted his camera to give a 'skull's eye view' of Cushing as Christopher Maitland in *The Skull* (1965), just one of many atmospheric effects in the film

'Ever hopeful, I am pursuing you once more,' wrote LeFaux, 'believing that the terrible waste of such a splendid actor cannot go on indefinitely.' Cushing replied: 'I received your letter just before I left home (sadly!) for location work in Israel. I am delighted at the prospect of working with you again and am so glad that you should think of me for this most exciting project. Unless the company's "first call" on my services intervenes, I should be free.'

Loyal Servant, by Ian Rodger, was recorded on 8th November and broadcast on the Home Service on 30th November. Cushing's fee was 60 guineas. Afterwards, LeFaux sent a letter of congratulation. 'It was a splendid performance on Sunday!' Cushing replied 'I'm surprised *Loyal Servant* hasn't been done already on sound or television...' concluding, 'now, on with the gardening!'

On 14th December 1964, Cushing recorded an interview at the TV Theatre, Shepherd's Bush for the BBC 1 series *First Impressions*. It was transmitted on 5th January 1965. Cushing's fee for this show was 25 guineas, plus a return fare London-Whitstable.

On 18th January, Cushing began work at Shepperton Studios on his second Amicus production, *The Skull*, based on a short story by Robert Bloch. Freddie Francis was once again the director and the supporting cast included Patrick Wymark, Christopher Lee, Jill Bennett and Peter Woodthorpe.

Writer Christopher Maitland (Cushing), a wealthy collector of arcane literature and relics, acquires the skull of Donatien Alphonse François, the infamous Marquis de Sade – 'the man whose name has become the symbol of cruelty and savagery in all of us.' His

friend Sir Matthew Philips (Lee) warns him that De Sade was possessed by an evil spirit which still inhabits the skull. During the nights of the new moon, the skull is animated by beings from another realm, driving whoever possesses it to murder...

Milton Subotsky stated that he had always wanted to make a movie without dialogue, and *The Skull* is very nearly it. In this respect, the film has much more in common with the continental horror film-making of Mario Bava than the script-and-character-driven Hammer films. As a cost-cutting measure, Subotsky usually wrote the scripts for his pictures, and the submitted script for *The Skull* was about half-an-hour short. Also there were few stage directions. This was not a problem for Freddie Francis, who maintained that scriptwriters put in too many stage directions and he generally ignored them anyway. He followed the maxims of John Huston (with whom he had worked) that every shot had to tell its own story, and had to be filled with as much information as possible. So, much time is given over to Cushing's appalled grimace and lingering shots of grotesque artefacts, including the skull itself. Occasionally though, Freddie Francis pulls off a genuine cinematic *tour de force*.

In one harrowing scene, made all the more distressing by Cushing's face of horrified confusion, Maitland is taken to a weird courtroom by two police officers. There, he is compelled to bring a revolver to his head. Francis closes in on Cushing's vivid blue eyes – he fires, but the chamber is empty. The bewigged judge laughs insanely, gas pours through a grille and, as the walls close in, the skull floats towards him with horrible purpose. It is the realisation of a nightmare, prefiguring by several years the bold colours and disorientating dream-imagery of *The Prisoner*. Later, as Maitland is dispatched to steal a statue from Philips, the skull bobs cheerfully out of its cabinet and settles itself down with De Sade's awful grimoire. Seen through the skull itself, Cushing's expression of utter dread dissolves into bland, hypnotised compliance. Francis had a specially-made cowl over the camera to present a 'skull's-eye view' – it is an obvious, almost childish, cinematic device, but its ghoulish simplicity makes it work.

Cushing plays Maitland as a rationalist, whose refusal to believe in every successive horror perpetrated by the spirit makes his fate at once harder to bear and all the more inevitable. There is a very genuine feeling that he is losing his mind. His final stand, as the skull closes in for the kill has distinct echoes of the conclusion of *Nineteen Eighty-Four* just over ten years before.

In France the film was called *The Dreadful Crimes of the Marquis de Sade* but in May 1966, the *Times* reported that a Paris court had ordered the title changed again after complaints from Count Xavier de Sade, a descendant of the Marquis and a landowner in the Aisne district.

Variety (4th August 1965) hailed a 'classy shudder film... script is sound except for dragging in some scenes for effect only. The right ascetic approach is given by Peter Cushing as the determined collector.'[4]

During the filming of *The Skull*, Cushing made a guest appearance on Bernard Cribbins' television show. Cribbins had been impressed with Cushing's renditions of music hall songs and invited him on the programme. Cribbins had hits with the comic songs 'Hole in the Ground' and 'Right Said Fred', both of which went top ten in 1962. The show, titled *Cribbins*, was recorded on 5th and 6th February in Studio 4, Television Centre.

In the early 1960s, Hammer had scored a considerable hit by issuing pirate movies (*The Pirates of Blood River*, *The Devil-Ship Pirates*) specifically timed to meet the demands of children on the school summer holidays. Milton Subotsky, who had successfully taken on Hammer at the horror game, saw the potential to rival these holiday films too. He acquired the rights to the first Dalek story from the BBC's *Doctor Who* series and gained co-financing from another American, Joe Vegoda, whose chief specification was that the films go out under the Aaru name rather than Amicus. Realising that they still needed an international name to front the picture, Subotsky cast Cushing as Dr Who without an audition.

Cushing considerably softened William Hartnell's portrayal of the mysterious alien time-traveller, making him everyone's favourite Uncle, a kindly, dotty, distinctly *terrestrial* boffin, though in his white wig, corduroy jacket and with perpetually bowed legs, he looks something like an elderly Wild West sheriff. Subotsky revised and simplified Terry Nation's TV script, making it unequivocally family entertainment. While missing the intensity of the black-and-white television serial, it remains a charming and endearing children's film, bursting with colour and spectacle and catching, at several moments, a real sense of the magic of outer space.

'I cannot guarantee your safety, but I can promise you unimagined thrills!' Dr Who and Susan (Roberta Tovey) are held captive on the planet Skaro in *Dr Who and the Daleks* (1965)

In his home-made time machine TARDIS (Time And Relative Dimension In Space) the eccentric Dr Who transports his grand-daughters Barbara and Susan, plus Barbara's accident-prone boyfriend Ian, to the distant planet Skaro. Here they encounter the mutated Daleks, who inhabit robotic shells, and the blond, humanoid Thals. Thousands of years of war have reduced the planet to ashes, and the Thals have become pacifists. But now the Daleks plan to explode a neutron bomb to wipe out the Thals once and for all.

The film was shot between 12th March and 23rd April 1965 at Shepperton Studios. The director was Gordon Flemyng, with Roy Castle as Ian, Jennie Linden as Barbara and Roberta Tovey as Susan.

There is some childish comic business at the beginning with Castle (Cushing's co-star in *Dr Terror's House of Horrors*) but once in his stride, Cushing is in total command. He gives an expression of undiluted wonder on seeing the surface of Skaro for the first time, and a terrific wink to Susan as he suggests they explore the futuristic city that they have seen in the distance. The petrified jungle set filled the whole of Stage H at Shepperton, at that time the biggest sound stage in England. It was partly lit from below with concealed lighting, and the anamorphic lenses were removed from the cameras for the jungle scenes to give a weird distortion to the picture. Director of photography John Wilcox came straight to the picture after finishing *The Skull*.

Roberta Tovey remembered that there was a magical atmosphere on the set. 'Peter Cushing was a great

Roy Castle, Jennie Linden, Roberta Tovey and Cushing step out at Shepperton Studios during the filming of *Dr Who and the Daleks* (1965)

the travellers are dying of radiation sickness from the planet's poisonous atmosphere. While this revelation is not quite as harrowing as it was on television, it is still a chilling touch for such an upbeat film.

Cushing provided a bewitching narration for the trailer – 'Come with us into that strange new world. I cannot guarantee your safety ... but I can promise you unimagined thrills!' – and, riding on the success of the Daleks on television, the film was one of the top ten British films of the year. Like *Dracula*, there were queues round the block at cinemas. 'Kids will love it,' said the *People*. 'Their parents will find this gigantic schoolboy lark Dalektable!'[7] 'The dotty Doctor is played by Peter Cushing rather in the manner of a mad hatter looking for a lost tea party,'[8] wrote Leonard Mosely in the *Daily Express* on 23rd June.

Although Terry Nation had reservations about the big-screen version of his story, his contract gave him a percentage of the profits. Nation recalled with some amusement that the film's blockbusting success meant that Subotsky was forced to pay up with the royalties after the first year.

There was also a windfall for Cushing from the Hammer film *Dracula Prince of Darkness*. This was the film that saw the return of Christopher Lee to the role of Dracula and it featured, as a prologue, the conclusion of the original Hammer *Dracula* with Cushing and the candlesticks. Cushing was formally contracted for the re-use of this footage on 1st July 1965 – in *Past Forgetting* he recalled that he needed work done on the roof at Hillsleigh Road and James Carreras generously covered the cost of the work as a 'repeat fee'.

There were more science fiction capers for Cushing in his next film, *Island of Terror*, which was directed by Terence Fisher and co-produced by Richard Gordon, who produced *Corridors of Blood* and *Grip of the Strangler* with Boris Karloff.

In *Island of Terror*, Cushing plays the eminent pathologist Doctor Brian Stanley, who is informed of a boneless corpse found on the remote Petrie's Island off the Irish coast. Stanley travels to the island with

flower man,' she recalls. 'For the scene when Susan finds a flower in the forest, he phoned up the Royal Horticultural Society and found the name, which I then had to remember.'[5] Before finishing the film Cushing agreed to do a sequel, on the condition that Tovey return as Susan.

The stars of the film are undoubtedly the Daleks themselves, possibly the most malevolent and certainly the most melodramatic robot-creatures in science fiction. ('The Daleks are beyond reason,' states the Doctor, 'they wish only to conquer!') £4500 of the budget was assigned for building the Daleks from the BBC's plans and they look magnificent. Most importantly, the Daleks' easily-imitated electronic voices were preserved intact from the television version, and in the echoing city they are genuinely unnerving.

Bryan Hands was one of the Dalek operators and had to control the Black Dalek during the climactic battle. 'I suppose being the Dalek leader was a kind of honour,' he said, 'except that I was still inside it when it exploded!' He remembers that Cushing was enthusiastic on set, and was concerned that the 'Dalek boys' were looked after. 'He would occasionally join us in the canteen but would generally take to his dressing-room when not required.'[6]

There are some breathtaking mattes for the crags of Skaro, Malcolm Lockyer's music is equally monumental and at times strangely moving. There is also a grim moment when the Doctor realises that bone specialist Doctor David West (Edward Judd) and West's girlfriend Toni (Carole Gray). There they discover that scientists working in secret to develop a cancer treatment have accidentally created a tentacled organism that eats bone. Worse, the silicone-based creatures, called silicates, are impervious to firepower and can multiply indefinitely.

Cushing was heartened, no doubt, by the presence of his friend Fisher and some old acting comrades including Eddie Byrne and Niall McGinnis. He gives a very relaxed performance as the modern-thinking doctor, who goes through the picture with an easy manner and a wry quip for every occasion.

The film is encumbered with often tortuous dialogue and a wildly improbable plot, but Fisher somehow manages to ride these problems out. Cushing, of course, delivers the scientific terminology as if it were Shakespeare and his wide-eyed disbelief as the silicates multiply in front of him makes up for the fact that they are uninspiring, immobile rubber props, festooned, for no very obvious reason, with spaghetti.

But Dr Stanley, who is shyly fond of Toni himself, is not so very brave. At the scientist's laboratory, he is all for sticking together. 'I wouldn't want to stay out here alone – it's too damn creepy!'

Fisher does not shirk from the chills, either. As Stanley and West gather the radiation samples that they believe will destroy the creatures, a prowling silicate's tentacle grabs Stanley's wrist. The organisms are as strong as steel, so West has no choice but to chop off Stanley's hand before his bones are liquefied. Even this doesn't dampen Stanley's spirits, however, and after his arm has been bandaged, he complains 'One more transfusion and I'll be a full-blooded Irishman.'

Malcolm Lockyer's thunderous music is very like his score for *Dr Who and the Daleks*, but fits the action and adventure well. Barry Gray, the composer of the *Thunderbirds* theme, who had also worked on sound effects for the Dalek movie, adds more electronic whoops and warbles here, plus some genuinely unpleasant sucking noises that add a horrible touch to the silicate attacks.

While not on a par with Fisher's Gothics, it is an appealing and exciting film. When it was released in the US (as late as March 1967) *Variety* was generous with its praise for the star. 'Cushing, whose performances in this type of role are always above average, is properly brusque and with a wryly objective point of view. He also varies between heroism and cowardice, creating a character with natural, not exaggerated fears and hesitations.'[9]

Despite Cushing's problems with appearing on stage in *The Sound of Murder* while filming *Suspect,* he was shooting *Island of Terror* while appearing on stage in the Ben Travers farce *Thark*. This production began a short run at the Yvonne Arnaud Theatre, Guildford and was directed by Ray Cooney. The cast included Alec McCowen (who had appeared in *Time Without Pity* as Michael Redgrave's son), Ambrosine Philpotts, Jennie Linden, who followed Cushing from *Dr Who,* and the veteran comedy actress Kathleen Harrison.

When the play transferred to London's Garrick Theatre at the beginning of August, Harold Hobson reviewed it in the *Sunday Times*. His review shows further evidence of Cushing's worldwide popularity in connection with the horror genre, and his particular attraction for the French.

'Tuesday's performance of *Thark* at the Garrick was a Travers triumph. My enjoyment owed nothing to nostalgia. It was fresh, vital, a thing entirely of today. It was a considerable pleasure to see Peter Cushing, who plays the part of a middle-aged gentleman with roving eyes. In these grievous times we should reverence all actors who build up Britain's reputation abroad. Though they remain in Britain, they are cultural exports. Mr Cushing is the idol of the *Midi-Minuit Fantastique* mob, and the mere mention of his name, coupled if possible with that of Christopher Lee, is enough to raise spirits in the Rue du Cherche-Midi. His rufous countenance, his formidable but flustered commands certainly raised mine. I wondered now and again why he was appearing in Mr Travers' girl-friend burlesque of the twenties instead of some tale of freezing horror. Mr Cushing falling off the whirlwind and misdirecting the storm with exasperated confidence is an inspiring sight. If only Mr Lee had emerged from the grandfather clock on that ominous

Doctor Stanley, Toni (Carole Gray) and David West (Edward Judd) on the *Island of Terror* (1965)

staircase, my pleasure would have been perfect. What am I saying? It *was* perfect.'[10]

Cushing remembered that the play called for his character, Sir Hector Benbow, to share a four-poster bed with nephew Ronnie (McCowen) in the 'haunted house' of Thark. The rake on the stage at Guildford was exceptionally steep and the bed, on castors, would edge closer and closer to the edge. 'We were,' wrote Cushing, 'in danger of going "over the top".'[11] Cooney's suggestion was that they push the bed back up the stage, to the encouragement of the audience.

Cushing had been engaged in an ongoing correspondence with the BBC since the *Cribbins* show because Moss Bros kept charging him for the hire of a suit used in that production. The situation was eventually resolved, with effusive apologies all round, by the time Cushing began rehearsals for a play in BBC 2's *30 Minute Theatre* series. It was called *Monica* by Pauline Macaulay and was rehearsed between 27th October and 3rd November 1965. It was broadcast live on 4th November from Studio G, Lime Grove. The director was Naomi Capon and Cushing's fee was £378. The play was thus described in the *Radio Times*: 'Simon (Gary Bond) is furious with his girlfriend Monica and fakes suicide, knowing that she will arrive in the nick of time to save him. A man arrives instead and what was intended as a joke takes a sinister turn.'[12]

The BBC had planned to repeat Cushing's groundbreaking performance in *Nineteen Eighty-Four* in 1962, but it was considered that the quality of the telerecording was not acceptable for rebroadcast. The only viable alternative was to remount the production, retaining the Kneale script, with a new cast. The production eventually went ahead on 28th November 1965, directed by Christopher Morahan, with David Buck as Winston Smith, Joseph O'Conor

as O'Brien and Jane Merrow as Julia. 'It was excellent,' Cushing remarked of the new production, 'with a good cast, but nobody turned a hair. Time had moved on. It just wasn't frightening any more.'[13]

Cushing appeared on *Late Night Line-Up* on BBC 2 on 27th November 1965 in a programme devoted to the old and new productions of *Nineteen Eighty-Four*. André Morell, Yvonne Mitchell, Nigel Kneale and Rudolph Cartier were all interviewed, along with Buck, Merrow, O'Conor and Morahan. Cushing delightedly pointed out that filming for his version of the play took place on the building-site that eventually became the BBC Television Centre. The remake of *Nineteen Eighty-Four* was long believed lost, until an almost complete print was found the the US Library of Congress. The 1965 production has many strengths, but Cushing's version remains undoubtedly the more powerful.

After Christmas, Cushing was back at Shepperton Studios from 31st January to 22nd March 1966, facing the Daleks again in his second film as Dr Who – *Daleks' Invasion Earth 2150 A.D.*

The film was based on another story from the television series (1964's *The Dalek Invasion of Earth*) and Gordon Flemyng returned as director. To match increased audience expectations, the film required exterior filming and a huge model of the Daleks' flying saucer so the budget was duly increased. Joe Vegoda came on board once again and the Sugar Puffs company added finance in return for prominently placed posters in the film advertising their cereal. The film was shot on Studio B at Shepperton. In Studio A, shooting was underway on *Casino Royale* with a host of stars including Cushing's former leading ladies Ursula Andress and Deborah Kerr.

The film sees policeman Tom Campbell (Bernard Cribbins) stumbling into TARDIS after being attacked in a smash-and-grab raid. Dr Who, with Susan and his niece Louise (Jill Curzon), takes Tom to London in the 22nd Century, where they discover that the Daleks have invaded and subjugated the people of Earth. The film (shot under the title *Daleks Invade Earth 2150 A.D.*), is rather more gritty in tone than its predecessor, with a strong supporting cast including Andrew Keir, Ray Brooks and Godfrey Quigley as the anti-Dalek freedom fighters. Bernard Cribbins once again makes a good partner for Cushing, and the Doctor seems less eccentric when with him. For the latter part of the film, however, Cushing is teamed up with Brooks and they work less well together.

Key scenes like a London street full of Daleks are thrilling, but there is noticeably less dialogue in this film than the first, and the conclusion, diverting the Daleks' planet-splitting bomb, seems rushed and muddled.

Dr Who and Tom Campbell (Bernard Cribbins) are apprehended by Robomen on the banks of the Thames. Worse is in store in *Daleks' Invasion Earth 2150 A.D.*

'I'm really a very gentle character, fond of long walks and reading. But no one believes it,' said Cushing, interviewed by William Hall for the *Evening News* (25th March 1966) behind-the-scenes on *Daleks' Invasion Earth 2150 A.D.* 'Outside his dressing room in darkest Shepperton, they were waiting for him to tangle with those grotesque pepperpots who never seem to take Not Wanted for an answer. Mr Cushing smiled thinly and said "A lot of people have accused me of lowering my standards but I've never felt I'm wasting myself. You have to have a great ego to want to play Hamlet all the time, and I just haven't got that ego. Challenge me on this, and I'll say: "Well, I've kept working." And surely that's the important thing. It was no surprise to me to learn that the first *Doctor Who* film came into the top twenty box-office hits last year, despite the panning the critics gave it. That's why they've done the sequel, *Daleks Invade Earth 2150*. And that's why they're spending almost twice as much on this one."

'At 50, Mr Cushing is reconciled to the oddities of show business. "I played Winston Smith in *Nineteen Eighty-Four* on TV and it was probably the high spot of my television career. I'd like to have done the film version, but they gave it to Edmond O'Brien. I still don't know why. Now I'm playing Doctor Who while Bill Hartnell is doing it on TV. But that's the way it goes. Down one minute up the next. After a time you get used to it." Today Mr Cushing has reason to be content. Having saved the world (a novel touch, using the earth's magnetic centre to pin the metal Daleks to the core) he is now considering several parts that will keep him occupied throughout the summer. "Among them – a Roman general, a French Legionnaire and dear old Frankenstein again."

'He hooked his thumbs into his luridly fancy waistcoat, sat back comfortably and said "It's nice to have people fighting over you. Rare too. Three years ago during that terrible slump in the industry I was out of work for 18 months. I'll never forget it. But ours is an unpredictable world. That's why I keep working."

'Apart from lone hikes in which he memorises the next day's lines (his wife Helen, 23 years married, waved him away this week on a 13-mile 'Fieldfare' walk) Mr Cushing's hobbies are collecting model soldiers and operating the miniature theatre he has built at his beachside cottage in Whitstable Kent.

'Mr Cushing's hobbies are collecting model soldiers and operating the miniature theatre he has built at his beachside cottage in Whitstable'

"We have no children and no animals. But all the kids and all the dogs in Whitstable are my mates" he said. They're used to having a monster in their midst.'[14]

Cushing fell ill during the making of the film, requiring Subotsky to re-arrange the shooting schedule to prioritise scenes without him. Subotsky was able to claim £30,000 on the film's insurance policy for a two-day hold-up until Cushing had recovered.

Daleks' Invasion Earth 2150 A.D. went on general release on 5th August 1966, with a strident trailer that set the mood: 'Planet Earth has been bombarded by meteorites, subjected to cosmic rays, savagely invaded by men of steel, who have no flesh to pierce, no blood to spill! 2150 A.D. – a year that will thrill you and terrify you!'

The craze for the Daleks was waning, however, and this movie was considerably less successful than the first Dalek film. The *Times* mentioned the 'long-suffering, ill-used Peter Cushing,'[15] but Alexander Walker in the *Evening Standard* said that 'the sets are quite an eyeful, so are the special effects, and director Gordon Flemyng can teach Disney a lot about packing in the action.'[16]

On the back of the Dalek films' success, Stanmark Productions and Watermill Productions put together a pitch for a *Dr Who* radio series starring Cushing. A pilot was recorded, entitled *Journey into Time*, in which the Doctor and his granddaughter travel back to the American Revolution. The script was written by Malcolm Hulke, who later wrote stories for the BBC series. Sadly, the pilot was not broadcast, and the plan for a series was dropped, but it is hoped that a recording of the pilot may still exist.

Chapter Eighteen

Back to Baker Street

Of the list of roles that Cushing was anticipating in the *Evening News* interview on 25th March 1966, it must have been aggravating that the only one to come to fruition was 'dear old Frankenstein again'. Cushing was at Bray at the beginning of July to begin his fourth Frankenstein film, *Frankenstein Created Woman*, a project that was mooted as early as 1958, when James Carreras coined the title as Hammer's answer to Roger Vadim's *And God Created Woman*. Cushing's contractual fee for the film was £5000.

Terence Fisher was back at the helm as director and the film is a definite return to form for the series. As if to prove the point, Fisher begins the film with a shot of a guillotine, as he did in *Revenge*. Anthony Hinds' script rids Frankenstein of the mawkish sentiment displayed in *Evil* and the Baron is back in total command, having now turned his attention to the soul. He even appears to *have* a soul – he certainly doesn't kill anyone, and his work here seems almost philanthropic. But he is still some distance from understanding human nature, and the forces of love and revenge are ultimately his undoing.

In this film, Frankenstein thinks nothing of experimenting on his own body, subjecting himself to freezing to prove that the soul can survive death. As the Baron is revived by his associate Doctor Hertz (Thorley Walters) with a massive electrical charge and some smelling salts, Cushing rises from his coffin rubbing his neck in a now-familiar bit of business to signify weariness or discomfort. Frankenstein's assistant Hans (Robert Morris) is sent to fetch champagne from the local café, setting the plot in motion as he encounters three wealthy, idle young 'bloods' who are taunting the scarred Christina (Susan Denberg), daughter of the café owner Kleve. Later, the bloods break into the café and kill Kleve, but Hans is accused of the murder and executed at the guillotine. Hertz acquires the body and Frankenstein captures the young man's soul. Christina, who was in love with Hans, commits suicide shortly after witnessing his execution. Frankenstein retrieves Christina's body and cures her disfigurement, but places Hans' soul inside her body.

At Hans' trial, Frankenstein appears before Peter Maddern's ferrety police chief. As ever with Cushing, the details are everything. He idly flicks through the bible when Frankenstein should be swearing on it, and when asked 'What is your occupation?' he replies 'I am a busy man.' In place of the buttonhole from *Revenge,* Cushing now uses the Baron's black opera cloak as his chief prop, swirling it flamboyantly or pulling it straight for effect on several occasions. There is continuity with *Evil* in that the Baron's hands have been burned and are useless for surgery.

The science is never elaborated upon, and the talk of 'frames of force' to give life after death is woolly indeed. Thorley Walters' wide-eyed, child-like Doctor Hertz is agog at every new scientific marvel, and comes very close to stealing the film. The soul-catching apparatus itself consists of two parabolic dishes and a tuning fork, but with Cushing manning it we are compelled to believe, bringing a glimpse of the metaphysical to the Hammer *Frankenstein* canon. And who can complain as Cushing, in black gloves with his sleeves rolled up, ministers to the dead, with the two artfully-teased streaks of grey at his temples giving a subliminal impression of a devil's horns.

Reviewers noted that Walters was playing Watson to Cushing's Holmes, but when the Baron is tending to the newly-beautified Christina – using her as an experimental subject – it becomes clear that this is

Frankenstein rises from the slab while Doctor Hertz (Thorley Walters) and Hans (Robert Morris) look on in *Frankenstein Created Woman* (1966)

Producer Anthony Nelson Keys, Cushing and Susan Denberg on location for *Frankenstein Created Woman* (1966)

nothing less than Hammer's *Pygmalion*, with Cushing as Higgins and Walters as Colonel Pickering. As Hans wreaks his terrible revenge through Christina, murdering each of the bloods in turn, the film takes a grisly and inevitably tragic turn. In one of the most disturbing scenes in any British horror film, Christina is seen kneeling in supplication before the head of her late lover. Then, tormented by her divided personality, she commits suicide by throwing herself off a cliff. As Christine brings his experiment to a premature end, Frankenstein looks on with a flicker of fury, frustration and possibly even sadness in his eyes. Then, with a glance to the Almighty, he sets off alone again.

The film, photographed by Arthur Grant, is beautifully coloured with rich reds and mouldy greens, with the Baron decked out in black-and-white to catch the eye. It is apparent, however, that the number of days Cushing was required on this film were kept to a minimum, as the juveniles (Morris, Denberg and the bloods) are given several long scenes to eke out the length. In the earlier *Frankensteins*, Cushing was barely off the screen for a minute. *Variety* remarked that 'Cushing could walk through the Frankenstein

part blindfold by now, but he still treats it seriously as though he were playing Hamlet.'[1]

It is easy with hindsight to see that Cushing was heading for a dispiriting run of low-brow and low-budget movies. It's difficult to wonder why he didn't try something new – if there was a point when he should have stepped off the horror treadmill, it should have been here. Perhaps typecasting was playing a part, certainly in film terms Cushing's name was now synonymous with horror. Perhaps he genuinely felt happiest with friends, or at least people who understood the way he worked and would consider the importance to him of Helen's care. An alternative would have been films in Europe or America, but he would not – could not – move away from London and Whitstable because of Helen's health.

To his credit, Cushing never denigrated the genre that had made him. 'I believe implicitly in everything I do in terror pictures,' he said later, 'because I believe there is a public demand for this type of escapist entertainment. They are, after all, harmless outlets for what might otherwise be awkward tensions in many people. I believe in the characters I play and the weird

Martha Hyer as Kate Meredith with her traitorous husband John in *Some May Live* (1967)

and peering, wall-eyed, into the middle distance. This sequence is reminiscent of the collecting mania theme of *The Skull*, and, like that film, was based on a story by Robert Bloch, who also wrote the screenplay. James Bernard provided the score and created a smothering atmosphere of obsession and menace. The sight of Poe himself, cobwebbed in his cell and desperate for death is chilly stuff, and the segment has more of the true flavour of Poe about it than several films based on his stories.

After a radio play for the BBC World Service called *The Strong are Lonely*, in the new year Cushing joined Joseph Cotten and Martha Hyer in the spy thriller *Some May Live*, directed by Vernon Sewell.

and uncanny games they get up to. I have to believe. It is the only way I prevent myself and my pictures being laughed out of the cinemas. By believing in what I'm acting in – an actor should do, whatever his part dictates – I am able to give greater credulity to the character and the picture, so to strike the necessary note of authenticity to capture the audience's true attention.'[2]

Cushing was at Shepperton Studios again from 14th November for a segment called *The Man Who Collected Poe* in the Amicus portmanteau film *Torture Garden*, directed by Freddie Francis.

The Torture Garden is a tawdry fairground attraction run by the bizarre Doctor Diabolo (Burgess Meredith), who invites members of the public to look into the shears of Atropos, a sibyl, who will give them a glimpse of their future. Three victims step up, and all of them see visions of their own destruction.

Then Ronald Wyatt (Jack Palance) steps up to the shears. He is an avid collector of the works of Edgar Allan Poe. In his vision of the future, he meets Lancelot Canning (Cushing), reputedly the world's greatest collector of Poe memorabilia. 'My whole life,' says Canning, 'is centred around Edgar Allan Poe in *every* respect.' Wyatt visits Canning's Maryland home, where Canning shows him a collection of first editions and memorabilia and proposes a toast to 'the immortal Edgar Allan Poe.' As the evening goes on, Wyatt gets Canning drunk. Canning takes him into a locked cellar, where he shows the fascinated Wyatt a collection of unpublished Poe manuscripts on modern paper. But the prize of Canning's collection is beyond Wyatt's wildest imaginings – the resurrected corpse of Edgar Allan Poe himself!

Cushing enjoyed working with Jack Palance and plays an excellent drunk, slurring his words merrily

In the early years of the Vietnam war, Kate Meredith (Hyer) is a Communist spy – working on ciphers for the US army in Saigon but passing information to the Viet Cong through her husband John (Cushing), a British foreign correspondent. When an attempt is made on the life of a visiting US senator, CIA agent Colonel Woodward (Joseph Cotten) suspects an inside job. Kate confesses to Woodward that her husband has been forcing her to spy, and she has complied for the sake of her son. She agrees to pass false information to the Viet Cong, knowing that it will mean John's execution when his Chinese masters learn of the deceit.

The film opens with an interminable voice-over and possibly the most excruciating theme song ever committed to film (sung by Vince Hill). Cushing's character is supposed to be on edge, but the actor just looks embarrassed and rather bored, the cramped sets (at Twickenham Studios) giving little room for expansive performances. There are a couple of effective moments – David Spenser as the youthful Chief of Police carries out an eye-watering torture scene using toothpicks, and Cushing has a touching scene when Meredith has to say a final goodbye to his son. But there are also some ridiculous money-saving shots of Martha Hyer's double on location, in raincoat and headscarf, filmed from behind and fooling nobody. Generally, the film is tedious and difficult to get through. For a long time it was impossible to find, and having finally seen a copy, it is clear why no one has rushed to put it out on DVD.

The screenplay was by David T Chantler, who had written the script for Hammer's *She*, but clearly Cushing was disinclined to write additional dialogue here. He clearly didn't have a problem with director Vernon Sewell, however, and was working with him again on *The Blood Beast Terror* later in the year.

Cushing's next film was at Pinewood studios with Terence Fisher – another science fiction subject, *Night of the Big Heat*, based on a novel by John Lymington. It had been made into an *ITV Play of the Week* in 1960.

The film begins with the island of Farah in the grip of a ferocious heatwave, and a small inn run by novelist Jeff Cullen (Patrick Allen) quickly becomes the centre of operations. The brusque Roderick Hanson (Christopher Lee) behaves suspiciously and has a room full of scientific equipment, but it transpires he is attempting to prove a theory that the heatwave is caused by extra-terrestrial invaders. When the islanders start dying, it becomes clear that there are aliens on Farah – creatures that can kill with a searing blast of heat.

The exteriors were shot in

Doctor Vernon Stone, Tinker Mason (Kenneth Cope), Jeff Callum (Patrick Allen) and his wife Frankie (Sarah Lawson) face an alien invasion in *Night of the Big Heat* (1967)

the freezing February of 1967, with the bare trees signifying the withering temperature of the heatwave. Cushing plays Doctor Stone, the affable island medic, who doesn't do much doctoring beyond providing a few aspirins and sedatives. Cushing is on the edge of the frame for many of the early scenes, wiping his forehead with his handkerchief and improvising 'my word, it's hot' dialogue. As the death toll rises, Stone bravely volunteers to go for help at the island's Met Office station. He reports back by radio, but is intercepted by one of the alien creatures. His dying scream of terror is chilling and provides one of the few highlights of the film. This has much in common with *Island of Terror* – an island menaced by largely unseen, non-humanoid creatures – although the scientific jargon is even more nonsensical here. The strong cast lurch from one unlikely set-up to the next, and the results are often deeply embarrassing. Harry Ringel wrote in *Cinefantastique* 'Not even Peter Cushing could enliven the flattened souls who inhabit Fisher's faintly printed science fiction universe.'[3]

On 26th February, Cushing took part in a radio production of Ugo Betti's play *The Burnt Flowerbed* but there was no more film or television work until the summer when Cushing joined the roll-call of British character actors who appeared in ABC's popular adventure

series *The Avengers*, starring in a science fiction-themed episode called *Return of the Cybernauts*. The story was directed by Robert Day, who had directed *She* in 1964. It also reunited Cushing with his old chum Patrick Macnee, co-star from Robert Helpmann's disastrous production of *The Wedding Ring* in 1952.

The Avengers was not given to sequels, so *Return of the Cybernauts* is one of the very few episodes to follow on directly from events in a previous story.

Dr Neville (Charles Tingwell), Benson (Frederick Jaeger), Professor Chadwick (Fulton McKay), Paul Beresford and Emma Peel (Diana Rigg) in *The Avengers: Return of the Cybernauts* (1967)

In Philip Levene's *The Cybernauts*, Michael Gough played electronics expert Doctor Armstrong, who intended to take over the world with an army of remote-controlled robots – cybernauts. In *Return of the Cybernauts* Peter Cushing plays Paul Beresford, Armstrong's brother, taking embittered revenge for his sibling's defeat and death at the hands of John Steed (Macnee) and Emma Peel (Diana Rigg).

Brian Clemens, producer of *The Avengers*, knew Cushing long before they worked together. He remembers 'at Elstree and Pinewood he would often be doing other things, and through mutual friends, including Albert Fennell [co-producer of *The Avengers*], who knew him very well, we would meet for lunch or a drink.' There was no conscious decision to bring Cushing in because of the horror connection in the story, it was simply a good part for a good actor. Cushing had a reputation for changing his lines, but guest stars on *The Avengers* were not allowed to alter their scripts, only to make suggestions. 'But Peter was a delight to direct,' Clemens adds, 'totally trusting our expertise.'[4]

So Cushing is relaxed, among friends and at the height of his powers. Consequently, Beresford is more three-dimensional than most *Avengers* villains, and seems more than usually unlikeable because Cushing is clearly playing it for real. He flirts effortlessly with Diana Rigg – 'Rapport and Peter went together,' said Clemens of the charming scenes between Beresford and Mrs Peel. Further to fuel Steed's jealousy, Beresford is notably one of only three people in *The Avengers* who calls Mrs Peel 'Emma'.

Return of the Cybernauts is comic-strip stuff, but done with huge panache and with some very good scares,

such as the cybernaut tearing the roof off a fleeing scientist's car, accompanied by Laurie Johnson's brilliantly effective 'heartbeat' theme. Cushing never loses control as Beresford's madness takes hold, and he is particularly chilling as he uses a mind-controlling device to turn Mrs Peel into a human cybernaut.

Production on *Return of the Cybernauts* was completed 15th June 1967. One month later, Cushing was filming *Corruption* at Isleworth Studios for director Robert Hartford-Davis.

'It was gratuitously violent, fearfully sick,' Cushing remarked of *Corruption*. 'But it was a good script, which just goes to show how important the presentation is.' Later he said, 'Audiences did not get the idea that it was supposed to be based on a dream, which in fact did not justify some of the scenes that were presented. With any film you participate in, the company, if they so wish, can destroy your original interpretation of the role.'[5]

Cushing plays the eminent surgeon Sir John Rowan, whose fiancée, model Lynn Nolan (Sue Lloyd), is disfigured when a photographic lamp falls onto her face. Rowan devotes himself to finding a cure for Lynn, but though her looks are temporarily restored, the trauma has driven her insane. When repeated skin grafts are necessary, Lynn drives Rowan to serial murder to acquire fresh donors.

That the murders are eventually presented as a dream on Rowan's part makes little difference – they are real in the course of the film. Bill McGuffie, who provided the music for *Daleks' Invasion Earth 2150 A.D*, underscores the frenzied killing with manic jazz riffs.

There were three different edits of the film, for Britain, Europe and Japan, and the European version was the most explicitly graphic. Seeking fresh supplies of the pituitary gland to continue the work on Lynn, Rowan goes to a Soho prostitute, whom he kills. In the British version, Cushing simply drops the knife from his sleeve and stabs the girl, who keeps her clothes on throughout and is given a couple of funny lines during an interrupting phone call ('Ring me back in 10 minutes ... perhaps you'd better make it 20...'). In the European version, the girl is topless, and immediately goes into Rowan's bag where she finds the knife. There is a voice-over of Lynn's distraught screaming goading Rowan on and we are given a brief shot of a doll with its head broken off. The stabbing is much more frenzied and Cushing grimly wipes his bloodied hands down the woman's breasts before literally hacking her head off.

Kate O'Mara shares several strong scenes with Cushing in *Corruption* (1967)

The Victorian trappings of the Frankenstein tales always put the horrors at one remove from reality, so Baron Frankenstein sawing off someone's head is acceptable in the context of fantasy. Watching a man cutting the head off a prostitute in 1960s Soho is a different matter altogether.

Nevertheless, in the midst of this revolting business, there are some clever ideas and as a document of the 'swinging' Sixties it is interesting – Anthony Booth, as photographer Mike, actually says 'Freak out, baby' at one point. Cushing's futile step forward as Booth leads his wife away is a tiny touch, but priceless. Kate O'Mara as Lynn's sister Val, is particularly impressive and shares several bitter scenes with Cushing. While Rowan explains that he is using the secrets of the ancient Egyptians to find a solution, Cushing delivers his lines tenderly, while reading a book and making notes. Val insists that John is becoming obsessed with Lynn's treatment, meanwhile Lynn is becoming suicidal. Rowan snaps, with Cushing giving one of his most natural and ferocious outbursts on the screen.

Robert Flemyng as Professor Mallinger with Inspector Quennell in *The Blood Beast Terror* (1967)

Cushing also regarded his next film, *The Blood Beast Terror*, with some distaste, but compared to *Corruption* it is almost as homely as a Hammer, and at least it is firmly back in the realms of the fantastic. It was shot at the tiny Goldhawk Studios at Shepherd's Bush by director Vernon Sewell, beginning on 7th August.

Apart from the early scenes that attempt to pass off an inlet of the Thames as darkest Africa – and the alarming title – there is much to recommend *The Blood Beast Terror*. Helped along by Paul Ferris' creeping, percussive score, there is an enjoyable sense of mystery as an unknown 'something' starts seeing off the locals. It's like an episode of *The Avengers* in Victorian dress. This was Cushing's first film for Tigon, the company formed by producer Tony Tenser, who had formerly made films with *Corruption*'s director Robert Hartford-Davis. Tenser had already produced Michael Reeves' *The Sorcerers* with Karloff and would oversee Vincent Price's *Witchfinder General* in September.

Cushing clearly provided some of his own touches for the good-natured Inspector Quennell, who sucks on sweets and nags his sergeant about slopping tea in the saucer. Robert Flemyng (replacing Basil Rathbone, who died shortly before filming started) plays sombre entomologist Professor Mallinger and Wanda Ventham his lovely daughter Clare. The plot makes little

sense, but includes some enjoyable touches, like the amateur dramatics put on by Mallinger's students – a melodrama about galvanism in which Clare is 'brought back from the dead'.

Cinematographer Stanley Long photographed the film in autumnal tones, giving it a look like one of Jack Asher's Hammer horrors. Glynn Edwards steals the show as the long-suffering Sergeant Allan, then Roy Hudd steals it back as a comic mortuary attendant. Some poor post-synching occasionally betray the low budget, but the film was done with conviction, particularly by the cast.

Peter Bryan, who wrote *The Hound of the Baskervilles* and worked on *The Brides of Dracula*, creates considerable suspense through the dialogue. A coachman who saw the flying monster is reduced to a raving maniac. ('It was a creature sir,' he tells Quennell, 'with wings sir. *Horrible* wings sir...') But then it is revealed, for reasons never clearly explained, Clare Mallinger is a giant death's head moth which has assumed human form. A cocooned moth, swathed in cobweb in the cellar, is very creepy, but the blood beast herself, when seen clearly, looks like an elaborately-sequinned fancy dress costume. 'What are we going to tell 'em?' asks Sergeant Allan as the moth perishes in a fire at the close. 'They'll never believe this at the yard.' 'They'll never believe it anywhere,' says Quennell.

When production was completed on *The Blood Beast Terror*, Cushing took a break, again dedicating himself to caring for his wife. When he returned to work in the spring of 1968, it was in one of his most celebrated roles and for his old employer, the BBC.

'The game's afoot!' Holmes and Dr Watson (Nigel Stock) in a 1968 BBC publicity still for *Sir Arthur Conan Doyle's Sherlock Holmes*

ITV viewers got a hint of what to expect when Cushing made a brief appearance at the televised 1968 British Film Academy Awards on 28 March. Cushing's good friend Kenneth More was put in charge of greeting the guests, and after a word or two about Cushing's model soldiers, asked 'Have you got anything up your sleeve for us?' Cushing replied 'If I'm allowed to say... I'm going to play Sherlock Holmes. A series for the television. Will you come and be Watson?' 'I wouldn't mind that!' More replied. More's participation in the series was not to be, but the show was destined to be one of the big successes of the BBC's autumn season.

The *Sherlock Holmes* series was one of the first drama serials for BBC 1 to be made in colour. However, as BBC 1 did not start broadcasting in colour until more than a year later, the full effect was not seen until the series was repeated in 1970.

For contractual reasons involving the Doyle estate (the Holmes stories were not yet in the public domain) the BBC had to make it clear that these stories formed the second season of *Sir Arthur Conan Doyle's Sherlock Holmes*. The first season had aired in 1965 and starred Douglas Wilmer as Holmes with Nigel Stock as Doctor Watson. Wilmer declined to appear in the second series, commenting on, as he put it, 'a large amount of

unwisdom at the helm'[6] during the first. So the BBC approached John Neville, who had played Holmes in the 1965 Compton-Tekli film *A Study in Terror*. Neville also declined, but Cushing accepted readily. Cushing was placed under exclusive contract to the BBC for seven months and shooting began in May.

'I think Peter wanted to raise his profile a bit,' says Donald Tosh, script editor and co-producer on the series. 'He had done some films which he thought were not tremendously wise choices. This was a prestige project, back at the BBC, back on his old ground. But it had changed beyond recognition. And I don't think he knew how much he was second choice to Douglas Wilmer, which would have upset him if he had known. Wilmer, good actor that he was, was nowhere near Peter in star terms, he'd just rather coined Holmes for the 1960s.'[7]

Nigel Stock, who had received much critical acclaim for his portrayal of Watson, continued in the role, providing a note of continuity. The 'hook' for the new series was to be its portrayal of 'the savagery of Victorian crime' taking a cue from Patrick Hamilton's *Gaslight*. Producer William Sterling fancied a Hitchcockian touch, and advised his directors to watch the Easter Bank Holiday screening of *Psycho* 'As I have been saying to everybody, it is a starting point to my production approach for Holmes.' Cushing agreed to the project on 16th February, and was placed under exclusive contract on 20th May at 735 guineas per programme. The decision to make the series in colour was not finalised until 13th May.

The first scenes filmed were for *The Hound of the Baskervilles*, and took place for the first time on genuine Dartmoor locations, near Newton Abbott in Devon, using a vintage steam train on the Dart Valley Railway. In the programme, the exteriors appear rich and are excitingly shot. While the interior sets are spacious, they are somewhat overlit. In comparing the BBC's production of *The Hound of the Baskervilles* with Hammer's, Cushing is noticeably gentler, which some felt was a mistake, although he still gives an unforgettable spin to lines like 'It's murder, Watson. Refined, cold-blooded, deliberate murder!'

It soon became clear that the project's reach was exceeding the BBC's grasp. The filmed Grimpen Mire sequence was unusable and had to be remounted at considerable cost at the BBC's Ealing film studios. In the electronic studio, a general unfamiliarity with the colour television equipment led to further expensive delays. For Cushing, who 15 years earlier had been in some chaotic live TV broadcasts from Alexandra Palace, it must all have seemed horribly familiar.

Donald Tosh had worked on the early days of *Coronation Street* and as a story editor on *Doctor Who* and was brought onto *Sherlock Holmes* to replace John Barber, who was leaving to become drama critic of the *Daily Telegraph*. He had something of a baptism of fire, as he recalls. 'The Head of Serials, Andrew Osborn, said, "We've just filmed the two episodes of *The Hound of the Baskervilles* and the series has now overspent by £13,000," which in those days was a *vast* sum of money. I was basically told to re-write the scripts so that the exterior sequences could be done in the studio.'[8]

Plans to feature stars like Leslie Caron, Orson Welles, Sean Connery and Peter Ustinov in supporting roles were quickly dropped. The supporting cast still featured many familiar faces, however, including, Brenda Bruce, Daniel Massey, Juliet Mills, Cecil Parker, Dennis Price, Corin Redgrave, Peter Woodthorpe and Edward Woodward.

Despite lengthy pre-production for the 100-minute *Hound of the Baskervilles*, the period of time between recording and transmission of subsequent episodes got shorter. Cushing was calmed considerably by the presence of Helen in the studios on 23rd August for the recording of *The Second Stain* but ill health prevented her from attending all the recordings.

William Sterling had to supervise the editing of *The Dancing Men* and a studio session for *The Boscombe Valley Mystery* on 23rd September. As a consequence, an unfinished edit of *The Dancing Men* was accidentally transmitted on 24th September. When this mistake was reported in the *Daily Mail* the following day, it was used as a stick to beat the BBC with. 'The unprecedented disasters in the showing of this week's *Sherlock Holmes* – they broadcast an unedited recording which included shots at rehearsal – were probably due to divine retribution. No series deserves it more! Admittedly it has some good things, notably the reconstructions of the original *Strand* illustrations and the playing of Nigel Stock and Peter Cushing, although in my judgement Holmes should be colder and more arrogant. Elsewhere it was the crudest attempt the BBC has made to crash the international market ... I was disgusted by the generally low aim of *The Dancing Men*, which stretched itself to fill its time by blowing up the character of the housekeeper into a figure of mysteriously unexplained menace by the crude device of dressing her in black and photographing her outside doors looking fierce. But it made no attempt to visualise Holmes' ingenious solution of the cipher, which was the point of the whole story. The series is even made with transparently obvious breaks for commercials. ITV can justify this sort of thing by reminding us that it is a commercial operation. The BBC operates a public service system and in the past has always refused to cater for the international market at the expense of the British audience. Now it is debasing a famous British literary possession to satisfy a market it doesn't need to sell in. The note of contempt for the mass audience in *Holmes* is nothing new. It indicates a disastrous change of policy towards its fictions which requires an explanation.'

David E Rose, Assistant Head of Series, Drama, wrote a personal letter to Cushing on the matter of *The Dancing Men*: 'I felt I must say how very regrettable it was that there should have been two interruptions to *The Dancing Men* transmission last Monday night; and coming so near to the start of this very important series. I would like you to understand that it was in no way due to carelessness with regard to the programme ... and further measures are being considered against a repetition, not only concerning drama but the service as a whole. May I add on a personal note that, having been close to the series for a couple of weeks, I am elated by your presence as "Holmes" on the screen both individually and together with "Watson"; I am deriving much warmth and pleasure.'

Andrew Osborn found that he had to be rather more hands-on with the project than had been expected. Will Sterling had directed several small films but was very inexperienced as a producer. He was effectively replaced by Osborn and Tosh, although his name was left in the credits. Cushing remained committed to the project but, as always, he liked to have the whole script memorised before the rehearsal period, and was dismayed by the number of last-minute rewrites. 'If I had to change a line,' Tosh remembers, 'Peter would say "Oh no, I can't take any more. It's too late. I can't make any more changes..." So we said, "OK, Peter, you say it your way, we'll get round it and shave

Holmes and Watson (Nigel Stock) consult *Peoples of All Nations* in the BBC adaptation of *The Sign of Four* (1968)

something else." Nigel Stock would take on anything, he just got on and did it, he didn't mind. Cushing was the star, he had to carry the whole series, that was why he was there – as a *major* star.'

There was drama off-screen at the conclusion of *The Solitary Cyclist,* however, on 25th November. Tosh recalls, 'Stanley Miller, a big fellow, long since dead, adapted *The Solitary Cyclist,* which has one of the worst endings of all time. The whole deduction hinged on this single line – Holmes suddenly says "I should have realised it was a false beard" or whatever. It really is pathetic, but it's Doyle. Stanley didn't really want to use it and Peter hated it. He said "I'm not going to say it." I said "You've got to say the line, it's the only explanation there is." Peter usually pulled us up because we weren't using the original Doyle lines. And now here was a line that *was* Doyle and he didn't like it. Stanley was jumping up and down in the gallery saying "That man will say that line! It's Doyle!" I think in the end they had to hold him down.

'Peter kept fluffing the line, so we couldn't use it. We'd got to about take 19 and somebody said "Do you realise we've got about three minutes and then they pull the plugs, or we're all on overtime?" The director, Viktors Ritelis, decided that he could edit around it and nobody would notice. I said "Don't tell Peter! Don't, for God's sake, say a word." I went storming out of the gallery, down onto the floor and accused Peter of unprofessionalism in front of the entire cast and crew. He was shocked to the core. He'd probably never been spoken to like that, or certainly

not recently. I said "I know you don't want to record this line, but we will record it once, if we have to pay overtime to everybody for the next week." Peter sailed through the rest of the scene, said it very quickly and it was all over and gone and wrapped up and we all breathed a sigh of relief.'[10]

Today, director Viktors Ritelis has nothing but happy memories of those troubled times. "I remember the *Holmes* series well," he says. "In fact some of my fondest work-related memories are of Peter Cushing, and his tiny wife who sat behind me in the gallery during recording. When she died he sent me a note thanking me for the way I treated her and it is one of my treasured possessions. Both were lovely people."

The Sign of Four and *The Blue Carbuncle* were the last two episodes of the series to be shot, and considering that emotions behind-the-scenes were becoming more and more strained, it is not perceptible on screen.

The Sign of Four was adapted from Doyle's 1890 novella by Holmes aficionados Michael and Mollie Hardwick, and features Ann Bell as Mary Morstan, who – in the book – became Mrs Watson. That particular romantic entanglement is not included in the script, although Stock's Watson is clearly taken with the lady. A lengthy filmed sequence, as Holmes, Watson and Toby the dog track the villainous Jonathan Small, was shot in York Street and Church Road in Twickenham, in Isleworth and on a boat on the Thames at Brentford.

As Christmas 1968 approached, a proposed version of *The Red Circle* by the Hardwicks had been shelved, so Donald Tosh dug out Stanley Miller's adaptation of the Holmes Christmas story *The Blue Carbuncle.* The script was too short and lacked incident, so Tosh rewrote it entirely to return it more or less to Doyle's original story of Mr Henry Baker, whose Christmas goose 'lays a beautiful blue egg' – the Countess of Morcar's priceless jewel, the Blue Carbuncle. The story features one of Holmes's most bewitching pieces of deduction, delineating Baker's entire character and situation by examining his discarded hat, and Cushing presents this with characteristic aplomb.

The Devonshire Club in St James Street was used as a location for the Cosmopolitan Hotel where the jewel theft takes place, while Great Goodwin Farm, near Guildford, became Mrs Oakshott's goose farm. Harry Wilde was engaged to tutor Cushing in miming with the violin and the Salvation Army were paid five guineas for recording carols. The filming was completed on 29th November but the studio scenes were recorded just a week before the programme's transmission.

Despite the problems, the series was a great success and Cushing was hailed as a definitive Holmes for a new generation. The series received awards in Italy and Hong Kong, with ten of the episodes repeated in colour in the summer of 1970.

Chapter Nineteen

Scientist, Surgeon, Madman, Murderer

Towards the end of the *Sherlock Holmes* recordings, Cushing selected his favourite television moments when he appeared on *Star Choice* for BBC 1, recorded on 10th December for a fee of 50 guineas. With just a fortnight off, Cushing was back at Hammer for *Frankenstein Must Be Destroyed*, which began filming on 13th January 1969. This was Cushing's fifth appearance as Frankenstein and he was again directed by Terence Fisher, with an exceptional supporting cast including Veronica Carlson, Simon Ward, Freddie Jones and Maxine Audley.

Although unremittingly grim, the film is a magnificent piece of work and regarded by many as Hammer's finest film. This is also Cushing's most detailed performance – the *Frankenstein* cycle gave Cushing and Fisher the opportunity to refine a characterisation of considerable depth and frightening conviction.

This was Cushing's first film for Hammer since they departed Bray Studios, and as a result, the exteriors (at ABPC Elstree) look bigger, more realistic and genuinely foreign, away from the storybook settings of *Frankenstein Created Woman*. The photography is gritty and grainy, and Fisher experiments with new techniques including many more close-ups. The film's grammar is fluent and more assured, and the script, by assistant director Bert Batt, makes the familiar set-ups fresh and fascinating.

The film opens as a mysterious cloaked figure makes his way through a European square – we don't see his face, but Cushing's distinctive gait gives the game away. James Bernard's hurdy-gurdy music mimics Anton Karas' 'Harry Lime' theme as the unsuspecting Doctor Heidecke approaches his consulting-room. The unseen figure raises a sickle, and blood splashes over the brass name-plate.

The close-ups, cuts and hand-held camerawork in this early sequence are not typical of Fisher, but we are back on more familiar ground with the appearance of Harold Goodwin as a reassuringly comic burglar. Cushing, his face still unseen, follows silently as the burglar descends into a basement laboratory. With effortless grace, Fisher tricks out the suspense,

until the burglar stumbles on a ghastly, pallid body suspended in a tank – a classic shock. But there's more to come. Cushing makes his way through the laboratory, his hand idly brushing the retorts. Suddenly we see the Baron's ghastly bald mask. It is a startling, repellent image and the previous shock is effectively topped. The Baron and the burglar fight – knocking over the body in the tank, of course – the whole urgently scored by Bernard. If the masked Frankenstein is occasionally a stuntman – there's no reason why it shouldn't be – there is one shot at least in which Cushing's body language comes across clearly. The burglar escapes and the Baron tears off his mask in fury. Cushing's wide eyes and panting, sweating face carry a genuine thrill of excitement. The music sounds a fanfare – '*Frank-en-stein Must-Be-Dest-royed!*' – and the Baron sets to work disposing of the body from the tank.

Later, the burglar, almost delirious with terror, is interviewed by Inspector Frisch (Thorley Walters), who rightly suspects that they are looking for a 'mad and highly dangerous medical adventurer.' Meanwhile Frankenstein, impeccably mannered and eminently charming, arrives at a guest house run by Anna Spengler (Veronica Carlson). Under the alias of Mr Fenner, the Baron makes himself at home. Anna's fiancé, Karl Holst (Simon Ward), works at the local asylum with the formidable Professor Richter (Freddie Jones). One of their patients is the deranged Doctor Frederick Brandt, who reputedly practised brain transplants. Holst is stealing drugs from the asylum to pay for treatment for Anna's invalid mother. Frankenstein immediately seizes this weakness and blackmails Holst into assisting him.

Cushing's performance is more measured than the flamboyance of *Created Woman*, informed, no doubt, by his work before the television cameras in *Sherlock Holmes*. Physically, he looks exactly like Holmes, his costume is almost identical, although his expressions are harder and he speaks in short, clipped sentences. Cushing's own hair is dyed to match the toupée, which he wore as Holmes – as a result, Frankenstein looks very slightly artificial, almost robotic.

Frankenstein and Holst (Simon Ward) hurry to remove the brain of Professor Brandt (George Pravda) in *Frankenstein Must Be Destroyed* (1969)

The rape scene proved exceptionally difficult for Veronica Carlson and Peter Cushing to film. 'I thought the world of Jimmy Carreras, but it was an error,' Carlson remembers. 'Peter didn't want to do it. He took me to dinner one evening to discuss it but it didn't make the scene any easier. I couldn't refuse to do it. Terence Fisher was very understanding but it was totally humiliating. Every alternative was more vulgar than the last ... Terry just said "Cut. That's it," and turned away. Peter and I just stayed there and held on to each other.'

Although the scene sits awkwardly in the continuity of the film, it is undeniably very powerful, played with a frenzied conviction by Cushing. Frankenstein repeatedly kisses Anna but there is no passion – the Baron is impotent of emotional feeling, and this is simply a monstrous act of violation. Properly, Anna should afterwards have been revolted by Frankenstein's very presence, but the rape was filmed *after* many of the subsequent scenes.

Frankenstein returns to work and begins surgery to put Brandt's brain in Richter's body, using little more than carpenter's tools – none of the electrical jiggery-pokery of the previous films. Here is some of the grimmest brain-work in any of the Hammer *Frankensteins*. As technology had moved on in the 1960s, so Frankenstein's methods seem to have regressed. Cushing handles it all grim-faced – he's even unshaven at this point.

Windsor Davies appears as a policeman, intent on searching the premises with his men. Bernard's strings create a diabolical tension while Davies simply walks up and down. Even after his three murders and a rape, the audience is placed in the unlikely position of *not wanting* Frankenstein to be caught. Even the Baron allows himself a small smile as the police are deflected and the surgery can continue. The experiment is a success. Pleased with himself, Frankenstein goes out for a constitutional. Unfortunately, as he buys himself a buttonhole, he is spotted by Brandt's wife, Ella. Frankenstein's vanity is his undoing once again.

The sudden burst of a water-main at the Spengler house temporarily exhumes the late Doctor Brandt. There is something obscene about Brandt's dead arm flapping in the plume of water that erupts from the flowerbed, and poor traumatised Anna – not far from insanity herself – has to drag Brandt's body out of

It is a tight script, full of highly concentrated action in a short space of time and, significantly, there is no subplot – Frankenstein is on screen nearly all the time.

On a raid to the asylum to steal equipment for a new laboratory, Frankenstein and Holst are apprehended by a nightwatchman. Panicked, Holst kills him and they flee back to the guest house. 'Who *are* you?' Holst demands. 'I am Baron Frankenstein,' says the Baron, with a glance aloft to an irate Jehovah. He explains that Brandt – with whom he had been in correspondence – had discovered a successful method of transplanting brains. He must now cure Brandt's madness to learn the secret.

The subsequent kidnap of Brandt from the asylum is botched and Brandt suffers a heart attack. Back at the laboratory, watched by the terrified Anna, Frankenstein massages Brandt's chest. With a single, deft movement Cushing takes out his pocket-watch to time the heartbeats. Before Brandt dies, his brain must be transplanted into another body – more specifically, into the body of another *doctor*, Frankenstein thus exacting his revenge on the medical profession that has disowned him. 'Professor Richter would be ideal...'

A little later, Anna discovers Frankenstein and Karl with Professor Richter's unconscious body. She is sent back to her room, where Frankenstein later rapes her. This scene was included shortly before shooting wrapped at the instruction of James Carreras, who claimed the distributor feared there was not enough sex in the picture. Ironically, the scene was ultimately cut from American prints.

the sodden earth and hide it elsewhere. Later, when Frankenstein returns, the water repair men have dug up the garden. Momentarily startled, he exchanges glances with Anna. 'There's nothing more to be seen here...' he tells the onlookers, before airily remarking to the workmen 'Ruined my plants!'

In the meantime, Ella Brandt has found a caricature portraying her husband and Frankenstein as vultures and she decides to pay a visit on the Baron. Greeted kindly by Frankenstein, Frau Brandt is taken to her husband – or at least to the bandaged *thing* he says is her husband. Cushing's scenes with Maxine Audley have a special finesse. She was an old friend from the *Caesar and Cleopatra* days and the rapport of these two theatre-trained actors is apparent. Cushing makes it seem that there is concern at the heart of Frankenstein's actions but we are aware that he is manipulating Frau Brandt with meticulous cruelty. The ruse works – he has bought the time they need.

After kissing Audley on the hand, Cushing turns back to camera, and his face fills the frame. 'Pack!' he spits. 'We're leaving!'

The next day, Ella returns and realises she has been deceived. Brandt's body is subsequently discovered in the outhouse. Meanwhile, Frankenstein, Karl and Anna have returned with Brandt/Richter to his earlier laboratory, seen at the beginning of the film. Freddie Jones wakes, pulls off the bandages and looks in disbelief at his 'wrong' hands. In a silver tray, Brandt sees his reflection – but not *his* reflection. Frankenstein discovers Karl in the stables, where the boy is planning his escape, and they fight. Anna encounters the desperate Brandt/Richter and

Cushing with Maxine Audley as Ella Brandt in *Frankenstein Must Be Destroyed* (1969). Audley had appeared on stage with Cushing in the 1950s

stabs him in panic before he runs off. Frankenstein, seeing what Anna has done, kills her.

Brandt/Richter goes back to Ella. He hides behind a screen and speaks like a frightened child. Jones carries the role with complete sincerity. 'I have become the victim of everything Frankenstein and I ever advocated.'

The next morning, bidding Ella leave, Brandt/Richter sets a trap. Frankenstein enters. 'I fancy that I am the spider and you are the fly, Frankenstein,' croons Jones. 'Better you had killed me...' A cat and mouse-chase ensues, with Brandt/Richter shying oil lamps onto the petrol-soaked floor. Frankenstein desperately tries to locate Brandt's notes. He finds them, and tries to

escape, but Brandt/Richter catches him and carries the screaming Frankenstein back into the burning house. The final end? Perhaps...

Work on *Frankenstein Must Be Destroyed* wrapped on 26th February 1969 and the film opened in May. For the *Sunday Telegraph,* brevity was the soul of wit. 'At the Warner, *Frankenstein Must Be Destroyed* – yet again! New monster, old tricks, with Peter Cushing reassuringly in charge.'[1]

The *Sunday Times* went into a little more depth. 'If you must have horror films, *Frankenstein Must Be Destroyed* is probably about as good as you can expect ... The good Doctor Frankenstein (Peter Cushing, of course) saws off the top of a victim's head and bores a hole in it with a handy brace-and-bit – the old elements of nausea, in fact, with redeeming ridiculousness. The comic effects in this series, always intentional, here are smarter than usual. After his exercise with the saw Frankenstein orders two lightly boiled eggs for breakfast.'[2]

When the film opened in America, *Variety* wrote enthusiastically: 'there's nothing tongue-in-cheek about the playing of Peter Cushing who gets his effect by an authority which carries along the audience and which he could hardly strengthen even if playing Lear for an Oscar.'[3]

This film shows the depths of Frankenstein's misogyny. He emotionally manipulates Ella Brandt and has completely brutalised Anna even before he rapes her. 'Let her go,' pleads Karl at one point. 'You don't need her.' 'I need her to make *coffee*,' spits Frankenstein. When Frankenstein finds Brandt in the asylum, he contemplates his friend through the bars of the cell door. We catch, in extreme close-up, the merest flicker of Cushing's eyes. This is truly film acting of the master class.

During *Frankenstein Must Be Destroyed*, the BBC filmed a documentary in the *Made in Britain* series called *Dracula and Frankenstein Make Money For Britain*. The programme was filmed at Elstree on 7 February and broadcast the following Monday, 10 February, and celebrated Hammer's receipt of the Queen's Award to Industry, which the company had been awarded in May 1968. As well as talking to James Carreras, interviewer Michael Sullivan spoke to Cushing on set

Cushing and Veronica Carlson consult the script with director Terence Fisher on the set of *Frankenstein Must Be Destroyed* (1969)

is rescued by Goodrich's agents and brought back to Oxford. However, his mind is disturbed. At the college's Quincentenary dinner, Fountain delivers a searing indictment of academic life, condemning the Doctors in scarlet as hypocritical vampires themselves. 'Let us beware of those who seek to possess our bodies and our minds,' Fountain cries, 'the thieves who come to take your souls. "Love me," says the academic "and do *exactly as I say*".'

After this outburst, Fountain finds Penelope and kills her by drinking her blood. He is chased onto the college roof but falls and is impaled on the railings below. As provost, Goodrich is empowered to act as coroner in respect of deaths which occur within the college precincts. Cushing brings a last note of eloquence to the film as he reports the death of his daughter and her fiancé with tears in his eyes. 'It is my verdict that Penelope Goodrich and Richard Fountain, being misused by the world, did in equal consent, take their own lives. The one by the letting of blood, the other by falling from a college building, while temporarily of unsound mind. May God have pity for their souls.'

There was not much money behind this production and it ran out altogether while Hartford-Davis was on location in Cyprus. The film was assembled later by the producers from the existing footage and Hartford-Davis took his name off it. The result looks like several different films have been cut together, and even within sequences there is little integrity. In Cushing's first scene – at a reception – there is such a wanton disregard for continuity that party-guests disappear from one side of a room to the other between lines. The Greek scenes fare a little better, featuring Patrick Macnee, newly de-mobbed from *The Avengers,* and some stunning scenery.

Cushing was featured in another cameo as Benedek in the Amicus/AIP collaboration *Scream and Scream Again*, which was filmed from 5th May 1969. The German-born director Gordon Hessler was a protegé of Roger Corman and though the cast also included Vincent Price and Christopher Lee, Cushing shared no scenes with them.

Scream and Scream Again is a surprisingly complex film for Amicus, based on Peter Saxon's 1967 novel *The Disorientated Man*, with a grotesque central premise about the take-over of the world by

and asked what sort of fan-mail he got. 'Oh, the most marvellous letters, literally from all over, some from Ghana … who write "My beloved father," which always makes my wife raise an eyebrow. One finished up by saying could he have a photograph and then he said "your occupational doings is very beautiful." …They come from China, Japan, everywhere you can think of. It's easier to say where they don't come from!'

Sullivan also asked Cushing whether he was worried about type-casting. Laughing, he replied 'Oh, it's never affected me! … I think as an actor you should and can do other things. But I love doing these pictures. People get enjoyment from them, so I'm very happy to be asked to do them.'

Behind-the-scenes footage from *Made in Britain* was included in the BBC's 1987 documentary *The Studio That Dripped Blood.*

Whatever Cushing thought of *Corruption*, it did not stop him taking part in another Titan film directed by Robert Hartford-Davis in 1969. This was called *Incense for the Damned*, based on Simon Raven's novel *Doctors Wear Scarlet*, and concerned the brilliant Oxford scholar Richard Fountain (Patrick Mower) who falls under the influence of vampirism. Cushing plays Doctor Walter Goodrich, Provost of Lancaster College, to whose daughter, Penelope, Fountain is engaged to be married. Goodrich is an intellectual bully, who has Fountain's career mapped out for him and whose only allegiance is to the honour of the college.

On holiday in Greece, Fountain becomes enchanted by the female vampire Chriseis (Imogen Hassall) but invulnerable synthetic beings. Cushing only took a day to shoot his appearance in an Eastern European segment, playing a neo-Fascist – he was asked to play similar roles, to his increasing discomfort, several times more in the 1970s. In the established Frankenstein tradition, Benedek is dispatched by one of the synthetic supermen.

In his autobiography, Cushing wrote with some pride that he was the first straight actor to appear on *The Morecambe and Wise Show*. Cushing's first for them was recorded on 30th and 31st May 1969 – as a concession to Eric Morecambe's heart condition, he and Ernie Wise recorded their 50-minute programme over two days. Cushing's first appearance was as King Arthur in a sketch with Ernie Wise as Merlin and Morecambe as Sir Lancelot – although Morecambe is dressed as Sherlock Holmes throughout, and says of Cushing, 'Watch him, he'll bite your neck.'

'What news of Carlisle?' splutters Cushing as Eric's foolery sets them giggling. 'They won 3-1!' says Eric.

Cushing became a regular guest on *The Morecambe and Wise Show* over the next ten years with a running gag that he was never paid for his first appearance. He *was* paid, of course – £367 and ten shillings – moreover he was paid the same again to attend the 16th and 17th August recording sessions to make his first 'complaint'.

Unlikely as it may seem, one of Cushing's biggest celebrity fans was the American entertainer Sammy Davis Jr, who had apparently seen every one of Hammer's films. Davis 'showed such kindness and hospitality to Helen and me,' Cushing wrote in *Past Forgetting*. 'First night tickets for his show at the Palladium, afterwards at the White Elephant Club, and endless appreciation for the enjoyment my performances had given him.' So, when Davis asked Cushing to join Christopher Lee in an unbilled cameo in his comic film *One More Time*, which was being directed at Shepperton by Jerry Lewis, Cushing readily agreed. In what amounted to little more than a morning's work, on 23rd July 1969 Cushing appeared once more as Baron Frankenstein, an unlikely resident (along with Count Dracula) of the cellar of Pepperworth Castle. As Sammy Davis stumbles onto the 'horror comics' scene after exploring a secret passage, he is greeted by the Baron with the line 'Aha! We have a visitor!' Dracula, with a glass of blood in his hand, asks 'Won't you join our little party?'

This vignette adds little to the film which concerns the misadventures of small-time crooks Charlie Salt (Davis)

and Chris Pepper (Peter Lawford), heroes of the 1968 movie *Salt and Pepper*. Although this cameo was only an excuse for Davis to appear with his heroes, he was clearly grateful for the opportunity and a fortnight later Cushing was the recipient of a dozen bottles of champagne and a colour television, with letters of appreciation from Davis and Jerry Lewis.

In 1969, Cushing spent much of the year looking after Helen. As her emphysema worsened, they decided to sell the Hillsleigh Road property and move down to Whitstable, where the sea air helped Helen's breathing. Cushing also had a stair-lift installed at the seaside retreat.

Cushing was called in to service in January 1970 to help Hammer out. They had struck up a co-finance deal with American International (the company that had produced Roger Corman's Poe pictures starring Vincent Price) to produce *The Vampire Lovers*, based on J S LeFanu's *Carmilla*. Ingrid Pitt, a Polish actress who had appeared in *Where Eagles Dare*, was cast by James Carreras as the vampire seductress Carmilla. However, AIP were concerned about financing a film with an unknown in the lead, and instructed Hammer to bring in Cushing to play General Spielsdorf. Shortly before filming began there was a press call, showcasing Cushing and Pitt, at the Savoy Hotel on 13th January.

The film was shot between 19th January and 4th March at ABPC Elstree Studios, with Roy Ward Baker directing. Baker had previously worked in Hollywood (where he directed the 1952 Marilyn Monroe thriller *Don't Bother To Knock*) and at Rank, where he was responsible for the classic *Titanic* drama *A Night To Remember* (1958). Baker's Hammer work included the

Cushing with director Gordon Hessler on the set of *Scream and Scream Again* (1969)

General Spielsdorf prepares to stake Carmilla Karnstein (Ingrid Pitt) in *The Vampire Lovers* (1970)

excellent *Quatermass and the Pit* (1967) and the black comedy *The Anniversary* (1968) with Bette Davis.

In the early scenes of *The Vampire Lovers* we see Cushing resplendent in a red uniform as the General. The studio scenes look a little underfunded, but the exteriors at Moor Park Golf Club are impressive and the acting does much to cover the joins as the plot rattles on with conviction. Soon after Marcilla (Pitt) comes to stay at the home of General Spielsdorf, his daughter Laura (Pippa Steel) begins to suffer nightmares in which she is molested by a monstrous cat. Soon she is becoming weak, and eventually, despite tender care from Marcilla, she dies.

There is still a relaxed quality to Cushing's performance. He has a good scene with Jon Finch as Laura's beau, Carl Ebbhardt, and later, in a deck-chair-striped waistcoat, he discusses Laura's illness with Ferdy Mayne's oblivious doctor, while Ingrid works her wickedness above. Cushing's bedside manner is touching, and spectacularly deft is his ultimate realisation that Marcilla is a fiend. When he rushes to Laura's bedside, unshaven, dressed in a splendid black nightgown, his howl of despair is truly touching. 'It is daylight now,' he breathes, 'and she is dead!' Finding the bite-marks on Laura's breast, he realises, aghast, what has been going on.

The General goes to consult his friend Baron Hartog (Douglas Wilmer) who seems to be a member of the middle-European vampire-hunting chapter of which Van Helsing is later a part. Carmilla moves on to the home of Sir Roger Morton (George Cole) where she begins turning her unhealthy affections to Morton's

daughter Emma (Madeline Smith), playing with her, praying with her and eventually preying *on* her. There is excellent support again from Kate O'Mara as Emma's governess Madame Peridot, who bemoans 'the trouble with this part of the world is that they have too many fairy-tales...' before herself being drawn into Carmilla's web of seduction. As Carl becomes informed of Carmilla's evil, he rides to save Emma from the same fate as Laura – and Jon Finch holds his sword hilt like a crucifix, as Olivier did in *Hamlet*.

At Karnstein Castle, the truth is revealed – Carmilla is the last of the vampiric Karnstein family. She is hunted down and there is a wonderful expression of revulsion from Cushing as he plunges the stake into Carmilla – it is his first bit of vampire-dispatching in nearly ten years.

'Often though I have thought to befriend the ill-used monsters of the screen,' wrote the *Sunday Times*, 'I had never thought of keeping a vampire as a pet – or so I felt until *The Vampire Lovers*. This is about a female vampire who battens by preference on the bosom of some sweet girl (vampirism, recognising the need to march or rather nuzzle with the times, has gone nudist). However she is ready to bite anyone of the male sex, too, beginning with a nibble at the ear and proceeding to a sanguinary gnaw at the throat. Pretty Madeline Smith, round-eyed and no wonder, provides some of the bosoms; the versatile vampire is played by Ingrid Pitt; and Peter Cushing is among the hosts who accept without demur her appearance, stunningly draped in scarlet, as a house-guest in the best Styrian families.

Later though, Mr Cushing mucks in, and I use the term advisedly, with the exterminating team. And now the film looks back on an earlier occasion when an executioner collapses, too tired to decapitate another thing. And suddenly you feel that Carmilla, temporary survivor of the massacre, deserves to join the martyred monsters of the screen. Somebody ought to set up a rehabilitation centre for delinquent vampires. Think, after all, of the scene when at breakfast after a night literally bloodthirsty, the sated girl is offered a dish of kedgeree or devilled kidneys. "I'm not hungry," she says pushing it away. You would have to go far to find a cheaper pet to feed.'[4]

Ingrid Pitt recalled her first meeting with Cushing as he chopped off her head, during the filming of Carmilla's climactic death scene when a dummy was set up for the decapitation. 'I mumbled something silly like "don't get cut up about it", but Peter was terribly sweet and offered to take me to tea to make up for it.' The friendship between Cushing and Pitt deepened on meeting Mrs Cushing. 'Helen could speak Russian, and I could manage a smattering, so we began sending cards to each other in Russian, with Peter acting as the postman. He did his job very well. Helen loved roses, and so I was sent cards with roses on them. I hadn't really been in London long, and I was a bit lonely, so it was kind of them to take me under their wing, if only for a short time. Then Peter found out that one of the last days of filming, 3rd March, was the 100th anniversary of my father's birth. At the end of the day's filming he brought out champagne and a cake, then took me and Helen off to a little restaurant. It was magical.'5

In early 1970, Hammer decided to ring the changes with the Frankenstein character and cast Ralph Bates as the Baron in Jimmy Sangster's *The Horror of Frankenstein*. Cushing duly appeared for a photocall to officially hand on the baton and participated in a behind-the-scenes promotional film, in which he talked about the character of Frankenstein.

From 29th June at Shepperton Studios, Cushing was working on another portmanteau film for Amicus called *The House That Dripped Blood*, directed by Peter Duffell. Because of Helen's worsening condition, Cushing had attempted to obtain a release from his contract, and while he was freed from Hammer's *Lust for a Vampire* (to which he was contracted and scheduled to begin on 6th July) he was held to the Amicus film.

Cushing appeared in a segment of *The House That Dripped Blood* called *Waxworks*, as retired stockbroker Philip Grayson, who becomes obsessed with the wax figure of Salome in a local wax museum. 'The story was nothing more than a contrivance to get Peter Cushing's head on a plate,' said Duffell. 'I decided to try to give the story a little resonance on the strictly human level by building up the loneliness of the character, taking refuge from the loneliness of life in his books, music and memories ... of the dead girl.'6 (The music included Schubert's 'Death and the Maiden', which gave Duffell his preferred – and rejected – title for the film.) For the scene when Grayson is seen flicking through some theatre programmes, Duffell provided the programmes himself, including one for Olivier's production of *The School for Scandal*, in which Cushing had played Sir Joseph Surface.

Joss Ackland and director Peter Duffell with Cushing on location in Weybridge for *The House that Dripped Blood* (1970)

The *Waxworks* segment, with able support from Joss Ackland and Wolfe Morris, is a grim enough little tale (based, like the other three segments, on stories by Robert Bloch), but let down by unappealing wax effigies and a thumpingly obvious twist. Of the other stories, Christopher Lee's tale of witchcraft is the best, while Jon Pertwee and Ingrid Pitt team up for a comic horror story about a vampire's cloak. Pitt remembers that, although they had no scenes together, she met Cushing for tea at the studios while filming, and they were together in the dubbing studio when the film was finished. The most affecting part of *The House That Dripped Blood* are the shots of Cushing, standing on a riverbank, lost in grief for his lost love. It is difficult not to think that he was anticipating the unendurable   Helen's death.

The critics were kind. 'Agreeable surprise,' said Dilys Powell in the *Sunday Times*. 'In *The House That Dripped Blood*, four stories go to make up a lively and intelligent essay, far better than its title suggests, in horror and joke-horror. Peter Duffell, directing his first feature film, has dealt admirably with a cast including Denholm Elliott, Peter Cushing, Christopher Lee and Nyree Dawn Porter.'7

Chapter Twenty

Losing Helen

When the volume of his fan mail had increased to huge proportions, Cushing decided to take on a secretary. But finding one who could stay the course was not easy. 'They came and went in bewildering succession,' he wrote, 'all to have babies (not guilty, m'lud). In September 1959, Mrs Joyce Buten arrived and promptly announced that she also wanted to start a family. In desperation, I told her that it didn't matter how many children she had, so long as she didn't leave us.'[1]

In 1974 Joyce remarried, to Bernard Broughton, and would remain as Cushing's secretary for the rest of his life.

In the late 1960s Helen began a correspondence course of breathing exercises which were improving her condition somewhat, until she was told by a locum doctor that what she was doing was waste of time. 'It was pitiful to see her spirit crumble,' Cushing said of that time. 'Although it wouldn't have made any difference to the inevitable outcome, that slap in the face took the heart out of her, and speeded her decline. Her weight went down to six stone – I had lost three myself – and we were both physically and mentally spent.'[2]

As Cushing no longer had a London home, when he was filming in Shepperton or Pinewood he would stay at Brown's Hotel in Mayfair – 'my favourite hotel in London'[3] he called it – and this accommodation would generally be included in his fee. For his next engagement, the Amicus film *I, Monster*, he did not want to be away from Helen in the evenings so travelled on the milk train from Whitstable at 6.00 am and returned home at 10.00pm at night. Joyce, who was living in Welling at this time, travelled to Whitstable to keep Helen company during the mornings and afternoons.

I, Monster, based on Robert Louis Stevenson's *Dr Jekyll and Mr Hyde*, was filmed from 10th October 1970, directed by 22-year-old director Stephen Weeks, with Christopher Lee in the dual role. In a transparent attempt by Milton Subotsky to duck copyright restrictions (MGM then owned the rights to the title), the central characters were re-named – Jekyll became Marlowe and Hyde became Blake – although most of Stevenson's other characters, including Cushing's character of the solicitor Utterson, were retained.

Subotsky also determined to make the film in 3-D, using a process that required constant lateral movement within the frame. This made conventional film grammar almost impossible and after a while, the process was abandoned, so in the finished film several interminable tracking shots are oddly cut together with static close-ups.

Despite the technical problems Christopher Lee gives an excellent central performance. The script, however, wastes no time on the subsidiary characters so Cushing spends an inordinate amount of time on the edge of the frame, nodding in agreement with colleagues Richard Hurndall and Mike Raven. Cushing loved the period furnishings, and wore

Cushing with Christopher Lee and 22-year-old director Stephen Weeks on the set of *I, Monster* (1970)

Contact sheet pictures recording Cushing's sole day of filming (alongside Valerie Leon) on Hammer's ill-fated Bram Stoker subject *Blood from the Mummy's Tomb* (1971)

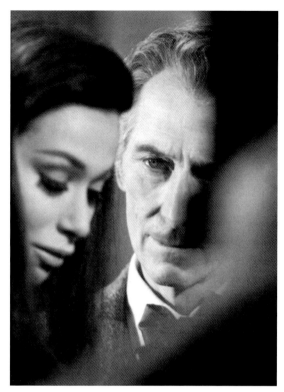

some of his own Edwardian styled clothes for the film, which were tailored for him by theatrical costumiers Montague Burton's – as a result, he seems completely at home in this era. He is even able to reprise the eye-up-to-the-magnifying-glass trick as he compares the identical signatures of Marlowe and Blake.

Although by turns tedious and confusing, the film has several startling scenes. A nightmare sequence features a distorted, faceless Marlowe; there is a spectacular chase through the massive turbines of a water-works and the monstrously ugly Blake's pathetic encounter with a small child in a park. The film has an authentically cluttered look and Carl Davis' lyrical score does much to unify the disparate elements.

Cushing's last job in 1970 was *The Morecambe and Wise Christmas Show*, recorded on 16th December 1970 at Television Centre for transmission on Christmas Day. Eric and Ernie's guests included William Franklyn, Edward Woodward and Eric Porter, with Cushing emerging from a grandfather clock at one point to complain once again that he hadn't been paid.

On 11th January 1971, Cushing began work as Professor Julian Fuchs in Hammer's *Blood from the Mummy's Tomb*, an adaptation of Bram Stoker's *The Jewel of Seven Stars*. The director was Seth Holt. Cushing completed only one day's work on the picture, which is recorded in a handful of stills with leading lady Valerie Leon.

'At the end of the first day,' wrote Cushing, 'Joyce rang to say Helen had been taken into Canterbury Hospital for a check-up, where she would be kept for a few days. She looked tired when I got there in the evening, but comfortable enough.' But that night, Helen had a relapse. 'I begged the doctor to let her come home, and he agreed, pointing out that she would need constant nursing.'[4]

Cushing asked John Redway to cancel his participation in *Blood from the Mummy's Tomb*. He brought Helen back to Whitstable and arranged

day-and-night nursing care. 'For a little while, she improved, amid familiar surroundings and loving care, but it was only temporary, like an electric light bulb, that sometimes seems to glow brighter for a few seconds just before the filament burns itself out, and is extinguished forever.' At two minutes past nine on the morning of 14th January 1971, with her husband by her bedside, Helen Cushing died.

'I went out onto the deserted beach,' Cushing recalled. 'It was blowing almost gale force ... I began humming "Happy Birthday To You". I think I'd gone a little mad. I found myself indoors again, wandering aimlessly about the house, then suddenly started rushing up and down stairs as fast as I could, in the vain hope of inducing a heart attack.'[5]

He would consider suicide more than once in the weeks that followed. But, he wrote, 'Deep down I knew I would never take such a step ... It wouldn't be fair, I thought. Someone would have to clear up the grisly mess; it is not allowed by God; it wouldn't get me what I wanted, anyway – to be reunited immediately with Helen and in any case I hadn't the necessary courage. Over-riding all these considerations, there was that message that Helen left me in her last letter. 'Let the sun shine in your heart. Do not pine for me, my beloved Peter, because that will cause unrest. Do not be hasty to leave this world, because you will not go until you have lived the

Gustav Weil contemplates the evil of the Karnsteins in *Twins of Evil* (1971)

14th February aged 47. Michael Carreras stepped in as director]. Then one of the art department boys was killed on his motorbike.'[8] The crew of *Blood from the Mummy's Tomb* organised a wreath of flowers to be sent to Helen's funeral.

More than two months would elapse after Helen's death before Cushing was able to return to work in late March 1971. He was reunited with some familiar faces to play Gustav Weil in Hammer's *Twins of Evil* at Pinewood Studios. The gaunt-looking Cushing was clearly very upset, although acute, stupefying grief would not engulf him until some four years later.

Cushing's burden of sadness does not get in the way of his performance; if anything, it lends it an added dimension. Weil is as powerful and detailed a characterisation as Frankenstein, and a real return to form after Cushing's unsurprisingly distracted turn as Utterson.

Twins of Evil was the third film in Hammer's Karnstein trilogy. The second was *Lust for a Vampire*, originally intended to be directed by Terence Fisher and to star Cushing – scriptwriter Tudor Gates had written the part of Giles Barton, a student of the occult, especially for the actor. When Fisher suffered a fall and was unable to participate, Jimmy Sangster took over as director, then Cushing declined the role so he could care for Helen.

Twins of Evil, like *Vampire Lovers* and *Lust for a Vampire*, was produced by Harry Fine and Michael Style, written by Tudor Gates, and featured the female vampire Carmilla Karnstein. The film retained the same Styrian locale from the first two Carmilla pictures but under director John Hough the tone was darker than Roy Ward Baker's fairy-tale *milieu*. A Western in all but the trappings it was clearly influenced by Michael Reeves' 1967 film *Witchfinder General* and Weil is not very far in manner and dress from Vincent Price's Matthew Hopkins.

'Peter Cushing takes a protective attitude to the questionable characters he has played over the years,' stated Hammer's publicity material for *Twins of Evil*. 'And his latest is no exception. "This chap is by no means a baddie," he said. "He's a fanatical puritan and believes that what he's doing is absolutely right.

life you have been given. And remember, we will meet again when the time is right ... this is my promise.'[6]

Blood from the Mummy's Tomb continued with Andrew Keir in the role of Fuchs. 'The producer, Howard Brandy, rang me to see if I'd help Hammer out,' Keir recalled. 'He said "We've tried to carry on, but it isn't going to work. Peter's very upset." The part was written for Peter, he had his own personality and style and that's what the writer saw. Obviously, if you're writing it for Peter, you must know his work. The character had something that it wouldn't have had if it had been written for me.'[7]

The production of *Blood from the Mummy's Tomb* was dogged by tragedy, as assistant director Derek Whitehurst remembers. 'First Peter left, then we lost the director, Seth Holt [who died of a heart attack on

His religion dictates that the way to rid the evil or sin from people is to burn them – a dreadful thing to do but he is not just doing it out of vengeance.'[9]

If Weil does have human feelings, they are buried very deep and even at his gentlest, he speaks in a kind of controlled roar. Before the credits, the Brotherhood burst in on a helpless village girl who is dragged out and summarily burned at the stake. Cushing gives her an expression of revulsion, pity, resignation – even self-disgust – all in a sneer. Weil can stop the Brotherhood from rioting with a word and then, with a flick of his head, set them off again. Later, he makes the simple act of washing his hands into an affecting gesture. Kathleen Byron is excellent as his gentle wife, who has to put up with a husband who rarely enters a room without first throwing open the door and then standing framed in the doorway, snarling.

As the story begins, Weil takes in his orphaned nieces, the twins Maria and Freda (Mary and Madeleine Collinson). Maria is virtuous but Freda is wicked, and soon rebels against her stern uncle who regards the two girls as 'birds of paradise' in their exotic travelling clothes. Freda is duly seduced and corrupted by the sybaritic Count Karnstein (Damien Thomas), who himself has been turned into a vampire by the spirit of his ancestor, Carmilla.

Weil's austerity serves to make Karnstein's debauchery more exotic. Damien Thomas counters as a handsome and cultured villain, spitting taunts at his dour adversary. 'Pray for me, Weil. That's what you're supposed to do for sinners, isn't it? *Pray for me!*'

The plotting is uneven, Cushing's lines become repetitive and there are three almost identical burnings before the film is halfway through. As in *The Vampire Lovers*, the vampires aren't bothered by daylight, and after a while it begins to seem ridiculous that Weil and his men spend their nights thundering about the countryside riding down every young girl they can find. ('Some men like a musical evening,' Karnstein glitters. 'Weil and his friends find their pleasure from burning innocent girls.') With Karnstein seeing off his share and the Brotherhood burning the rest, it's a wonder there are any girls left in the village at all. The showdown at the finale sees Weil with an axe in his back and Karnstein impaled on a spear – a fittingly grim conclusion to a bleak morality play.

While reviews generally assessed *Twins of Evil* as 'more of the same', it fell to the burgeoning fan press, which now included genre magazines like *Cinefantastique*, to give the film due credit for shifting the goalposts – Cushing was particularly praised for bringing sympathy to the 'twisted witch-hunting uncle [who] travels the lonely road of evil-doing in the Lord's name.'[10]

On 11th July, a short item appeared in the *Sunday Express*. 'On most days around lunchtime, actor Peter Cushing cycles away from his home in Whitstable.

He returns after four or five hours and goes straight to bed. "My wife Helen died in January and I cycle to stop thinking about her. I set off in one of three directions, towards Faversham, Margate or Canterbury. It's about 14 miles there and back to Canterbury. I stop off for cups of tea in tea shops I used to go to with Helen. Everywhere I cycle holds memories of her. We went everywhere together. She's with me all of the time … I've given up many of the things we used to do. The memory is too harrowing. That's why I cycle every day."'[11]

Thus the general public was informed of the desperate straits of one of its most beloved stars. There was immediately an enormous outpouring of affection. 'I have been deeply moved by the many letters I have received following the article last week,' wrote Cushing to the *Sunday Express* on 18th July 1971. 'I shall answer them all in time. No doubt through my own fault, I was misquoted. I never could – and would never try – to forget my beloved wife Helen. My cycling is for a number of reasons but not that. I suffer a great deal of remorse for certain things done, and certain things not done – and it is these destructive elements which I am trying to exorcise. If self-pity crept into what I said then it must be true. But I had no wish to give that impression. If it were not the certain Truth and Knowledge that I shall be reunited with my loved one when my pilgrim journey on this strange land is finished – then I could not face up to anything. Without that promise, the whole of this life would be a mockery and a waste. The best is yet to come for all of us. In the mean time, this life must go on. And I shall endeavour to give of my best in work and diverse activities. Thank you again for your kind thoughts of me. May God's blessing be with you always.'[12]

On 27th July 1971, Cushing travelled to Harpenden to film the BBC 2 *Nature Spectacular* for producer Richard Brock. The fee was £100 (plus the rail fare from Whitstable to London, £2.10).

'Work – a problem to solve is all I ask. Give me work.' So said Cushing as Sherlock Holmes at the conclusion of *The Sign of Four*, and Cushing, perhaps also remembering Holmes' advice to Watson that 'work is the best antidote to sorrow', launched himself into a gruelling schedule of five films in the next four months. An unmade project from this period was Peter Bryan's script *Dead…?* which would have seen Cushing as Mainard, the leader of a psychic society who becomes involved with the horrible consequences of a séance at a carnival.

At the beginning of September he was back with Amicus and director Freddie Francis for *Tales from the Crypt*, a $500,000 adaptation of five stories from the American EC horror comics. Cushing's name had been linked with these maligned publications as far back as the *Nineteen Eighty-Four* outcry.

Cushing is made up by Roy Ashton for the role of the zombie Grimsdyke in *Tales from the Crypt* (1971)

The finished make-up as seen on screen in *Tales from the Crypt* (1971)

Grimsdyke is a poignant creation, meticulously drawn and played with care and subtlety. The plucky old man is first seen entertaining the local children while his spoiled and affluent neighbour James Elliot (played by Robin Phillips) looks on and decides to destroy him for no reasons other than jealousy and spite.

Dressed in a blue bobble-hat and threadbare cardigan, with stubbly grey whiskers, Grimsdyke is everyone's favourite grandad – the accent is basically Dr Who-with-the-corners-taken-off. 'As written, all his lines were spoken to himself,' said Cushing of Grimsdyke. 'A lonely sad figure, with only his faithful dog for company, but somehow the situation didn't ring true to me. I drew inspiration from personal experience, as I was in similar circumstances, apart from the dog. I found I could address some of the dialogue to this pet, as one so often does in real life, but for the major portion, I needed something else. At home, a photograph of Helen hangs on the wall above my writing-desk, and during those dark days I often found myself looking at it and speaking to her. I thought this would be the answer to my problem with Grimsdyke, and Freddie Francis agreed. We didn't use Helen's picture, as it would have been wrong "casting", but a suitable face was found and put in a cheap wooden frame, upon which the old boy whom I was to play could gaze longingly.'[15]

It is difficult to watch the scenes where Grimsdyke's hands tremble over a ouija board to contact his late wife (who, of course, is called Helen) but the scene is undeniably powerful. Her message warns of danger and Cushing's eyes widen in terror. 'Danger? Who to? Is it one of the children?' Like Job, Grimsdyke bears his persecutions stoically – by Elliot's machinations, the old man loses his job, his pension, his beloved dogs. Even the children are told to stay away from him. 'Just one more turn of the screw' promises Elliot.

Then, on Valentine's Day, Grimsdyke receives a bundle of cards. 'But you're my only sweetheart,' he tells his wife. The cards are full of hateful verses. Cushing reads and re-reads them in bewilderment. 'Some people live in the country, some people live in

Cushing was sent the script but disliked the part he was offered – the role of Ralph Jason in the *Monkey's Paw*-styled episode *Wish You Were Here*, which was eventually taken by Richard Greene. He spotted the role of Arthur Grimsdyke in the *Poetic Justice* story and asked John Redway to suggest this. 'The role in the script,' Cushing said, 'was originally nothing. The story as written was about the young man. Subotsky said, "Of course, let him have it!"'[13]

With the assistance of Freddie Francis, Cushing virtually ad-libbed the part. 'I based the character of Grimsdyke on an old man I once knew. He was rich but wore shabby clothes all the time, and was good to the kids in the neighbourhood.'[14]

the town. Why don't you do us a service? Jump in the river and – ' The final, disbelieving, heartbroken quiver of his mouth is profoundly moving.

Grimsdyke hangs himself and Elliot discovers the body. Cushing helped to choreograph the details – one shoe off, revealing a woolly sock, a withered pot-plant and the shattered frame of his wife's photograph. Grimsdyke, who studied books on spiritualism, has the last laugh, however, and a year later he rises from the grave set on revenge.

The old man's resurrection is cleverly done, with a double-exposure effect that captures the half-glimpsed quality of a nightmare, and Cushing himself insisted on playing the zombified Grimsdyke rather than employing a stand-in. The heart-stopping effect of putting gauze over his eyes to suggest gaping sockets was worked out in the lunch break between Cushing and his good friend, make-up artist Roy Ashton.

As Grimsdyke approaches Elliot in his study, he steps stiffly from the blackness of the shadows and places his rotting hand delicately on the desk, a touch Cushing put in himself, recalling a similar detail from Boris Karloff's shock appearance in *The Mummy* (1932).

'Peter Cushing – What would a horror film be without him?' asked the Amicus press notes. 'Certainly my public image overshadows reality,' admitted Cushing, 'but that's what the movie business is all about, isn't it? It means I'm doing something right.'[17]

In *Cinefantastique*, Dan Scapperotti stated '*Poetic Justice* was the best of the five tales. Freddie Francis elicits the finest performance from Cushing as the aged Grimsdyke. The veteran actor presents a character both pathetic and noble. As the persecuted junk man, Cushing maintains his dignity as his world crumbles around him.'[18]

The *New York Times* thought that *Tales from the Crypt* was not 'strictly speaking, a horror film at all, although it has its share of silly supernatural effects. Its people are small and spiteful and their bad ends exhibit the kind of heavy morality I associate less with fine horror fiction than with cautionary literature designed to persuade children to brush their teeth.'[19]

Cushing went from Amicus straight back to Hammer to reprise the role of Van Helsing for the first time since 1960 in *Dracula A.D. 1972*. Filming started on 27th September at MGM-EMI Elstree (formerly ABPC), directed by Alan Gibson, with Christopher Lee as Dracula, Michael Coles, Christopher Neame

Lee and Cushing on Hadley Common with producer Josephine Douglas, during filming of the prologue for *Dracula A.D. 1972* (1971)

and Stephanie Beacham. The producer was Josephine Douglas who, as a BBC producer, had worked with Cushing in the 1950s.

Dracula A.D. 1972 begins well as Dracula and Lawrence Van Helsing fight it out on top of a coach in 1872 – the coach crashes and Dracula is impaled on a broken carriage-wheel. Cushing is wide-eyed as Dracula decomposes in front of him once again, before a classic double-take-and-fade-away as Van Helsing drops dead of his exertions. It is a thrilling sequence, lent a bluish phosphorescence by the day-for night filters. If the film had maintained this pitch it would have been much the better. As it is, the early 'modern' scenes are almost unwatchable.

Things cheer up as we see Lorrimer Van Helsing, grandson of the above, approaching in long shot – a rather old-fashioned-looking figure in the London of 1972. He berates his grand-daughter Jessica (Beacham) for putting her feet on his writing-desk and reading his books – 'This is my place of work, not W H Smith and Son' – but becomes genuinely concerned when he discovers that she is dabbling with the occult.

Van Helsing hunts Dracula in modern-day Chelsea in *Dracula A.D. 1972 (1971)*

Cushing's almost imperceptible expression of confusion as Jessica tells her grandfather 'I've never dropped acid, I'm not shooting up...' shows a man struggling to keep up with a changing world.

Cushing has several fine scenes, particularly an exchange with Michael Coles' Inspector Murray that gives the lie to the theory that Cushing was out of his depth in a modern setting. When it becomes clear that Dracula has been resurrected, Van Helsing visits a church to fill a bottle of holy water from the stoup and Cushing's slightly guilty look around as he adds to his vampire-hunting accoutrements is priceless. When Jessica is kidnapped by Dracula's minions, Van Helsing pelts up and down the King's Road before

falling exhausted against a shop window in a state of genuine despair. There's even a touch of the old Van Helsing's fierce athleticism in the fight between Cushing and Christopher Neame. 'I think it's valid ... that Van Helsing should be viewed by Scotland Yard as an elderly eccentric,' Cushing said. 'Any man who leaves home in the morning with a doctor's bag filled with crucifixes and sharpened stakes just in case he should run into a few vampires ... He's got a few problems of his own.'[20]

In his handful of scenes, Christopher Lee looks magnificent as Dracula, but has practically nothing to do. In the final confrontation with Van Helsing, however, the vampire is as animalistically savage as in 1958, and even gets a genuine Stoker line – 'You would play your brains against mine? Against me, who has commanded nations?' Cushing conceded that the role of Van Helsing offered much more potential than the role of Dracula. 'Christopher doesn't want to keep playing the sort of Dracula films he has been playing – *Dracula in the Dark, Dracula Meets Frankenstein, Search the House for Dracula*. All he has to do as Dracula is stand in a corner, show his fangs and hiss.'[21]

Marjorie Bilbow, in *Cinema TV Today*, found the film 'a not particularly convincing attempt to bring old Drac up to date that even undemanding addicts are unlikely to find very exciting.' Her review encapsulates the contemporary opinion of the film, although there is high praise for Cushing. 'The idea of Count Dracula coming to life in the present day is good and it is perfectly feasible to assume that the vogue interest in the black arts should provide him with his chance to return. The film would be much more successful if it did not make such desperate efforts to be up-to-the-minute with slang expressions that manifestly do not come naturally to the cast or the characters they are portraying, or waste so much plot time on party and disco scenes that are old-hat telly. What with music that is more bang-bang thriller than spooky, and direction that emphasises the crime and detection element rather than the supernatural, Dracula and his activities get pushed into the background. Only Peter Cushing, moving serenely and sincerely through the thicket of trite dialogue and over-anxious performances, achieves moments of chilling conviction.'[22]

On 30th September, Cushing appeared on Radio 2's *Late Night Extra* programme

Inspector Murray (Michael Coles), Van Helsing and his grand-daughter Jessica (Stephanie Beacham) in *Dracula A.D. 1972 (1971)*

to talk about the new Hammer *Dracula*. A week later he was interviewed at Brown's Hotel by John Doran for *Be My Guest*, broadcast on Radio 2 on 19th November. On returning to Whitstable, he was interviewed at home for a documentary on comics in BBC 2's *Man Alive* series, recalling the days of the *Gem* and the *Magnet* with examples from his own collection.

Another assignment for Hammer followed quickly, with a film called *Fear in the Night*. Jimmy Sangster was producer, director and co-writer, with a small cast comprising newcomers Judy Geeson and Ralph Bates, with Joan Collins – although all of Cushing's scenes were with Geeson.

The film was shot between 15th November and 17th December 1971 on location and at MGM-EMI Elstree. The total budget for the film was a mere £141,000, and Cushing's fee for four days' filming was £1000.

'You must think me a very dry old stick.' Michael Carmichael meets Peggy Heller (Judy Geeson) in Jimmy Sangster's *Fear in the Night* (1971)

The story involves the fragile Peggy Heller (Geeson) who, while recovering from a nervous breakdown, is attacked in her home by an unseen assailant – all she can remember later is tearing off the attacker's false arm. However, because of her emotional state, her claims of the assault are disbelieved. She goes to stay at the school where her husband Robert (Bates) works, but there she discovers that the school has no pupils, and the headmaster has an artificial arm...

Cushing's place in the story, as the improbably named headmaster Michael Carmichael, is simply to play the bogeyman, but this he does very effectively indeed. His initial appearance, as he looms out of nowhere, is splendidly creepy. With his hairpiece rigidly set, Cushing maintains a suitably robotic bearing and adds off-putting little touches like sniffing Geeson's hair. Carmichael is one of the rare instances of Cushing playing a genuinely damaged character. We learn that the headmaster was injured in a terrible fire at the school and that the whole building is kept operational, with tape-recordings standing in for the pupils, for him to play-act his former role.

Unfortunately, *Fear in the Night* is a case of very little meat and an awful lot of gravy. "We had such fun on the set," recalled Jimmy Sangster. "Judy Geeson was rather a dear and Peter was just super. The problem was when we'd nearly finished shooting and I realised it was likely to be very short. So I had to hold a lot of walks and entrances and exits far longer than one normally would."[23]

On 20th November 1971, Cushing travelled to Bristol to take part in a series called *Sounds Natural* for Radio 4. He was interviewed on his interest in wildlife and the countryside, and the talk was illustrated with sound recordings from the BBC Sound Archive.

In November of the previous year, director Robert Fuest had wanted Cushing to play Doctor Vesalius in Vincent Price's art deco horror extravaganza *The Abominable Dr Phibes*. Cushing chose instead to spend his time nursing Helen, and Vesalius was played by Joseph Cotten. In December 1971, however, Cushing filmed a cameo at Elstree for the second Phibes film, *Dr Phibes Rises Again*, again directed by Fuest.

Disfigured genius Anton Phibes (Price) is racing against time – and the mysterious archaeologist Biederbeck – to reach the sacred 'river of life' in Egypt, where Phibes intends to revive his late wife Victoria. On board a passenger steamer, the *Elsinore Castle*, Phibes sees off a meddlesome scholar of antiquities called Ambrose, dumping him overboard in a giant gin bottle. Cushing appears as the ship's captain in a short scene with Robert Quarry as Biederbeck, insisting that they continue looking for Ambrose. Biederbeck says, on the contrary, that they must continue on their way with all speed. Cushing looks smart and sober in his captain's uniform, with his own moustache neatly trimmed. He gets one joke in his minute-and-a-half-long conversation. "I suppose," he asks Biederbeck of the late scholar, "he never ... touched the bottle?" Legendary tippler Hugh Griffith, Cushing's TV co-star in *The Moment of Truth*, played Ambrose.

Chapter Twenty-One

Can You Cure Unhappiness?

In December, Cushing joined the cast of Spanish/British co-production *Panico en el Transiberiano* (in English territories, *Horror Express*), made at the Studio 70 Complex, Madrid, by director Eugenio Martin, with Christopher Lee and Telly Savalas co-starring. Cushing disliked overseas filming but his intention here was clearly to be as far away as possible from familiar things for his first Christmas without Helen. When he got to Spain, however, he was all ready to come straight home again. It was only the kind words of producer Bernard Gordon and Christopher Lee that persuaded him to stay. To further bolster his spirits, Cushing was invited to spend Christmas with Lee, his wife Gitte and their young daughter Christina.

It would have been a pity to lose Cushing's performance as Doctor Wells opposite Christopher Lee's Alexander Saxton – they are a monster-beating version of Charters and Caldicott, from Hitchcock's *The*

Doctor Wells and Professor Saxton (Christopher Lee) realise the truth about their extra-terrestrial enemy in *Pánico en el Transiberiano* (*Horror Express*) (1972)

Lady Vanishes, on the Trans-Siberian express. Saxton has discovered a fossilised primate in the Szechuan province of China – he believes it is an example of the 'missing link' between ape and man. But even before the creature is loaded on the train, it returns to life and begins drawing the life from the passengers, absorbing their knowledge. Saxton and Wells eventually theorise that the fossil is inhabited by a formless alien intelligence which can pass itself from victim to victim, acquiring knowledge as it goes. Now the alien intends to build a machine in which to return home.

Like the train, the film rattles along with a thrilling sense of mystery and horror bolstered by John Cacavas' eerie score. It is all very elegantly presented, the match of any of the later Hammers, despite the conditions at Studio 70 which Lee maintained were spartan in the extreme. Throughout, Cushing and Lee behave with gentlemanly aplomb and both look magnificent, revelling in the understated rapport of 15 years' work together. ('Both Lee and Cushing have developed a dapper way of saying an idiotic line straight,' wrote Margaret Hinxman of the *Sunday Telegraph,* 'while still communicating the joke of it to the audience.'[1]) Only Cushing, immaculate in a dinner jacket, could enquire, with sublime seriousness, 'Is Professor Saxton's fossil still at large?' or, when it is pointed out that either Saxton or Wells could be the monster, exclaim 'Monster? We're British, you know!'

'Old trains are nice,' said the *Daily Telegraph,* 'and it is the saviour of Gene Martin's *Horror Express,* that takes us on a journey from Peking westwards in a lovely old steam specimen about 1900. On board are the inseparable Peter Cushing and Christopher Lee, as a couple of square scientists escorting a curious fossil found in Shangri-La country, which duly comes to life with eyes that fatally flash red, rather like traffic signals. I rather thought this might be Telly Savalas in disguise.'[2]

Considering the decline in the British film industry from the late 1960s it is scarcely believable that at this time so many horror films were being made in Britain, and that an actor like Cushing could go from one film to the next without a break. In fact, only Cushing or

Lee could have done this – testament to their unique position in the industry and unshakable reputation for reliability.

From 31ˢᵗ January 1972, Cushing was at Shepperton Studios to play another Victorian scientist, Professor Emmanuel Hildern, in Freddie Francis' *The Creeping Flesh*. The film was made for Tigon, with Tony Tenser as producer. Like *Horror Express*, the plot revolves around an ancient fossilised creature which comes back to life, although the tone here is much more disquieting, with many of the expressionistic touches that Francis first used in *The Skull*.

Professor Hildern theorises that evil is a living organism, a disease 'which infects humanity like cholera or typhoid.' He lives in dread

Doctor James Hildern (Christopher Lee) looks down on his distraught half-brother Emmanuel in *The Creeping Flesh* (1972)

that his beloved daughter Penelope (Lorna Heilbron) will succumb to the madness that confined her mother Marguerite to an asylum. As part of his research, he has brought back from New Guinea the skeleton of a monstrous primitive creature which he believes is a legendary being called 'the Evil One'.

From the flesh of the creature, which reconstitutes in water, Hildern creates a serum that he believes will inoculate his daughter against evil. To his dismay, the treatment turns her into a murderous savage. Meanwhile, Hildern's jealous half-brother James (Christopher Lee) steals the skeleton, but his coach is overturned in a thunderstorm and, reanimated, the Evil One walks again...

Cushing's commitment to the role was as strong as ever and his professionalism absolute. He still concerned himself not only with his performance but also with every aspect of filmmaking. His copy of the script is enthusiastically annotated with character details and instructions to himself. 'Don't gabble. Don't overact. Don't be conventional absent-minded professor.' 'Both eyes open when looking into microscope.' And there, mixed up with notes about hairpieces and how to prepare a microscope slide are the words 'Bois' 'Helen' 'Us'.

Hildern is a much more fragile creature than the gung-ho Doctor Wells. His overpowering, almost childlike scientific curiosity leads him to some rash and dangerous hypotheses, ultimately destroying that which he holds dearest – his daughter – and leaving

him a gabbling lunatic. 'Peter related to me as a father and was tremendously caring and supportive,' Lorna Heilbron remembers. 'He felt that I resembled Helen, so we had a rather intense relationship where I felt he really lived his part in the film.'[3] To play the deranged Hildern in the prologue and epilogue, Cushing again sacrifices any shred of vanity – without the toupée, which he wore for practically every film now, his hair is whitened and disarrayed and his cheekbones are strongly emphasised with make-up. A quavering voice, insisting 'I alone can save the world', completes the impression of the character's tragic mental collapse.

Cushing and Lee have only a few scenes together, and though they work well, there is little of the banter that infused *Horror Express* – Lee maintained that they worked better together when playing antagonists. James Hildern is a cold intellectual whose brutal and arcane experiments are motivated by greed for money and prestige. His smug smile of triumph in the last reel brings to an end a story with distinct overtones of Shakespearean tragedy.

Freddie Francis acclaimed the work of producer Norman Priggen in giving the film higher than usual production values for a horror movie. The sepia-toned photography is beautiful, the settings are sturdy and Hildern's cell – a kind of white void dressed with a jumble of laboratory equipment – is an interesting abstract idea. Paul Ferris, who also scored Cushing's film *The Blood Beast Terror* in 1967, here uses insistent, minimal percussion to fray the nerves.

As in *The Skull*, Francis dwells on lingering close-ups of the grotesque bony face of the 'Evil One', peering into – and eventually out of – the dead eye-sockets. The huge cowled shape that thumps up the stairs in the finale is monstrously powerful and Cushing's quaking terror as he faces it provides a direct line of sight back to the climax of *Nineteen Eighty-Four*.

On 6th and 7th April 1972, Cushing was at Shepperton for his role in another Amicus portmanteau film, *Asylum*. This was directed by Roy Ward Baker from a script by Robert Bloch, again from his own short stories. Cushing played Mr Smith in a segment called *The Weird Tailor* with his old friend Barry Morse.

Morse plays the tailor Bruno who is instructed, by a strange and insistent client called Mr Smith, to make a suit from a bizarre shimmering material. Bruno must follow the instructions in an ancient book, and can only work during the hours of darkness. It transpires, however, that Smith is a diabolist, and the suit is intended to raise his son from the dead. As Mr Smith, Cushing keeps his expressions bland and benign and wears his own black-rimmed glasses. His voice is gentle but his diction is of course, impeccable. Initially, Smith seems like Bruno's saviour, but we are given clues to Smith's bizarre intentions – he enters Bruno's shop in silhouette, and later leads the tailor to his bare study in a low-shot full of foreboding. Smith cannot pay Bruno. His research into the forbidden arts, he explains, his voice breaking with emotion, cost him his fortune. He draws a gun and insists that Bruno give him the suit. Roy Ward Baker creates a touching and iconic set-up with Cushing clutching a revolver and with tears in his eyes, standing over the white cadaver of his dead son.

'I believe that reactions must be instinctive rather than planned,' Cushing revealed, 'because I do not find planned reactions believable. The unschooled actor or director would have the character ... with tears running down his face, moaning "I can't go on." When my wife passed away I was very quiet, almost

'I play rather an impetuous gentleman with the wonderful name of Mr Smith,' said Cushing of his role in *Asylum* (1972)

stunned. Mr Smith in *Asylum* loses his son and does not go to pieces, he quietly seeks a way to regain his son by means of this occult book and magic suit. I don't approve of the occult business but the reaction of Smith is entirely my own, based on my own experience ... more believable than if I played it for histrionics.'[4]

Cushing listed his costume on the script as 'Blue 3-piece suit (red stripe, white piping), shirt (cream), tie (blue), blue socks, black shoes, overcoat, black trilby hat (hair piece when not wearing hat), dark suede gloves'. As an indication of Smith's penurious state – 'no watch and chain'.

Cushing's next film was for a new company in the horror field, but the faces behind it could not have been more familiar. 'I hear that Christopher Lee is to become the temporary "boss" of his friend Peter Cushing,' the *Evening Standard* reported in March 1972, 'Mr Lee has formed a production company with producer Anthony Nelson Keys to make a film called *Nothing But The Night*. They have asked Mr Cushing to appear in it. "It's a psychological thriller," says Cushing, "I play a pathologist, which I have never done before, and Chris is an ex-Army officer with Special Branch connections. I am happy to say that Hammer films are not at all disturbed, in fact they are bending over to help us. It will be the third consecutive film I've made with Christopher in three months. We've become a sort of Laurel and Hardy act."'[5] Lee and Nelson Keys' company was christened Charlemagne Film Productions, and shooting began on 18th April on location (later at Pinewood) under the direction of Peter Sasdy. The diverse cast included Diana Dors, Duncan Lamont, Georgia Brown and Fulton MacKay. Cushing plays Sir Mark Ashley, who investigates a series of deaths linked to the wealthy patrons of the Van Traylen orphanage. Eventually it becomes clear that the orphans themselves are part of a plan by the patrons to achieve immortality by transferring their minds to the bodies of the children.

The film, based on a novel by John Blackburn, is effectively a whodunnit, but so relentlessly does the script mislead and misdirect on the way (throwing

all the suspicion onto Diana Dors'
character, Anna Harb) that when the
twist is revealed the viewer can't be
blamed for feeling roundly conned.
Cushing plays the pathologist well,
even shouting Christopher Lee down
at one point, but the character is
flatly written and does nothing in
second half of the film. Diana Dors
and Georgia Brown work very hard
and to the credit of director Peter
Sasdy, there are some lingering
moments in what is effectively a film
about institutional child abuse.

At the conclusion of the film, the
children, dressed in the uniforms of
the adults who have possessed them,
realise the folly of the experiment
and one by one, jump over a cliff to
their deaths. *Nothing But The Night* is
clearly a film ahead of its time but is
hampered by an impenetrable and
humourless script. It suffered from
poor distribution and was not widely
seen. Sadly, it was Charlemagne's only film.

During the filming of *Nothing But The Night* at
Pinewood, Cushing gave his first significant interview
on the subject of Helen's death to Ray Connolly of
the *Evening Standard*. 'They say that time heals, well,
in this case it hasn't,' he said. 'Not after a year and
three months ... Mediums? I neither believe in them
nor disbelieve. But I would never go to one. And
sometimes one might think what is one doing here?
and why one doesn't do what dear George Sanders
did the other day, or what poor Tony
Hancock did. But I know I've been
left for a reason. There is no waste. No
waste.'[6] In July the *Standard* reported
that Cushing had persuaded his close
friend Paddy Smith – his stand-in and
driver – to take his wife and small son
on holiday in Cushing's Jaguar. 'I can't
bear waste' said Cushing. 'It seems
such a shame to have the car lying
idle in my barn. I used it quite a lot to
take Helen for treatment and for quiet
holidays. But it's only done 25,000
miles since I bought it ten years ago
which is ridiculous.'[7]

After an appearance as the 'mystery
voice' on Radio 4's *Twenty Questions*,
recorded on 2nd June 1972, and an
appearance on BBC TV's amiable
antiques quiz *Going for a Song*,
recorded on 9th June in Bristol,
Cushing started work on another
film for Amicus. Based on the novel

Cushing larks about with his stand-in and driver Paddy Smith on location for *Nothing But The Night* (1972). Co-star Diana Dors and director Peter Sasdy can be seen behind them

Fengriffen by David Case, it was known for a while
as *Bride of Fengriffen* before eventually coming to the
screen as *~~And Now The Screaming Starts!* Roy Ward
Baker was the director and the cast included Patrick
Magee, Herbert Lom, Rosalie Crutchley, Stephanie
Beacham and Ian Ogilvy. Filming began on 17th July
1972 at Shepperton, with Oakley Court doing service
once again, here as the Fengriffen family pile.

In 1785 Charles Fengriffen (Ogilvy) brings his new
bride Catherine (Beacham) to live at the family estate.

Sir Mark Ashley talks to Mary Valley (Gwyneth Strong) while Dr Haynes (Keith Barron)
looks on in Charlemagne Productions' *Nothing But The Night* (1972)

Soon she is having hallucinations – an eyeless spectre appears outside her window and a severed hand attacks her. She later learns that she is pregnant and fears that she has somehow been impregnated by the ghost. The family Doctor, Whittle (Magee) sends for a doctor from London 'well versed in a new science' – psychiatry. Doctor Pope (Cushing) arrives and discovers that the debauched behaviour of Charles' grandfather has led to a curse on the bride of Fengriffen.

The story is simple – 'the sins of the fathers visited upon the sons' – but told in convoluted style. It is enlivened greatly by Cushing's gentle performance, in Regency duds and a rather effeminately tousled blond hairpiece. 'Can you cure unhappiness, Doctor?' asks Stephanie Beacham's troubled Catherine. He cannot, sadly, despite spending three-quarters of an hour trying. Cushing's scenes with Beacham are touching but the film is repetitive and wearing.

Derek Whitehurst was assistant director on the picture – the first of three in a row with Cushing. 'After Helen's death,' he says, 'I can't say Peter became difficult to work with, but you had to be careful. There was never a question of his grief interfering with a film or a part. He would always learn the script, which was a very rare thing, but he became very concerned about eyelines. When he was acting, if he caught someone's eye behind the camera, even me, who'd worked with him before, it would put him off. In the end everybody had to duck out of sight so that he wouldn't see them. He would call me to one side very gently and I'd have to move the sparks out of the way and they would complain that their tea was getting cold. It became a bit of a routine. Perhaps it stopped him working with people who didn't know him. But

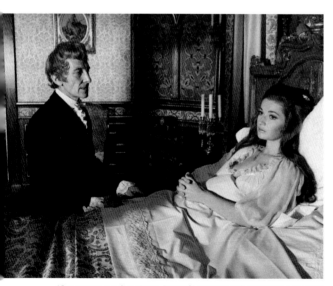

'Can you cure unhappiness, Doctor?' Dr Pope with Catherine Fengriffen (Stephanie Beacham) in ~~And Now The Screaming Starts! (1972)

there wouldn't be any drama. He was still easy-going, gracious to other actors, there was no camera hogging, no exasperation with lines being forgotten or people that weren't very good. And he was still always charming to the young ladies – we had many in Hammer films, and some of them were pretty grim."[8]

After the Amicus production, a new *Frankenstein* was on the cards at Hammer with Terence Fisher, in an early 19th Century setting. On 31st August 1972, Cushing wrote from Whitstable to producer Roy Skeggs about reusing the hairpiece from ~~*And Now The Screaming Starts!* which was hired from a London company called Wig Creations. 'They are keeping it for me, and I would be grateful for your confirmation.'

The next day there was another note to Skeggs, listing props for Baron Frankenstein and surgical instruments required for the operation scenes. By 6th September, Cushing was installed at Brown's Hotel and in the few days before filming began on 18th September Cushing worked on Anthony Hinds' script with Skeggs and Fisher.

Frankenstein and the Monster from Hell would be Hammer's final *Frankenstein* and Terence Fisher's last film. In finishing, it returned to the very beginning of the canon – *Frankenstein and the Monster* was the title of the Milton Subotsky script that led to *The Curse of Frankenstein* in 1956. The title was rejected in 1956, but with the words 'from Hell' tacked on it obviously passed muster in 1972. Cushing, ever one to expose the wiles of the front office, observed 'But people will be expecting a Monster from Hell, and we haven't got one.'[9] Terence Fisher rationalised that the monster came 'from Hell, from evil, from Frankenstein's mistaken belief that he is the creator of man, which of course he isn't, and will never succeed in being.'[10]

Cushing here gives a last, rather distant performance as the Baron. When Simon Helder (Shane Briant) a follower of Frankenstein's theories, is committed to an asylum for the criminally insane, he discovers that the Baron is resident in the asylum also.

To introduce Frankenstein, Fisher uses a powerful three-step cut, from long-shot, to mid-shot, to close-up, reminiscent of the way James Whale introduces the creature in *Frankenstein* in 1931. Here we are drawn into Cushing's porcelain face as James Bernard's strings weave their spell, giving an immediate familiarity. We learn that the Baron has the run of the asylum and is cynically manipulating the inmates to engineer his newest creation. Helder joins him enthusiastically, however, after years of being a rational, driven scientist – always coldly sane – Frankenstein has finally tipped over the brink into irredeemable madness.

Fisher's revelation of his new creature echoes the unveiling in *Curse*, but the monster is poorly designed – eyeless and slumped in his cage, it looks like a hairy old soak in joke shop mask. David Prowse

Frankenstein about his grisly business with Simon Helder (Shane Briant) and the Angel (Madeline Smith) in *Frankenstein and the Monster from Hell* (1972). The monster (David Prowse) awaits his new brain in the background.

is able to imbue the monster with some character when he can use his eyes, and enacts a very affecting scene as he looks on his own hideous reflection.

Frankenstein and Helder are aided by a mute girl called Sarah, known to the inmates as the Angel. She is played by Madeline Smith, who had prevously appeared in *The Vampire Lovers*. Smith has a thankless task, running around after everyone, and yet she still manages to invest Sarah with a kind of luminous innocence. 'I look at that film now and wonder who the girl is,' says Madeline Smith. 'With her very dark hair, a bit podgy in the fizzog, nothing like me at all! I remember that Peter was lovely to work with, but I was still rather nervous because he was such a big star. He got on well with Shane, who was as ferocious in his way about what he did as Peter was.

'It was terrible to see what grief had done to Peter. He was so painfully thin, and it was as if the light had gone out of his eyes. With Helen gone, he was half a person. I remember also that he used to cover his script with the most beautiful, tiny writing, like a little old mathematician or the Brontës! He paid no heed to the hoot-and-hollerers and just got quietly on with the business of making our little film.'[11]

As Frankenstein fits his monster with a new brain, Cushing is almost licking his lips as Helder's saw slices through the skull – he later kicks over the old brain in a gesture of supreme indifference. Then as the monster awakens, to a plaintive fiddle motif from James Bernard, there is a glitter in Cushing's eye as Frankenstein faces his creation. Suddenly, the Creature turns on Helder with a broken bell-jar and

Cushing displays his old, familiar athleticism as he smashes a bottle of chloroform into his coat and leaps onto the monster's back.

With the Creature subdued, Frankenstein explains his latest and most insane scheme – to mate Sarah with the creature and finally produce a perfect human being. The Baron smiles as he reveals his plan to Helder, but there's something dead and dreadful in those water-blue eyes. Cushing was concerned about the logic of Frankenstein wanting to mate his creature with a mute girl and rewrote two pages of the script to explain that Sarah's inability to speak was due to a shock, not a physical condition.

Outside in the asylum the inmates are on the rampage, having suspected foul play from the Baron for some time. They eventually round on the Creature and tear it to pieces, echoing the similar scene in *Revenge*. As the monster lies in a heap, Frankenstein repeats his first line 'Go back to your rooms, now. There's nothing more for you to see. It's all over.'

The film is preoccupied with failure and death, following the downbeat trend of *Frankenstein Must Be Destroyed*. It is Fisher's last grim fairy-tale, with genuine moments of power and poetry, providing a fitting conclusion to the story of the Baron that does not disgrace the director or the star. Derek Whitehurst could see that it was the end of an era. 'Terry said he didn't think he'd be directing any more,' he recalls. 'The strain was just too great for him. In a few years, the film business had changed completely, and we'd lost a lot of the old Hammer personnel. It was rather a sad atmosphere when we finished that one.'[12]

Cushing and Lee battle it out one last time as Van Helsing and Dracula in the fiery climax of *The Satanic Rites of Dracula* (1972)

For Cushing and Whitehurst however, it was straight on with the next one, and on 13th November, Cushing began work as Lorrimer Van Helsing again, in *The Satanic Rites of Dracula* (in production the film was known as *Dracula is Dead and Well and Living in London*). Cushing's fee was now £6000, plus accommodation at Brown's Hotel and £25 per week for his driver. The director was *A.D. 1972*'s Alan Gibson, with Christopher Lee and Michael Coles also returning from that film. Stephanie Beacham was not available to

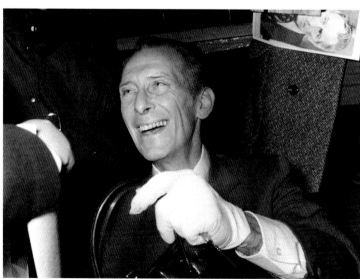

Gentleman Cushing obliges with a lady's handbag during an autograph session at the NFT. The white smoking glove was worn to prevent nicotine stains on his fingers

play Jessica Van Helsing so the role was taken by Joanna Lumley. Old comrades Freddie Jones, Patrick Barr and William Franklyn also joined in.

'My family have an affectionate joke with me about Peter,' Franklyn remembered. 'If I eulogise about someone, praising their character, humour, etc, they say in unison "it's one of Dad's 'Peter Cushing' saints." Because in my professional lifetime I've seldom met a person of such generosity of spirit, humour, natural courage and non-judgemental reactions. He was an icon of the non-egotistical, totally professional and immensely companionable actor team-spirit. On a film set, Peter always wore an immaculate white glove, as if being expected to serve crumpets and pour tea. As if by magic, it disappeared the moment the preparation for a take was sounded, and on the word "print" from the director it would miraculously appear again, with the inevitable cigarette between the first and second fingers. A nicotine-stained professor of whatever branch of horror was, to Peter, unthinkable. Unless forbidden by the director on safety grounds, Peter would always do his own stunts. We have ridden and jumped and sworded with the same fun that we swapped anecdotes on military manoeuvres and board games. He was a leading consultant on the subject. Knowing him and remembering him brings warmth and smiles.'[13]

In *The Satanic Rites of Dracula*, Van Helsing is called in once again by Inspector Murray when several well-known establishment figures are involved in a black mass at a country estate called Pelham House. One of the sect is an old friend of Van Helsing's, the Nobel Prize-winning bio-chemist Professor Julian Keeley (Freddie Jones). Van Helsing visits Keeley who is in a state of terrified agitation having developed an accelerated strain of *bacillus pestis* – bubonic plague.

Later, Murray and Jessica discover vampirised girls in the cellar at Pelham house, and it is revealed that Keeley's research was sponsored by a reclusive tycoon called D D Denham. Van Helsing confronts Denham and exposes him as

Dracula, but is captured and taken to Pelham House. Here, on the 23rd day of the 11th month, the Sabat of the Undead, Dracula will release the plague and fulfil the biblical prophecy of Armageddon.

Cushing's scenes here are limited again, but there is a marvellous exchange with Freddie Jones as the dribbling, cow-faced Julian Keeley, who is totally in thrall to Dracula. 'Evil and violence are the only two measures that hold any power...' he drools. 'And nothing is too vile, nothing is too dreadful. You need to feel the thrill of disgust, the beauty of obscenity.'

Cushing seems a little bored at having to relate the list of anti-vampire precautions yet again, and the list of items that can repel Dracula has now taken on ludicrous proportions. But there is real steel in Van Helsing's confrontation with 'D D Denham' as he draws the pistol to fire the

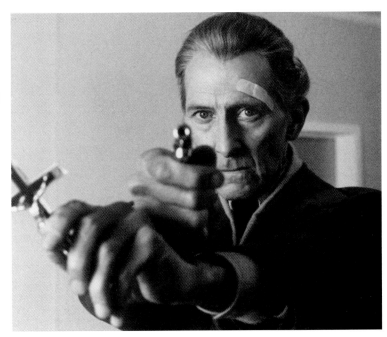

Van Helsing shows his steel in *The Satanic Rites of Dracula* (1972)

silver bullet. Lee looks powerful and handsome, and his delivery, including a Bela Lugosi-inspired accent at one point, reveals nothing of his utter disappointment with Hammer's treatment of the character. This was the last film in which Lee and Cushing would face each other as Van Helsing and Dracula.

Cushing gets the best speech in the film with William Franklyn's disbelieving Colonel Torrence, who asks if they are dealing with 'hob-goblins and witches and things that go bump in the night'.

'Hobgoblins are fantasy creatures of the nursery,' states Van Helsing. 'As for witches they certainly exist, although 90 per cent of them are charlatans... Things do go bump in the night. Quite often.'

Again, Cushing was responsible for rewriting Van Helsing's lines. He was notably concerned about the line which says that the vampire lives in mortal dread of silver. 'This bothers me,' he wrote on the script 'because of the silver ring Dracula wears,' but the reference remained unchanged. Cushing clipped a biblical quotation from a newspaper and pasted it into his script. It read 'Be not overcome of evil, but overcome evil with good. Romans XII, 21.'

Cushing began 1973 with two BBC television shows in one day. On the afternoon of 4th January, he was a guest on *Ask Aspel*, in which children requested clips from favourite TV shows be shown again. In the evening, Cushing appeared on the magazine programme *Nationwide*, to talk about his recent films.

In mid January, Cushing took to the stage of the National Film Theatre in London to take part in one of the John Player Lectures sponsored by the famous tobacco company. He spoke at length about his early life, his trip to Hollywood and his stage career, although there was little about Hammer or his horror roles. A transcript of the interview with David Castell would form the basis for his autobiography, which he began after Helen's death 'as a form of therapy.'[14]

A fortnight later, on 5th February 1973, Cushing was back at the BBC recording another *Morecambe and Wise Show* – broadcast in March. In this programme, Cushing tells Eric and Ernie, 'I'm not letting you out of my sight until I get paid. Until I get my money, wherever you go, I shall go.' 'That'll be a bit awkward at about 11 o'clock tonight,' says Morecambe. As a result, Cushing has to join in the song-and-dance routine 'We're a Couple of Swells'. He is a little unsteady, but he seems to be enjoying himself greatly. Suffice to say, even by the end of the show, he has still not been paid.

In April, Cushing attended The Second International Horror Film Festival in Paris, organised by Alain Schlockoff, and on 17th April received a standing ovation as he collected the Licorne D'Or award for best actor in a horror film (for *Tales from the Crypt*) and a special award for his horror film work over the last decade. While in France he visited the Riviera to film the location work for an episode of ITC's adventure series *The Zoo Gang* entitled *The Counterfeit Trap*. Here Cushing played another Frenchman, Judge Gautier, who has fallen on hard times. He is painfully insecure about his much younger wife (played by Jacqueline Pearce) and becomes involved with a smuggling ring

Accusations fly between horror stars Oliver Quayle (Robert Quarry), Herbert Flay and Paul Toombes (Vincent Price) in *Madhouse* (1973)

to keep her in luxury. The episode was directed by John Hough (from *Twins of Evil*) and the regular cast of *The Zoo Gang* included John Mills and Barry Morse.

Back in England, on 14th May, Cushing began work at Twickenham Studios on *Madhouse*, an Amicus/American International co-production based on Angus Hall's novel *Devilday* and directed by Jim Clark. Filmed under the rather more evocative title *The Revenge of Dr Death* it featured Cushing as Herbert Flay, an embittered screenwriter and former actor. Flay plots a diabolical revenge on horror star Paul Toombes (played by Vincent Price) whom he believes has robbed him of the chance of stardom in the role of 'Dr Death'. When a figure dressed up as the Dr Death character begins committing murders, Toombes is a suspect but Flay is the killer all along. Location work was carried out at Pyrford Manor in Surrey (for Flay's mansion) and at the London Weekend Television Studios on London's South Bank.

The film is peppered with clips from Roger Corman's Poe movies (starring Price), features several grisly deaths and a climactic fight between Flay and Toombes which Cushing described as 'a titanic ding-dong.'[15] The bout concludes with Flay tumbling into a tank of spiders. 'It was me,' Cushing told his American fan club, 'and I like spiders.'[16]

Perhaps *Madhouse* is an appropriate title after all for a film which involves everyone in an inordinate amount of running around. Because Cushing is the actual villain of the piece, he plays it quietly while the red herring characters go hell-for-leather. One of those herrings was actor Robert Quarry, who had recently found fame as the vampire Count Yorga in two American International films. Quarry had appeared with Cushing briefly in the *Dr Phibes* film and befriended the actor during filming.

The BBC's cinema programme *Film 73* featured a behind-the-scenes item on *Madhouse*, with director Jim Clark, Cushing and Price. Clark acknowledged his debt to the 'gods' of the horror genre, Tod Browning and James Whale, and said of his stars 'One couldn't work with easier people. They respond marvellously to direction and know instinctively what to do. They're both extraordinarily pleasant people anyway, and one is terribly lucky to have them.'

Price revealed that at the time he was 'very anxious to do a ...thriller for children, where there is no blood, but with all the marvellous old things like creaking doors... Kids are the biggest audience in the world.'

'Look how they love *Doctor Who*!' Cushing pointed out enthusiastically. 'Do you know it? We did two films and it's been such a success on television.'

While shooting *Madhouse*, Cushing took part in an episode of Price's BBC radio anthology *The Price of Fear*. Entitled *The Man Who Hated Scenes* and recorded on 16th June 1973, the story presented Cushing as a cuckolded husband again, a timid man who will go to any lengths to avoid a 'scene' but who engineers an appalling fate for his adulterous wife. The *Film 73* interview and the radio work reveals a rapport and genuine friendship between Cushing and Price which is perhaps not apparent in their film work.

On 14th May, Cushing wrote from Twickenham Studios, in reply to an invitation from Kay Evans, producer of *Woman's Hour*, to be guest of the week on 20th June. 'My belovèd wife derived so much enjoyment from *Woman's Hour* over the years and so did I. I am currently engaged on two films with overlapping schedules – either one could require my services on 20th June. Hope I will be free!' Kay Evans was prepared, if need be, to record the interview 'between shots at the studio'. Cushing wrote again from the Royal Station Hotel in Hull on 3rd June to inform her that he would be at Shepperton Studios on 20th June (filming *From Beyond The Grave*). The interview was recorded at Broadcasting House on 18th June with presenter Sue MacGregor and was clearly an emotional experience. 'Dear Miss MacGregor,' wrote Cushing the following day, 'thank you for your compassionate interest in the interview. I do hope the end result is what you desired.'

In Amicus's film *From Beyond the Grave*, a weird curio shop called Temptations Ltd provides the linking device for the four stories, and in his role as the proprietor of this emporium, Cushing has excellent co-stars like Ian Carmichael and Ian

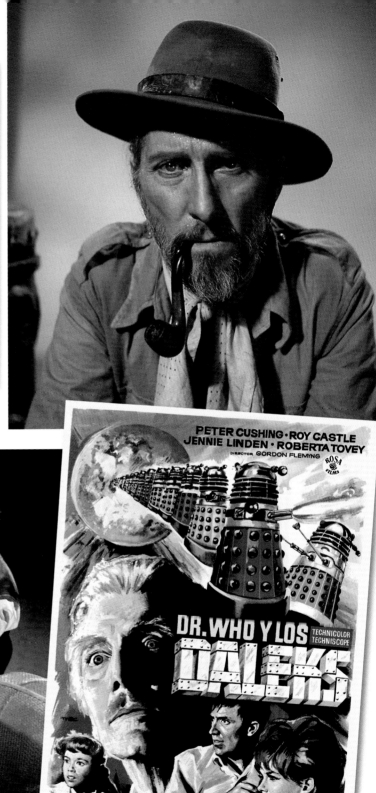

Above: The French poster for *The Skull* (1965)
Right: Major Holly in Hammer's epic *She* (1964)

Above: Frankenstein tends his most beautiful creation
in *Frankenstein Created Woman* (1966)
Right: A Spanish poster for *Dr Who and the Daleks* (1965)

La 20th Century-Fox presenta

LA MALEDIZIONE DEI FRANKENSTEIN

con
PETER CUSHING - SUSAN DENBERG
e con
THORLEY WALTERS

SCENEGGIATURA ORIGINALE DI   PRODOTTO DA
JOHN ELDER   **ANTHONY NELSON KEYS**
REGIA DI
TERENCE FISHER
UNA PRODUZIONE
SEVEN ARTS-HAMMER PRODUCTION

DISTRIBUZIONE   Colore De Luxe

Prima Edizione Italiana 1968

The dramatic Italian locandina for *Frankenstein Created Woman* (1966)

Lancelot Canning and Ronald Wyatt (Jack Palance) in a segment called *The Man Who Collected Poe* from *Torture Garden* (1967)

Sir John Rowan with his fiancée Lynn Nolan (Sue Lloyd) in *Corruption* (1967)

Right: Cushing on location on Dartmoor for the BBC version of *The Hound of the Baskervilles* (1968)

As 'The screen's most fantastic fiend' on the British poster for *Frankenstein Must Be Destroyed* (1969)

Sherlock Holmes and Dr Watson (Nigel Stock) with Inspector Gregson (George A Cooper) in the BBC's *A Study in Scarlet* (1968)

With Veronica Carlson in a promotional shot for *Frankenstein Must Be Destroyed* (1969)

Above: Van Helsing and Dracula (Christopher Lee) face to face in modern London in *Dracula A.D. 1972* (1971)

Below: Kindly Mr Grimsdyke entertains the local children in *Tales from the Crypt* (1971)

Above left: The Spanish poster for *Horror Express* (1972). Above right: The desperate Mr Smith in *Asylum* (1972)

Below: Sarah (Madeline Smith), Baron Frankenstein, Helder (Shane Briant) and Durendel (Charles Lloyd Pack) in *Frankenstein and the Monster from Hell* (1972)

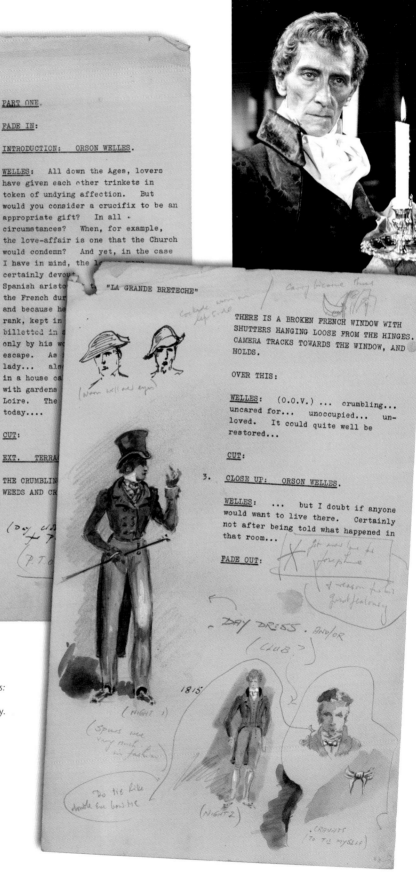

"LA GRANDE BRETECHE"

PART ONE.

FADE IN:

1. INTRODUCTION: ORSON WELLES.

WELLES: All down the Ages, lovers
have given each other trinkets in
token of undying affection. But
would you consider a crucifix to be an
appropriate gift? In all ·
circumstances? When, for example,
the love-affair is one that the Church
would condemn? And yet, in the case
I have in mind, the l... ...
certainly devou...
Spanish aristo... ...t...
the French dur...
and because he...
rank, kept in...
billetted in...
only by his wo...
escape. As...
lady... ale...
in a house ca...
with gardens...
Loire. The...
today....

CUT:

EXT. TERRA...

THE CRUMBLIN...
WEEDS AND CR...

"LA GRANDE BRETECHE"

THERE IS A BROKEN FRENCH WINDOW WITH
SHUTTERS HANGING LOOSE FROM THE HINGES.
CAMERA TRACKS TOWARDS THE WINDOW, AND
HOLDS.

OVER THIS:

WELLES: (O.O.V.) ... crumbling...
uncared for... unoccupied... un-
loved. It could quite well be
restored...

CUT:

3. CLOSE UP: ORSON WELLES.

WELLES: ... but I doubt if anyone
would want to live there. Certainly
not after being told what happened in
that room...

FADE OUT:

Cushing's watercolour sketches and
annotations on his script for his role as
Count Gerard De Merret (top right) in
Anglia TV's *Orson Welles Great Mysteries:
La Grande Breteche* (1973). Cushing
illustrated many of his scripts in this way.

Above: A study in villainy – The Grand Moff Tarkin with Darth Vader (David Prowse) in *Star Wars* (1976)

Right: Professor Abner Perry in *At the Earth's Core* (1976)

Below: The malevolent Baron Corofax in *The Devil's Men* (1975)

Chuck Spillers (Brian Cox) with Martin Blueck in *Hammer House of Horror – The Silent Scream* (1980)

As William T Kolderup, the richest man in America, with Ana Obregón as Meg in *Misterio en la isla de los Monstruos* (*Mystery on Monster Island*, 1981)

With Christopher Lee, John Carradine and Vincent Price in *House of the Long Shadows* (1982)

Proudly displaying the Order of the British Empire, presented in 1989

Bannen to play against. This is one of the strongest Amicus portmanteau films, directed by Kevin Connor and based on stories by R Chetwynd Hayes.

As David Warner enters the shop to buy an old mirror, Cushing appears from out of the knick-knacks in bushy eyebrows, wielding a crocodile and a peculiar Northern accent. '250 *pound...*' he drawls, sucking on his pipe, 'a *gen-you-wine* antique...' Warner knocks the price down, swindling the old man, and as a result, meets a grisly end.

The extravagantly made-up Cushing appears even more goblin-like when seen through a wreath of smoke or the dimpled glass of the shop-window. 'You have *cer-tiffy-cate*?' he enquires of Ian Bannen, who is attempting to buy himself a Victoria Cross. 'Otherwise every Tom Dick and Harry would be after one, and that wouldn't be *fur*, would it?' Bannen nips back and steals the medal anyway. Cushing is unimpressed. '*Naughty...*' he tuts to himself. 'Shouldn't have done that...' And Bannen duly receives his comeuppance. For Ian Carmichael, who swindles him out of a silver snuff-box, Cushing has the glorious parting shot 'I hope you enjoy snuffing it!'

On 12th July 1973, John Redway wrote to BBC producer Anthony Cornish about a radio script by Brian Hayles called *Lord Dracula*. 'Peter Cushing thought it very good and even talks about it as the basis for "a splendid, definitive Dracula epic film". He would be interested to take it further as a radio series.' Later, the script was reworked as a one-off radio production, but Cushing was not involved. Hayles had provided the script for *Nothing But The Night*, and later wrote *Arabian Adventure* in which Cushing appeared. Hammer reworked the story as a screenplay called *Vlad the Impaler* which spent more than 20 years in the development wilderness without seeing production.

On 16th July 1973, Cushing began work on Amicus's werewolf film *The Beast Must Die*. This was directed by Paul Annett and starred Calvin Lockhart as millionaire big game hunter Tom Newcliffe, who invites a disparate group to his country estate knowing that one of them is a werewolf.

Cushing plays Doctor Christopher Lundgren, a Norwegian expert on werewolf lore, and is required to deliver a lengthy, dull treatise – most of it nonsensical – about the lymphatic

Cushing as the proprietor of Temptations Ltd in *From Beyond the Grave* (1973)

system and the science of werewolfism. Calvin Lockhart is powerful and enigmatic, but even he has little to do. The film features some agonisingly poor day-for-night shooting, a considerable amount of running around and a fake-looking werewolf played by a large dog. The film's on-screen 'werewolf break', a gimmick like those used by horror huckster William Castle, serves only to protract the agony.

Cushing, with no character to fall back on, seems unsettled and out of place, although as usual, his script was covered with annotations. 'Be – don't act, eyes up – don't look aslant or down. Smile when I can.'

The following month he would be back on fine form, in 1815 costume, in a segment of the *Orson Welles Great Mysteries* TV series entitled *La Grande Breteche*.

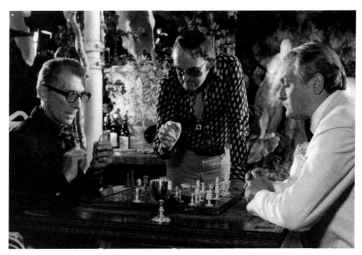

Director Paul Annett supervises a chess game between Professor Lundgren and Arthur Bennington (Charles Gray) in *The Beast Must Die* (1973)

Chapter Twenty-Two

Treading Time

Orson Welles Great Mysteries was a collection of 25 half-hour stories produced in the UK by Anglia Television, with guest stars including Claire Bloom, Donald Pleasence, Dean Stockwell and Christopher Lee. Cushing did not work with Welles, however, whose role in the series was simply to heave into view at the beginning of each story and deliver a cryptic introduction. Welles' scenes were shot in Paris by Peter Bogdanovich.

La Grande Breteche is the story of Count Gerard de Merret (Cushing) and his faithless wife Josephine (Susannah York) who is having an affair with a Spanish prisoner from the Napoleonic war. Knowing that Josephine's lover is hiding in her closet, the Count makes her swear on a crucifix that the cupboard is empty, then proceeds to have it bricked up. The story, which recalls Poe's favourite theme of burial alive, was adapted from Balzac by Martin Worth and the director was Peter Sasdy, who the previous year had worked with Cushing on *Nothing But The Night*.

Under harsh studio lights, Cushing's physical appearance is startling. His Regency coat hangs on his shoulders, his skin is almost transparent and his cheeks are quite hollow. But even in a half-hour playlet, he was mindful of his character's motivation. 'Get across love for Josephine' he wrote on his *Grande Breteche* script, 'and the reason for his great jealousy.' He annotated the script with a wealth of detail, including three watercolour drawings of costumes from 1815 and sketches on how to tie a cravat and how to wear and carry a bicorne hat. His list of personal props includes gloves and cane and a fob-watch and winding-key, many of which he provided himself.

By 1973, Hammer were finding money difficult to come by from their English and American backers. With hopes of making inroads into the successful kung-fu genre, chairman Michael Carreras struck a co-production deal with the Shaw Brothers of Hong Kong for two films, to be made in the colony. In his position as Hammer's remaining trump card, Cushing was contracted to appear in both, playing Van Helsing in *The Legend of the 7 Golden Vampires* and British agent Rattwood in the kung-fu thriller *Shatter*.

Before he left for Hong Kong, Cushing was involved in Carreras' plans to create a Hammer museum.

Cushing's famous model-building skills were to be showcased prominently, and he was asked to produce a series of 1:24 scale tableaux representing Dracula's castle, two prehistoric scenes and the vampires' temple from *7 Golden Vampires*. The deadlines were very tight and Cushing worked for five weeks on the first model, which was the temple. Cardboard, paper and balsa wood were the principal materials, with a variety of nails, nuts and washers used for fixtures and fittings. Cushing was determined not to let Carreras down, and became so completely preoccupied with the project that he worked all day and frequently all of the night. When the model was completed he had to burn his clothes. Sadly, the plans for the museum came to nothing and the other models were never made, but a full-sized wax model of Cushing as Baron Frankenstein later appeared in an exhibition co-organised by Carreras and mounted in the cellars of the London Palladium. Cushing admitted that he would not go to see his effigy, because 'I'd be too embarrassed!'[1]

The Legend of the 7 Golden Vampires began filming on 22nd October 1973 on location in Hong Kong and at the Shaw Brothers' studios. The director was Roy Ward Baker, working on his final Hammer assignment.

The year is 1904. While giving a lecture in Chung King University in China, Professor Laurence Van Helsing meets Hsi Ching (David Chiang), a young man whose ancestral village of Ping Kuei is at the mercy of the legendary seven golden vampires. Van Helsing joins an expedition to Ping Kuei, financed by the wealthy Vanessa Buren (Julie Ege) but discovers an old foe – Count Dracula (John Forbes-Robertson) – controlling the vampires and zombies that plague the region.

The Legend of the 7 Golden Vampires has many powerful and strange moments, and Cushing brings his usual quiet dignity to the bizarre conclusion of the Hammer Dracula cycle. But the film was made under the most extreme circumstances, as Roy Ward Baker told *Shivers* magazine: 'It could have been much better. Michael Carreras was in charge and was trying to freshen it up – very bold and praiseworthy – but the whole set-up was slip-shod and nobody knew what anyone was doing. The Shaw Brothers' studios weren't soundproofed. They were huge but they were made of corrugated iron ... and nobody had thought it through whether to shoot direct sound or dub it all afterwards ... The film was a failure, an absolute failure.'

Baker had some praise for Cushing, however. 'I made several films with Peter and he was an absolute charmer. Before his appearance in every scene, he would check how he was dressed, what he had in his pockets. Meticulous detail. He was very straightforward, but strait-laced, I'd say. A nice person who made a career by specialising, and what he did he was very good at.'[2]

This Edwardian incarnation of Van Helsing contradicts Hammer's continuity (he was supposed to have died in 1872), but the Professor has lost none of his old vampire-hunting zeal. In his grey wig and russetty velvet coat, Cushing looks charmingly like a rather more sober Dr Who, and while slighter in frame, is not much different from the Van Helsing of *The Brides of Dracula*. Cushing is at his best in the quiet scenes, musing by the campfire over whether he has been sent by divine intervention, or feeling a prickly sensation in his neck when evil is approaching.

Van Helsing tracks down Dracula in China with his friends Vanessa Buren (Julie Ege) and Hsi Ching (David Chiang) in *The Legend of the 7 Golden Vampires* (1973)

The scenes of corpses pulling themselves out of the grave are very good indeed, owing much to the Chinese tradition of 'hopping' vampires, and there is something unsettling about the mixture of styles. However, the muddle of religion and vampirology gives rise to some amusing conjecture. 'They abhor anything which has a holy significance,' Van Helsing explains. 'In Europe, the vampire walks in dread of the crucifix, here it would be the image of the Lord Buddha.' Thankfully he was not called upon to knock two candlesticks together and make one of those.

As the battle gets underway, Van Helsing grabs a flaming brand and has a go at the vampires himself. Cushing falls into a bonfire at one point, which looks exceptionally dangerous. The stunt is cut short on screen, and looks alarmingly impromptu. Otherwise, Cushing seems to be enjoying himself in the lengthy fight sequences, punctuating the martial arts mayhem with shouts of advice – 'strike at their hearts!'

The chief let-down in the film is the representation of Dracula. The Shaw Brothers insisted that the Count was included simply for the box-office, but the character is shoddily represented and given nothing to do. John Forbes-Robertson's pantomime Dracula, plastered with make-up, is the first significant image in the film and is an embarrassing throwback to Lugosi's theatrics. In the finale, Dracula all but *trips* onto Van Helsing's outheld spear, before disintegrating

via some fake-looking rubbery make-up. Not even Cushing's expression of disgust can save this one.

This was to be Van Helsing's final screen adventure (although Cushing subsequently narrated an LP based on the film). Hammer planned a further foreign excursion that sadly never saw production – *Kali, Devil Bride of Dracula* would have seen the professor opposing a vampiric Thuggee cult in India.

Shatter, the companion picture to *7 Golden Vampires*, began filming in December 1973. Stuart Whitman stars as Shatter, a past-his-prime hit-man who assassinates the tyrannical African president M'Goya, then finds he has been the unwitting agent of a powerful drugs cartel. Shatter ultimately turns the tables on Leber (Anton Diffring) the cartel's unscrupulous banker.

In a couple of brief scenes, Cushing plays Rattwood, a weary and cynical British security operative. He makes his first appearance after Shatter has been beaten up in an alleyway. It's an unfamiliar performance for Cushing – unsympathetic, sarcastic – and he uses an affected upper-class drawl. 'You're marked, Shatter,' he tells him. 'You're wearin' a neon sign ... If the British government or the CIA ... had wanted M'Goya dead, they would have staged a simple accident. Your little operation had all the subtlety of a three-ringed circus.' Full of gentle menace, Rattwood tells Shatter to leave Hong Kong by the morning, 'or we'll have you floatin' face down in the harbour. It's a promise.' 'You're a bastard...' Shatter tells him later. 'Aren't I?' says Ratwood.

Retired horror star MacGregor greets his guests with a wink in *La grande trouille* (1974)

Work began on the film with Roger Corman's former editor Monte Hellman as director, although Hellman left the production after several weeks. Cushing had flown home by Boxing Day (26th December) so it is likely that Hellman shot all of Cushing's scenes. The remainder of the film was directed by Michael Carreras. Hammer's plans to develop *Shatter* as a television series starring Stuart Whitman and Cushing were dropped when distribution company Avco-Embassy did not release the film. And so, quietly, Cushing's last Hammer film ended. He would appear in the television series *Hammer House of Horror* in 1980 and in a couple of subsequent Hammer documentaries, but the film work ended in Hong Kong, a very long way from Bray Studios. To his credit, Cushing was always enthusiastic to support any new suggestions that the company presented to him, and even in the last years of his life did not rule out a return to the role of Van Helsing 'as long as they give me a nice comfy chair to sit in.'[3]

Cushing flew from Hong Kong to France to make a film called *La grande trouille* for first-time director Pierre Grunstein. The title means 'The Big Shock' but the film is also known as *Tendre Dracula*. It concerns the misadventures of two scriptwriters (Bernard Menez and Stephen Shandor) who are sent to the castle home of horror star MacGregor (Cushing) to persuade him to continue in a successful TV horror serial. But MacGregor has been told to avoid emotional strain, and so has devoted his life to romance. On the way, the writers are joined by two beautiful actresses (Miou-Miou and Nathalie Courval) who are not quite what they seem...

The film trades shamelessly on Cushing's horror reputation. MacGregor makes his appearance in a puff

of smoke in a cavernous rock staircase, and greets his guests in a dress suit and cloak like Lugosi's *Dracula*. He has a shaft of light across his eyes and this manifestation is accompanied by a tinkle of romantic piano music. Cushing opens his cloak with a flourish, and bids his guests welcome.

MacGregor's emotional instability is immediately established when he suddenly becomes enraged. Cushing bares his fangs and practically bellows his lines, and so violent an outburst from the quietly-spoken actor is oddly disturbing. Thankfully, from then on, the shouting is kept to a minimum as Cushing delivers some prophetic words about the death of horror and some bewitching lines about the immutability of love. 'Without romance, my dear young friends, we are lost, we are all lost. It is romance that separates man from beasts...' Cushing wrote these lines himself – they resemble those he wrote for *She* – but brevity is not MacGregor's strong suit and these musings on romance become interminable. Alida Valli plays the love of MacGregor's life, a witch-like creature whom he has rechristened Heloise, 'because I find it more romantic. She is my claim to humanity, my soul ... Now, you cannot call your soul *Mabel* – I ask you!'

Even for a comic French softcore porn film *La grande trouille* is an incomprehensible piece. People die and then come back to life, and MacGregor seems to be engaged in constructing android simulacra in the cellar. Things become no clearer as the film goes on and at the conclusion, a turret in MacGregor's castle takes off like a rocket in a scene that is pure *Monty Python*. Several scenes are delightfully photographed however, and there is a gorgeous flashback, in which Cushing plays MacGregor's grandfather, a grumpy Scottish gravedigger with a great grey beard who drives a hearse with plumed horses. (The old man drops dead of shock when young MacGregor says he is going off to be an actor.) But it's a long way from Hammer horror to see Cushing cracking some rather blue jokes and at one point, spanking Miou-Miou over his knee.

While Cushing was still in Hong Kong, he was offered a role in a film called *The Ghoul*, which was to be made by a new production company called Tyburn. 'I'd just got back from the studios one evening,' Cushing related, 'when the phone rang and a young man announced himself as Kevin Francis, Freddie's son, whom I'd last seen as a boy. He was ringing from London to ask if I would star in *The Ghoul* under his father's direction. Of course, I was delighted to accept.'[4] Tyburn's first film was *Persecution*, starring

Lana Turner, Ralph Bates and Trevor Howard. This was followed quickly by *The Ghoul*, which began filming on 4th March 1974 at Pinewood Studios.

Cushing plays Doctor Lawrence, a defrocked clergyman who hides a terrible secret in his remote moorland home. Some years ago in India, his son was corrupted by a depraved prince and as a result become a ghoul, feeding on human flesh. Lawrence's wife committed suicide and the priest brought his son back to England to keep him shut away in the attic. When four young people, lost on the moor, seek shelter at Lawrence's house, only one of them will survive...

Francis father and son assembled a strong cast for the film, including a young John Hurt as the backward gardener Tom. Gwen Watford, Cushing's *Winslow Boy* co-star, rather improbably plays the ghoul's devoted Ayah in dusky make-up, while Ian McCulloch, Alexandra Bastedo, Veronica Carlson and Stewart Bevan are the young things. Don Henderson, who later appeared alongside Cushing in *Star Wars*, played the ghoul, the actor enduring considerable discomfort from the green contact lenses required for the role.

While shooting *The Ghoul*, Cushing gave a frank interview to journalist David Montgomery. Perhaps because of its upsetting portrait of a man shattered by grief, the interview was not published for more than three years, eventually surfacing in the *Sunday Times* in August 1977 when *Star Wars* had opened in America.

'To work,' he said, 'it's the only thing left, isn't it? What else would I do? My whole life now is work because work is literally the only thing that helps time pass in any bearable way. Up out of bed as usual at the crack of, and then ... what? A book, a nap, some tea, a stroll. Another day winding out like an open road. I'm a complete recluse now. No one can take the place of Helen. Ever. So one's alone. And I'm killing time by working harder than ever I have before. I'm reminded of Helen all the time, d'you see, 24 hours a day. And it isn't that it makes it any worse or any better being with people, but I just find, mentally and physically, that I can't cope in company. It's false. And one thing I hate is falseness. "Hate" – I hate the word "hate". I *don't like* falseness. What many don't understand, and I hope they never have the experience, is that I'm lonely *all* the time, whether I'm with hundreds of people, say in a film studio, or if I'm on my own.

'Out of pure kindness, they think – some of them – that I should forget, make a complete break, sell the house, her belongings, live in London. And some of them say "Oh, you'll meet someone else." They can't understand. There is no-one else. There is no-one else

A warm greeting between two old friends as Cushing appears on Christopher Lee's *This Is Your Life* (1974)

I can ever dream of sharing life with. To me it is so repugnant that the very idea almost makes me physically sick, that people can think of that. And yet it's only out of kindness that they do. Bless them, they don't quite see.'[5]

There was to be one bright spot in the making of *The Ghoul* however, as Cushing explained to Montgomery. 'I have really appeared in a film with Helen now. In this film there is required a photograph of Mrs Lawrence, the wife of the man I play. And I asked Freddie Francis, the director, if we could use some photographs of Helen, and he thought it a marvellous idea. They blew them up and sepia'd them, and had these marvellous close-ups of Helen ... So at last we made a film together.'[6]

Quite whether this blurring of art and life was a sensible idea or not is debatable. Veronica Carlson recalls that when Cushing had to deliver the lines about Mrs Lawrence's death, he was so overcome that he broke down in tears and had to leave the set. 'I wanted to go up to him and just give him a hug,' says Carlson. 'But you couldn't. He wanted to be on his own.'[7]

If there was any uneasy feeling that his private grief was being exploited, Cushing went on record in *Past Forgetting* and elsewhere to state the contrary and said how enormously grateful he was to Kevin Francis for his continued support. The actor and producer enjoyed a warm friendship until Cushing's death.

Also during *The Ghoul*, Cushing appeared with Carlson on a *This Is Your Life* programme to pay tribute to Christopher Lee. Other guests included Vincent Price, Oliver Reed and Trevor Howard and the programme was broadcast on 3rd April 1974.

At Easter, Cushing followed the lead of Spike Milligan and Cliff Richard to appear on a late-night religious programme called *What Was He Like?*, explaining his own interpretation of the life of Christ. There were also appearances on the BBC's *Film 74* and *Horizon* programmes.

In May 1974, at Pinewood Studios, Cushing starred in a episode of Gerry and Sylvia Anderson's big-budget science-fiction series *Space: 1999* entitled *Missing Link*. The series starred Martin Landau as Commander Koenig with Barbara Bain and Barry Morse. Guest stars for the series included Joan Collins, Christopher Lee, Roy Dotrice and Leo McKern. Cushing played Raan, an ancient being, with Joanna Dunham as his daughter Vana.

508-year-old scientist Raan in *Missing Link*, an episode of *Space: 1999*

Cushing admitted that he did not read science fiction, but he seemed to enjoy playing it, and he was doubtless attracted to the role of a 508-year-old scientist who lives in a city made of light.

Raan is described in Edward Di Lorenzo's script thus. 'On the surface he is all charm and rather amusing. However, there is an underlying menace about him – it is not intentional, but nevertheless it weaves through his words somewhat like a surgeon describing the operation to a patient before actually performing it.'

Raan intends to study Koenig as an example of the missing link between 'primitive' man and his civilisation, but Vana will not let her father experiment on a living specimen. 'The perfect balance between thought and feeling must be found,' Raan admits. 'Both our worlds have yet to discover it.' Cushing's costume for Raan consisted of a diaphanous gown and a long white wig, and the make-up used a heavy gold face-paint which proved very difficult to remove.

Cushing was back in more familiar costume, and on fine form in his second Tyburn film, *The Legend of the Werewolf*, as Paul Cataflanque, police pathologist and amateur detective. The film was directed by Freddie Francis from 19th August 1974 at Pinewood Studios co-starring Ron Moody, Roy Castle and Hugh Griffith.

Cushing seems to be enjoying himself enormously – almost all of his scenes, until the last, have a ghoulish humour about them. It is never forced, it is just a witty, clever, concentrated performance. Cataflanque is eating his tea as the newest cadaver is brought in. '*Ooh dea*r,' Cushing clucks, with his mouth full, peering under the sheet, 'that's very nasty...' He gets rid of his pompous superiors by mischievously presenting them with a gullet and when he does a bit of undercover research in the local brothel he is left bashfully holding a frilly garter. Perhaps his best one-liner is his resigned 'C'est la vie' as he melts down his silver walking-stick handle to make a silver bullet. David Rintoul is equally effective as the wolf-boy Etoile, whose torment at becoming a werewolf is genuinely harrowing.

Unfortunately, though beautifully shot in parts, *The Legend of the Werewolf* is a haphazardly-plotted film, over reliant on repetitive red-filtered werewolf's-point-of-view shots. The film has much in common with its stablemate *The Ghoul*, but Cushing seems much happier than he was in that film, and his performance as Cataflanque is one of his most enjoyable in the 1970s, a classic example of the actor being a great deal better than the lines he is given to say.

After the collapse of the Hammer museum project, Michael Carreras was busy looking for other outlets for the Hammer name. He followed the lead of another great British institution, the *Carry On* films, and began plans for a theatre show. When the popularity of the *Carry Ons* in cinemas began to wane, producer Peter Rogers staged *Carry On London*, which enjoyed a successful run at the Victoria Palace Theatre in London in 1973. A Hammer stage show might have been a going concern if Cushing had participated, but he wrote an apologetic letter to Carreras on 25th April 1975.

'My dear Michael, John Redway has told me of your kind thought regarding your new venture, and I want you to know how much I appreciated it. But I'm afraid the 'legitimate' theatre is now a thing of the past as far as I'm concerned. Many years ago, it was part cause of a nervous breakdown I had, which – perforce – kept me out of work for nearly twelve months. I have of course, been on the stage many times since then and each occasion was anathema to me. I wish you good luck and great success in all you assay.'

The letter was signed 'Helen and Peter'. At this time, Cushing was also offered the role of Sherlock Holmes in a Broadway production of *The Crucifer of Blood*, based on *The Sign of Four*, which he also declined.

From the beginning of June 1975, New York independent filmmaker Ken Wiederhorn made a $300,000 film provisionally called *Death Corps* – later retitled *Shock Waves* – shot on 16mm and blown up to 35mm. Wiederhorn, who with partner/producer Reuben Trane had won an Oscar in 1973 for the Best Dramatic Student Film, sought advice on making a low-budget horror film from producer Richard Gordon, who had made *Island of Terror*. Gordon recommended Cushing, who readily agreed – 'I felt if my name could help them at all, it would be a good thing to do.'[8] Cushing's four days of shooting took him to Florida's Biscayne Bay, where he kept a low-key presence on set, making coffee for the cast and crew and helping the ladies in the cast through the swamp.

The film stars Brooke Adams as Rose, who joins a group of friends to charter a seedy yacht for a cruise – the boat's curmudgeonly captain is played by John Carradine. One night the boat is rammed by the hulk of a freighter which has run aground near a small island. Exploring the island, the friends discover an abandoned hotel, whose single inhabitant keeps the secret of a bizarre Nazi experiment from the Second World War.

As the classical music from a gramophone bleeds through the colonnades of the deserted villa and slurs to a halt, Cushing's voice rings out 'Why have you come to this place?' It is an entrance to match Christopher Lee's in *Dracula*. In a gently lilting German accent, he continues, 'I am waiting. You will please answer my question.' Cushing here plays a strange and sinewy figure, but an undeniably powerful one, even in his ragged clothes and filthy neckerchief. He is surprisingly athletic too – as can be seen when he sprints across the beach later in the film. He is made-up with a livid scar across his forehead and right eye. This weird recluse is a former SS commandant, who was in charge of a division of troops which were surgically altered to exist underwater, to crew submarines which would never have to surface. 'They were the most vicious and bloodthirsty of all the SS divisions,' the commandant explains. 'We created the perfect soldier from cheap hoodlums and thugs and a good number of pathological murderers and sadists as well. We called them the *Toten Corps* – the Death Corps – creatures more horrible than any you can imagine. Not dead, not alive, but somewhere in between.'

The collision with the cruiser has awakened the Death Corps, who stride across the seabed toward the island. The underwater scenes of the zombies (photographed by Irving Pare) have a balletic grace and a fairy tale otherworldliness. These sequences,

accompanied by discordant synthesized score (by Richard Einhorn) are as compelling as any Hammer scene and the albinoed zombies, with their pallid, goggled faces, were described by *Fangoria* as 'one of the best monster gangs to come down the pike in a long time'.[9] Some of the acting, however, is unintentionally hilarious and the zombie who pursues and finally drowns the commandant looks suspiciously like David Hockney. But *Shock Waves* is not a bad film, and prefigures many of the late 1970s horrors. The commandant provides Cushing with a chance to play a menacing character, but one who is haunted by a terror from the past. His tiny, guilty glance to the swastika banners that decorate his retreat is exceptional. It is one of his last really satisfying horror roles.

On his return to Britain, Cushing was to have starred in a film version of Dennis Wheatley's *The Satanist* for Tyburn, with a planned cast including Shirley Bassey and Orson Welles. This film fell through at the last minute, so Cushing was able to film two cameo scenes as Sir Edward Gifford in Kevin Connor's film *Trial by Combat*.

In *Trial by Combat* (1975) Ben Willoughby (Neil McCarthy) and Sir Edward Gifford educate the young John Gifford (Marc Harrison) in the ways of chivalry

The film stars Donald Pleasence as the leader of the Knights of the Order of Avalon, who recreate medieval jousts in full armour. But these displays have nothing to do with pageantry – the knights of the order are being used as a kind of vigilante group, bringing 'justice' to criminals who have escaped the law. Director Connor was obviously keen to work with Cushing again after *From Beyond the Grave*, it is a shame, however, that he could not be given more to do. Sir Edward is effectively the embodiment of the knights' true code and as such is seen off even before the credits have run. Cushing appears later in a flashback, as Sir Edward's son remembers how

Ingrid Pitt watches Cushing addressing a capacity crowd at the Famous Monsters Convention in 1975

in Basingstoke. Cushing suggested that they open their season with *The Heiress*, a play by Ruth and Augustus Goetz, based on *Washington Square* by Henry James. Set in 1850, the play tells the story of the dominating Doctor Austin Sloper (Cushing) and his awkward daughter Catherine (Ryan), and her one chance for escape and fulfilment with former playboy Morris Townsend. Is he the reformed character and honourable suitor he claims to be, or is he merely after her money?

The Heiress played to full houses between 21st October and 1st November 1975 and Cushing stated that the few weeks he spent on the production were the happiest he had

his father taught him fencing and the importance of chivalry. The film features John Mills as the unconventional ex-Scotland Yard man Bertie Cook, and with knights on horseback seeing off underworld criminals, it has the spirit and feel of an extended episode of *The Avengers*.

Cushing made several appearances on television in 1975. He appeared on *The Amazing World of Cinema* in a show entitled *The Mad Scientists* for VPS/Polymedia. He was also a guest on *Looks Familiar*, the nostalgic quiz game hosted by Denis Norden in which a panel of celebrities recall personalities, films and events from the early part of the century. Cushing also provided the on-screen narration for Paul Annett's documentary on the supposedly-haunted *Herstmonceaux Castle*.

Despite telling Michael Carreras that his career in the 'legitimate' theatre was over, in October Cushing took one last turn on the boards to pay tribute to a favourite actress. He had watched and enjoyed the television series *Edward the Seventh*, starring Timothy West, and he was particularly taken with the actress Helen Ryan's portrayal of Princess Alexandra. 'Miss Ryan,' he wrote 'played the royal personage as if she had lived and breathed and had her being during that period of ... history. I was deeply impressed by this remarkable recreation and wrote her a fan letter.'[10]

Ryan was married to Guy Slater, who was about to start a season as director of the Horseshoe Theatre

spent since 1971. Helen Ryan remembers 'Peter was wonderful, super in the play, but he was so terribly nervous. The play opened at 7.30 and Peter would be at the theatre three hours beforehand to check his props and his costume.'[11]

Later in November, Cushing was the guest of honour at 'Monstercon', a New York event run by horror fan and *Famous Monsters of Filmland* editor Forrest J Ackerman. This gave many American fans their first chance to meet Cushing in person. Ingrid Pitt and Michael Carreras were also guests, and Pitt remembers Carreras taking herself and Cushing to a jazz club where Carreras displayed his exceptional talent for playing the trumpet. At the convention, Carreras unveiled plans for a new Hammer film based on the comic strip *Vampirella*, to star Cushing, directed by John Hough. This, like so many Hammer plans at the time, never came to fruition. While in America, Cushing made a guest appearance with Ackerman on Tom Snyder's *Tomorrow* TV programme in New York. They were joined by Professor Leonard Wolfe, author of *The Annotated Dracula*, who dominated the conversation. Although Snyder had no knowledge of the genre, Cushing played along cheerfully, and scoffed at Wolfe's theories of the sexual connotations of vampire-staking.

Shortly afterwards, Cushing went to Greece to film *The Devil's Men*. This muddled story of ancient rites and blood sacrifice was directed by Costa Carayiannis with Donald Pleasence, Luan Peters and Nikos Vewrlekis, with Cushing as the occultist Baron Corofax, a nobleman from Dracula's homeland of Carpathia. Corofax is sinister and severe, but Cushing seems far too noble to be a villain. He is given little to do, but maintains a great stillness when delivering his lines, giving them a subtle, implied menace. 'I have little in common with the local people...' he coos to the heroine, Laurie Gordon (Luan Peters). 'I am an exile – you being an American will find that hard to understand.' Pleasence plays Corofax's opponent, the Van Helsing figure Father Roche – a sympathetic, heroic priest with a core of steel.

The sound in the film is hollow and indistinct, the photography flat and the script feeble. The camera prowls around picture-postcard ruins, underscored by Brian Eno's unsettling synthesised score and far too much is made of the pagan idol, a pint-sized statue of a minotaur with two gas-burners up its nose. There are several big close-ups of Cushing's green-tinted face, shot through distorted lens, and he looks formidable striding through the caves in his crimson robes. 'The old customs remain,' he intones endlessly, 'and the ancient gods live on.'

Corofax's invulnerable disciples cannot be killed even by the force of an oncoming car, but in a nice reversal of fortune, Cushing is stopped in his tracks when Pleasence brandishes a crucifix. In a final insane twist, Corofax and his people are sprinkled with holy water and literally explode. The film could have done with more surreal touches like this earlier on.

Only three years later, John Carpenter made *Halloween* with a teen heroine, an unstoppable robot-like killer and a synthesized score. He wanted Peter Cushing too, for the lead role of psychiatrist Doctor Loomis, but Cushing turned the role down, as did Christopher Lee – although Lee later admitted this was a mistake. The part of Loomis went to Donald Pleasence, but it would have been interesting if Cushing had completely made the transition from old horror to the new. He had gone some way with *Shock Waves* and *The Devil's Men*, although it was clear that this new style wasn't really *his* style.

Back in England after Christmas, Cushing was filming from 20th January 1976 in an AIP/Amicus co-production based on Edgar Rice Burroughs' fantasy novel *At the Earth's Core*. The director was Kevin Connor again. Cushing plays eccentric inventor Dr Abner Perry, who has built a fantastic burrowing machine dubbed the 'Iron Mole' and intends to drill through the Welsh hillside for a trial run. We first see Perry in his dust-coat supervising the building of the machine, when Cushing somehow manages to sum up the inventor's whole character in a little wave of encouragement.

The mole is launched and immediately goes out of control, depositing Perry and his American backer David Innes (Doug McClure) in a palaeolithic jungle with a pink sky. ('The land of pink jelly' the *Evening Standard* called it.) 'This cannot be the Rhondda valley!' Perry mutters gravely, before declaring 'David, we are not *on* Earth... from my observations, dear friend, I can positively state that we are *under* it – at the Earth's core!'

As they dismount the Mole and explore the new terrain, Perry and David are interrupted by a dinosaur, of the man-in-a-rubber-suit variety, which lumbers past on a back-projection screen while Cushing and McClure dash about in the foreground. Ten years on, Cushing all but repeats his Dr Who performance, needing less make-up.

Escaping the dinosaur, David and Perry are captured and imprisoned by a group of vicious, pig-faced creatures called Sagoths. 'They're so excitable...' says Perry, 'like all foreigners.' (As the Sagoth guard approaches later, Cushing, clearly ad-libbing, clucks 'Here comes cheerful Annie again!')

The travellers meet fellow captives Ghak (Godfrey James) and Dia (Caroline Munro) who tell them that the land is called Pellucidar, which is ruled by the Mahars, a savage race of telepathic reptile-birds. Soon

With Caroline Munro and Doug McClure in *At the Earth's Core* (1976)

Perry and David are leading the rebellion against the Mahars and the scenes of Cushing drilling the Pellucidans in archery are delightfully funny. So too is his line, delivered into the impassive milky eye of the chief Mahar, 'You cannot mesmerise me, I'm British!'

The *Standard* concluded that the film-makers should have 'success with the wide-eyed child that is in all of us.'[12] while the *Telegraph* praised the 'often very funny Peter Cushing.'[13]

Milton Subotsky's name is down as screenwriter, but Cushing recalled that, as ever with Amicus, there wasn't much of a script. He had to make up his own lines – chiefly 'By jove!' or cries for help from the thick of various predicaments.

Mike Vickers created a score of electronic bleeps and burbles and a stirring orchestral theme, ideal for this sort of scientific romance. Behind the camera was veteran cinematographer Alan Hume who had photographed many Cushing films.

There is still something wonderfully nostalgic in this very British genre of brass-bound Victorian

'It's hideous! Obscene!' Mebach Von Claus faces the resurrection of the Third Reich, with Karl (Frank Gatliff) in *The New Avengers: The Eagle's Nest* (1976)

derring-do, which was all but obliterated by the coming of *Star Wars*. There was even the potential for a sequel in Perry's innocent enquiry to David 'Have you ever thought of going to the moon?'

When the film was released at end of July in time for the school summer holidays, Thames TV's cinema programme for children *Clapperboard* dedicated a whole show to exploring behind the scenes of *At the Earth's Core* and for many young viewers it was a thrilling introduction to the world of film-making.

In 1975, producers Brian Clemens and Albert Fennell had made a deal with French television backer to bring *The Avengers* back to the screen after a break of nearly seven years. *The Satanic Rites of Dracula's* Joanna Lumley was the new *Avengers* girl, with Gareth Hunt on hand for the fisticuffs, as Patrick Macnee, now 53, was considered to be too old for that kind of thing. The series went under the title of *The New Avengers*, but in most respects, the old order was unchanged. Clemens wasted no time in inviting Cushing back as a guest star for the first episode of his new series, *The Eagle's Nest* which was filmed in April on location on the Isle of Skye and at Pinewood studios. 'It was sad to see how fragile Peter was,'

Clemens remembers. 'He told me he was just treading time until he could join his wife.'[14]

Cushing plays Doctor Mebach Von Claus, an eminent German scientist whose field of expertise is suspended animation. It's a gently humorous performance, and there is a good deal of fun with a deep-frozen frog called Albert in a scene that recalls a similar revivification in *The Curse of Frankenstein*. Von Claus is kidnapped and taken to the Scottish island of St Dorca, where Father Trasker (Derek Farr) leads a group of Nazis disguised as monks. Von Claus is asked to attend to a sick member of the order who has been placed in cryogenic suspension, little suspecting he is part of a plot to resurrect the greatest evil of the Twentieth Century – Adolf Hitler.

To leaven the wilder excesses of the plot, there is some artfully-played comedy that shows the series is back on top form. Joanna Lumley has a beautiful scene with Sydney Bromley as a bewildered old local who saw a German plane come down nearby, while Macnee interrupts a squadron of jackbooted, saluting Nazis with a hopeful 'Rule Britannia?'

The Eagle's Nest is a more complex piece of work than *Return of the Cybernauts*, the action more realistic and less cartoonish. Von Claus is beaten up savagely – and gives a reaction of genuine horror when he discovers that the monks have nothing less than Hitler's body in suspended animation. 'It is hideous! Obscene!' Cushing spits, on seeing the Fuhrer's face. 'You'll have to kill me first...'

It was rarely easy for Cushing to discern, on the studio floor, the fate of the film he was making. Occasionally, he had been upset when he felt that the context of his performances had been changed (*Corruption*, for example) and he even maintained that *The Curse of Frankenstein* could have been 'another picture that came and went and nobody took any notice.'[15] What importance did he place, then, on a few days' filming at the end of April 1976 on a children's science fantasy adventure? The sets were small and the young American leads were homesick and disgruntled at their lack of direction. But from its troubled beginnings, the film became one of the biggest cinema sensations of all time. That film was *Star Wars*.

Chapter Twenty-Three

Still Dancin'

Cushing did have an inkling of what to expect from *Star Wars*, perhaps. 'I thought the kids would adore it'[1] he said. He was not wrong. A lot of kids adored it very much indeed – and a lot of adults, too. His participation in this blockbuster granted him another piece of immortality.

With *Star Wars*, George Lucas – as writer, producer and director – changed the face of filmmaking. The movie became one of the highest-grossing pictures of all time and audiences came to expect action and spectacle. The developments in special effects required for the film set new standards for the industry, and John Williams' sweeping orchestral score raised the film's soundtrack to the status of classical music.

The adventures of young farmboy Luke Skywalker (Mark Hamill), 'a long time ago, in a galaxy far, far away....' have become a modern myth. Luke dreams of leaving the desert planet Tatooine and joining the rebellion against the oppressive forces of the evil Galactic Empire. He acquires two robots which have escaped from a rebel ship – one of them, R2-D2, is carrying the plans to the Empire's secret weapon, a massive battle station of terrifying power called the Death Star. Luke's journey sees him join forces with the exiled Jedi knight Obi-Wan Kenobi (Alec Guinness) and the space pirate Han Solo (Harrison Ford) to face the evil Darth Vader.

In his script, originally entitled *The Star Wars*, Lucas mixed elements of classic fairy-tale and Arthurian legend with knowing cinematic references. He assembled elements from all his favourite childhood films – the dog-fights from *Tora! Tora! Tora!*, the cliffhangers from *Flash Gordon*, the bar-room brawl from any number of Westerns – and the greatest screen villains were represented by Peter Cushing.

Lucas originally considered Cushing for the role of Obi-Wan Kenobi before deciding that his lean features would be better employed as the villain, Grand Moff Tarkin. ('I've often wondered what a "Grand Moff" was,' said Cushing later. 'It sounds like something that flew out of a cupboard.') Tarkin is a charming and calculating villain, at his best in a confrontation with Carrie Fisher as Princess Leia. 'Governor Tarkin,' she spits. 'I recognised your foul stench when I was brought on board.' 'Charming to the last,' replies Tarkin blithely. 'You don't know how hard I found it signing the order to terminate your life.'

Tarkin's second-in-command, Darth Vader, would achieve greater significance as the *Star Wars* trilogy continued. Here, though, Tarkin exerts some control over Vader – with a word, he stops him from telepathically throttling an underling and Leia observes that Tarkin is 'holding Vader's leash'. By an occasional haunted glance, however, Cushing is able to imply that Vader holds the real power, and Tarkin is uneasy in his presence. Thus both characters are made more frightening.

'Peter Cushing is a very good actor...' George Lucas said in an interview for *Rolling Stone* magazine. 'Adored and idolised by young people and by people who go to see a certain kind of movie. I too he will be fondly remembered for the next 350 years at least.'[3] Certainly, Cushing was adored by those who worked with him on *Star Wars*, including *Monster from Hell* David Prowse (Darth Vader), Don Henderson (General Tagge) and Leslie Schofield (Imperial Commander). Carrie Fisher remembers that Cushing was very kind to her, giving her the benefit of his years of experience in film acting.

There is a final shot of Tarkin, a split second before Luke and his friends destroy the Death Star, as he stands alone, having refused to abandon the station 'in our moment of triumph'. With his hand at his mouth, he is almost chewing his nails. In his moment of quiet terror, we see the humanity of the monster – classic Cushing.

Cushing's filming at the EMI-Elstree Studios (formerly MGM-EMI) was sandwiched between *The New Avengers* and flying to America to appear in *The Great Houdinis*. Like all the *Star Wars* 'guest stars', apart from Guinness, Cushing was on a specially arranged flat fee of £1000 for a week, which he finished on 4th May 1976, and he received no further payment.

'One spares a grain of compassion for Grand Moff Tarkin, Governor of the Imperial Outlands, despite his unconscionable villainy,' said *Films and Filming*, 'simply because he is so excellently played by the immaculately-spoken Peter Cushing, who regardless of their cross purposes in the plot, seems in effect to share with Guinness a Movement Towards The Perpetuation Of Clear Speech."[4]

On board the Death Star, Governor Tarkin interrogates Princess Leia (Carrie Fisher), watched by Darth Vader (David Prowse) in *Star Wars* (1976)

Cushing's chief memory of *Star Wars* was the trouble with his boots. Close to the opening of *Star Wars*, the *Evening News* revealed: 'The reason Peter Cushing's size twelves led to a knees-up', accompanied by a helpful picture of the Cushing feet. 'Sharp-eyed cinema-goers may note, when the fabulously successful film *Star Wars* opens here at Christmas, that Peter Cushing only ever appears on screen filmed from the knees up. The reason is that wafer-thin Mr Cushing – he is six feet tall but weighs only nine stone – has such enormous feet that the film's wardrobe department was unable to cater for him. As the Grand Moff Tarkin ... the man who made horror respectable was supposed to wear proper dictator-style riding-boots and the wardrobe duly supplied a pair of size nines. "But alas, I have taken a size twelve since my youth," Cushing said. "When I crammed on the size nine boots I could hardly walk. So I persuaded the director George Lucas to shoot me from the knees up – which meant I could wear comfy plimsolls." Surprisingly, Mr Cushing's partner in horror, Mr Christopher Lee, who can give him a good four inches in height, takes only a size eleven – and a *narrow* at that.'[5] For the record, Cushing is seen wearing the boots in one brief long-shot.

Then Cushing was off to Hollywood, invited by 20th Century-Fox to appear in *The Great Houdinis*, a TV movie on the life of the celebrated illusionist Harry Houdini. *Starsky and Hutch*'s Paul Michael Glaser played Houdini, with Ruth Gordon, Wilfred Hyde-White, Bill Bixby, Vivian Vance, Sally Struthers and Clive Revell. Cushing played Sir Arthur Conan Doyle – the *Sherlock Holmes* author who investigated spiritualism and the occult with Houdini – while Maureen O'Sullivan played Doyle's wife.

Cushing arrived in America on Tuesday 11th May and was called the following day at 7.00 am. 12th May was Wilfred Hyde-White's birthday, which was celebrated with a party on set at which Cushing cut the cake. On 13th May scenes were filmed in a prison cell set on Stage 20 at the Fox studios. By this time, the film was over budget and behind schedule due to problems with a séance sequence, and work went on until midnight on all of Cushing's filming days. The scene in which Doyle tries to persuade Harry that his wife has received a warning for Harry from his late mother is one of the strongest scenes in the film.

Between takes, Cushing was happy to chat with his American fans, recalling his days on stage with Tod Slaughter in *The Gay Invalid* and his recent experience in *Tendre Dracula*, while revealing his fondness for buckwheat pancakes.

At this time, the American Peter Cushing Club Journal featured a revealing section in which Cushing answered readers' questions. In a simple question and answer fashion, Cushing gave brief responses on a host of subjects. He seemed to find the questionnaires taxing, would rarely be drawn on a particular topic but by his occasionally terse replies would often say much by saying nothing. As witnessed here –

Is humour an important ingredient in a horror film? 'It is an important ingredient in all walks of life.'

What is the first step to make a good horror film? 'Sincerity.'

Have you ever considered ending your career in horror films like Mr Lee? 'No. Nor has Mr Lee, I think you'll find.'

Do you think young adults aged 13 or 14 should be able to see your 'R' ('X') rated films? Why or why not? 'I have a feeling they *do* – on television if not in the cinema.'

You have stated that you avoid seeing certain types of movies. Would you mind giving examples of these types? '*The Exorcist, Last Tango in Paris, Shampoo, The Graduate*, etc.'

What did you think of the film *Jaws*? 'First-class entertainment.'

How did you like being guest of honor at the Famous Monsters Con? If asked would you make a return visit? 'It was a most wonderful and moving occasion. I was completely overwhelmed by the warmth of the welcome I received and the genuine affection extended by all those in attendance. Indeed I would come again if asked and circumstances allowed.'[6]

Cushing revealed to the fan club that he did not watch fantasy movies, but nevertheless he would consider appearing in another *Frankenstein* if the script was good. He explained that he no longer had his collection of toy soldiers, which were sold after Helen's death. He expressed his preference for ragtime music and thought the BBC's production of *War and Peace* 'Quite excellent – beautifully produced.'

He also revealed that he had read Nicholas Meyer's Sherlock Holmes novel *The Seven Per Cent Solution*. 'It was very ingenious and had a style of its own, and as such I thought it was splendid. But to my mind no one has ever been able to catch the atmosphere of the original Conan Doyle stories.'[7]

On 28th August 1976, Cushing appeared on the *Jim'll Fix It Bank Holiday Special* for the BBC. In the show, presenter Jimmy Savile helped to grant the wishes of viewers and two boys wrote in wanting to know about horror make-up. They were duly made-up to look monstrous, but they had a further request – to scare Peter Cushing. Cushing happily joined in the fun. Sadly, the programme is now completely overshadowed by the distressing allegations made about Savile's behaviour.

In the autumn of 1976, there was a reunion for Cushing with Vincent Price for a radio serial called *Aliens in the Mind*. Developed from an idea by former *Doctor Who* script editor Robert Holmes, the serial is a *Quatermass*-like story of a genetic mutation on the remote Scottish Island of Lewigh which breeds a race of powerful telepaths. Cushing plays Doctor John Cornelius, an eminent British brain surgeon and Price plays Professor Curtis Lark, a bohemian American explorer, scientist and Nobel Prize winner whose research has been in the field of telepathy and telekinesis. Together they form a rather waspish Holmes and Watson partnership, with Cornelius gently educating Lark in the finer points of British life while facing a mysterious and relentless foe. Richard Hurndall from *I, Monster* also starred, with Cushing's good friend Irene Sutcliffe.

As the British film industry continued to decline, Cushing increasingly found that he had to travel abroad more and more to find work – only one of his next seven films was made in England. In October 1976 he travelled to Spain to play another German, Major Von Hackenberg, in Ottokar Runz' film *Die Standarte* (*Battleflag*). Cushing joined several former Hammer co-stars, included Simon Ward (*Frankenstein Must Be Destroyed*) and Jon Finch (*The Vampire Lovers*) for this lavish production, which was filmed in German and Spanish. We see Cushing striding across the battlefield, in a splendid grey uniform, kepi and boots – the proper size, this time, hopefully. 'Will the gentlemen permit me to join them?' he inquires politely as he languidly lights a cigarette. He begins interrogating the senior cadet officer Count Heister, claiming some abilities in fortune-telling, looking at the soldier's hand and stating 'one should always be prepared for death, fella. Some people seem to know when it will intervene.' By a series of questions, Von Hackenburg exposes Count Heister as a fraud – his father was a gypsy. 'I have no doubt that there are normal men among the gypsies,' says the major, 'but they don't try to pass themselves off as aristocrats.' Von Hackenburg orders that Heister surrender the standard to Menis (Simon Ward), who must now guard the battleflag with his life. Menis' adventures take up the rest of the film.

In November Cushing flew to Canada for *The Uncanny*. This was yet another portmanteau picture – produced by Milton Subotsky as an Anglo-Canadian co-production, and directed by Denis Heroux. It was originally entitled *Brrr!* and was based on Michel Parry's short story anthology *Beware of the Cat*. Cushing's scenes were filmed on location in Senneville and at the Panavision Studios, Montreal, from 16th November 1976, although the 'Malkin' segment was filmed at Pinewood Studios.

Heinrich Haussner sizes up a recruit in *Hitler's Son* (1977)

The Uncanny saw Cushing back in top-billing position, and once again providing the linking device for a series of eerie tales. In this instance he is Wilbur Gray, a down-at-heel eccentric who believes that cats are agents of the Devil. With Canadian locations, the film looks very different from the usual home-grown product and Cushing's performance of barely-controlled hysteria is eminently watchable – in other hands it could have been merely aggravating. He makes the idea of a man being hunted by cats convincing and rather disturbing.

Gray takes the evidence to his wearily sceptical publisher Frank Richards (Ray Milland). 'It's all here!' he tells him. 'Years of research! Evidence from all over the world proving beyond a shadow of doubt that cats have been exploiting the human race for centuries!' Richards, himself a cat-fancier, says that the public may not yet be ready for such tales. 'You said that about my book on flying saucers!' wails Gray, and proceeds to present the evidence from his manuscript. The first, and best, story is set in London in 1912, starring Joan Greenwood as Miss Malkin, a wealthy, bedridden old lady who is ultimately nibbled to death by her feline charges.

The following black magic episode with Chloe Franks is dull and the third segment, a film studio farce with Donald Pleasence and Samantha Eggar set at 'Haemorrhage Film Productions', becomes a histrionic runaround. The whole is saved by Cushing's detailed performance of preoccupied seediness – he is wearing two cardigans, wipes his nose on his gloves – but because his theories are proven true, Gray ultimately achieves a kind of nobility. In several scenes, Cushing directs his lines to a low camera and

seems to be carrying on a suspicious 'conversation' with his tormentors. Gray meets a grisly end when his is set upon by a pack of moggies and falls down a flight of steps.

In 1977 Cushing returned to Australia to make an eight-part series called *A Land Looking West* with John Izzard of Swan Television.

Cushing is not only the narrator for this marathon documentary on the history of Australia from the time of the Aborigines to the present, he also appears on screen in seven of the eight episodes, generally striding over a dusty hill. He makes an excellent presenter, particularly in the segments about the first British colonists, but it does beg the question as to why an Australian wasn't used, especially as Cushing has to relate the sometimes appalling treatment of the native Australians by the British.

Cushing recalled how they used a small plane to cross the vast areas of outback between their Perth base and the various locations. Their pilot would routinely doze off because, he said 'the plane knows the way' 'There's faith for you, I thought.'[8]

For his next role, in *Hitler's Son*, Cushing travelled to Munich's Arri Studios in September 1977. The premise of the film is that Hitler's naive son Willi (played by Bud Cort) is taken in by a group of neo-Nazis and used as a figurehead for their new Reich. Filmmakers were eager to follow the success of black comedies like Mel Brooks' *The Producer*s, but *Hitler's Son*, filmed under the rather less incendiary title of *Return to Munich*, is a surprisingly charming piece.

Cushing looks fit and seems genuinely happy to be doing something different, although the 'exiled Nazi' role became a typecasting headache as much as the 'stitcher of limbs'. Cushing enjoys the comedy in the part, and has a sublimely funny running gag involving several perfectly-timed comic falls.

Cushing played Heinrich Haussner, the leader of the Fascist League, but even in the wake of *Star Wars*, little was made of his contribution. *Hitler's Son* was featured on the cover of the May 1978 edition of *Films and Filming*, but Cushing was nowhere to be seen, even in the two-page photo spread. Shooting on *Hitler's Son* over-ran by six weeks, causing Cushing to miss an appearance in John Dark and Kevin Connor's Edwardian science-fiction adventure *Warlords of Atlantis*. Cushing was to have played Atraxon, Imperator of the Supreme Council of Atlantis, a ruthless Martian scientist who intends to pervert the course of human development. It would have been a good cameo in a popular and well-publicised film, which was a great summer holiday hit in the post-*Star Wars* summer of 1978. Atraxon was eventually played by Daniel Massey, the cast also included Cyd Charisse, Peter Gilmore and Doug McClure.

At the end of 1977, Cushing wrote to his British and American fan clubs requesting that they be disbanded. He felt that he was too old, and that his work, now mostly cameo appearances, did not warrant such attention. The British club concurred with his wishes, but the Americans embarked on a campaign to prove that their star was still loved and wanted. After heartfelt letters from club organiser Deborah Del Vecchio (née Bennett) and the members, appealing to Cushing to let the club continue, he, of course, agreed. Del Vecchio and Tom Johnson went on to write the first detailed, invaluable Cushing filmography in 1992.

On 27th July 1978, Cushing flew to Zambia to take part in a film called *A Touch of the Sun*. This low-budget comedy was directed by Peter Curran, who had been a film editor on Hammer's *When Dinosaurs Ruled the Earth*, later becoming a producer with films including *Male Bait* (1971) and *Penelope* (1975). *A Touch of the Sun* was something of a family affair as Curran wrote, directed and edited the picture, which was produced by his wife Elisabeth. Unfortunately, the film, also known as *No Secrets*, is a shambolic piece of work, with added-on softcore porn sequences that look as if they were filmed in a suburban living room.

With his solar-powered ray, Emperor General Samumba of the African state of Akasuba (Edwin Manda) downs a US space capsule and holds it to ransom for $25 million. US Captain Nelson (Oliver Reed) and CIA Agent Coburn (Bruce Boa) are sent to retrieve the capsule, allying themselves with the wily District Commissioner Potts (Cushing), who was left behind in his jungle outpost when World War II ended and has no idea that Akasuba is independent. The role of Commissioner Potts was originally intended for comedy actor Terry-Thomas, who had to drop out because of other commitments.

Most of Reed's slapstick, with a bawling Keenan Wynn as General Spellman, is unbearable. However, it is difficult to dislike a film which features Cushing's broadest comedy performance. In shorts and pith helmet, Cushing does some Oscar-class double-taking and ad-libs wildly, whether singing along to Samumba's propaganda broadcasts or complaining that the war is stopping his deliveries of champagne. 'I've been writing to Winston for 20 years,' he says, 'but he never replies.' Captain Nelson politely points out that the War ended in 1945 and Churchill has died. But Potts is a sly old bird, and attempts to turn every situation to his financial advantage. He ropes in a group of local Chief Zawe's tribesmen as bearers and charges the Americans $1000. ('What's that in Sterling?' he inquires, twirling his beard furiously.) When they later run into Samumba's

solar-powered force field, Potts knocks on it with his swagger stick and remarks that Captain Nelson has been 'reading too much H G Wells'.

Amidst all the mayhem, though, there is a touching scene as the commissioner expresses his bewilderment with the modern world. 'I think I'm goin' mad...' he says. 'Stark starin' mad. First the war's over. Then Winston's dead, then invisible sun-walls...' When he discovers all the off-duty Zawe tribesmen wearing smoking jackets and drinking cocktails, it's the final straw. 'Now all my bearers think they're Noël Coward!'

'The quiet Zambian temperament appeals to Cushing,' explained the publicity brochure for *A Touch of the Sun*. 'He finds the local people gentle, sympathetic and more inclined to be content without the luxuries of life than their European counterparts. Cushing describes himself as an old-age pensioner from the seaside village of Whitstable in Kent. The colours of Africa are glorious, and as a painter Cushing delights in the purple bourgainvillaes, scarlet poinsettias ... flame trees, and the endless vistas of green forests under pale blue skies. The prospect of handling some of the country's wild creatures, such as a cheetah and a python, in his role as the animal-loving Potts, bothers Cushing not at all; nor does the heat, which is nothing compared with the scorching air of Israel where he has been on location before.'[9]

The film has some touches of inspired craziness, such as General Samumba's troops dressed as Highland pipers travelling in a double-decker London bus marked '11A – Piccadilly to Akasuba via Oxford Circus.' Melvyn Hayes appears as a camp Tarzan, with his accident-prone mate Jan (Mike Cross) but Commissioner Potts remains delightfully unfazed. 'Last week he thought he was Ginger Rogers,' he tuts. 'Wonderful "Black Bottom".'

Christopher Lee and Oliver Tobias join Cushing (in costume as the Wazir, with added smoking glove) behind the scenes on *Arabian Adventure* (1978)

Cushing's only other role in 1978 was in *Arabian Adventure*, filmed in September at Pinewood Studios, directed by Kevin Connor. A reworking of the *Arabian Nights* stories, it is set in the fictional region of Jadur where the evil wizard Alquazar (Christopher Lee) sends a young prince, Hasan (Oliver Tobias) on a quest for the magical blue rose of Elil. Cushing appears in a cameo as the deposed ruler of Jadur, the imprisoned Wazir Al Wuzara. He pops up in a dungeon cell near the beginning of the story, where Prince Hasan has been confined by Alquazar. When Hasan says 'Allah helps those who help themselves' the Wazir retorts 'Well, he doesn't seem to have done you much good, has he?'

The film is exciting enough, but in the post-*Star Wars* days there was little time for any film that did not deliver androids, spaceships and laser battles. In referring back to Alexander Korda's 1940 film *The Thief of Bagdad*, *Arabian Adventure* allowed Christopher Lee to pay tribute to one of his boyhood heroes by taking the role originally portrayed by Conrad Veidt. Lee is magnificent, and Cushing (with the white whiskers he grew for Commissioner Potts) is delightful when he is on screen – which is not long enough.

On television meanwhile, Morecambe and Wise had made a highly publicised departure from the BBC, joining Thames Television for a new series. Cushing continued as a regular guest, with his old routine, still demanding money for his original appearance. Cushing appeared in the show broadcast on 18th October 1978, with guest stars including Donald Sinden and Judi Dench, and Cushing's co-star from *Nineteen Eighty-Four*, Leonard Sachs.

Apart from providing the narration for a short film called *The Detour*, directed by Rodney Holland, which concerned the adventures of a young boy and his dog (whom the boy believes to be a reincarnation of the Egyptian god Anubis) Cushing did no more work until mid-1980.

In 1979, with Hammer Film Productions in receivership, former board-members Roy Skeggs and Brian Lawrence formed an alliance between their own company Cinema Arts and ITC. The result was a series of 13 50-minute horror films for television called *Hammer House of Horror*, produced 'in association with Hammer Film Productions'. With its memorable ponderous theme, high production values and many old Hammer personnel, the series was a fitting last hurrah for the old firm. The series was filmed from 28th June 1980 on location in Buckinghamshire.

The Silent Scream is the best-remembered of the *Hammer House of Horror* episodes, doubtless because of the participation of Cushing. The actor is reunited with Alan Gibson, director of the modern-dress Draculas and the familiarity is obviously reassuring. Cushing gives a masterfully underplayed performance, once again with a German accent as benign pet shop owner Martin Blueck, who says he was a former inmate of a concentration camp. Blueck is a genuinely horrific figure, all the more so for the hint of pathos that remains even after his true colours are revealed. Francis Essex's script gives Cushing and a young Brian Cox some excellent interplay, and the claustrophobic pet-shop setting (which recalls the *What Big Eyes* episode of Nigel Kneale's *Beasts*) is disturbing from the outset. The story has several unexpected twists and the gruelling ending provides the series with one of its most potent and lingering images. Producer Roy Skeggs recalls that Cushing was very reluctant to take on the role, another Nazi, but participated out of loyalty to Hammer.

Following *The Silent Scream*, Cushing worked on the Hallmark Hall of Fame TV production of Charles Dickens' *A Tale of Two Cities*. This splendid production was directed by Jim Goddard, written by John Gay

Martin Blueck falls into his own trap in *Hammer House of Horror: The Silent Scream* (1980)

and filmed from 30th July 1980 for six weeks at Shepperton Studios and on location in England and France.

In Paris, shortly before the French Revolution, Doctor Alexander Manette (Cushing) is released from wrongful imprisonment in the Bastille and is reunited with his beloved daughter Lucy (Alice Krige). Lucy marries a French nobleman, Charles Darnay (Chris Sarandon), who has left his title in France to live in England. But when Darnay returns to France to rescue a faithful servant from the hands of the revolutionaries, the aristocrat is himself captured. Doctor Manette cannot save him, but a dissolute English lawyer called Sidney Carton, who resembles Darnay, is able to switch places with him in the prison of La Force. Carton knows, however, that this means certain death at the guillotine.

This film features a cast of Britain's finest actors. Billie Whitelaw is a powerfully malicious Madame Defarge, Kenneth More bumbles endearingly as Jarvis Lorry, while none less than Flora Robson, Robert

Cushing's last great role – Doctor Manette appeals to the revolutionaries of France in *A Tale of Two Cities* (1980)

Urquhart and Barry Morse fill the minor roles. In the last great role of his career, Cushing gives an understated and unsentimental performance as the long-suffering Doctor Manette. First seen in straggling beard and long matted hair, he plays the reunion between Manette and his daughter with consummate skill, turning his face out of shadow as a flicker of recognition crosses his vivid blue eyes. There is an obvious affection between Cushing and Krige. 'She is everything to me,' Manette says of his daughter, 'more than life itself.'

When Manette was in the Bastille, he worked as a cobbler. Later, when he suffers a relapse, he is compelled back to his old prison trade and the camera lingers on a haunting close-up of Cushing's eyes as the horror of his imprisonment clouds his reason.

In his best scene, Cushing enthusiastically rouses the revolutionaries and pleads for Darnay's life. 'For sixteen years I was a prisoner in the Bastille. I know the pain, I know the suffering you endure!' He is taken up on the shoulders of the mob. 'I beg you ... as a citizen ... as a patriot, not to take his life!'

Chris Sarandon later appeared as a vampire in the horror comedy *Fright Night* (1985) with Roddy McDowall as movie vampire-hunter 'Peter Vincent', a gentle Cushing/Price parody.

It was possibly a conflict of schedules with *A Tale of Two Cities* that stopped Cushing from taking the role of Robert Miles in Lucio Fulci's Italian horror film *Il gatto nero* (*The Black Cat*) which was due to film from 11th August. The script, by Harry Alan Towers and Biagio Proietti, was sent to Cushing in May, and

as usual he meticulously annotated it with costume requirements and instructions to himself on his performance ('Play Miles oddly. Slightly mad to start with'). As ever, Cushing's notes show his concern for his co-stars ('No cruelty to cats – vet standing by') and in red letters across the top of the script it reads 'Helen' 'Us'. It is unlikely that Cushing would have been comfortable with the explicit gore of the Italian horror school, but whatever his reasons for ultimately declining, the film went ahead without him and his role was taken by Patrick Magee.

After *A Tale of Two Cities*, Cushing travelled to Spain for *Misterio en la isla de los monstruos* (*Mystery on Monster Island*, sometimes simply *Monster Island*), directed by Juan Piquer Simon.

Cushing plays William Kolderup, a shipping magnate and 'the richest man in America' – and as if to prove it, almost as soon as he appears, he is seen buying an island for five million dollars. The island is reputedly infested with monsters, but Kolderup's rival Taskinar knows that hidden on the island is a fortune in gold. Kolderup's heir is his nephew Jeff, who is eager to see the world before his impending marriage and despite his uncle's reluctance, Jeff is sent off for a trip on a ship called the *Dream*. After some days, the boat is attacked by monstrous fish-like humanoids and is seen to explode, leaving Jeff and his dance tutor Artelett shipwrecked on Kolderup's 'Monster Island'. The pair meet a female castaway, rescue a man from cannibals, build a stockade to defend themselves from predatory dinosaurs and battle masked marauders. In the nick of time, Kolderup arrives to declare that the whole set-up has been a sham, a test of manhood for young Jeff, but he has reckoned without the greedy and devious Taskinar.

For the few scenes in which he appears, Cushing plays the richest man in America with panache, but notably *without* an American accent. He wears several suits best described as 'natty', and it is a shame he didn't get some more scenes. His dialogue with Ian Serra's endearingly vulnerable hero is strong and affecting. Terence Stamp is as underused as Cushing, but smoulders with style as the villain, and gets to squareoff against Cushing in the finale.

The film is a close cousin of *At the Earth's Core*, although the dinosaurs here are clumsier and even more rubbery. Though Cushing doesn't face the monsters in this outing, Abner Perry could easily have replaced the twittering dance master who is embroiled in the action. The creatures that attack the *Dream* are ludicrous sub-*Doctor Who* costumes with grumpy-looking faces, but their fake look is explained when we learn that they were made by a San Francisco toymaker. On the plus side, there are some very interesting monsters composed of seaweed, which rise up in great slippery heaps from the beach and pursue Jeff and his friends.

In *Starburst #27* Tony Crawley made a spectacularly vitriolic outburst about the forthcoming *Monster Island*. 'Now the bad news... Jean Piquer is directing a new movie... He'd have difficulty directing traffic as evidenced in ruining Jules Verne in his tawdry version of *Journey to the Centre of the Earth* with Kenneth More...'[10] Crawley reported that James Stewart was to star in *Monster Island* – Cushing replaced Stewart in the role of Kolderup.

Juan Piquer was interviewed by Manuel Valencia for *Cinefantástico y de terror espanol 1900-1983*. 'What surprised me... was the tremendously professional approach of Peter Cushing during shooting of *Monster Island*. I was really amazed. As a person he was a true gentleman, so charming and kind. He was, a genuine living legend, and as advanced in years as he was, his enthusiasm during the shoot was unbelievable. I remember ... he told us that he believed in reincarnation, and that he wanted to die so that he could join his wife who had died some time before. I recalled this story years later and used it as the beginning of *Cthulhu Mansion* (1991)'[11]

Monster Island featured a cameo by another genre star, Paul Naschy, who is still as big a horror hero to the Spanish as Cushing was to the British. 'Peter Cushing was the first person to congratulate me when I won the Méliès award at the Paris Festival in 1972. Oliver Reed, Christopher Lee and Terence Fisher were all present, but Peter was the first to come over with all his usual elegance and style and shake me by the hand. I later dined with Peter and Terence Fisher and I have very fond memories of them. Some years later

we both appeared in *Monster Island* although we didn't have any scenes together. I was a 'special guest star' and Peter didn't have much screen time either but Piquer knew the 'marquee value' of the names Terence Stamp, Paul Naschy and Peter Cushing...'[12]

Back home, Cushing was a guest on the *Morecambe and Wise Christmas Show*, which went out on Christmas Day 1980. An exceptional guest cast included Peter Barkworth, Jill Gascoine, Peter Vaughn, Gemma Craven and Alec Guinness.

At the end of 1980, Cushing went to Spain for the Cinespana production *Asalto al casino* (*Black Jack*) directed by Max H Boulois. The film concerns an attempt on a casino by a gang disguised as a rock group, and the attempts by a dogged policeman to foil them. Cushing's character of Sir Thomas Bedford is behind the robbery, and sits at the gaming table while the heist is underway. Cushing appears at the beginning of the film, and at the end, with a couple of lines in the middle. 'There are only two pleasures in life,' he says. 'A good whisky and a good horse.' The heist fails, but Sir Thomas at least escapes with his freedom. Francisco R Gordillo, assistant director on *Black Jack* and later director of Paul Naschy's *Licántropo,* recalls: 'Peter Cushing worked on that film for three days. I remember between scenes Peter and I were talking, with the aid of an interpreter, because Peter only knew a few words of Spanish, but we had quite a lengthy conversation about the *cinefantástico* genre that he'd done such a lot of great work in. It's a funny thing that in the space of that one conversation we became so friendly. Peter told me that he would like to work with me again in a new film I was then trying to get off the ground, *El cepo* (*The Trap*, 1982, in which Jack Taylor played the proposed Cushing role). I felt flattered by that because Peter didn't know me at all ... but I thought that was a most generous gesture on his part. Unfortunately *Black Jack* didn't have much luck. As far as I know it was never shown theatrically – I don't know what happened to it.'[13]

The only other British actor in the cast was Brian Murphy, at the time a national hero as the henpecked husband George in the TV comedy *George and Mildred*. Murphy had no scenes with Cushing, and they did not meet during the filming, but the actor's 'star treatment' gives a clue as to how Cushing was looked after. Murphy remembers 'I was rushed over to Spain to be included in the film because *George and Mildred* was a huge success in Spain and it was thought at the time to get hold of Murphy was a great coup! As to what the story was about, I had very little idea, but the money was excellent – and they wined and dined me. I suspect I was cheaper than Alec Guinness.'[14]

Cushing's career would only take in four more films, but among those was the chance for a last reunion with the three other great names of horror cinema – John Carradine, Vincent Price and Christopher Lee.

Chapter Twenty-Four

A Saint in Retirement

In May 1982, Cushing was rushed by ambulance to the Kent and Canterbury Hospital. His left eye had become swollen to about three times its normal size. It was, he remembered, 'not a pretty sight and extremely painful' but with his usual deference, he decided that 'as this eruption occurred on a public holiday... I didn't want to pester the overworked doctors.'[1] Thinking the swelling to be merely an oversized stye, Cushing bathed his eye and laid down on the couch. He was found unconscious the next day by his housekeeper, Maisie, who rang for a doctor. Finally, having been examined by no less than three doctors, he was taken to hospital. He was diagnosed with prostate cancer, which was affecting his eye, and given – at best – 18 months to live. He was looked after by Mr Darvill and Doctor Rake of the Cancer Care Unit and put on a permanent course of drugs. To the amazement of the doctors, and without surgery, Cushing made an almost complete recovery. He nearly lost his eye but it was saved, although he was left with slight double vision. His secretary Joyce Broughton and her husband Bernard, who were now taking a more active role in the day-to-day running of things, requested that the specialists did not tell Cushing of the seriousness of his condition. They managed to keep the details of his illness from him for nearly four years, by which time he had completely outstripped the doctors' expectations anyway.

Joyce Broughton remembers that the upheaval of the illness was responsible for rousing Cushing from ten years of grief. 'He came out of his "blue study" as he called it, when he was really ill,' she says. 'He hated hospital and desperately wanted to come home, but the specialist said he could not go home alone, so he came to live with us in Hartley. Suddenly he was thrown into a household with two teenage girls, cats, dogs and many friends around, I don't know how the poor man coped after living a quiet and orderly life then coming almost to a madhouse with telephones ringing, different music in different rooms, boyfriends and girlfriends always around. But he was marvellous, and he began to slowly enjoy life a little more, although he continued to miss his beloved wife until the day he died. After this period he would come and stay for a few days most weekends. But eventually

we moved to Whitstable to be near him and he only came to us when he wasn't well. He loved his home so much with his books and things around him. Thankfully ... with the tremendous care of Doctor John Ribchester, he lived for another 13 years.'[2]

'I must record how deeply touched I've been,' Cushing wrote, 'and always will be, by the love and devotion showered on me by Joyce and Bernard Broughton. I am so grateful to them, and so blest.'[3]

By August 1982, Cushing was well enough to take part in *House of the Long Shadows*, filmed on location at Rotherfield Park, East Tisted, Hants. The film was directed by Pete Walker for the Cannon Group, with a script by Michael Anderson adapted from Earl Derr Biggers' novel *Seven Keys to Baldpate*. Walker had been successful in the 1970s with a series of grisly low-budget shockers including *House of Whipcord*, *Frightmare* and *House of Mortal Sin*, and Sheila Keith, who appeared in these three films, took a part in *House of the Long Shadows* that was originally intended for Elsa Lanchester. Cushing was to co-star with three friends, John Carradine, Vincent Price and Christopher Lee – making a gruesome foursome.

Author Kenneth Magee (Desi Arnaz Jr) bets his publisher Sam Allyson the sum of $20,000 that he can write a novel in 24 hours. Allyson suggests that Magee stay at the isolated Baldpate Manor in Wales, but when Magee arrives at Baldpate, he suddenly finds it 'busier than Times Square'. Gradually, the Grisbane family, the original owners of the Manor, assemble – father Elijah (Carradine) daughter Victoria (Keith), sons Sebastian (Cushing) and Lionel (Price). They are met on this night because 40 years ago they imprisoned the third son, Roderick, in his room after he murdered a pregnant girl. But Roderick's room is empty – and who is the mysterious Mr Corrigan (Lee), who claims that he now owns the property?

Cushing plays the timid and tipsy Sebastian Grisbane with an endearingly affected lisp. When Price appears, resplendent in cloak and fedora, to announce 'I am Lionel Grisbane', Sebastian gives an exasperated 'Oh, Lord!'. After years of playing commanding characters, Cushing revels in a poor soul who is frightened of his own shadow. 'I've never been a particularly cou*wag*cous man,' he stammers. 'And the

Wicked Roderick (Christopher Lee), timid Sebastian (Peter Cushing) and flamboyant Lionel (Vincent Price) – three Grisbanes who are not what they seem. *House of the Long Shadows* (1982)

events of this evening have been most disconcerting.' He creates a real sense of pathos as he says 'It's a tewwible thing you know, living one's entire life in a state of fear. It is all I have ever known, fear...'

All the principals work hard – they are playing to their reputations, but what reputations! Price is glamorous and Lee has authority, both are magnificently lit by Norman Langley, and despite some wearing performances from the juveniles and a bland script, the film staggers on. There is an unnecessarily grisly death scene involving a washstand full of vitriol, but Walker manages a fine crescendo of horror as Corrigan reveals that he is the wicked brother Roderick, then runs amok with an axe. As Lee takes a climactic tumble down the stairs, however, and finishes up with an axe in his chest, the whole thing is revealed as a hoax. The Grisbanes are all actors, and the events of the night are a mere charade to inspire Magee to write a better novel. So

why do several murders take place when Magee is not even present? The film and its stars are thrown away for the sake of the cheesiest 'happy ending' in film history and a few limp comic scenes. Reviewers quite rightly felt cheated. Derek Malcolm in the *Guardian* said the film 'brings together Price, Cushing, Carradine and Lee for the first time. It then proceeds to waste them utterly. The worst thing about the film is its total lack of ambition.' The *Sunday Telegraph* thought the 'daft-beyond words plot' could not give the quartet 'anything remotely worth getting their teeth into.'[4] It should have been so much better.

Cushing followed this with a role in *Sword of the Valiant*, another Cannon production and another wasted opportunity. The film was made in Ireland, Wales and France, in September and October 1982, with Miles O'Keeffe as Sir Gawain who, after an encounter with the mysterious Green Knight (Sean Connery) embarks on a quest to the ends of the Earth.

The film was directed by Stephen Weeks, the 'poor dear boy' who had struggled to make something out of *I, Monster*, and who had already made a film of *Gawain and the Green Knight* in 1972, starring Murray Head as Gawain and Nigel Green as the Knight. Here Cushing is wasted in a handful of blink-and-you'll-miss-'em scenes – it is possible he took part simply as a favour to Weeks. He plays Gaspar, Seneschal to the Lord Fortinbras (John Rhys Davies). Ronald Lacey plays Fortinbras' scheming son, reuniting two of the stars of *Raiders of the Lost Ark* (1980), although Rhys Davies was ten years younger than his 'son' Lacey. Apart from one mordant scene opposite Lacey, Cushing is reduced to twittering around Fortinbras as he stomps about a huge model castle and knocks over armies of toy soldiers. The film is ultimately sunk by O'Keeffe's leaden central performance and even Connery, spectacular in gold-green make-up and a twiggy beard, cannot save the day.

Cushing's icon status was played upon in his next film *Top Secret!*, a frantic, gag-a-minute comedy from Jim Abrahams, Jerry Zucker and David Zucker, the directors of *Airplane!* Val Kilmer is rock star Nick Rivers, who foils a plan by the lunatic General Streck (Jeremy Kemp) to take over the world. Lucy Gutteridge also stars, with cameos by Michael Gough and Omar Sharif. Cushing appears in a brief scene as a bookshop proprietor who is in league with the resistance. The entire bookshop segment is a gag however – the scene was recorded backwards, with the actors, Cushing, Kilmer and Gutteridge, going through a series of pre-rehearsed movements to finish 'at the beginning'. The scene begins by spoofing Cushing's magnifying glass trick. The proprietor has a magnifying glass at one eye, then when he removes the glass, the prosthetic eye is still huge. 'We had to do the whole scene in *one take*,' Cushing recalled. 'We had to do everything backwards. We had to walk backwards. If a book was thrown up it was really thrown *down*. I knew that this magnifying glass was going to be there at the end of every take we did. And it terrified me!'[5]

Cushing's next assignment was a rather more gentle experience, in *Tales of the Unexpected*. This was Anglia's follow-up to the *Orson Welles* mystery series and was originally produced by John Rosenberg. The first two series were fronted by Roald Dahl, who introduced half-hour dramatisations of his famous stories with chilly geniality. By the time Cushing appeared in the series, it had moved away from Dahl's grisly fables and was using stories by other authors. *The Vorpal Blade*, shown on 28th May 1983, was adapted by Robin Chapman from a story by Edward D Hoch and was directed by John Jacobs, the producer for *La Grande Breteche*. In a castle garden, an elderly German, Von Baden (Cushing), recounts his university days at Heidelberg as a member of the White Corps, led by the brilliant and tyrannical fencing champion Rudolf Cassan (Anthony Higgins). Cushing looks fragile, but brings a poignancy to his sedate role as narrator, sharing his scenes with another television veteran, John Bailey. Anthony Higgins would show his fencing prowess again as Moriarty in the film *Young Sherlock Holmes* (1985), and would play the Great Detective in the 'updated' TV movie *Sherlock Holmes Returns* (1993).

Cushing was a studio guest on the BBC's *Breakfast Time* on 14th June 1983. The interview included clips from *House of the Long Shadows* which was on release at the time.

Then Cushing went to Hollywood for the cameo role of Professor Copeland in the television biopic *Helen Keller: The Miracle Continues,* directed by Alan Gibson. The film was shot in 1983 with Mare Winningham as Helen Keller, the blind and deaf girl who overcame the odds to become a celebrated scholar and lecturer, with Blythe Danner as Annie Sullivan, Keller's beloved 'Teacher', who interpreted the outside world to the girl via touch-signing. Keller enrolls in Radcliffe College in 1904, where the potential of her work is spotted by Professor Copeland. He is responsible for getting Keller her first professional commission – a series of magazine articles which are then collected as

Von Baden with Winterluck (John Bailey) in *Tales of the Unexpected – The Vorpal Blade* (1983)

a book. Cushing looks elegant in his academic gown, and gives Copeland a wry sense of humour. He screws in a monocle to examine the dull essays submitted by the other Radcliffe girls. '*Spring finds Cape Cod?*' he hoots. 'I wasn't aware that it was lost!'

Back in 1980, plans had been announced for Cushing to appear again as Sherlock Holmes, in a project that would have seen Holmes being encouraged out of retirement by Watson for one last case. This idea ultimately emerged in 1984 as Tyburn's *The Masks of Death*, a film for Channel 4 directed by Roy Ward Baker, who described the project as a film made by Holmes enthusiasts for Holmes enthusiasts. Cushing played an elderly but still spry Holmes, with John Mills as Dr Watson and Anne Baxter as Irene Adler. Production started on 21st July 1984.

In 1913, Holmes and Watson uncover a plan by the German nobleman Graf Udo Von Felseck to leak poison gas into London's homes through the domestic gas supply. Cushing gives a surprisingly active final performance as Holmes, adopting various disguises including a bespectacled parson and a swarthy boatman with an eyepatch. (Make-up by Roy Ashton, who created Grimsdyke.) Several strong horror moments include Russell Hunter's inebriated tramp Mr Coombes raving about monsters on the streets of London – 'Devils! With bodies of men but faces of pigs ... holes for eyes and snouts for noses. Evil ones in search of evil!' Holmes eventually deduces that 'the masks of death' are gas-masks, used by the workers in the Graf's diabolical plan.

The script was by N J Crisp from a story by Anthony Hinds, but the dialogue is mostly unmemorable and the few good lines are hijacked from Doyle. Cushing's scenes with Mills have a dewy-eyed sentimentality, as if all concerned knew that this was a farewell performance of sorts.

Even though Jeremy Brett was making a very good job of playing Holmes in the award-winning Granada series at the same time, the *Times* on Christmas Eve 1984 was full of praise for *The Masks of Death*. 'Peter Cushing and John Mills were combined with what are known on television as "special guest stars", to suggest that only the great can be on familiar terms with Conan Doyle – or for that matter, with his most famous creation. After all the attempts at parody and the no less frequent inflictions of sexual innuendo or psychoanalysis, Holmes has emerged unscathed – the reason that he has so vigorous and emblematic a character that he can be neither diluted nor obscured. He has even survived the transition to television, which is more than can be said for most real people. And as Peter Cushing proved last night, age cannot wither him; he was Prospero in this production rather than Hamlet, but none the worse for that. Once again, the Holmes adventure becomes an opportunity for the exploration of characters and settings on a Grand Guignol scale, And once again it can become the vehicle for that peculiarly English combination of genuine horror and spirited comedy.'[6]

Cushing was filming again from 21st January 1985 on *Biggles*, directed by John Hough. For a fee of £35,000, Cushing played Air Commodore William Raymond, with a young cast including Neil Dickson, Alex Hyde-White (son of Wilfrid), Fiona Hutchison and Marcus Gilbert. Rather than produce a straight adaptation of Captain W E Johns' stories about the World War I flying ace James 'Biggles' Bigglesworth, the film-makers unwisely decided to update the character. The result looks just as badly dated for being set in 1986 as if it had been set in 1917.

However, Cushing is on fine form as Raymond, who appears during the credits in a thunderstorm, walking deliberately with a stick. Raymond arrives at the New York apartment of Jim Fergusson (Hyde-White) and politely introduces himself, saying 'It should have happened by now.' Fergusson is a busy man, however, and sends the old man away, then moments later is time-warped back to the Western Front in 1917 where he rescues Biggles from a crashed plane. When Fergusson is subsequently warped back to New York, he wastes no time in locating the Commodore in his London home – inside Tower Bridge. ('When they raise the bridge it gets a bit noisy' Raymond admits.) Cushing then has to explain that Biggles and Fergusson are 'time twins'. The time-travel business needs someone like Cushing to make it believable, and as ever, he does it brilliantly. 'I do not know *why* it happens,' he says, a flicker of firelight catching his cheek, 'only that it *does*.' Raymond served with Biggles many years ago and maintains 'he is a fine officer. You'll be in good hands,' before sending Fergusson on his way with a thump on the shoulder. When Biggles is later reunited with Raymond, there are tears in the Commodore's eyes – and doubtless the audience's – as he says, with complete sincerity 'How I've missed you, old friend.'

The *Times* review said pertinently 'Just when British films seem to be doing so well, *Biggles* comes along to show the other side of things ... The flying ace might well have been made over into a sort of period James Bond, instead there is a misguided and inept attempt to give the film an appeal for imagined mid-Atlantic teenage audiences ... The script is witless, the direction is showy and the performances of the twin heroes are weakly amiable.'[7]

The film is slightly better than its reputation. The dogfights are exhilarating, especially the scrap between a modern helicopter and a German biplane and the sonic weapon which the Germans are developing in secret in No-Man's Land is a genuinely frightening conceit. On the downside, the synthesised score is weak and aggravating, and the scenes set in New York but filmed in London are excruciating. Cushing rises above it all as Commodore Raymond, who keeps a raven and takes tea beneath a huge portrait of Queen Victoria. It is nothing less than an amalgam of Cushing's on and off-screen personas – initially sinister but ultimately strong and reassuring, as British as the flag and yet slightly out of place in the modern world. It is an appropriate salute. *Biggles* was Peter Cushing's final film.

Nevertheless, the actor was still going strong. In late 1985, he came back to *Jim'll Fix It* as a 'Fixee'. One of his remaining ambitions was to have a rose named after Helen, and wrote to the BBC hoping that the programme could 'grant the wishes of people who were over 70 as well as those who are 7'. Rose-grower Christopher Wheatcroft took Cushing around the rose beds at his nursery to choose an appropriate bloom to bear the name 'Helen Cushing', and they eventually settled upon a solitary whitish rose with pink edges. It was, said Cushing 'a beautiful way to keep in perpetuity and loving memory the name of a most wonderful lady.'

In 1985, Stephen Weeks wanted Cushing to appear as Professor Hodgson in his film *The Avalon Awakening,* which Cushing described in his notes on the script as a cross between *Nineteen Eighty-Four, Star Wars* and the legend of King Arthur. A young woman called Lynda is troubled by disturbing dreams and consults Hodgson. It transpires that Lynda is possessed by the spirit of Guinevere and calls on Merlin to arise. Cushing made extensive notes on the script, and was encouraged by the fact that Christopher Lee would also be involved, but the film never reached production.

Another near miss was *A Drop in the Ocean,* by *Dracula A.D. 1972* scriptwriter Don Houghton. This was a proposed TV satire about the tiny island of Valtaray, off the coast of Scotland, which existed in isolation for many years until oil was discovered in the harbour. Cushing would have played Neil MacNaughton, 18th Thane of Valtaray, and Houghton provided him with a set of documents outlining the invented culture and history of the island. In 1982 Cushing had also been suggested for the role of President Borusa in the *Doctor Who* story *Arc of Infinity,* a role eventually taken by Leonard Sachs, and in 1985, Cushing was offered a

Cushing points out 'Mother's little girl' during a signing of his autobiography in Harrods in 1986

role in the TV series *Knights of God* that was ultimately taken by another Doctor Who, Patrick Troughton.

March 1986 saw the publication of Cushing's first volume of autobiography by Weidenfeld and Nicholson. He had begun writing his life story in the 1960s, and had taken up the task again as a form of therapy after Helen's death. The finished volume is similar in structure to *The Peter Cushing Story,* published in instalments in the *TV Mirror* in 1955, and in dealing chiefly with his early life follows closely the outline of the John Player Lecture from 1971. In some cases, the same story is remembered with different details in each.

By 1986, there was a generation of fans who had come to know the actor from *Star Wars* and regular TV screenings of the Hammer films, but who knew little about Cushing's early life, and so came new to *Peter Cushing – An Autobiography.* It is a warm and often funny book, detailing his early life and influences, his adventures in America, his meeting with Helen and his rise to fame in the theatre and on television. With uncompromising honesty, he described his early hardships, his nervous breakdown and the utter anguish of Helen's death. On first reading, many admitted they were moved to tears. Some fans were disappointed, however, that the book said little about Cushing's work at Hammer, and that Cushing chose to end the story in 1971, when he said 'my life, as I knew and loved it, ended.' To promote the book, Cushing embarked on a nationwide round of book-signings and was interviewed on television and radio and in the national press. The book was a massive success.

'The book could have been rather mawkish,' wrote Quentin Falk in the *Guardian,* 'if it was not for the disarming sincerity which Cushing still brings to everything he does. Not only his book but his work – even if the framework has often been frankly mediocre – and his demeanour which is unreservedly and endlessly lauded by that most cynical body of men, film technicians.' Falk also accurately pointed out that 'if it wasn't for the brilliantly-crafted screen persona that was forever transplanting him into exotic mittel-European settings, Cushing might forever have been locked into Semi-Detached Suburban Mr Brit.'[8]

'I never dreamed I'd end up sitting here,' Cushing told *Time Out,* 'with everyone interested in such a very old man's memoirs.' The interview described the actor as 'dressed in muted early Dr Who style, with a discreetly floppy bow tie, checky sort of trousers and watch-chain.' In the interview, Cushing expressed his dismay at the horror inherent in modern life 'watching a *Dracula* picture made 25 years ago must be rather like watching *Noddy in Toyland*' but admitted guarded admiration for Jeremy Brett's Holmes. 'He obviously went into tremendous detail, everything is dead right, but *you don't like the man.* You should like Holmes. Whether he was nice or not doesn't matter.'⁹

Cushing was delayed on his way to the BBC's Birmingham studios for *Pebble Mill at One* on 24ᵗʰ March 1986, but this only meant that his interview with Paul Coia received an even more rapturous reception when he turned up at last. In this interview, Cushing was more outrageous than usual, playing to the audience shamelessly and even impersonating Kenneth Williams at one point. He stated, however, that 'the only thing I was ever good at was playing rugby. Union, I hasten to add.'

Also on 24ᵗʰ March, an interview appeared in the *Daily Express* in which Cushing made several heartfelt revelations. 'Was Helen as much mother as lover?' asked Victor Davis. 'Oh, very much so,' Cushing admitted. 'I'm so glad that comes across in the book because it is the truth. It wasn't the coddling of a mother's boy but her whole instinct was motherly. She realised that in me, here was someone who needed taking in hand.'

Davis continues; 'In the memoir ... there's a cryptic line that suggests something other than devotion to Helen. It reads "There were times when I was human and erred." Does this mean what I think it means? He doesn't look like a man who had erred. "Bless you but I'm afraid I did. I didn't want to dwell on it, but I felt compelled to tell the truth." Was this a one-off temptation? Sigh. "About two or three one-off temptations. They were actresses and I was about 35-years-old. It is not something I'm proud of. I never intended it to happen. The first time I rang Helen from the nearest phone box and said 'I've done something terrible. I'll be home in a while, put the kettle on.' I told her the same evening. You see it was too much on my conscience. Helen's reaction was truly amazing." Hadn't she biffed him with a saucepan and called her lawyer? "Oh no. She said, 'There is too much sorrow in the world to worry about a little thing like that. You must get things in proportion. If you left me and had babies all over the place, that would distress me terribly because I like and respect you. But what has happened is no more important than cleaning your teeth. It is a natural bodily function. Forget it'." Once might have been an accident, twice a misfortune but *three* times going home to

confess? Says Peter, "I don't say I did not hurt her. She would not have been human. But she never let it be apparent. And she meant it when she said I was just being a bit of an old fuss-pot. Mind you, I'll never forgive myself. I was human and she was divine."'¹⁰

On Tuesday 25ᵗʰ March, Cushing was on the main stage of the National Film Theatre at Waterloo for a *Guardian* Lecture, interviewed by Wayne Drew. This interview covered similar ground to the John Player Lecture and was preceded by a brief signing session for the autobiography. At the end of the lecture, Cushing received a standing ovation from the capacity audience, and was visibly moved to tears.

At the charity première of *Biggles* on 22ⁿᵈ May 1986 Cushing was presented to the Princess of Wales at the Empire cinema, Leicester Square, when he broke with protocol to bend and kiss her hand. The Princess was delighted. Prince Charles remarked how much he had enjoyed Cushing's portrayal of Sherlock Holmes.

Cushing was once again interviewed about the autobiography on the BBC's regional programme *Look North* on 5ᵗʰ June 1986. He later appeared on the BBC's *Everyman* documentary *The True Story of Frankenstein,* which looked at the character of Mary Shelley herself (shown on 19ᵗʰ October 1986) and took part in an excellent documentary in the *Omnibus* strand, *Hammer – The Studio That Dripped Blood.* This included comments from Christopher Lee, Anthony Hinds, Jimmy Sangster, Aida Young, Ingrid Pitt and James Bernard. Cushing was interviewed at his home in Whitstable. On the Bank Holiday edition of *Wogan,* 22ⁿᵈ May 1987, Terry Wogan hosted the first part of a two-show celebration of the *Golden Days of British Cinema,* with a star cast including Cushing, Christopher Lee, Bryan Forbes, Bernard Cribbins and Irene Handl.

On 1ˢᵗ June 1987, *Today* quietly reported the announcement of Cushing's retirement. 'After making some of the world's best-known horror films during his 50-year career, Peter Cushing has decided that he will never make another movie. He's just finished filming two television advertisements and he says the experience is enough to make him realise enough is enough. "I did them because I'd been offered two film parts and I didn't know if I was going to be up to the work," he admits. "I didn't want to let anyone down so I thought I'd cut my teeth on these commercials. But having spent four days shooting, I've decided not to do any more films. These adverts will be my swan song. It's just too much for me." In the adverts, for Borthwick's roasts and steaks, Cushing plays a professor who discovers a Neanderthal man. "It sounds bizarre, doesn't it," he laughs. "I have never done a TV commercial before – even though film clips of me were used in the Griff Rhys Jones adverts for Holsten Pils. I thought it would be rather fun. And I was amazed at the amount of money they spend on just one commercial. Hammer could have made a whole film on the budget we had!"[11] Another film that went by the wayside as Cushing retired was Tyburn's proposed Holmes adventure *The Abbot's Cry*, which Cushing described as the story of a village menaced by the wandering ghost of a monk.

May 1988 saw the publication of Cushing's second volume of autobiography, *Past Forgetting: Memoirs of the Hammer Years*. This book did little to make up for the lack of attention paid to Hammer in the first autobiography, but it did contain another range of funny stories and theatrical anecdotes. The *Scotsman* carried a perceptive review which said 'Peter Cushing is one of those actors we take for granted ... he has never attained the glamour of a Connery or the critical respectability of a Guinness. However the subtitle of his second volume ... is a misnomer. Hammer's initial *Dracula* is not mentioned. A more reasoned examination of the subject would have been particularly interesting as the criticisms of the Hammer films were much the same as those levelled at the original books when they appeared. This book ... is never more than a collection of random memories, unstructured in a way that suggests a perverse game of word association, so illogical at times is the link between one anecdote and the next. What does emerge is the confirmation of the screen persona of a gentleman, sometimes lofty, sometimes child-like. This is the combination which made his performances as Dr Who so effective. He quotes an interview with his late wife in which she says that he loathes gossip, and there is not a malicious word in the book. His peers are "magnificent" "excellent" and "outstanding". Through this short, rambling volume shines the warm personality of one of the nice men of the movie business.'[12]

In the *Daily Telegraph*, Jeffrey Richards stated 'Peter Cushing is a star cherished by millions as if he were an old family friend, for the very odd reason that he has been frightening the life out of them for the past 30 years ... Cushing's considerable gifts as an actor have been insufficiently appreciated because of his long association with the unfashionable genre of horror films. But his acting has a precision and classical purity. There are glimpses of real distinction in the recordings that survive of his haunted Winston Smith and Cassius in *Julius Caesar* ... It is high time that his achievement in British cinema was publicly recognised. A knighthood would not be an inappropriate reward for a man who has become one of the best-loved and most widely respected of British film actors.'[13]

There was no knighthood, but on 30th December 1988 Cushing was informed that he was to be awarded the Order of the British Empire in the Queen's New Year's Honours List. A mishap on the very same day, however, put him back in hospital and ended his daily routine of a bicycle ride through Whitstable – he fell off his bike as he swerved to avoid a runaway dog.

Cushing revealed that the accident happened as he was cycling to the bottle bank with an empty bottle of brandy. 'I'm virtually teetotal,' he said, 'but my doctor said it would do me good, so I have a watered down brandy with sugar on Sunday as a little treat. After the crash Bernard brought me in half a bottle to the hospital and the doctor rang my GP to find out how much I drink. To this day, in his mind, I'm a drunk.'[14]

On 22nd March 1989, Cushing was duly presented with the OBE by Her Majesty the Queen at Buckingham Palace. In appreciation of all the messages of good wishes he had received, Cushing wrote a letter to the *Whitstable Times*. 'I wish I could thank everyone personally,' he said. 'But that is not possible ... I suppose I am an incurable romantic, because I would like to have slain a dragon or saved the Queen's life, or done some other brave deed which would make me feel I really deserve this honour. But I love this country of ours and its people so very much, and am deeply proud of this recognition, because it must mean that I have done something during my life for it and for them.'[15]

Cushing's last association with Tyburn was the filmed interview *Peter Cushing: A One-Way Ticket to Hollywood*, shown on Channel 4 on 4th June 1989. This comprised 90 minutes of Cushing in conversation with writer Dick Vosburgh, illustrated with photographs and excerpts from Cushing's performances including *Vigil in the Night*, *Hamlet*, *Nineteen Eighty-Four*, *Dracula* and the Tyburn films. As a record of his engaging, sincere, rambling style of conversation, the interview is priceless.

'I hadn't expected to be trotting around until the summer,' Cushing told Katie Ekberg for her article 'The Rather Friendly Baron Frankenstein' in the *TV Times* which dealt chiefly with his recent accident. 'The doctor said to me "Don't forget an anaesthetic puts you as near to death as possible and then brings you back again" and at my age that's no fun. I'm a bit short of breath now but there's no pain, just an ache. I'll always have a limp so I'll just have to play the wounded soldier in my next role. No more cycling though. The doctor said anyone over 70 shouldn't really cycle and to be honest I've lost my confidence.' On 4th June 1989, the same day that *A One-Way Ticket to Hollywood* was screened, Cushing took part in 'The Great Hip Walk' for the British Orthopedic Association. 'Everyone walks a mile' he explained. 'That's three times round the Kent County Cricket Ground, though I think I'll be lucky to make it once.'[16]

There is one sadness in Cushing's later life that he mentions only in passing in his autobiography, but one on which some light was shed by Christopher Lee. 'He didn't really talk about family matters to me,' Lee recalls. 'He was closer in that respect to Peter Gray. But he said to me once, "I'm sorry I don't see my brother any more." I said "What do you mean, you don't see your brother?" He told me that his brother's wife didn't approve of actors, and wouldn't have anything to do with him, so he hadn't been in contact with his brother for many years. It seemed very sad indeed.'[17] Perhaps if Cushing had been able to re-establish contact with David it might have alleviated the sadness of Helen's passing a little. David Cushing died in 1987.

This Is Your Life featured Cushing on 21st February 1990. The guests included a statuesque Ursula Andress, who reminded him that her character was called 'She Who Must Be Obeyed'. 'Yes, darling, and you still are,' said 'Saint' Peter with a saucy grin, 'what would you like me to do?' Also appearing were Caroline Munro, David Rintoul, David Prowse, Joanna Lumley, Freddie Jones, Kevin Francis, Gwen Watford, a hale-and-hearty Peter Gray and Peter Ustinov. John Mills and Christopher Lee sent pre-recorded announcements – Lee telling Cushing that he was 'a delight and a despair ... the only actor who can read the *Times*, drink his whisky and soda, light his pipe and deliver his lines all at the same time'. Lee finished with the Holmesian exhortation – 'Step out!'. Roy Ward Baker, Anthony Hinds and Sir James Carreras were also among those present.

Joyce revealed that Cushing was actually aware beforehand that he was going to be featured on the programme, and was worried that he would not appear sufficiently alarmed when Michael Aspel presented him with the famous red book. His actor's talents were undimmed, and when 'surprised' he delivered the priceless – if unlikely – line, 'It's just as well I wore my toupée, isn't it?'

Also in 1990, TVS's series *The Human Factor* featured Cushing in a special programme called *For the Love of Helen*. Cushing talked about his life and his faith, and displayed some of his paintings. As part of his recuperation after the cancer treatment and the accident, he had taken up painting again.

As late as 1990, Cushing was still defending causes close to his heart. On 12th July 1990, *Newsroom South East*, BBC 1's regional news programme for London and the South East reported on the threat of demolition hanging over Bray Studios, and Cushing was interviewed along with another longstanding Bray 'resident', cameraman Len Harris. Later, on 9th August 1990 on the same programme, Cushing officially joined the fight to save Bray Studios from closure.

On 29th December 1990, Cushing's last acting assignment was transmitted. To commemorate the 50th anniversary of the Battle of Britain, BBC Radio Kent broadcast *Human Conflict*, a dramatisation of the life of Air Chief Marshal Hugh Dowding, commander-in-chief of Fighter Command (played by Laurence Olivier in the film *Battle of Britain*). Alan Dobie played Dowding and Cushing played a fictional character, a former RAF pilot obsessed with restoring the Air Marshall's reputation. Michael Bath, the

producer, told the *Times*: 'Both are working virtually for nothing. They are doing it out of respect for Dowding. The play portrays him as one of the great men of the 20th Century, the man who won the Battle of Britain.' Cushing added, 'I looked forward to taking part in such a moving tribute to a much maligned man to whom so much is owed.'[18] Because of Cushing's increasing fragility, the play was recorded in his Whitstable home.

Cushing never considered himself as a singer, and thought rapping was 'something you got round a parcel'.[19] Nonetheless, at the age of 78 he provided the rap for a rock single called 'No White Peaks'. The single began life as a poem about a homesick soldier by Peter Kayne which Cushing was asked to record. It was then combined with a rock track by Assegai Records and released on 11th November 1991. Cushing made an appearance on Granada's magazine show *This Morning* around the same time, promoting the single and turning his still considerable charm on co-presenter Judy Finnegan.

In early 1992, Cushing's long association with Whitstable was commemorated when a newly built sea-viewing platform at Keam's Yard was officially named 'Cushing's View'. 'Incurable romantic' Cushing donated a special bench, designed for two canoodlers. The seat bears a plaque saying 'Presented by Helen and Peter Cushing, who love Whitstable and its people so much.' Cushing's 80th birthday on 26th May 1993 was celebrated by a magnificent party organised by the Broughtons, attended by friends including Peter Gray, Michael and Ann Redington, Don Henderson, Paul Eddington, Ernie Wise and many more.

The next year, his 81st birthday saw the publication of *The Bois Saga*, his phonetic history of Britain, which had begun life with 'silly old Bloggs' locked in the lavatory in 1950. Five hundred copies of 'The Saga of the Famully Bois and Their Rival Fakshun The Poleish Born Blogs' were printed, and comparisons were made between Cushing's book and the work of James Joyce.

Cushing's last professional engagement was, appropriately, in celebration of Hammer films, and reunited him with Christopher Lee. On 17th May 1994, the 'old firm' of Cushing and Lee provided the narration for *Flesh and Blood: The Hammer Heritage of Horror*, an American documentary co-produced with Hammer and directed by Ted Newsom. Those who saw Cushing at the recording session in Canterbury were alarmed at how painfully gaunt the actor appeared and his voice, on the finished commentary, is almost unrecognizable. No one, other than Christopher Lee and Joyce Broughton, knew how terribly ill he was. The cancer, valiantly kept in abeyance for so long, had returned. Nevertheless, Cushing insisted on attending the scheduled recording, and kept bright throughout the session, ad-libbing and joking with Lee. The exertions of the day kept Cushing in bed for two days afterwards and Joyce admitted that she couldn't fathom how he had done it. The broadcast of the documentary was well-publicised in Britain, with a photo-feature in the *Radio Times*. The programme went out in two instalments, on consecutive Saturday nights in August.

Shortly before the first part of *Flesh and Blood* went out, Cushing was taken into the Pilgrim's Hospice at Canterbury. 'We always promised to keep him at home for as long as was possible' Joyce recalls, 'and he would decide when things became too much for him. This we did by me staying with him all day and Bernard all night. We kept our promise until he told us that he was ready to go into the hospice ... The hospice staff were wonderful, not only to him but to everyone in their care, and to Bernard and to me.'[20] After a fortnight in the hospice, and between the two instalments of *Flesh and Blood*, the long fight with cancer came to an end. Peter Cushing died on 11th August.

Obituaries in the national newspapers were uniformly enthusiastic in their praise – 'He was a considerable actor,' said the *Telegraph*, 'whose precise, unapologetic theatrical technique was a boon to Hammer's potentially risible subject matter ... He could imbue superstitious rituals with sincerity and spiritual force, and in all his Gothic efforts kept his tongue very firmly out of his cheek.'[21] The BBC assembled a very moving tribute from various carefully chosen clips, from *Nineteen Eighty-Four*, *Hamlet*, *Dracula*, *The Ghoul*, *Dr Who and the Daleks* and more, scored with John Williams' poignant violin theme from *Schindler's List*. The montage was broadcast after the second part of *Flesh and Blood*.

Some unsavoury newspaper speculation followed when it was discovered that Helen's headstone had been removed from its place in the churchyard at Seasalter. Joyce Broughton later revealed that it was one of Cushing's last wishes that Helen's headstone not become a place for fans to gather. 'He asked us to take certain measures concerning both his own and Helen's ashes and to put them in a secret last resting-place. We have never revealed the details of those instructions, but I can say that we carried them out to the best of our ability.'[22]

Despite Cushing's determination that he did not want a 'big splashy affair', his funeral on 19th August

'I'm very old, you know,' Cushing admitted, but the mischievous twinkle was undimmed

brought Whitstable to a standstill. The funeral procession, led by the frock-coated Mr Terry Davis carrying one of the actor's walking-sticks, first visited Cushing's View which was decked with flowers, then stopped outside Cushing's favourite restaurant, the Tudor Tea Rooms in Harbour Street, which was closed for the day as a mark of respect. Whitstable residents, many of whom followed the cortège on foot paid warm tribute. In the *Daily Telegraph*, Roger Dilley said 'We were so used to seeing him about the place. I don't think Whitstable will be quite the same without him.' David Ruddock added, 'His were old world values, from an age of courtesy that has gone.'[23]

On Thursday 12th January 1995, there was a memorial service at St Paul's Covent Garden, 'the Actors' Church', attended by Joanna Lumley, Paul Eddington, Ingrid Pitt and many other friends and colleagues. Christopher Lee and Ron Moody read the lessons, actor James Bree recalled Cushing's early career and Kevin Francis his films. Rosie Ashe, a young singer whose work Cushing greatly admired and who had sung at his 80th birthday party, sang Noël Coward's 'If Love Were All' accompanied by Jonathan Cohen.

The following summer there was an exhibition of Cushing's paintings, along with other items such as painted scarves and playing cards, at the Brook Arts Centre in Chatham, Kent.

'Peter Cushing was one of the handful of actors who defined the horror movie,' said the obituary in the *Independent*, 'Whether playing Baron Frankenstein, witnessing the awful results of his brilliance or Professor Van Helsing in hot pursuit of Dracula, he brought an air of refinement and nobility to the genre ... His name on the cast list was a constant and reassuring guarantee of quality.'[24]

Peter Cushing was one of Britain's finest actors. He believed in the impossible and compelled us to believe too. On screen, he championed the forces of good or presented a villain you knew wasn't all bad. His classic films are as popular as ever and his reputation will continue to grow wherever and whenever they are shown. He bore his own private terrors of nerves and grief for so long, but if he is now reunited with his beloved Helen then the Peter Cushing story has a very happy ending after all.

Afterword

The remarkable coda to the Peter Cushing story is that even today, new material is coming to light, sometimes after more than fifty years and it is Cushing's fans around the world, now affiliated online, who have helped to locate many of these discoveries.

As well as the films in the Pathé newsreel archive (showing Cushing at a meeting of the 'Waistcoat Club' in 1954, at home in his 'den' in 1956 and on the set of *Frankenstein Created Woman* at Bray) we can now see online the Milk Marketing Board film for *The Legend of the 7 Golden Vampires*, showing the cast on location. Hopefully other films like this will appear. Another gem is a promotional reel for Hammer's *The Horror of Frankenstein* with Cushing chatting so enthusiastically about the role of Frankenstein that new incumbent Ralph Bates scarcely gets a word in. Cushing doesn't seem unduly worried about handing over the part – it may even have been something of a relief. (And he was to return, of course, as the Baron in *Frankenstein and the Monster from Hell*, Hammer's equivalent of Sean Connery's return as James Bond in *Diamonds Are Forever*.)

Behind-the-scenes footage also recently came to light from the making of both Amicus Dalek films. The brief scene of Cushing with Roy Castle doing an impromptu dance during the shooting of *Dr Who and the Daleks* is delightful, and shows the sort of larks that Cushing enjoyed on set at this time.

How Cushing would have cheered the return of Hammer as a film-making concern, with worldwide hits such as 2010's *Let Me In* and the 2012 adaptation of *The Woman in Black*, which is the highest grossing horror film in the UK for at least 20 years. The huge success of these new films has raised the profile of the original Hammer output, increasing the demand for restored and remastered prints, some of which have been given a limited cinema release. (Also, there are some surprises, such as the discovery of a Japanese print of *Dracula* with a longer version of the climactic disintegration.) The meticulous details of Cushing's performances are faithfully represented in high definition on Blu-ray discs, which also convey the films' original colours more sumptuously than ever before. It has been a great pleasure for me to participate in commentaries and documentaries for several Cushing Blu-rays. The commentary for *The Blood Beast Terror*, alongside Jonathan Rigby, was particularly enjoyable – I hope the listeners agree.

In Whitstable, the seaside town in Kent where Cushing had a home for nearly 40 years, he is still considered a local hero. As well as a blue plaque, 'Cushing's View' and 'Cushing's Walk', there is now a pub, 'The Peter Cushing'. Appropriately, the building was once a cinema. Actor, writer and producer Mark Gatiss, who helped so much with the first edition of this book, visited Whitstable to pay a heartfelt tribute to Cushing in his excellent *History of Horror* series in 2011. In recent years the Whitstable Museum has hosted several exhibitions celebrating Cushing's life and work, providing an opportunity to see some of Cushing's most treasured items – his miniature theatre sets, the scarves he painted for Helen, his easel and watercolours.

At a Hallowe'en gathering in London in 2010, Joyce Broughton kindly displayed Cushing's scrapbooks, including some of the original artwork for his book *The Bois Saga*, along with other pieces, including figures sketched in the margins of newspapers. The *Bois Saga* pictures are exquisite, but what fascinated me most was a little picture of Frankenstein's monster – the Boris Karloff version – painted by 'the Baron' himself.

George Lucas said that Cushing would be 'fondly remembered for 350 years at least'. So thankfully, we've got a little while yet to revisit Frankenstein, Van Helsing, Sherlock Holmes, Dr Who and all the other characters brought to such vivid life by the irreplaceable Peter Cushing.

Inspector Quennell investigates Dr Mallinger's laboratory in
The Blood Beast Terror (1967)

Chronology

New Connaught Theatre, Worthing
from June 1936
Cornelius by J B Priestley
(*PC as Creditor*)
It Pays to Advertise
(*PC as Johnson*)
Week commencing 15th June 1936
Producer W Simson Fraser
Bees on the Boatdeck
by J B Priestley
(*PC as Mr Tooke*)
Week commencing 29th June 1936
Producer W Simson Fraser
The Man at Six
(*PC as Police Surgeon*)
Week commencing 20th July 1936
Producer W Simson Fraser
Potash and Perlmutter
(*PC as Expressman*)
Week commencing 3rd August 1936
Producer Peter Coleman
Aloma
(*PC as Boano*)
Week commencing 17th August 1936
Producer Peter Coleman
The Midshipmaid
(*PC as Kingsford*)
Week commencing 24th August 1936
The Middle Watch
(*PC as Captain Randall*)
Anthony and Anna by St John Ervine

Grand Theatre, Southampton
1937, including
Lean Harvest
(*PC as John Fairweather*)
Winter Sunshine
(*PC as Elderly Traveller*)
Lady Precious Stream by S I Hsiung
(*PC as Chinese Servant*)
Dick Whittington
(*PC as King Rat*)

With Harry Hanson's Court Players,
including Rochdale, 1938
Marigold
(*PC as Army Officer*)

Penge Empire 21st - 27th March, 1938
Blondie White
With Betty Bowden, John Ayres, Ursula
Gilhepie, Reginald Marsh
28th March – 3rd April 1938
The Greeks Had a Word for It
by Zoë Akins
(*PC as Stanton*)
4th April 1938 –
Fresh Fields by Ivor Novello

Nottingham Theatre Royal
30th May – 5th June 1938
This Money Business
by Cyril Campion
(*PC as Mr Lilywhite*)

6th – 12th June 1938
Love From A Stranger
by Frank Vosper
Based on *Philomel Cottage*
by Agatha Christie

The Man in the Iron Mask (United Artists)
(*PC as Captain of the Guard*)
Filmed February – March 1939, United Artists
Studios, Hollywood, California
Directed by James Whale
with Louis Hayward, Joan Bennett

A Chump at Oxford (Hal Roach)
(*PC as Jones*)
Filmed April 1939 Hollywood, California
Directed by Alfred Goulding
with Stan Laurel, Oliver Hardy

Vigil in the Night (RKO Pictures)
(*PC as Joe Shand*)
Filmed July – September 1939
RKO Radio Studios
Directed by George Stevens
with Brian Aherne, Carole Lombard

Palm Springs, July 1939,
including tour of West Coast, USA
Love From A Stranger
by Frank Vosper
(*PC as Bruce Lovell*) *with Ida Lupino*
(During break in *Vigil in the Night*)

Laddie (RKO Pictures)
(*PC as Robert Pryor*)
Filmed at RKO Radio Studios
Directed by Jack Hively
with Tim Holt, Virginia Gilmore

The Howards of Virginia
(Columbia Pictures)
(*PC as Leslie Stevens*)
Filmed at Columbia Studios
Directed by Frank Lloyd
*with Cary Grant, Martha Scott,
Cedric Hardwicke*

The Passing Parade
Your Hidden Master (MGM) (short)
(*PC as Clive of India*)
Filmed 1940 at MGM
Directed by Sammy Lee
with Emmett Vogan, John Nesbitt

Dreams (MGM) (short)
Directed by Felix E Feist
with John Nesbitt

Woman in the House (MGM) (short)
Directed by Sammy Lee
(*PC appears in clip from* **Dreams** *only*)

Women in War (Republic Pictures)
(*PC as Captain Evans*)
Filmed 1940
Directed by John H Auer
with Elsie Janis, Patric Knowles

They Dare Not Love (Columbia Pictures)
(*PC as Sub-Lieutenant Blacker*)
Filmed at Columbia Studios
December 1940 – January 1941
Directed by James Whale
and Charles 'King' Vidor
with George Brent, Martha Scott

Outward Bound NBC Radio (US)
(*PC as Tom Prior*)

The Grandpa Family (Serial)
NBC Radio (US)
(*PC as Alf, the son*)

Scenes from Bitter Sweet NBC Radio (US)
by Noël Coward
(*PC as The Music Master*)

Summer Season at Warrensburg, New York
State, USA, May – September 1941
Night Must Fall by Emlyn Williams
(*PC as the Inspector*)

Macbeth by William Shakespeare,
presented in modern dress
(*PC as Banquo and Doctor*)

Pound on Demand
(*PC as the Irish Policeman*)
presented with **Fumed Oak**
by Noël Coward
(*PC as Henry Gow*)

The Ghost Train
by Arnold Ridley
(*PC as Teddy Deakin*)

The Petrified Forest
by Robert E Sherwood
(*PC as Alan Squire*)

Biography
by S N Behrman
(*PC as Leander Nolan*)

Mansfield Theater, Broadway, New York
21st - 29th November 1941
The Seventh Trumpet
by Charles Rann Kennedy
(*PC as Police Constable Percival*)

Canadian Ministry Films
We All Help
(*PC as Captain Roberts,
Royal Canadian Mounted Police*)
Filmed Montreal, February 1942

ENSA Tour, including Wolverhampton,
Canterbury, Dover, Oxford, Taunton,
Oswestry from April 1942
Private Lives by Noël Coward
(*PC as Elyot Chase*)
*with Sonia Dresdel, Humphrey Morton,
Yvonne Hills, Helen Beck*

Manchester Opera House, July 1943
War and Peace
(*PC as Captain Ramballe and Alexander I,
Emperor of Russia*)
Directed by Julius Gellner
*with Barry Morse, Peter Illing,
Paulette Preney, Frederick Valk*

Phoenix Theatre
War and Peace
6th – 21st August 1943
(20 performances)

Mendelssohn (BBC Home Service)
(PC as Paul)
Broadcast 8th September 1943 from
The Corn Exchange, Bedford
Producer Stephen Potter
with Basil Langton, Peggy Ashcroft,
Austin Trevor, Deryck Guyler, Carleton Hobbs

Destination Unknown (BBC Home Service)
Recorded 11th November 1943
at Studio C, Bedford College
Producer V C Clinton Baddely

'Q' Theatre, Richmond
The Morning Star
by Emlyn Williams
(16th – 21st November 1943, 9 perfs)
(PC as Cliff Parrilow)
Produced by Charles Hickman
with Margaret Johnston, Irene Handl

The Lay of Horatius
(BBC Home Service)
Broadcast 16th December 1943
from Studio C, Bedford College
Producer John Burrell

'Q' Theatre, Richmond
The Dark Potential
(transferred as **This Was A Woman**)
by Joan Morgan
(25th – 30th January 1944, 9 perfs)
(PC as Valentine Christie)
Produced by Henry Kendall
with Sonia Dresdel, Shelagh Fraser,
Peter Copley

The Fifth Column
by Ernest Hemingway
(27th March – 2nd April 1944, 9 perfs)
(PC as Robert Preston)

The Crime of Margaret Foley
by Percy Robinson and
Terence De Marney
(2nd – 7th May 1944, 9 perfs)
(PC as Kevin Ormond)
Produced by Richard Bird
with George Merritt, Percy Robinson,
Judy Kelly, Ian Fleming

Watch on the Rhine
by Lillian Hellman
(13th – 18th June 1944, 9 perfs)
(PC as Kurt Muller)
with Netta Westcott,
Charles Farrell, Alice Darch

Private Lives
by Noël Coward
(PC as Elyot Chase)

Cambridge Theatre, West End
Happy Few by Paul Anthony
(from 10th October 1944 –)
(PC as Private Charles, a Free Frenchman)
Directed by William Mollison
with Wally Patch, Tony Quinn, Derek
Blomfield, John Slater

Globe Theatre, West End
While the Sun Shines
by Terence Rattigan
(Play opened 8th November 1943,
PC from December 1944)
(PC as Lieutenant Colbert)

Directed by Anthony Asquith
for H M Tennent Productions
with Michael Wilding, Douglas Jefferies,
Brenda Bruce
Subsequent tour of **While the Sun**
Shines including Bolton

Criterion Theatre
The Rivals
by Richard Brinsley Sheridan
25th September 1945 – 16th February 1946
(166 perfs)
(PC as Mr Faulkland)
Directed by William Armstrong
and Edith Evans (with Tyrone Guthrie)
with Edith Evans, Michael Gough,
Anthony Quayle, Reginald Beckwith

The Rivals (BBC Home Service)
(PC as Faulkland)

'Q' Theatre, Richmond
They Came To A City by J B Priestley
(one week, 1946)
(PC as Joe Dinmore)
with Roberta Huby

The Seagull by Anton Chekhov
(one week, 1946)
(PC as Doctor Dorn)

While the Sun Shines
by Terence Rattigan (one week, 1946)
(PC as Lieutenant Colbert)

Tonight at 8.30
by Noël Coward (one week, 1946) including
The Astonished Heart
(PC as Chris Faber)
We Were Dancing
(PC as Karl Sandys)
Fumed Oak
(PC as Henry Gow)
with Joan Greenwood

Orley Farm by Anthony Trollope
(BBC Home Service)
(PC as Mr Round, Jr in episodes 3, 5, 6, 11)
Broadcast 24th November, 8th December,
15th December 1946, 20th January 1947
from Broadcasting House
Producer Howard Rose

'Q' Theatre, Richmond
The Curious Dr Robson
by J Lee Thompson
26th November – 1st December 1946
(9 perfs) *(PC as Dr Robson)*
Produced by Eileen Pollock

Wednesday Matinee:
A Fourth for Bridge (BBC Home Service)
(PC as Henry Forum)
Broadcast 11th December 1946

Theatre Royal, Windsor
The Rivals by Richard Brinsley Sheridan
(PC as Mr Faulkland)
with Peter Gray

The Face of Theresa
(BBC Home Service)
(PC as Blane)
Broadcast 25th January 1947
from the Langham Hotel, London
Producer Hugh Stewart

Radio Theatre: It Speaks for Itself
(BBC Home Service)
Broadcast 1st May 1947
from Broadcasting House
Producer Peter Watts

Hamlet (Two Cities)
(PC as Osric)
Filmed May – November 1947
at Denham Studios
Directed by Laurence Olivier
with Laurence Olivier, Terence Morgan,
Jean Simmons, Felix Aylmer

UK Ministry of Information Films
The New Teacher
(PC as Steve)
It Might Be You (aka **Safety First**)
(PC as Doctor)

The High Toby by J B Priestley
(A puppet show)
Single performance at Heals,
Tottenham Court Road
with Ralph Richardson, Meriel Forbes,
Phyllis Calvert
Produced by George Speaight

Old Vic tour of Australia and New Zealand
(Depart 14th February –
return 16th October 1948)
The School for Scandal
by Richard Brinsley Sheridan
(PC as Joseph Surface)
Directed by Laurence Olivier
with Laurence Olivier, Terence Morgan,
Vivien Leigh, George Relph

Richard III by William Shakespeare
(PC as George, Duke of Clarence and
Cardinal Bouchier)
Directed by Laurence Olivier
and John Burrell
with Laurence Olivier, Vivien Leigh,
George Relph, Terence Morgan

The Skin of Our Teeth
by Thornton Wilder
(PC as The Professor/Convener)
Directed by Laurence Olivier
with Laurence Olivier, Vivien Leigh,
George Relph, Terence Morgan

Beau Brummell (ABC Radio Australia)
(PC as George Bryan Brummell)

Twenty Questions (ABC Radio Australia)
(PC as guest)

New Theatre, London
The School for Scandal
by Richard Brinsley Sheridan
(in repertory, 20th January 1949 to
4th June 1949, 74 perfs)
(PC as Joseph Surface)
Directed by Laurence Olivier
with Laurence Olivier, Terence Morgan,
Vivien Leigh

Richard III by William Shakespeare
(in repertory 26th January 1949 – 2nd June
1949) *(PC as George, Duke of Clarence and*
Cardinal Bouchier)
Directed by John Burrell
with Laurence Olivier, Vivien Leigh,
George Relph, Terence Morgan

The Proposal 'A Jest in One Act'
by Anton Chekhov
(in repertory, 10th February to
1st June 1949, 39 perfs)
(PC as Ivan Vassilyevitch Lomov)
Directed by Laurence Olivier
with Derek Penley, Peggy Simpson

Saturday Night Theatre:
The Alien Corn
(PC as Undergraduate)
Broadcast: 8th October 1949
Producer Hugh Stewart

Opera House, Manchester
from 6th November 1950
    Malvern Festival Theatre
    1st – 7th January 1951
    Garrick Theatre, London
    24th January – 24th March 1951 (68 perfs)
    The Gay Invalid
by Sir Barry Jackson and Robert Brenon
adapted from Molière's
La Malade imaginaire
*(PC as Valentine, an Officer
in the King's Guard)*
*with Elisabeth Bergner, A E Matthews,
Tod Slaughter, Daphne Slater*

**St James' Theatre: Laurence Olivier's
Festival Season**
    Caesar and Cleopatra
by George Bernard Shaw
(in repertory, 10th May to 23rd October
1951, 76 perfs)
(PC as Bel Affris, later as Brittanus)

    Antony and Cleopatra
by William Shakespeare
(in repertory, 11th May to 22nd October
1951, 76 perfs)
(PC as Alexas Diomedes)

From the London Theatre
excerpt from Antony and Cleopatra
(BBC Home Service)
Broadcast 13th August 1951
(PC as Alexas Diomedes)

PC 49 #10 The Case of the Tenth Green
by Alan Stranks (BBC Home Service)
(PC as Edgar Abigail)
Broadcast 27th November 1951
Recorded 9th November 1951
Producer Vernon Harris
with Brian Reece, Joy Shelton, Leslie Perrins

Eden End by J B Priestley (BBC TV)
(PC as Charles Appleby)
Tx: 2nd and 6th December 1951,
from Alexandra Palace
Rehearse 12th November – 5th December
1951, Inns of Court, Drury Lane
Producer Harold Clayton
with Helen Shingler, Julien Mitchell, Rachel Gurney

When We Are Married
by J B Priestley (BBC TV)
(PC as Gerald Forbes)
Tx: 25th December 1951
Rehearse 10th – 21st December
at 60, Paddington St
Producer Fred O'Donovan
*with Frank Pettingell, Raymond Huntley,
Gabrielle Daye*

Pride and Prejudice 6-episode serial
(BBC TV)
(PC as Mr Darcy)
Tx: 2nd, 9th, 16th, 23rd February, 1st, 8th
March 1952, from Alexandra Palace
Rehearse 14th January – 1st February 1952 at
Mansergh Woodall Boys' Club
Producer Campbell Logan
*with Gillian Lind, Daphne Slater, Prunella
Scales, David Markham*

Bird in Hand (BBC TV)
by John Drinkwater
(PC as Cyril Beverley)
Tx: 13th and 17th April 1952 from Studio D,
Lime Grove
Rehearse 31st March – 12th April
Producers Michael Barry and Dennis Vance
with Basil Appleby, Leslie Dwyer

Manchester Opera House, August 1952
The Wedding Ring
by Kieran Tunney and Simon Wardell
(PC as Cyril Soames)
Directed by Robert Helpmann
*with Gladys Henson, Irene Browne, Irene Handl,
Shelagh Fraser*

Moulin Rouge (Romulus)
(PC as Marcel de la Voisier)
Filming July – September 1952
at Shepperton Studios and on location
Directed by John Huston
*with José Ferrer, Zsa Zsa Gabor, Suzanne Flon,
Christopher Lee*

If This Be Error by Rachel Grieve (BBC TV)
(PC as Nick Grant)
Tx: 11th November 1952 from Lime Grove
Rehearse 27th October – 10th November
Producer Stephen Harrison
*with Gillian Lind, Shelagh Fraser, Frank Allenby,
Dandy Nicholls*

Asmodée by Francois Mauriac,
translated by Basil Bartlett (BBC TV)
(PC as Blaise Lebel)
Tx: 9th December 1952 from Lime Grove
Producer Harold Clayton
*with Eileen Peel, Elizabeth Henson,
Michael Meacham*

For the Children: The Silver Swan
by C E Webber (BBC TV)
(PC as Lord Henriques)
Episode 1: **Francis**
Tx: 30th December 1952, from Lime Grove
Rehearse 17th – 19th December
Producer Rex Tucker
with David Kossoff

Number Three by Charles Irving,
adapted by George F Kerr and Nigel Kneale
(BBC TV)
(PC as Simpson)
Tx: 1 and 5th February 1953,
from Lime Grove
Rehearse 16th January – 1st February at
the Jewish Lads' Club, 5 Hanway Place,
Lime Grove
Producer Stephen Harrison
*with Ursula Howells, Jack Watling,
Raymond Huntley, Terence Alexander*

Asmodée by Francois Mauriac (BBC TV)
(PC as Blaise Lebel)
Tx: 17th February 1953
Rehearse 28th December – 16th February
(Released from rehearsal 28th – 31st January)
Producer Harold Clayton
*With Eileen Peel, Elizabeth Henson,
Michael Meacham*

Epitaph for a Spy
by Eric Ambler (BBC TV)
Episodes 1 – 6
(PC as Josef Vadassy)
    1: Arrest Tx: 14th March 1953
    2: Go Spy the Land 21st March
    3: Violence 28th March
    4: Ultimatum 4th April
    5: All Men are Liars 11th April
    6: Epitaph 18th April
Broadcast from Alexandra Palace
Producer Stephen Harrison
with Ferdy Mayne

Wednesday Theatre Presents:
A Social Success by Max Beerbohm
(BBC TV)
(PC as Henry Robbins)
Tx: 29th April 1953, from Lime Grove
Rehearse 20th April 1953 – 28th April
Producer John Irving
*with Dan Cunningham, Marjorie Stewart,
Audrey Fildes*

Rookery Nook by Ben Travers (BBC TV)
(PC as Clive Popkiss)
Tx: 23rd May 1953, from Scala Theatre
Kingsway
Rehearse 5th – 21st May at North Paddington
Boys' Club
Producer Lionel Harris
*with Lally Bowers, David Stoll, Beryl Bainbridge,
David Kossoff*

The Road from the play *Nationale Six* by
Jean-Jacques Bernard, adapted by Alfred
Shaughnessy (BBC TV)
(PC as Antoine Vanier)
Tx: 21st and 25th June 1953
Rehearse 5th – 20th June at Mary Magdalen
Hall, Holloway
Producer Peter Cotes
*with Wilfrid Lawson, Josephine Griffin,
Ellen Pollock, Bryan Forbes*

Anastasia by Marcelle-Mauret,
adapted by Guy Bolton (BBC TV)
(PC as Piotr Petrovsky)
Tx: 12th and 16th July 1953
Rehearse 29th June – 10th July at
60 Paddington St, London
Producers Michael Barry, John Counsell,
Rosemary Hill
with Helen Haye, Mary Kerridge, Anthony Ireland

The Noble Spaniard (BBC TV)
by W Somerset Maugham from the French by
Grenet-Dancourt
(PC as the Duke of Hermanos)
Tx: 4th August 1953 from Lime Grove
Rehearse 17th July – 3rd August 1953
Producer Stuart Latham
*with Frances Rowe, Terence Alexander,
James Gilbert, Elisabeth Gray*

Portrait by Peko by P N Walker-Taylor
adapted by Guy Bolton (BBC TV)
(PC as Seppi Fredericks)
Tx: 23rd and 27th August 1953, Lime Grove
Tx: 31st August from Dusseldorf
Rehearse 5th to 21st August 1953
Producer Lionel Harris
*with Patrick Barr, Ursula Howells,
Irene Handl, Basil Appleby*

The Black Knight (Warwick)
(PC as Sir Palamides)
Filmed September – October 1953 on
location, England, Wales and Spain
Pinewood Studios from 2nd November
(3 weeks)
Directed by Tay Garnett
*with Alan Ladd, Patricia Medina, André Morell,
Anthony Bushell, Patrick Troughton,
Basil Appleby*

Tovarich by Jacques Deval,
adapted by Robert Sherwood (BBC TV)
*(PC as Prince Mikhail Alexandrovitch
Ouratieff)*
Tx: 24th and 28th January 1954, from
Studio E, Lime Grove
Rehearse 4th – 22nd January 1954
Producer Eric Fawcett
*with Ann Todd, Clive Morton,
Frances Rowe, Andrew Laurence*

Beau Brummell by Anatole de Grunwald
(BBC TV) *(PC as George Bryan Brummell)*
Tx: 14th and 18th March 1954,
from Lime Grove
Rehearse 22nd February – 13th March
Producer Campbell Logan
*with Daphne Slater, Ferdy Mayne, Walter
Fitzgerald, David Peel, Prunella Scales*

A Book at Bedtime: Natural Causes
by Henry Cecil (BBC Light Programme)
Monday 8th – Friday 26th February 1954

Morning Story: The Bride in the Bath
(BBC Light Programme) *(PC as narrator)*
Broadcast 2nd March 1954

The Gay Lord Quex
by Arthur Wing Pinero (BBC Home Service)
(PC as the Marquess of Quex)
Tx: 5th April 1954, from Broadcasting House
Recorded 31st March
Rehearse 28th – 31st March 1954
Producer Archie Campbell

May Day (BBC TV)
(PC as narrator)
Tx: 1st May 1954, from Studio E, Lime Grove
Producer Paul Johnston

Men of Mystery (BBC TV)
(PC as Celebrity Guest)
Tx: 14th May 1954, from Lime Grove
Producer Bill Ward
with David Nixon, David Berglas, Chandu

Wimbledon Theatre 31st May 1954
Devonshire Park Theatre, Eastbourne
24th June 1954
    The Soldier and the Lady
    by Ian Stuart Black
    (PC as The Soldier)
    Directed by Sam Wanamaker
    with Sheila Sim

Woman's Hour (BBC Home Service)
Woman, Lovely Woman: 1930 – 1940
Tx: 24th June 1954
Producer Isa Benzie

The End of the Affair (Coronado)
(PC as Henry Miles)
Filmed 29th June – 10th September 1954
at Shepperton Studios
Directed by Edward Dmytryk
*with Deborah Kerr, Van Johnson, John Mills,
Stephen Murray, Michael Goodliffe*

Down You Go! (BBC TV)
(PC as Celebrity Guest)
Tx: 29th July 1954, from the
Television Theatre, Shepherds Bush
Producer Ernest Maxim

The Face of Love (BBC TV)
(PC as Mardian)
Tx: 5th October 1954, from Lime Grove
Rehearse 17th September – 4th October
Producer Alvin Rakoff
with Mary Morris

Magic Fire (William Dieterle/Republic)
(PC as Otto Wesendonk)
Filmed October 1954 on location in Bavaria
Directed by William Dieterle
*with Alan Badel, Yvonne De Carlo, Valentina
Cortese, Carlos Thompson, Rita Gam*

Nineteen Eighty-Four
by George Orwell, adapted by Nigel Kneale
(BBC TV)
(PC as Winston Smith)
Tx: 12th and 16th December 1954, from
Studio D, Lime Grove
Location filming at Alexandra Palace from
10th November 1954
Rehearse from 22nd November 1954
Producer Rudolph Cartier
*with Yvonne Mitchell, André Morell,
Donald Pleasence, Wilfrid Brambell*

The Creature by Nigel Kneale (BBC TV)
(PC as John Rollason)
Tx: 30th January and 3rd February 1955,
from Studio D, Lime Grove
Filmed Switzerland 3rd – 7th January 1955
Filmed Lime Grove 10th January
Rehearse from 17th January,
at 60 Paddington St, London
Producer Rudolph Cartier
*with Stanley Baker, Eric Pohlmann,
Wolfe Morris, Arnold Marle*

Find the Link (BBC TV)
(PC as celebrity guest)
Tx: 1st March 1955
Producer Ernest Maxim
*with Leslie Mitchell, Josephine Douglas,
Moira Lister, Kenneth Horne*

The Moment of Truth
by Peter Ustinov (BBC TV)
(PC as the Prime Minister)
Tx: 6th and 10th March 1955
Rehearse from 14th February
– 5th March 1955,
Producer Rudolph Cartier
*with Peter Ustinov, Jeanette Sterke, Donald
Pleasence, Hugh Griffith, Noel Hood*

Alexander the Great (United Artists)
(PC as General Memnon)
Filmed March – June 1955 in Spain
Directed by Robert Rossen
*with Richard Burton, Fredric March,
Harry Andrews, Stanley Baker, Claire Bloom*

The Browning Version
by Terence Rattigan (BBC TV)
(PC as Andrew Crocker-Harris)
Tx: 12th July 1955
Rehearse from 25th June – 11th July 1955
Producer Campbell Logan
*with Joyce Heron, Michael Gwynn,
Andrew Ray*

Wife for Sale by David Tutaev
adapted from Anton Chekhov's
Live Merchandise (BBC Home Service)
(PC as Grigori Vassilich Groholsky)
Recorded 9th September
Broadcast 12th September 1955
Producer Charles LeFaux
with Marjorie Westbury, Deryck Guyler

Richard of Bordeaux by Gordon Daviot
(BBC TV)
(PC as Richard II)
Tx: 29th December 1955, from Lime Grove
Rehearse: 5th – 28th December 1955
Producer Victor Menzies
with Jeanette Sterke, Joseph O'Conor, Robin Bailey

Curtain Up! *Stars in Their Choices*
Seagulls over Sorrento
by Hugh Hastings
(BBC Light Programme)
(PC as Able Seaman Badger)
Broadcast 4th Jan 1956
Producer Charles LeFaux
*with Shaun O'Riordan, Gordon Jackson,
Deryck Guyler*

Stars in their Choices
Escape Me Never
by Margaret Kennedy
(BBC Light Programme)
(PC as Sebastian Sanger)
Broadcast 11th Jan 1956
Producer Hugh Stewart
with Mai Zetterling, Brewster Mason

Duchess Theatre
    The Silver Whistle by Robert McEnroe
    (1st – 12th May 1956, 15 perfs)
    (PC as Oliver Erwenter)
    Directed by Martin Landau
    *with Ernest Thesiger, Robin Bailey, Alfie Bass,
    Peter Vaughn, Olga Lindo, Mary Merrall*

Time Without Pity (Harlequin)
(PC as Jeremy Clayton)
Directed by Joseph Losey
Filmed from June – August 1956 at British
National Studios, Elstree
(PC from 25th June – 20th July 1956)
*with Michael Redgrave, Leo McKern, Ann Todd,
Alec McCowen*

Home at Seven
by R C Sherriff (BBC TV)
(PC as David Preston)
Tx: 12th August 1956, from Lime Grove
Rehearse from 25th July – 11th August
Producer Stephen Harrison
with Helen Shingler, Raymond Francis

House Magazine (BBC TV)
(PC to talk about Film Producers' Award)
Tx: 28th October 1956

The Curse of Frankenstein
(Hammer)
(PC as Baron Victor Frankenstein)
Filmed 19th November 1956 – 3rd January
1957 at Bray Studios
Directed by Terence Fisher
with Hazel Court, Robert Urquhart,
Christopher Lee

Gaslight by Patrick Hamilton (BBC TV)
(PC as Manningham)
Tx: 13th January 1957, from Lime Grove
Rehearse 27th December – 12th January
Producer Stephen Harrison
with Mervyn Johns, Mary Morris,
Billie Whitelaw

The Abominable Snowman (Hammer)
(PC as Dr John Rollason)
Filming 28th January – 5th March 1957,
at Bray Studios
Directed by Val Guest
with Forrest Tucker, Maureen Connell,
Richard Wattis, Arnold Marle, Wolfe Morris

Hobbies: Model Soldiers
(BBC Light Programme)
Tx: 26th April 1957, interviewed at home

Picture Parade (BBC TV)
(PC interviewed about
The Abominable Snowman*)*
Tx: 19th August 1957

Violent Playground (Rank)
(PC as Father Laidlaw)
Filmed July – September 1957,
Pinewood Studios
Directed by Basil Dearden
with David McCallum, Stanley Baker,
Anne Heywood, John Slater, Melvyn Hayes

Dracula (Hammer)
(PC as Van Helsing)
Filmed 11th November 1957 – 3rd January
1958, at Bray Studios
Directed by Terence Fisher
with Christopher Lee, Melissa Stribling,
Michael Gough, Valerie Gaunt

The Revenge of Frankenstein (Hammer)
(PC as Baron Victor Frankenstein)
Filmed 6th January – 4th March 1958,
at Bray Studios
Directed by Terence Fisher
with Francis Matthews, Eunice Gayson, Michael
Gwynn, Oscar Quitak, Richard Wordsworth

What's My Line? (BBC TV)
Tx: 9th February 1958
Presented by Harry Carlisle
with Isobel Barnett, Barbara Kelly, Gilbert
Harding, David Nixon, Eamonn Andrews

Follow The Stars (BBC Light Programme)
(PC featured in specially recorded excerpt
from **Violent Playground***)*
Broadcast 9th March 1958
(Recorded 5th March)
Producer John Simmonds
with Stanley Baker, David McCallum,
Terry Scott, Bernard Cribbins

The Winslow Boy
by Terence Rattigan (BBC TV)
(PC as Sir Robert Morton)
Tx: 13th March 1958, from Studio D,
Lime Grove
Rehearse from 20th February 1958
Producer Rudolph Cartier
with John Robinson, Gwen Watford

Uncle Harry by Thomas Job (BBC TV)
(PC as Uncle Harry)
Tx: 8th May 1958,
from BBC Cardiff Studios
Rehearse 21st April – 8th May 1958
Producer David J Thomas
with Mary Morris

John Paul Jones (Samuel Bronston)
(PC as Captain Pearson)
Filmed May – August 1958,
on location in Spain
Directed by John Farrow
with Robert Stack, Marisa Pavan,
Charles Coburn, David Farrar

The Hound of the Baskervilles (Hammer)
(PC as Sherlock Holmes)
Filmed 13th September 1958 – 31st October
1958, at Bray Studios
Directed by Terence Fisher
with André Morell, Christopher Lee,
Francis De Wolff, Marla Landi

Today (BBC Home Service) *(interview about*
filming of **The Hound of the Baskervilles***)*
Broadcast 10th September 1958

Desert Island Discs
(BBC Home Service) *(PC as castaway)*
Broadcast 23rd February 1959
Recorded 17th December 1958

The Mummy (Hammer)
(PC as John Banning)
Filming 25th February – 16th April 1959,
at Bray Studios
Directed by Terence Fisher
with Christopher Lee, Yvonne Furneaux,
George Pastell, Felix Aylmer

Calling Australia: H for Horror
(BBC World Service) Tx: 13th April 1959
Recorded at Bray Studios

The Flesh and the Fiends (Triad)
(PC as Dr Knox)
Filmed from 25th May 1959
Directed by John Gilling
with Donald Pleasence, Billie Whitelaw,
June Laverick, George Rose, Renee Houston

Dateline London
(BBC Light Programme)
(PC as interviewee)
Tx: 17th July 1959

Aldwych Theatre
   The Sound of Murder
   by William Fairchild
   (5th August 1959 to 20th February 1960,
   227 perfs)
   (PC as Charles Norbury)
   Directed by Fred Sadoff *with Patricia Jessel,*
   Elisabeth Sellars, Terence Longden
   (Michael Goodliffe played Norbury after
   PC left during filming of **Suspect**)

Interview (BBC Light Programme)
(PC interviewed about his collection
of model soldiers)
Recorded 28th November 1959

Suspect (Boulting Brothers)
(PC as Professor Sewell)
Filmed December 1959   January 1960
Directed by John and Roy Boulting
with Ian Bannen, Raymond Huntley, Thorley
Walters, Donald Pleasence, Spike Milligan

The Brides of Dracula (Hammer)
(PC as Dr Van Helsing)
Filmed 26th January – 18th March 1960,
at Bray Studios
Directed by Terence Fisher
with Yvonne Monlaur, David Peel, Andrée Melly,
Martita Hunt, Freda Jackson, Henry Oscar

Cone of Silence
(Bryanston/British Lion)
(PC as Captain Judd)
Filmed March – April 1960
Directed by Charles Frend
with Michael Craig, Bernard Lee, George Sanders,
André Morell, Marne Maitland, Noel Willman

Sword of Sherwood Forest (Hammer)
(PC as the Sheriff of Nottingham)
Filmed 23rd May – 8th July 1960
Directed by Terence Fisher
with Richard Greene, Niall MacGinnis,
Oliver Reed, Richard Pasco, Sarah Branch

The Hellfire Club (New World)
(PC as Mr Merryweather)
Filmed July – August 1960
Directed by Robert S Baker
with Keith Michell, Adrienne Corri, Peter Arne,
David Lodge, Francis Matthews

The Naked Edge (Pennebaka/Baroda)
(PC as Mr Evan Wrack)
Filmed December 1960, at Elstree Studios
Directed by Michael Anderson
with Gary Cooper, Deborah Kerr, Eric Portman,
Michael Wilding

Cash on Demand (Hammer)
(PC as Harry Fordyce)
Filmed at Bray Studios, 4th April – 26th April
1961 *with André Morell, Richard Vernon,*
Norman Bird

Fury at Smugglers' Bay (Mijo)
(PC as Squire Trevenyan) Filmed from 15th
June 1961, at Twickenham Studios
Directed by John Gilling
with John Fraser, Bernard Lee, William Franklyn,
Liz Fraser, George Coulouris

Captain Clegg (Hammer/Major)
(PC as Captain Nathaniel Clegg/Dr Blyss)
Filmed 25th September – 8th November 1961,
at Bray Studios
Directed by Peter Graham Scott
with Patrick Allen, Oliver Reed, Michael Ripper

Im Namen des Teufels
(The Devil's Agent) (Criterion/Constantin)
(PC does not feature in release print)
Directed by John Paddy Carstairs
with Peter Van Eyck, Christopher Lee,
Billie Whitelaw, Jeremy Bulloch,
Helen Cherry, Peter Vaughn

The Man Who Finally Died
(Magna/British Lion)
(PC as Peter Von Brecht)
Filmed 1962 at Shepperton Studios
Directed by Quentin Lawrence
with Stanley Baker, Mai Zetterling,
Eric Portman, Niall MacGinnis

Peace with Terror (ABC TV)
(PC as Parsons)
Tx 3rd June 1962 was postponed
Final Tx: n/k
Directed by Quentin Lawrence
with Brian Wilde

Living Today (BBC)
(interview, 'to talk about your hobby, painting')
Tx: 16th April 1963
Recorded 9th April 1963

The Spread of the Eagle
Episodes 4-6 (BBC TV)
Julius Caesar by William Shakespeare
(PC as Caius Cassius)
Part 4: **The Colossus**
    Tx: 24th May 1963
    Recorded 7th – 8th March 1963, Studio 4
    Television Centre
Part 5: **The Fifteenth**
    Tx: 1st June 1963
    Recorded 24th – 25th March, TC4
Part 6: **The Revenge**
    Tx: 8th June 1963
    Recorded 4th – 5th April, TC4
    Rehearse 25th February – 3rd April
Produced and directed by Peter Dews
with Keith Michell, Barry Jones,
Paul Eddington

New Comment: 'The Macabre'
(BBC Third Programme)
(PC as interviewee)
Tx: 26th September 1963
Recorded 10th September 1963
Producer Joseph Home

Comedy Playhouse: The Plan
by Richard Harris and Dennis Spooner
(BBC TV)
(PC as Albert Fawkes)
Tx: 2nd November 1963
Recorded 7th Oct 1963 TC3
Rehearse 1st – 6th October 1963
Filming 22nd – 23rd September 1963
Producer Sydney Lotterby
with Graham Stark, Francis Matthews,
P G Stephens

The Evil of Frankenstein (Hammer)
(PC as Baron Frankenstein)
Filmed 14th October – 16th November 1963,
at Bray Studios
Directed by Freddie Francis
with Peter Woodthorpe, Sandor Elès, Katy Wild,
Duncan Lamont, Kiwi Kingston

The Gorgon (Hammer)
(PC as Dr Namaroff)
Filmed 9th December 1963 – 16th January
1964, at Bray Studios
Directed by Terence Fisher
with Christopher Lee, Richard Pasco,
Barbara Shelley, Patrick Troughton

Star Story
Story Seven: The Yellow Cat
by Michael Joseph (BBC TV)
Recorded 22nd March 1964, TC5
Not broadcast
Director David Bellamy

Story Parade: The Caves of Steel by Isaac
Asimov, adapted by Terry Nation (BBC 2)
(PC as Elijah Baley)
Recorded 5th – 7th May 1964, TC1
Rehearse 15th April – 4th May,
Filming 17th April
Directed by Peter Sasdy
with John Carson, Kenneth J Warren

Dr Terror's House of Horrors (Amicus)
(PC as Dr Sandor Schreck)
Filmed 25th May – 12th June 1964
at Shepperton Studios
Directed by Freddie Francis
with Christopher Lee, Roy Castle,
Donald Sutherland, Alan Freeman

In Town Today (BBC Home Service)
(PC as interviewee)
Broadcast 20th June 1964
Recorded 11th June 1964,
at Shepperton Studios
Producer Richard Dingley

She (Hammer)
(PC as Major Horace L Holly)
Filmed 24th August – 17th October 1964,
at Elstree Studios
Directed by Robert Day
with Ursula Andress, John Richardson, Bernard
Cribbins, Christopher Lee, André Morell

Let's Find Out
(BBC Light Programme)
(PC as guest)
Broadcast 20th October 1964
Recorded 3rd September 1964
Producer David Carter

Loyal Servant by Ian Rodger
(BBC Home Service)
(PC as Lord Churchill)
Broadcast 30th November 1964
Rehearse 6th, 7th, 8th November 1964
Recorded 8th November 1964
Producer Charles LeFaux

First Impressions (BBC 1)
(PC as interviewee)
Tx: 5th January 1965
Recorded 14th December 1964,
TV Theatre Shepherd's Bush

The Skull (Amicus)
(PC as Christopher Maitland)
Directed by Freddie Francis
Filmed 18th January – March 1965,
at Shepperton Studios
with Patrick Wymark, Christopher Lee,
Jill Bennett, Peter Woodthorpe

Cribbins (BBC 1)
(PC as guest)
Tx: 27th February 1965
Rec 5th – 6th February TC4
Rehearse 1st – 4th February
Producer Dennis Main Wilson
with Bernard Cribbins

Dr Who and the Daleks (Aaru)
(PC as Dr Who)
Filming 12th March – 23rd April 1965,
at Shepperton Studios
Directed by Gordon Flemyng
with Roy Castle, Jennie Linden, Roberta Tovey,
Barrie Ingham

Yvonne Arnaud Theatre, Guildford
    Thark by Ben Travers
    (PC as Sir Hector Benbow, Bart, MFH)
    Directed by Ray Cooney
    with Kathleen Harrison, Jennie Linden,
    Alec McCowen
Garrick Theatre, London
    from 3rd August – December 1965

Island of Terror (Planet)
(PC as Dr Stanley)
Filmed August – September 1965,
at Pinewood Studios,
Directed by Terence Fisher
with Edward Judd, Carole Gray,
Niall MacGinnis, Eddie Byrne

30 Minute Theatre: Monica (BBC 2)
(PC as Leonard)
Tx: 4th November 1965,
from Studio G, Lime Grove
Rehearse 27th October – 3rd November 1965
Producer Naomi Capon

Line-Up (BBC 2)
Tx: 27th November 1965
Interview re Nineteen Eighty-Four,
recorded 18th November

Daleks' Invasion Earth 2150 A.D. (Aaru)
(PC as Dr Who)
Filmed 31st January – 22nd March 1966, at
Shepperton Studios
Directed by Gordon Flemyng
with Bernard Cribbins, Ray Brooks, Andrew Keir,
Roberta Tovey, Jill Curzon

Frankenstein Created Woman (Hammer)
(PC as Baron Frankenstein)
Filmed 4th July – 12th August 1966,
at Bray Studios
Directed by Terence Fisher
with Thorley Walters, Susan Denberg,
Robert Morris

Torture Garden (Amicus)
(PC as Lancelot Canning)
Filmed from 14th November 1966,
at Shepperton Studios
Directed by Freddie Francis
with Jack Palance, Hedger Wallace

The Strong are Lonely
(World Service Drama)
Recorded 27th November 1966,
at Bush House
Producer James Vourden
Rehearse 26th November

Some May Live (Krasne)
(PC as John Meredith)
Directed by Vernon Sewell
Filmed from 1st January 1967,
at Twickenham Studios
with Joseph Cotten, Martha Hyer,
David Spenser

Night of the Big Heat (Planet)
(PC as Dr Vernon Stone)
Filmed from 20th February 1967,
at Pinewood Studios
Directed by Terence Fisher
with Christopher Lee, Patrick Allen, Sarah Lawson, William Lucas, Kenneth Cope

The Burnt Flowerbed (BBC Radio)
by Ugo Betti
Rehearse 25th February 1967
Record 26th February 1967
Producer Sunday Wilshin

The Avengers (Telemen/ABC)
Return of the Cybernauts by Philip Levene
(PC as Paul Beresford)
Tx: 30th September 1967
Production completed 15th June 1967
Directed by Robert Day
with Patrick Macnee, Diana Rigg, Fulton Mackay, Frederick Jaeger, Charles Tingwell

Corruption (Titan)
(PC as Sir John Rowan)
Filmed 15th July 1967 – August 1967, at
Isleworth Studios
Directed by Robert Hartford-Davis
with Sue Lloyd, Kate O'Mara, Noel Trevarthan

The Blood Beast Terror (Tigon British)
(PC as Inspector Quennell)
Filmed 7th August – 12th September 1967,
at Goldhawk Studios, Shepherd's Bush
Directed by Vernon Sewell
with Robert Flemyng, Wanda Ventham

Line-Up (BBC 2)
(PC as interviewee 'about yourself and Sherlock Holmes')
Tx: 29th April 1968

Sir Arthur Conan Doyle's
Sherlock Holmes (BBC 1)
Producer William Sterling
(PC as Sherlock Holmes)
with Nigel Stock

1: The Second Stain
Tx: 9th September 1968
Directed by Henri Safran
Dramatised by Jennifer Stuart
with Daniel Massey, Cecil Parker, Penelope Horner, William Lucas
Recorded 23rd August 1968
(5th in recording order)

2: A Study in Scarlet
Tx: 16th September
Directed by Henri Safran
Dramatised by Hugh Leonard
with Grace Arnold, Joe Melia, William Lucas, George A Cooper, Edina Ronay
Recorded 2nd August 1968 (3rd)

3: The Dancing Men
Tx: 23rd September
Directed by William Sterling
Dramatised by Michael and Mollie Hardwick
with Judee Morton, Maxwell Reed, Brenda Bruce
Recorded 2nd September 1968 (6th)

4: The Hound of the Baskervilles #1
Tx: 30th September
Directed by Graham Evans
Dramatised by Hugh Leonard
with Gary Raymond, Gabriella Licudi, Philip Bond, Gerald Flood
Recorded 8th July 1968 (1st)

5: The Hound of the Baskervilles #2
Tx: 7th October
Directed by Paul Ciappessoni
Dramatised by Hugh Leonard
with Gary Raymond, Gabriella Licudi, Philip Bond
Recorded 22nd July 1968 (2nd)

6: The Boscombe Valley Mystery
Tx: 14th October
Directed by Viktors Ritelis
Dramatised by Bruce Stewart
with John Tate, Nick Tate, Peter Madden
Recorded 23rd September 1968 (8th)

7: The Greek Interpreter
Tx: 21st October
Directed by David Saire
Dramatised by John Gould
with Peter Woodthorpe, Nigel Terry, Ronald Adam
Recorded 4th October 1968 (9th)

8: The Naval Treaty
Tx: 28th October
Directed by Anthony Kearey
Dramatised by John Gould
with Dennis Price, Corin Redgrave, Peter Bowles, Jane Lapotaire
Recorded 13th September 1968 (7th)

9: Thor Bridge
Tx: 4th November
Directed by Anthony Kearey
Dramatised by Harry Moore
with Juliet Mills, Isa Miranda, Grant Taylor, Willoughby Gray
Recorded 14th October 1968 (10th)

10: The Musgrave Ritual
Tx: 11th November
Directed by Viktors Ritelis
Dramatised by Alexander Baron
with Georgia Brown, Brian Jackson
Recorded 25th October 1968 (11th)

11: Black Peter
Tx: 18th November
Directed by Anthony Kearey
Dramatised by Richard Harris
with James Kenney, Ilona Rodgers
Recorded 12th August 1968 (4th)

12: Wisteria Lodge
Tx: 25th November
Directed by Roger Jenkins
Dramatised by Alexander Baron
with Richard Pearson, Derek Francis
Recorded 4th November 1968 (12th)

13: Shoscombe Old Place
Tx: 2nd December
Directed by Bill Bain
Dramatised by Donald Tosh
with Nigel Green, Edward Woodward, Kevin Lindsay, Peter Miles
Recorded 15th November 1968 (13th)

14: The Solitary Cyclist
Tx: 9th December
Directed by Viktors Ritelis
Dramatised by Stanley Miller
with Carol Potter, Charles Tingwell
Recorded 25th November 1968 (14th)

15: The Sign of Four
Tx: 16th December
Directed by William Sterling
Dramatised by Michael and Mollie Hardwick
with Ann Bell, Paul Daneman, John Stratton
Recorded 6th December 1968 (15th)

16: The Blue Carbuncle
Tx: 23rd December
Directed by Bill Bain
Dramatised by Donald Tosh
and Stanley Miller
with Madge Ryan, James Beck, Frank Middlemass
Recorded 16th December 1968 (16th)

Star Choice (BBC 1)
(PC as guest)
Recorded 10th December 1968

Frankenstein Must Be Destroyed
(Hammer)
(PC as Baron Frankenstein)
Filmed 13th January – 26th February 1969,
at Elstree Studios
Directed by Terence Fisher
with Veronica Carlson, Maxine Audley, Freddie Jones, Simon Ward

Made in Britain:
Dracula and Frankenstein
Make Money For Britain
(PC as interviewee)
Filmed at Elstree 7th February 1969
Tx 10th February 1969
Interviewer Michael Sullivan
with James Carreras, Veronica Carlson

Incense for the Damned
(PC as Dr Walter Goodrich)
Filmed April – May 1969
Directed by Robert Hartford-Davis
with Patrick Macnee, Patrick Mower, Edward Woodward

Scream and Scream Again (Amicus)
(PC as Benedek)
Filmed from 5th May 1969
Directed by Gordon Hessler
with Vincent Price, Christopher Lee, Michael Gothard

One More Time
(PC, uncredited, as Baron Frankenstein)
Directed by Jerry Lewis
PC's appearance filmed at Shepperton
Studios 23rd July 1969
with Sammy Davis Jnr, Peter Lawford, Christopher Lee, Percy Herbert

The Morecambe and Wise Show (BBC TV)
Tx: 27 July 1969
Recorded 30th – 31st May 1969
Rehearse 23rd – 29th May Forrester's Hall,
269 Kilburn High Rd, London
Producer John Ammonds
with Eric Morecambe, Ernie Wise, Bobbie Gentry, Vince Hill, Kenny Ball, Janet Webb

The Morecambe and Wise Show (BBC TV)
Recorded 16th – 17th August 1969
Rehearse 11th – 15th August
Producer John Ammonds
with Eric Morecambe, Ernie Wise

The Vampire Lovers (Hammer/AIP)
(PC as General Spielsdorf)
Filmed from 19th January 1970 – 4th March
1970, at Elstree Studios
Directed by Roy Ward Baker
*with Ingrid Pitt, Pippa Steel, Madeline Smith,
George Cole, Dawn Addams*

Line-Up
(PC as guest) Recorded 22nd February 1970

While We're On The Subject: Television
(PC as interviewee) Tx: 26th February 1970

London This Week
(PC as guest) Tx: 8th June 1970
Recorded 5th June 1970

The House That Dripped Blood (Amicus)
(PC as Philip Grayson)
Filmed from 29th June 1970,
at Shepperton Studios
Directed by Peter Duffell
with Joss Ackland, Wolfe Morris

I, Monster (Amicus)
(PC as Frederick Utterson)
Filmed from 10th October 1970,
at Shepperton Studios
Directed by Stephen Weeks
*with Christopher Lee, Mike Raven,
Richard Hurndall, Susan Jameson*

**The Morecambe and Wise Christmas
Show** (BBC 1)
Tx: 25th December 1970
Recorded 16th December 1970
Rehearse 11th – 15th December
Producer John Ammonds
*with Eric Morecambe, Ernie Wise, William
Franklyn, Eric Porter, Edward Woodward*

Blood from the Mummy's Tomb
(Hammer)
Filming 11th January 1971
Directed by Seth Holt
(Cushing completed only one day's filming
and does not appear)
with Valerie Leon

Twins of Evil (Hammer)
(PC as Gustav Weil)
Filmed 22nd March 1971 – 30th April 1971,
at Pinewood Studios
Directed by John Hough
*with Mary and Madeleine Collinson, Dennis
Price, Damien Thomas*

Nature Spectacular (BBC 2)
(PC as guest)
Recorded 27th – 29th July 1971
Locations Harpenden, Kent
Producer Richard Brock

Tales from the Crypt (Amicus)
(PC as Arthur Edward Grimsdyke)
Filmed from 13th September 1971,
at Shepperton Studios
Directed by Freddie Francis
with Robin Philips, David Markham

Dracula A.D. 1972 (Hammer)
(PC as Lawrence and Lorrimer Van Helsing)
Filmed 27th September – 5th November 1971,
at Elstree Studios
Directed by Alan Gibson
*with Christopher Lee, Michael Coles,
Stephanie Beacham, Christopher Neame*

Late Night Extra (BBC Radio 2)
(PC as interviewee)
Broadcast live 30th September 1971
from Broadcasting House
Producer Tony Luke

Be My Guest – Peter Cushing
(BBC Radio 2)
Broadcast 19th November 1971
Recorded 7th October 1971 at Brown's Hotel,
Mayfair
Producer John Knight

Man Alive: Comics (BBC 2)
(PC as interviewee)
Recorded 20th – 22nd November 1971
Producer James Clark

Fear in the Night (Hammer)
(PC as Michael Carmichael)
Filmed 15th November – 17th December 1971,
at Elstree Studios
Directed by Jimmy Sangster
with Judy Geeson, Joan Collins, Ralph Bates

Sounds Natural (BBC Radio 4)
(PC as guest)
Recorded 20th November 1971 at BBC Bristol
Broadcast 10th January 1972

Dr Phibes Rises Again (AIP)
(PC as Captain of the Elsinore Castle*)*
Filmed December 1971, at Elstree Studios
Directed by Robert Fuest
*with Robert Quarry, Vincent Price,
Terry-Thomas, John Cater*

**Pánico en el Transiberiano
(Horror Express)** (Granada /Benmar)
(PC as Dr Wells)
Filmed December 1971 – January 1972,
at Studio 70 Complex, Madrid
Directed by Eugenio Martin
With Christopher Lee, Telly Savalas

The Creeping Flesh
(Tigon British/World Film Services)
(PC as Professor Emmanuel Hildern)
Filmed from 31st January 1972,
at Shepperton Studios
Directed by Freddie Francis
with Christopher Lee, Lorna Heilbron

Asylum (Amicus)
(PC as Mr Smith)
Filmed from 1st April 1972,
at Shepperton Studios
PC filming 6th, 7th April 1972
Directed by Roy Ward Baker
*with Barry Morse, Ann Firbank,
John Franklyn-Robbins*

Nothing But The Night (Charlemagne)
(PC as Sir Mark Ashley)
Filmed from 18th April 1972,
at Pinewood Studios
Directed by Peter Sasdy
with Christopher Lee, Georgia Brown, Diana Dors

Twenty Questions (BBC Radio 4)
(PC as Mystery Voice)
Rehearse/Record 2nd June 1972,
at the Central Hall, Chatham
Broadcast 5th July 1972
Producer John Cassells

Going for A Song (BBC 1)
Recorded 9th June 1972 at Studio A,
BBC Bristol
Producer John King

~~And Now The Screaming Starts!
(Amicus)
(PC as Dr Pope)
Filmed from 17th July 1972,
at Shepperton Studios
Directed by Roy Ward Baker
with Stephanie Beacham, Ian Ogilvy

**Frankenstein and
the Monster From Hell** (Hammer)
(PC as Baron Frankenstein)
Filmed from 18th September – 27th October
1972, at Elstree Studios
Directed by Terence Fisher
with Shane Briant, John Stratton, Madeline Smith

The Satanic Rites of Dracula (Hammer)
(PC as Lorrimer Van Helsing)
Filmed from 13th November 1972 –
3rd January 1973, at Elstree Studios
Directed by Alan Gibson
*with Christopher Lee, Joanna Lumley, Freddie
Jones, Michael Coles, William Franklyn*

Ask Aspel (BBC 1)
(PC as guest)
Tx: 7th January 1974
Recorded 4th January 1973
Producer Granville Jenkins
with Tony Blackburn

Nationwide (BBC 1)
(PC as guest *'to talk about your latest film,
Nothing But The Night')*
Tx: 4th January 1973

The Morecambe and Wise Show (BBC 1)
Tx: 23rd March 1973
Recorded 13th February 1973
Rehearse 5th – 11th February 1973
Producer John Ammonds
*with Eric Morecambe, Ernie Wise, Georgie Fame,
Alan Price, Ann Hamilton*

P.M. (BBC Radio 4)
Tx: 18th April 1973
Produced by Helen Wilson
(PC interviewee)

The Zoo Gang (ITC)
The Counterfeit Trap *(PC as Judge Gautier)*
Tx 26th April 1974
Filmed April 1973, in France
Directed by John Hough
*with John Mills, Barry Morse, Lilli Palmer,
Jacqueline Pearce, Philip Madoc*

Madhouse (Amicus)
(PC as Herbert Flay)
Filmed from 14th May 1973,
at Twickenham Studios
Directed by Jim Clark
*with Vincent Price, Adrienne Corri,
Linda Hayden*

Film 73 (BBC 1)
Featuring filming of **Madhouse**
on location at Pyrford Manor

From Beyond the Grave (Amicus)
(PC as the Proprietor)
Filmed from 4th June 1973
Directed by Kevin Connor
*with Ian Carmichael, Ian Bannen,
David Warner, Ian Ogilvy*

The Amazing World of Kreskin
(Tyne Tees Television)
(PC as guest)
Recorded June 1973 *with David Kreskin*

The Price of Fear
The Man Who Hated Scenes (BBC Radio 4)
Recorded 16th June 1973
Producer John Dyas
with Vincent Price

Woman's Hour (BBC Radio 4)
Broadcast 20th June 1973
Producer Kay Evans

The Beast Must Die (Amicus)
(PC as Dr Christopher Lundgren)
Filmed from 16th July 1973,
at Shepperton Studios
Directed by Paul Annett
*with Calvin Lockhart, Charles Gray,
Michael Gambon*

Orson Welles Great Mysteries (Anglia TV)
La Grande Breteche by Honoré De Balzac,
adapted by Martin Worth
(PC as Count Gerard De Merret)
Directed by Peter Sasdy
Filmed September 1973
US Tx: 23rd November 1973
UK Tx: 27th July 1974
with Susannah York, Michael Gambon

The Legend of the 7 Golden Vampires
(Hammer/Shaw)
(PC as Professor Van Helsing)
Filmed 22nd October – 11th December 1973,
at Shaw Studios, Hong Kong
Directed by Roy Ward Baker
(and Chang Cheh, uncredited)
*with Julie Ege, David Chiang, Robin Stewart,
John Forbes-Robertson*

Shatter (Hammer/Shaw)
(PC as Rattwood)
Filmed 17th December 1973 – 15th January
1974 Directed by Michael Carreras
(and Monte Hellman, uncredited)
*with Stuart Whitman, Anton Diffring,
Ti Lung, Lily Li*

La grande trouille (aka Tendre Dracula)
(Vincent Malle-Renn)
(PC as MacGregor)
Filmed January 1974, in France
Directed by Pierre Grunstein
with Alida Valli, Miou-Miou

The Ghoul (Tyburn)
(PC as Dr Lawrence)
Filmed from 4th March 1974,
at Pinewood Studios
Directed by Freddie Francis
*with John Hurt, Don Henderson,
Gwen Watford, Veronica Carlson*

This Is Your Life: Christopher Lee
(Thames Television)
(PC as guest)
Tx: 3rd April 1974
*with Vincent Price, Oliver Reed, Veronica
Carlson, Trevor Howard*

What Was He Like? (ITV)
(PC explains his ideas about the life of Christ)
Recorded Easter 1974

Space: 1999 (ITC/Rai/Group Three)
Missing Link by Edward Di Lorenzo
(PC as Raan)
Filmed May 1974, at Pinewood Studios
Directed by Ray Austin
Tx: 27th February 1976
*with Martin Landau, Barbara Bain, Barry Morse,
Joanna Dunham*

Start The Week (BBC Radio 4)
(PC as guest)
Broadcast 15th August 1974 (live)
Producer Hugh Purcell

Legend of the Werewolf (Tyburn)
(PC as Paul Cataflanque)
Directed by Freddie Francis
Filmed from 19th August 1974,
at Pinewood Studios
*with David Rintoul, Ron Moody, Roy Castle,
Hugh Griffith*

Taste for Adventure: Fists of Fire (BBC 1)
Tx: 16th January 1975
Documentary re the boom in kung-fu films,
featuring behind-the-scenes footage of
The Legend of the 7 Golden Vampires

Shock Waves (Joseph Brenner/Zopix)
(PC as SS Commander)
Filmed June 1975, on location in Florida
Directed by Ken Wiederhorn
with Brooke Adams, Fred Buch, Jack Davidson

Trial by Combat (Weintraub/Heller)
(PC as Sir Edward Gifford)
Filmed 1975 on location in London
Directed by Kevin Connor
*with John Mills, Donald Pleasence,
Barbara Hershey*

Haunted – Herstmonceaux Castle
(PC as on-screen narrator) Filmed 1975
Directed by Paul Annett

Horseshoe Theatre, Basingstoke
   The Heiress
   by Ruth and Augustus Goetz
   21st October – 1st November 1975
   (PC as Dr Austin Soper)
   Directed by Guy Slater
   with Helen Ryan, Jonathan Newth

Tomorrow (NBC)
(PC as guest) November 1975
with Tom Snyder, Forrest J Ackerman

The Amazing World of Cinema
(VPS Polymedia)
The Mad Scientists
(PC as narrator/presenter)

Looks Familiar (ITV)
(PC as guest)
with Denis Norden, Dilys Powell

The Devil's Men (Getty/Poseidon)
(PC as Baron Corofax)
Directed by Costas Carayiannis
Filmed in November 1975,
on location in Greece
*with Donald Pleasence, Luan Peters,
Nikos Vewrlekis, Costa Skouras*

At the Earth's Core (Amicus)
(PC as Dr Abner Perry)
Filmed from 20th January – March 1976,
at Pinewood Studios
Directed by Kevin Connor
with Doug McClure, Caroline Munro

The New Avengers (Mark One)
The Eagle's Nest by Brian Clemens
(PC as Dr Mebach Von Claus)
Filmed April 1976, on location (Skye)
and at Pinewood Studios
Tx: 17th October 1976
Directed by Desmond Davis
*with Patrick Macnee, Joanna Lumley,
Gareth Hunt, Derek Farr, Frank Gatliff*

Star Wars (Lucasfilm)
(PC as Grand Moff Tarkin)
Filmed March – June 1976 at Elstree Studios
PC filming 'one week' to 4th May 1976
Directed by George Lucas
*with Carrie Fisher, David Prowse,
Leslie Schofield, Don Henderson*

The Great Houdinis (ABC Circle Films)
(PC as Sir Arthur Conan Doyle)
Filmed in Los Angeles, May 1976
(PC filming 12th – 15th May)
Directed by Melville Shavelson
Tx: 8th October 1976 (US)
*with Ruth Gordon, Paul Michael Glaser,
Maureen O'Sullivan, Wilfrid Hyde-White*

Clapperboard (Thames TV)
Behind-the-scenes on At the Earth's Core
Tx: 12th July 1976
with Chris Kelly

Magpie (Thames TV)
Tx: 20th July 1976
Behind the scenes on At the Earth's Core
*with Jenny Hanley, Douglas Rae,
Mick Robertson*

Jim'll Fix It Bank Holiday Special
(BBC TV)
('Horror make-up with Peter Cushing')
Tx: 28th August 1976
*with Jimmy Savile, Freddie 'Parrot Face' Davis,
Guys 'n' Dolls*

Aliens in the Mind
(BBC Radio 4 / Radio Scotland)
(PC as Dr John Cornelius)
A six-part serial
   1: **Island Genesis** 2nd January 1977
   2: **Hurried Exodus** 9th January
   3: **Unexpected Visitations** 16th January
   4: **Official Intercessions** 23rd January
   5: **Genetic Revelations** 30th January
   6: **Final Tribulations** 6th February
Produced by John Dyas
Script by Rene Basilico from an idea
by Robert Holmes
*with Vincent Price, Richard Hurndall,
Fraser Kerr, Irene Sutcliffe, Sandra Clark*

Die Standarte (Battleflag)
(Ottokar Runz)
(PC as Major Von Hackenberg)
Filmed October – December 1976
in Spain and Vienna
Director Ottokar Runz
With Simon Ward, Jon Finch, Viktor Staal

The Uncanny (Cinevideo/Tor)
(PC as Wilbur Gray)
Filmed from 16th November 1976,
in Panavision Studios, Montreal
and Pinewood Studios
Directed by Denis Heroux
with Ray Milland

A Land Looking West (Swan)
(PC as on-screen narrator)
Filmed in Australia, 1977
Producer John Izzard

Hitler's Son (Naxos)
(PC as Heinrich Haussner)
Filmed in September 1977 – January 1978
at Arri Studios Munich and on location
in Bavaria
Directed by Rod Amateau
with Bud Cort

A Touch of the Sun (Fusetcourt)
(PC as Mr Commissioner Potts)
Filmed 19th June 1978 – 20th August 1978
(PC from 27th July)
on location in Zambia
Directed by Peter Curran
*with Oliver Reed, Keenan Wynn, Bruce Boa,
Sylvaine Charlet, Melvyn Hayes*

Arabian Adventure (Badger)
(PC as Wazir Al Wuzara)
Filmed September 1978, at Pinewood Studios
Directed by Kevin Connor
*with Christopher Lee, Oliver Tobias,
Milo O'Shea*

The Morecambe and Wise Show
(Thames TV)
(PC as guest)
Tx: 18th October 1978
*with Donald Sinden, Judi Dench,
Leonard Sachs*

The Detour (short)
(PC as narrator)
Filmed 1978
Directed by Rodney Holland
with John Galdes

**Misterio en la isla de los monstruos
(Mystery on Monster Island)**
(Fort/Armena)
(PC as William Kolderup)
Directed by Juan Piquer Simon
Filmed 1980, in Puerto Rico,
Canary Islands and Spain
with Terence Stamp, Ian Serra, Paul Naschy

A Tale of Two Cities (Hallmark)
(PC as Dr Alexander Manette)
Filmed 30th July 1980 for six weeks,
at Shepperton Studios and on location
in England and France
Directed by Jim Goddard
*with Chris Sarandon, Billie Whitelaw,
Alice Krige, Flora Robson, Kenneth More*

**Hammer House of Horror:
The Silent Scream**
(ITC/Cinema Arts/Hammer)
by Francis Essex
(PC as Martin Blueck)
Tx: 25th October 1980
Shooting of series from 28th June 1980
on location in Buckinghamshire
Directed by Alan Gibson
with Brian Cox, Elaine Donnelly

**The Morecambe and Wise Christmas
Show** (Thames TV)
(PC as guest)
Tx: 25th December 1980
Thames Television
*with Peter Barkworth, Jill Gascoine,
Alec Guinness, Peter Vaughn, Gemma Craven*

Asalto al casino (Black Jack)
(Diffusion SA/Cinespana)
(PC as Sir Thomas Bedford)
Directed by Max H Boulois
Filmed December 1980/January 1981
*with Claudine Auger, Hugo Stiglitz,
Brian Murphy*

Top Secret! (Abrahams, Zucker, Zucker)
(PC as Bookshop Proprietor)
Filmed 1982
Directed by Jim Abrahams, Jerry Zucker,
David Zucker
*with Val Kilmer, Lucy Gutteridge, Michael
Gough, Jeremy Kemp*

House of the Long Shadows
(Golan Globus/Cannon)
(PC as Sebastian Grisbane)
Directed by Pete Walker
Filmed August – September 1982,
on location at Rotherfield Park,
East Tisted, Hants
*with Vincent Price, Christopher Lee,
John Carradine, Julie Peasgood, Sheila Keith,
Desi Arnaz Jr*

Sword of the Valiant
(Golan Globus/Cannon)
(PC as Gaspar, the Seneschal)
Filmed September – October 1982,
in Ireland, Wales and France
Directed by Stephen Weeks
*with Miles O'Keeffe, Ronald Lacey, John Rhys
Davies, Cynelle Claire*

Tales of the Unexpected (Anglia TV)
The Vorpal Blade by Edward D Hoch
adapted by Robin Chapman
(PC as Karl Von Baden)
Tx: 28th May 1983
Directed by John Jacobs
with John Bailey, Anthony Higgins

Breakfast Time (BBC 1)
Tx: 14th June 1983
PC as guest of the day, including clips from
House of the Long Shadows

Helen Keller: The Miracle Continues
(PC as Professor Copeland)
Filmed 1983
Directed by Alan Gibson
with Blythe Danner, Mare Winningham

The Masks of Death (Tyburn)
(PC as Sherlock Holmes)
Filmed from 21st July 1984
Directed by Roy Ward Baker
*with John Mills, Ray Milland, Anton Diffring,
Anne Baxter*

Biggles (Compact Yellowbill/Tambarle)
(PC as Air Commodore William Raymond)
Filmed 21st January – March 1985,
at Pinewood Studios
Directed by John Hough
*with Neil Dickson, Alex Hyde-White,
Fiona Hutchison*

Wogan (BBC 1)
(PC as interviewee, with Nicholas Rowe)
Tx: 10th March 1986 (live)

Jim'll Fix It
(PC as 'fixee' choosing the Helen Cushing Rose)
Producer Roger Ordish
with Christopher Wheatcroft

Pebble Mill at One (BBC 1)
(PC as interviewee)
Tx: 24th March 1986

Look North (BBC 1)
(PC as interviewee)
Tx: 5th June 1986

Everyman: The True Story of Frankenstein
(BBC 1)
(PC as interviewee)
Tx: 19th October 1986

**Omnibus: Hammer – The Studio That
Dripped Blood** (BBC 2)
(PC as interviewee)
Tx: 26th June 1987
Producers Nick Jones and David Thompson
Narrator Charles Gray

Wogan (BBC 1)
(PC as interviewee)
Tx: 22nd May 1987
'Terry Wogan hosts the first in a two-part
holiday celebration of the golden days
of British cinema'
*with Christopher Lee, Bryan Forbes,
Bernard Cribbins*

Wogan (BBC 1)
(PC as interviewee)
Tx: 19th December 1987

Wogan (BBC 1)
(PC as interviewee)
Tx: 24th February 1988
*with Colonel John Blashford-Snell, Joan Chen,
Aztec Camera*

**Peter Cushing: A One-Way Ticket to
Hollywood** (Tyburn)
Tx: 4th June 1989
Directed by Alan Bell
with Dick Vosburgh

This Is Your Life: Peter Cushing
(Thames TV)
Tx: 21st February 1990
*with Christopher Lee, Caroline Munro,
David Rintoul, David Prowse, Freddie Jones,
Gwen Watford, Peter Ustinov, Anthony Hinds,
Sir James Carreras, Ursula Andress*

The Human Factor (TVS)
For the Love of Helen
(PC as interviewee)

Newsroom South East (BBC 1)
(PC as interviewee)
Tx: 12th July 1990
with Len Harris

Newsroom South East (BBC 1)
(PC as interviewee)
Tx: 9th August 1990

Human Conflict (BBC Radio Kent)
Broadcast 29th December 1990
Producer Michael Bath
with Alan Dobie

Pebble Mill (BBC 1)
(PC as guest)
Tx: 31st October 1991

Behind the Headlines (BBC 2)
(PC as guest)
Tx: 2nd December 1992
with Linda Agran

BBC News (BBC 1)
(PC as interviewee)
Tx: 5th August 1993

Flesh and Blood:
The Hammer Heritage of Horror
(Heidelberg/Bosustow/Hammer)
(PC as narrator)
  Part One
  Tx: 8th August 1994
  Part Two
  Tx: 15th August 1994
  Recorded 17th May 1994
Directed by Ted Newsom
with Christopher Lee

Front endpapers
Top row: *A Chump at Oxford, Laddie, The Curse of Frankenstein, The Revenge of Frankenstein, Dracula*
Middle row: *The Black Knight, The End of the Affair, The Curse of Frankenstein, The Brides of Dracula*
Bottom row: *The Abominable Snowman, Sword of Sherwood Forest, The Evil of Frankenstein, The Hellfire Club, The Flesh and the Fiends*

Back endpapers
Top row: *Frankenstein and the Monster from Hell, The Legend of the 7 Golden Vampires, Twins of Evil, Dracula A.D. 1972*
Middle row: *Scream and Scream Again, Tales from the Crypt, A Tale of Two Cities, At the Earth's Core, Horror Express*
Bottom row: *The Vampire Lovers, ~And Now The Screaming Starts!, I, Monster, Corruption, From Beyond the Grave*

Cushing as the brilliant, Byronic, bad Baron Frankenstein in Hammer's *The Curse of Frankenstein* (1956)

Source Notes

1   Little Horror
1   *Hammer House of Horror* #18,
    interview with Alan Frank, March 1978
2   *ibid*
3   *TV Mirror*, 'The Peter Cushing Story'
    3rd April 1954
4   Interview with Alan Frank, *op cit*
5   *An Autobiography* Peter Cushing 1986
6   *ibid*
7   *ibid*
8   *TV Mirror*, 'The Peter Cushing Story'
    3rd April 1954, *op cit*
9   *ibid*

2   The Madman of Purley
1   Cushing, 1986, *op cit*
2   *ibid*
3   *TV Mirror*, 'The Peter Cushing Story'
    3rd April 1954, *op cit*
4   *TV Times* interview with
    Katie Ekberg, 3rd June 1989
5   *TV Mirror*, 'The Peter Cushing Story'
    3rd April 1954, *op cit*
6   Cushing, 1986, *op cit*
7   *TV Mirror*, 'The Peter Cushing Story'
    3rd April 1954, *op cit*
8   *ibid*
9   *ibid*
10 *Past Forgetting* Peter Cushing 1988

3   Hooray for Hollywood
1   *TV Mirror*, 'The Peter Cushing Story'
    10th April 1954
2   *Little Shoppe of Horrors* #8, interview with
    James Kravaal (Ian Jennings) May 1984
3   *TV Mirror*, 'The Peter Cushing Story'
    10th April 1954, *op cit*
4   *ibid*
5   Cushing, 1986, *op cit*
6   *TV Mirror*, 'The Peter Cushing Story'
    10th April 1954, *op cit*
7   Cushing, 1986, *op cit*
8   *James Whale* James Curtis 1982
9   Cushing, 1986, *op cit*
10 *TV Mirror*, 'The Peter Cushing Story'
    10th April 1954, *op cit*

4   Back to Dear Old Blighty
1   Cushing, 1986, *op cit*
2   *TV Mirror*, 'The Peter Cushing Story'
    17th April 1954
3   Interview with the author 1999
4   *TV Mirror*, 'The Peter Cushing Story'
    17th April 1954, *op cit*
5   *TV Mirror*, 'Peter is so Patient'
    29th October 1955
6   *A One-Way Ticket to Hollywood*,
    Tyburn, 1989
7   Cushing, 1986, *op cit*
8   Interview with the author 1999
9   *TV Mirror*, 'Peter is so Patient'
    29th October 1955
10 Interview with the author 1999
11 Cushing, 1986, *op cit*
12 Interview with the author 1999
13 Cushing, 1986, *op cit*
14 Tyburn documentary, 1988, *op cit*
15 *Illustrated* Magazine 7th August 1943
16 *TV Mirror*, 'The Peter Cushing Story'
    17th April 1954, *op cit*

17 *Times* 7th August 1943
18 Cushing, 1986, *op cit*
19 *On Q* Kenneth Barrow London 1992

5   French Without Tears
1   Cushing, 1986, *op cit*
2   *Evening Standard* 10th October 1944
3   Interview with the author 1999
4   Cushing, 1986, *op cit*
5   *Times* 26th December 1944
6   *Tatler and Bystander* 26th December 1944
7   Quoted in *Peter Cushing*, Fearney, 1995
8   Cushing, 1986, *op cit*
9   *ibid*
10 *TV Mirror*, 'The Peter Cushing Story'
    24th April 1954
11 *The Life of Laurence Olivier*,
    Thomas Kiernan, 1981
12 *Laurence Olivier – A Biography*,
    Donald Spoto 1991
13 Tyburn documentary, 1989, *op cit*
14 Spoto, *op cit*

6   Down Under And Back Again
1   *Darlings of the Gods* by
    Garry O'Connor, 1984
2   Spoto, *op cit*
3   Interview with the author 1999
4   Interview with the author 1999
5   Cushing, 1986, *op cit*
6   Interview with the author 1999
7   Cushing, 1986, *op cit*
8   Interview with the author 1999
9   *What's On in London* 18th February 1949
10 *Old Vic Yearbook* 1949
11 *Evening Standard* 28th March 1972
12 Interview with the author 1999
13 'The Peter Cushing Story'
    24th April 1954, *op cit*
14 *Tatler* September 1950
15 Cushing, 1986, *op cit*

7   The Pride of Alexandra Palace
1   Cushing, 1986, *op cit*
2   *Sight and Sound*, 'Not Quite so Intimate',
    by Nigel Kneale, Spring 1959
3   *TV Mirror* 'The Peter Cushing Story'
    1st May 1954
4   Letter to the author 1999
5   *Radio Times* 1st March 1952
6   'The Peter Cushing Story'
    1st May 1954, *op cit*
7   Cushing, 1986, *op cit*
8   Interview with the author 1999
9   Letter to the author 1999
10 Interview with Mark A Miller,
    Christopher Lee and Peter Cushing, 1995
11 Letter to the author 1999
12 Cushing, 1986, *op cit*
13 *Radio Times* 14 March 1953
14 Cushing, 1986, *op cit*

8   Busy Days and a Black Knight
1   *Radio Times* 4th August 1953
2   *Radio Times* 22nd August 1953
3   *Radio Times* 23rd January 1954
4   *ibid*
5   *Radio Times* 13th February 1954
6   *Evening Standard* 15th March 1954
7   *Daily Cinema* 9th September 1954

9   Nineteen Eighty-Four *And All That*
1   Interview with the author 1999
2   Tyburn documentary, 1988, *op cit*
3   *Daily Worker* 14th December 1954
4   *Daily Express* 14th December 1954
5   *Daily Sketch* 14th December 1954
6   Nigel Kneale, *op cit*
7   *Times* 31st January 1955
8   *Observer* 6th February 1955
9   *Radio Times* 6th March 1955

10   Richard II, Irving Nil
1   *Radio Times* 12th July 1955
2   Letter to the author 1999
3   Interview with the author 1999
4   Interview with the author 1999
5   *Radio Times* 29th December 1955
6   *Daily Telegraph* 30th December 1955
7   Quoted in *Hammer Films*,
    Johnson/Del Vecchio, 1996
8   *Radio Times* 12th August 1956

11   Enter Baron Frankenstein
1   *Tall Dark and Gruesome*,
    Christopher Lee 1997
2   Interview with the author 1999
3   Interview with the author 1999
4   C A Lejeune, the *Observer* 2nd May 1957
5   *Tribune* May 1957
6: *New York Journal* 7th August 1957
7   *Famous Monsters of Filmland* interview
    with Steve Swires, August 1978
8   *Daily Telegraph* 14th January 1957
9   *Hammer Horror* #7, interviewed by
    Marcus Hearn, September 1995
10 Interview in *Peter Cushing*,
    Johnson/Del Vecchio, 1996
11 Interview in *Hammer Films*,
    Johnson/Del Vecchio, 1996
12 *Times* 3rd March 1958

12   A Feast for the Horror-Gobblers
1   *The Films of Peter Cushing*
    Gary Parfitt 1998
2   Quoted in *A History of Horror*,
    Denis Meikle, 1996
3   Tyburn documentary, 1988, *op cit*
4   Interview with Ian Jennings, *op cit*
5   *Shivers* #22 October 1995
6   *Video Watchdog* #25, interview
    with Bill Kelley, September 1994
7   *Daily Telegraph* 31st May 1958
8   *Times* May 1958
9   *Variety* 7th May 1958
10 *New York Daily News* 29th May 1958
11 *New York Herald Tribune* 29th May 1958
12 *Daily Cinema*
13 *Kinematograph Weekly* 20th January 1958
14 *Daily Cinema* 2nd January 1958
15 Letter to the author 1999
16 Interview with the author 1999
17 *Observer* 31st August 1958
18 *Evening Standard* 28th August 1958
19 *Daily Express* 29th August 1958
20 *Radio Times* 12th March 1958
21 *Times* 14th March 1958
22 *Radio Times* 7th May 1958
23 *Daily Telegraph* 9th May 1958
24 *Evening Standard* 26th May 1958
25 *News of the World* 25th May 1958

13 Elementary Exercises
1 *TV Mirror* 'Toys? They're Not Child's Play' says Peter Cushing, July 1956
2 *Holmes of the Movies* David Stuart Davies, 1976
3 *Films and Filming* March 1959
4 Quoted in *A History of Horrors* 1996
5 *Daily Cinema* 5th September 1958
6 *Evening Bulletin*, quoted in *Hammer Films*, 1996
7 *Newsweek* quoted in *Shivers #22*
8 *Observer* 29th March 1959
9 *Sunday Times* 29th March 1959

14 That C-r-e-e-p-y Character
1: David Stone, *Everybody's* magazine 7th February 1959
2: Cushing, 1986, *op cit*
3: *Past Forgetting* 1988
4: Steve Swires, *Monsters of Filmland*, August 1978
5: *Christopher Lee and Peter Cushing*, Mark A Miller, 1994
6 *Video Watchdog* #25, interview with Bill Kelley, September 1994
7 Parfitt, *op cit*
8 *Little Shoppe of Horrors #4* 1978
9 *Variety* 10th February 1960
10 *Times* 8th February 1960
11 *Daily Telegraph* 6th August 1959
12 *Times* 7th August 1959
13 Vivien Hislop in *Evening News*, 7th November 1959
14 Parfitt, *op cit*

15 Swashing His Buckle
1 *Times* 7th July 1960
2 *New York Herald Tribune* 6th September 1960
3 *Observer* 10th July 1960
4 *Kinematograph Weekly* 19th November 1963
5 *Variety* 11th January 1961
6 *New York Herald Tribune* 10th October 1963
7 *Kinematograph Weekly*, *op cit*
8 Cushing, 1988, *op cit*
9 *ibid*
10 Letter to the author 1999
11 *Variety* 12th May 1962
12 Interview with the author 1999

16 Abdication, Restoration
1 Patricia Lewis, *Daily Express*, 9th January 1962
2 William Hall, *Evening News* 25th March 1963
3 Cushing, 1988, *op cit*
4 *TV Times* 3rd June 1962
5 *ibid*
6 *Daily Telegraph* 4th June 1962
7 *Daily Mirror* 24th May 1963
8 *Radio Times* 2nd November 1963
9 *A History of Horrors* 1996, *op cit*
10 *ibid*
11 Quoted in *The Hammer Story*, Hearn/Barnes, 1997
12 *Times* 16th April 1964
13 Hammer publicity for *The Gorgon*
14 Interview with the author 1999
15 *Films and Filming* December 1963
16 *Daily Telegraph* 8th June 1963
17 *Monthly Film Bulletin* October 1964

17 Men of Steel
1 Cushing, 1988, *op cit*
2 John Doran *Film Review* March 1965
3 *New York Times* 2nd September 1965
4 *Variety* 4th August 1965

5 Interview in *Dalekmania*, Lumiere Pictures, 1995
6 Letter to the author 1999
7 *People* 22nd June 1965
8 *Daily Express* 23rd June 1965
9 *Variety* 22nd March 1967
10 Harold Hobson in *Sunday Times* 6th August 1965
11 Cushing, 1988, *op cit*
12 *Radio Times* 4 November 1965
13 Cushing, 1988, *op cit*
14 William Hall in *Evening News* 25th March 1966
15 *Times* 21st July 1966
16 *Evening Standard* 20th July 1966

18 Back to Baker Street
1 *Variety* 15th March 1967
2 Quoted in Parfitt, *op cit*
3 *Cinefantastique*
4 Letter to the author
5 Quoted in Parfitt, *op cit*
6 Interview in *Peter Cushing*, 1994
7 Interview with the author 1999
8 *ibid*
9 *Daily Mail* 25th September 1968
10 Interview with the author 1999

19 Scientist, Surgeon, Madman, Murderer
1 *Sunday Telegraph* 25th May 1969
2 *Sunday Times* 25th May 1969
3 *Variety* 11th June 1969
4 *Sunday Times* 3rd September 1970
5 Interview with the author 1999
6 Interview in *Christopher Lee and Peter Cushing*, 1995
7 *Sunday Times* 28th February 1971

20 Losing Helen
1 Cushing, 1986, *op cit*
2 *ibid*
3 Cushing, 1988, *op cit*
4 Cushing, 1986, *op cit*
5 *ibid*
6 *ibid*
7 *Shivers #44*, interview with Adam Jezard, September 1997
8 Interview with the author 1999
9 Hammer publicity material
10 *Cinefantastique* Vol 2, #3
11 *Sunday Express* 11th July 1971
12 *Sunday Express* 18th July 1971
13 Cushing, 1988, *op cit*
14 Amicus publicity material
15 Cushing, 1988, *op cit*
16 *Shivers #22*, *op cit*
17 Amicus publicity material
18 *Cinefantastique* Vol 2, #3
19 *New York Times* 9th March 1972
20 Interview with Bill Kelley, *op cit*
21 *The Horror People* John Brosnan 1976
22 *Cinema TV Today* 7th October 1972
23 *Shivers #35*, interview with Jonathan Rigby and the author, November 1996

21 Can You Cure Unhappiness?
1 Margaret Hinxman *Sunday Telegraph* 23rd June 1973
2 *Daily Telegraph* 24th June 1973
3 Mark A Miller interview, *op cit*
4 Amicus publicity material
5 *Evening Standard* 6th March 1972
6 *Evening Standard* 29th April 1972
7 *Evening Standard* July 1972
8 Interview with the author 1999
9 Interview with Bill Kelley, *op cit*
10 *The Hammer Story*, 1997, *op cit*

11 Interview with the author 1999
12 Interview with the author 1999
13 Letter to the author 1999
14 Cushing, 1988, *op cit*
15 *ibid*
16 *American Peter Cushing Fan Club Journal #16*

22 Treading Time
1 *News of the World* 9th June 1972
2 *Shivers #38*, interview with Adam Jezard, February 1997
3 Quoted in *Hammer Horror Collectors' Special*, 1994
4 *The Ghoul* publicity material, Tyburn
5 David Montgomery *Sunday Times* 11th August 1977
6 *ibid*
7 *Shivers #69*, interview with Mark A Miller, September 1998
8 *Famous Monsters of Filmland #146* August 1978
9 *Fangoria*, quoted in *The Films of John Carradine* 1999
10 Cushing, 1988, *op cit*
11 Interview with the author 1999
12 *Evening Standard* 15th July 1976
13 *Telegraph* 16th July 176
14 Unpublished interview with Simon Flynn, 2000
15 Parfitt, *op cit*

23 Still Dancin'
1 Quoted in *Peter Cushing* 1994
2 Tyburn documentary, 1988, *op cit*
3 *Rolling Stone* 25th August 1977
4 *Films and Filming* October 1977
5 *Evening News* 27th October 1977
6 *American Peter Cushing Club Journal #13*
7 *ibid*
8 Cushing, 1988, *op cit*
9 *Touch of the Sun* publicity material
10 *Starburst #27* September 1980
11 Manuel Valencia *Cinefantástico y de terror espanol 1900-1983* 1999
12 Interview with Mike Hodges 1999
13 Interview with Mike Hodges 1998
14 Letter to the author 1999

24 A Saint in Retirement
1 Cushing, 1988, *op cit*
2 Afterword in the Midnight Marquee reprint of *An Autobiography* 1999
3 Cushing, 1988, *op cit*
4 *Sunday Telegraph* 25th June 1983
5 Tyburn documentary, 1988, *op cit*
6 *Times* 24th December 1984
7 *Times* 23rd May 1986
8 Quentin Falk *Guardian* 22nd March 1986
9 *Time Out* 12th March 1986
10 *Express* 24th March 1986
11 *Today* 1st June 1987
12 *Scotsman* 23rd May 1988
13 *Daily Telegraph* 22nd May 1988
14 *TV Times* 3rd June 1989
15 *Whitstable Times* 29th March 1989
16 *TV Times* 3rd June 1989
17 Interview with the author 1999
18 *Times* 29th December 1990
19 Quoted in *Peter Cushing* 1994
20 Afterword in the Midnight Marquee reprint of *An Autobiography* 1999
21 *Telegraph* 18th August 1994
22 Afterword in the Midnight Marquee reprint of *An Autobiography* 1999
23 *Telegraph* 20th August 1994
24 *Independent* 12th August 1994

Bibliography

The British Film Yearbook 1947-48
Edited by Peter Noble
Skelton Robinson British Yearbooks

The Year That Made The Day
The British Broadcasting Corporation 1953

The Television Annual for 1954
Edited by Kenneth Baily
Odhams Press 1954

The British Film and Television Yearbook 1957-58
Edited by Peter Noble
British and American Press 1957

Three Men and A Gimmick
Including *The Peter Cushing Story* as told to
Robert Hirst
The World's Work 1957

The Television Annual 1960
Edited by Kenneth Baily
Odhams Press 1959

The Gary Cooper Story
George Carpozi Jnr
W H Allen 1970

The Horror People
John Brosnan
Macdonald and Jane's 1976

Holmes of the Movies
David Stuart Davies
Bramhall House 1976

Helpmann
Elizabeth Salter
Angus and Robertson 1978

Olivier – The Life of Laurence Olivier
Thomas Kiernan
Sidgwick and Jackson 1981

James Whale
James Curtis
Scarecrow Press 1982

The Avengers
Dave Rogers
ITV Books/Michael Joseph 1983

Darlings of the Gods
*A Year in the Lives of Laurence Olivier
and Vivien Leigh*
Garry O'Connor
Hodder and Stoughton 1984

Coming To You Live!
Behind the Screen: Memories of Forties and
Fifties Television
Denis Norden, Sybil Harper and
Norma Gilbert
Methuen 1985

The Avengers Anew
Dave Rogers
Michael Joseph 1985

An Autobiography
Peter Cushing
Weidenfeld and Nicholson 1986

Noël Coward: Collected Plays Two
Noël Coward
Methuen Publishing 1986

The Royal Almanac
Paul James
Ravette 1986

Past Forgetting
Peter Cushing
Weidenfeld and Nicholson 1988

Rattigan Plays: One
Terence Rattigan
Methuen 1988

Laurence Olivier – A Biography
Donald Spoto
HarperCollins 1991

On 'Q'
Kenneth Barrow
De Leon Memorial Fund 1992

Peter Cushing: The Gentle Man of Horror and his 91 Films
Deborah Del Vecchio and Tom Johnson
McFarland and Company 1992

British Television: An Illustrated Guide
Compiled for the BFI by Tise Vahimagi
Oxford University Press 1994

Christopher Lee and Peter Cushing and Horror Cinema
A Filmography of their 22 Collaborations
Mark A Miller
McFarland and Company 1995

Peter Cushing
Editor/Publisher Donald Fearney 1995

James Whale: A Biography
Mark Gatiss
Cassell 1995

A History of Horrors
The Rise and Fall of the House of Hammer
Denis Meikle
Scarecrow Press 1996

Hammer Films: An Exhaustive Filmography
Tom Johnson and Deborah Del Vecchio
McFarland and Company 1996

The Hammer Story
Marcus Hearn and Alan Barnes
Titan Books 1997

Tall Dark and Gruesome
Christopher Lee
W H Allen 1977/Victor Gollancz 1997

The British Television Drama Research Guide
Richard Down and Christopher Perry
Kaleidoscope 1997

The Films of Peter Cushing
Editor/Publisher Gary Parfitt 1975
Revised and updated 1998

1956 And All That
The Making of Modern British Drama
Dan Rebellato
Routledge 1999

John Carradine: The Films
Tom Weaver
McFarland and Company 1999

English Gothic: A Century of Horror Cinema
Jonathan Rigby
Reynolds and Hearn 2000

Christopher Lee: The Authorised Screen History
Jonathan Rigby
Reynolds and Hearn 2001

Sherlock Holmes On Screen
Alan Barnes
Reynolds and Hearn 2002

Periodicals
Cinefantastique
Daily Cinema
Doctor Who Magazine
Doctor Who Magazine Spring Special
Famous Monsters of Filmland
Fangoria
Film Review
Films and Filming
Films Illustrated
Hammer Horror
Hammer Horror Collectors' Special
The House of Hammer/Halls of Horror
Kinematograph Weekly
Monthly Film Bulletin
Radio Times
Shivers
Sight and Sound
Starburst
Starlog
The Tatler and Bystander
TV Mirror
TV News
TV Times
TV Zone

Fanzines
The American Peter Cushing Club Journal
(editor Deborah Bennett)
The Cushing Courier
(editor Brian Holland)
Little Shoppe of Horrors
(editor Richard Klemensen)

Index

Professor Lundgren with Davina Gilmore (Ciaran Madden) in *The Beast Must Die* (1973)

Vincent Price and Cushing on location at Pyrford Manor for *Madhouse* (1973)

Peter Cushing, Eunice Gayson and Richard Wordsworth in *The Revenge of Frankenstein* (1958)